Italian and Italian American Studies

Series Editor
Stanislao G. Pugliese
Hofstra University
Hempstead, NY, USA

This series brings the latest scholarship in Italian and Italian American history, literature, cinema, and cultural studies to a large audience of specialists, general readers, and students. Featuring works on modern Italy (Renaissance to the present) and Italian American culture and society by established scholars as well as new voices, it has been a longstanding force in shaping the evolving fields of Italian and Italian American Studies by re-emphasizing their connection to one another.

Caterina Romeo

Interrupted Narratives and Intersectional Representations in Italian Postcolonial Literature

palgrave
macmillan

Caterina Romeo
Department of Modern Literatures and Cultures
Sapienza Università di Roma
Rome, Italy

Translation by Ellen McRae (with the exception of Chapter 2 and Section 4.4).

ISSN 2635-2931   ISSN 2635-294X   (electronic)
Italian and Italian American Studies
ISBN 978-3-031-10042-0   ISBN 978-3-031-10043-7   (eBook)
https://doi.org/10.1007/978-3-031-10043-7

This Palgrave Macmillan imprint is published by the registered company Springer Nature Switzerland AG.
The registered company address is: Gewerbestrasse 11, 6330 Cham, Switzerland

To our wonderful planet.
And to my beloved daughter, Maddalena.

ACKNOWLEDGMENTS

This book came to life during the COVID-19 pandemic. I am especially grateful to my close and extended family (human and otherwise) and beloved friends who helped me through very difficult times and numerous lockdowns. Thank you all for making my life easier in many creative ways.

I would like to thank the colleagues on whose support I can constantly count: Peter Covino, Giulia Fabbri, Edvige Giunta, Beatrice Manetti, Áine O'Healy, and Monica Cristina Storini.

I would like to thank Peter Covino for his invaluable assistance and advice in writing the book proposal, for his affection and constant support, for his bright and precious presence in my life.

My deepest gratitude goes to the book reviewers, Rosetta Giuliani Caponetto and Clarissa Clò, for putting their bright minds at my disposal, for their time and intellectual energy, their hard work, pointed feedback, and generous support. I would also like to thank Rosetta and Clarissa, together with Edvige Giunta, Áine O'Healy, and Emma Bond, for their wonderful and insightful blurbs.

I would like to thank Ellen McRae (translator) and Derek Pollard (editor). Thank you for your work, your competence, your professionalism, your ability to work as a team, and for keeping me going when I did not think this project would ever be completed.

The whole project of translating, writing, and rewriting this book began while I was Academic Visitor at the University of Auckland. I am truly appreciative of Bernadette Luciano for inviting me to do research at her institution: our stay in New Zealand was one of the most beautiful experiences in our lives. I am truly grateful to Bernadette Luciano to visit their institutions in Australia while I was in the Southern hemisphere: Francesco Ricatti at Monash University; John Hayek and Laura Lori at the University of Melbourne; and Giorgia Alù at the University of Sidney.

This translation and my sabbatical in New Zealand were financed through research funds from my institution, Sapienza University of Rome.

This volume is not a mere translation of *Riscrivere la nazione. La letteratura italiana postcoloniale* (Le Monnier-Mondadori 2018). Parts of the Italian text have been expunged, parts have been written anew (including the introductory chapter in its entirety), parts have been rewritten, and the whole volume has been updated and made presentable and understandable to an Anglophone audience.

This book is dedicated to our wonderful planet and to my beloved daughter, Maddalena Lehmann.

Praise for *Interrupted Narratives and Intersectional Representations in Italian Postcolonial Literature*

"This is an impressive study dedicated to migrant authors and their descendants who in the last thirty years have rewritten Italy with their work, sketched a culture in flux, presented a geography colored with new meanings, and filled a society with faces and talents that have struggled to enter into the publishing, film, television, or academic canon. Time and again, Romeo presents the reader with the same question (who can call themselves Italian and based on what criteria) in order to reveal the contradictions, the denials, and the excuses. Romeo transitions from one argument to another with dense and rich analysis, never losing sight of the real context and real life of the authors she so passionately describes."

—Rosetta Giuliani Caponetto, author of *Fascist Hybridities: Racial Mixing and Diaspora Cultures under Mussolini*

"With *Interrupted Narratives and Intersectional Representations in Italian Postcolonial Literature*, Caterina Romeo paints a compelling and comprehensive picture of Italian postcolonial literature from its inception in the early 1990s through the most recent cultural production. Adopting an intersectional and transdiasporic methodology, Romeo lucidly highlights the political implications of these works as they uncover how notions of race, gender and sexuality developed during the colonial period are still present in contemporary Italy. With an ambitious archive and its use of the most current scholarship, the book effectively maps the field and forcefully argues for its relevance not only in Italy, but in relation to other regions in Europe, the Mediterranean, and North America."

—Clarissa Clò, *Professor of Italian and European Studies, San Diego State University*

"Caterina Romeo's brilliant analysis illuminates the layers of Italian postcolonial literature and the ways in which it carries in its bones the weight of a haunting past. A must-read for anyone interested in transnational Italian culture, *Interrupted Narratives and Intersectional Representations in Italian Postcolonial Literature* shows how a vibrant literature can emerge from histories of oppression and, in the process, forever transform the culture of a nation."

—Edvige Giunta, coeditor of *Talking to the Girls: Intimate and Political Essays on the Triangle Shirtwaist Factory Fire*

"Deploying postcolonial, decolonial, and transnational perspectives, Caterina Romeo offers a compelling exploration of the writings of Italian immigrants, their descendants, and other authors of the Italian diaspora who have made their voices heard over the past three decades. Attentive to questions of national identity, gender, race, ethnicity, and the construction of space, her work provides an intersectional analysis of one of the most innovative currents animating cultural production at present. By mapping out the rich vein of Italian postcolonial literature, Romeo recalibrates our understanding of contemporary Italian culture and challenges conventional notions of Italianness."

—Àine O'Healy, author of *Migrant Anxieties: Italian Cinema in a Transnational Frame*

CONTENTS

CHAPTER 1

Introduction: Decolonizing Italian Literature

Italian postcolonial literature is one of the most historically significant, culturally incisive, and artistically revitalizing literary and cultural phenomena that have developed in Italy in recent decades. It has consistently provided a symbolic representation of the numerous social changes that have taken place in Italy since the late 1980s as a result of transnational migrations, encouraging society to question the very concept of a monolithic and immutable Italian identity, to rethink itself, and to conceive of migrants and Italians of foreign origins in ways that go beyond rejection and victimization. Since the early 1990s, Italian postcolonial literature has contributed to the reconfiguration of the numerous narratives—including cultural canons, disciplinary fields, documents, monuments, and memories—that in different ways, but through common trajectories, have constructed and stabilized the notion of an Italian national identity and culture articulated within (and only within) national boundaries and expressed (almost) only in the Italian national language. Such reconfiguration systematically challenges the notion of an imagined national

C. Romeo, *Interrupted Narratives and Intersectional Representations in Italian Postcolonial Literature*, Italian and Italian American Studies,
https://doi.org/10.1007/978-3-031-10043-7_1

homogeneity[1] and promotes a transnational and postnational approach. The present volume is a tribute to the social importance, cultural relevance, and literary significance of Italian postcolonial literature.

The expression "Italian postcolonial literature"—over 30 years after its inception, which conventionally dates back to 1990—is far from widely accepted: the term "postcolonial" until a few years ago was "an almost clandestine word in the context of Italian studies in Italy"[2] (Derobertis 2014, 153), a field that still struggles to acknowledge the cultural significance of this literary production.[3] The marginality to which Italian postcolonial literature is confined in Italy translates into a number of academic practices that tend to constantly delegitimize not only this body of literature but also the critical and theoretical work associated with it as

---

[1] Here I reference the subtitle of the collection *Postcolonial Italy: Challenging National Homogeneity*, which I coedited in 2012 with Cristina Lombardi-Diop and which constituted our first joint theorization of the Italian postcolonial. The theoretical framework we elaborated in *Postcolonial Italy* and developed in subsequent publications informs my knowledge of the Italian postcolonial that is at the core of this book. For a broad and detailed mapping of texts that have contributed to activating and developing the field of Italian postcolonial studies, see the extensive bibliographies in Lombardi-Diop and Romeo (2012, 2014a).

[2] "un lemma pressoché clandestino nel contesto degli studi dell'italianistica italiana." [All translations are the translator's unless noted otherwise].

[3] The reaction of the literary establishment to the announcement that Abdulrazak Gurnah was awarded the 2021 Nobel Prize in Literature is a clear example of how this establishment denies not only the literary value of Italian postcolonial literature but often also that of postcolonial literature outside national borders, especially when it interrogates and deconstructs the usual, pervasive, stereotyped colonial imaginaries. The news, received with a certain coldness, was accompanied by concerns from several parties that the prize had been awarded to the author for political rather than artistic reasons (as if the two were mutually exclusive). This position reproposes the binary "pure knowledge"/"political knowledge" artfully created by the US academy, as Edward Said (1979) claims, to discredit some epistemologies (together with the subjects that produce them) and canonize others. Said famously claimed that apolitical knowledge does not exist because all knowledge is produced by situated subjects (since the universal subject does not exist). For a reflection on the reaction of the Italian cultural establishment to the news of Gurnah's Nobel Prize, see Boscolo (2021). See also Sara Scarafia's interview with Alessandra Di Maio (Scarafia 2021) and Igiaba Scego's article written on the occasion (2021) for a countervailing position that underscores the importance of awarding the Nobel Prize to Gurnah.

articulated by scholars in the field.[4] Even if in the past decade postcolonial literature has become increasingly more visible in the Italian culturescape—at cultural events and in the publishing industry, school and university programs, academic essays, and newspapers and magazines—the term "postcolonial" is seldom used and is often replaced by expressions such as "migration literature," but also "migrant," "post-migrant," "multicultural," "intercultural," "Italophone," "expatriate," and "translingual" literature, among others.[5] Such terminology obliterates the connection with

---

[4] In 2014, I co-authored an article titled "The Italian Postcolonial: A Manifesto" with Cristina Lombardi-Diop (Lombardi-Diop and Romeo 2014b). Cristina and I used to jokingly refer to the final section of the article as "la polemica," our critique of the subtle (and not so subtle) mechanisms deployed by Italian academics, especially in the field of *italianistica*, to maintain the status quo and to keep postcolonial studies and postcolonial literature outside the national literary canon. As we wrote in 2014, "traditional approaches to literature and culture dominate the field of *italianistica* and severely curtail any attempt at innovation. In this field, the risk of exclusion and delegitimization is constantly looming, and it materializes through apparently innocuous or unrelated strategies, which include considering the literature that Italian postcolonial writers produce as sociological explorations rather than literature in its own right; cataloguing their texts as 'foreign literature' and therefore deeming the study of their work as legitimate only in comparative literature courses, rather than Italian courses; keeping scholars in the field at the margins of the academic system by regarding postcolonial studies, race studies, and gender studies as lesser fields of inquiry and publications in these fields as irrelevant for the advancement of academic careers; considering the postcolonial exclusively as an Anglophone theoretical and cultural paradigm that has no relevance for Italy or, if it does, as a nonetheless 'minor' and insignificant one" (433). I would love to say that, upon reading our article again while writing this introductory chapter, I found our work in the "la polemica" section obsolete, but that was not the case. However, I should add that such an attitude is not indicative of the whole of Italian academia and that even in the most conservative academic circles things are slowly changing.

[5] It must be noted that Italian postcolonial literature is still predominantly absent from university texts on contemporary Italian literature. For example, in three critical texts on contemporary Italian fiction published in recent years (Donnarumma 2014; Simonetti 2018; Tirinanzi De Medici 2018), not even an allusion is made to Italian postcolonial literature, almost as if it did not exist or was not worthy of being considered literature. In another very recent text (Bazzocchi 2021), a brief section is devoted to the literature of migrants and subsequent generations, but this is not defined as postcolonial or even as "literature": in fact, the title reads "Scritture della migrazione, scritture del dispatrio" ("Writings of Migration, Writings of Dispatriation"). The term *dispatrio* ("dispatriation"), borrowed from Luigi Meneghello, unlike *espatrio* ("expatriation"), does not indicate a distance from the homeland but rather a loss of the social and emotional patrimony tied to the concept of homeland. This term is often used in Italian *italianistica* to include all writings marked by migrations in different ways. As already pointed out, such a process obscures the power relations inherent in postcolonial societies.

Italian and European colonial history and the legacy of such history in contemporary Italy, and it fails to highlight, investigate, and question the power relations European colonial systems have put in place or the ways in which such relations are reactivated in contemporary times—especially through mechanisms of border control, production of clandestinity and illegality, processes of othering and racialization, and restrictions on citizenship.

Determining how to define and categorize literature written in Italian in Italy by migrant writers and their descendants, therefore, acquires a strong social and political valence because it means reflecting not only on the criteria of inclusion and exclusion operated by the Italian (and European) literary and cultural canons but also on who can be considered Italian (and European) and what the social and cultural role of these subjects is and can be. It means interrogating what constitutes *italianità* and to what norm—be it somatic, chromatic,[6] cultural, or other—it is necessary to conform in order to be included in this "privileged" category. Postcolonial writers in contemporary Italy—and in other European countries—contribute to bringing colonial archives to light and rewriting colonial history, to denouncing contemporary racism as a legacy of colonialism and revealing the processes of racialization that are structural in the formation of an Italian national identity, to highlighting the intersection of racism and sexism, to questioning the social and cultural privileges of normative Italians and rearticulating the dynamics of power, and to underlining the strong resistance to considering the intersection between Blackness and Italianness as viable in a society that has historically constructed itself as white and Catholic.

The postcolonial perspective deployed in this volume examines the temporal as well as the spatial continuum that connects "Italy's many diasporas"[7] in different historical periods and geographical areas, demonstrating the ways in which transnational and intranational mobilities (mass emigration, intranational migrations from the South to the North,

---

[6]With the expression "somatic norm," Nirmal Puwar (2004) designates the implicit norm that regulates the access of bodies to certain spaces. My category of "chromatic norm" is modeled on that of Puwar's "somatic norm," but while Puwar privileges the intersection between race and gender, the "chromatic norm" is instead centered on the intersection between race and color. Such an expression (strategically) essentializes the category of color to analyze the way in which space is constructed as white through the systematic elision of non-white bodies and focuses on their social visibility, invisibility, and hypervisibility.

[7]The reference here is to Donna Gabaccia's book by this title (2000).

contemporary immigration, new mobilities) have caused Italians to occupy positions of hegemony, as well as subalternity, in the past and in the present (including the current position of Italy within the EU).[8] Considering different migrations as lying on a continuum rather than being independent from one another "aims to overcome the methodological nationalism embedded in the study of the experiences of Italian mobility when these are considered as separate phenomena" (Burdett et al. 2020, 20). This also allows the contemporaneity of Italy to be connected with that of other European countries that took part in colonization and/or shared a widespread colonial culture,[9] a conspicuous legacy of which is still present in the mechanisms of social and cultural exclusion and differential inclusion of migrants, refugees, asylum seekers, and their descendants. The common postcolonial condition of contemporary Italy and of other European countries creates transnational trajectories among diasporic communities affected by the legacy of colonialism. This occurs in ways similar to those noted by Paul Gilroy (1993) among different Black communities and cultures around the world that have, from the common experience of the African diaspora, developed shared characteristics and aesthetics in different geopolitical contexts.

In the past few years, a transnational approach has informed the debate in the Anglophone world on both sides of the Atlantic around the redefinition of Italian studies. Such debate has questioned the very notion of a literary canon—which historically has sustained and consolidated an Italian identity as shaped within national boundaries and expressed in the national language—and has underlined the need to develop a "transnational turn in Italian studies" that would "stretch … or go … beyond the confines of national boundaries … in cultural, spatial or temporal terms" (Bond 2014, 416). More recently, the discussion has pointed to the meaning and the destiny of the nation-based discipline of Italian studies (and other modern

---

[8] For an analysis of how the status of "minor colonial empires" such as Italy and Portugal produces a condition of subalternity in the present-day European Union, see Lombardi-Diop and Romeo (2015b). For an analysis of the postcolonial condition in continental Europe, see, among many others, Lombardi-Diop and Romeo (2015a), Ponzanesi and Colpani (2016), Jensen et al. (2017), and Jensen (2020).

[9] Some countries do not have a direct history of colonization; however, they share a colonial culture (see Lombardi-Diop and Romeo 2015a). A particularly significant case in this regard is that of Switzerland: see, among others, Purtschert et al. (2016). For a reflection on the processes of othering through racialization in Europe and how such processes have contributed to the formation of a European identity, see Hine et al. (2009).

languages) in an increasingly globalized world characterized by transnational mobilities, by an extensive digitalization that crosses the boundaries of nations and continents,[10] by a climate crisis that affects the entire planet, and, I will add, by a pandemic that has, over the course of three years, profoundly changed our way of thinking, living, breathing, being (or not being) with and for others, and considering ourselves as a community beyond the borders of individual national states. Rethinking the concepts of Italian identity and culture, therefore, appears to be a necessary operation in order to highlight the transnational nature of shaping a national Identity. This process, as far as Italy is concerned, is the result of widespread migrations and mobilities and of the circulation of personal and collective stories and memories, cultural products that exceed literature as it is conventionally defined, and narratives articulated in different places and in different languages.

However, the process of preserving a national perspective and the identity politics that accompany it can be a strategic necessity to safeguard the rights of migrants and subsequent generations in contemporary Italy. The emphasis on fluid dynamics of identification rather than on static notions of national identity and "the transnational dimension of cultural life [that focuses] on what people do, not on normative or idealized notions of identity and belonging" (Burdett and Polezzi 2020, 14) may obliterate the fact that among those who claim their right to shape an Italian national identity are subjects (born and) raised in Italy who are denied the right to citizenship—still granted mostly according to a biologist and racist principle[11]—and Black Italians who are often excluded from—or differentially included in—the national body because they do not comply with the Italian chromatic norm. If, as Derek Duncan points out, elaborating on Walter Mignolo's thought, "to think from the border is not to re-think the nation but to think despite it" (Duncan 2019, 9), then it is necessary to remember that being able to think of oneself as having a place *within* the nation and its borders—not to mention risking one's own life and the lives of one's children to reach it—is still not an available option for many. In order to keep all these trajectories together, the transnational perspective needs to be intersected with the postcolonial and decolonial perspectives—more attentive to power relations inherent in a given society and

---

[10] In this regard, however, it is worth remembering that large areas of the planet remain excluded from the global network.

[11] On the process of acquiring citizenship in Italy, see note 57 in Chap. 4.

the history that produced them—so as to create transformative approaches to analysis and research that can lead to a reshaping of Italian society and, subsequently, to a reconceptualization of *italianistica*.

The analysis of the literature presented in this volume—even though it is produced primarily (but not exclusively) in the Italian language and within the borders of Italy—is therefore not driven by a desire to reinforce the national perspective, but rather the opposite. This body of literature, in fact, has thus far not benefited (and in Italy still does not benefit) from full cultural citizenship, just as many of the subjects that produce it do not benefit from political citizenship. The inclusion, therefore, of these subjects and their cultural production within the confined enclosure of *italianità* and *italianistica* promotes a profound change in the very notion of a nation still not sufficiently capable of accepting greater diversity from a social or a cultural and literary point of view. The writers and artists included in this book, who mostly do not identify with "Italy" as a national construct but rather with the localities in which they live and with broader transnational communities, are each contributing to the reconstitution of the very concept of national literature from a transnational and postnational perspective and to the decolonization of Italian culture.

This process of decolonizing Italian studies was initiated in the United States and is aimed at defying "systemic racism at large and its insidious infection in specific arenas throughout society, which include the academy" and interrogating Italian studies "with regard to diversity, equity, and inclusion" (Gibby and Tamburri 2021, i). The conversation started by Deborah Parker in 2018 presented considerations on what it means to be a professor of Asian heritage in the field of Italian studies, where very few minorities are represented and where an elitist attitude based on the notion of a presumed "originality" is widespread. According to this approach, a more diverse and inclusive faculty would not only promote the idea of a more diverse and inclusive discipline but also potentially attract students with different cultural and ethnic backgrounds who would be presented with subjectivities that resemble their own and issues that are important to them (such as processes of racialization and marginalization) represented in academia. However, as Rosetta Giuliani Caponetto observes in recounting the experience of study abroad student Nicole Phillip (2018) in Italy, the process of promoting diversity in academia in the United States "would be hindered if students visit Italy and discover that their teacher's diversity, and in turn their own, is not necessarily a value in that country" (Caponetto 2021, 46). The decolonization of Italian culture abroad, as Caponetto points out, must be coupled with the decolonization of Italian society and culture *in* Italy, where the debate on race, colonial legacy, and postcoloniality needs to be further implemented.

The representations of migrants and subsequent generations outside of consolidated stereotypes of undesirability and victimization that are elaborated in this volume through a complex analysis of their powerful and diverse production strengthen this necessary process of social and cultural decolonization. The analysis presented in the following chapters of the theoretical work about race recently (and less recently) produced in Italy in the Italian language (mostly) by Black and non-white female and non-binary Italian writers, intellectuals, artists, and artivists, including Geneviève Makaping, Igiaba Scego, Marie Moïse, Angelica Pesarini, Mackda Ghebremariam Tesfaù, Espérance Hakuzwimana (Ripanti), Djarah Kan, Oiza Queens Day Obasuyi, Nadeesha Uyangoda, Kwanza Musi Dos Santos, Ndack Mbaye, Lucia Ghebreghiorges, Leaticia Ouedraogo, Addes Tesfamariam, Alesa Herero, and Wissal Houbabi (aka Wii), and Sabrina Efionayi, among many others, demonstrates how such production participates in a transnational conversation articulated with other Black subjects around Europe (and beyond), reflecting on the European chromatic norm that relegates Blackness to the symbolic space of otherness.[12] If, as Fatima El-Tayeb states, "all parts of Europe are arguably invested in 'whiteness' as the norm against which ethnicization is read as a tool of differentiation between insiders and outsiders" (2011, xiv), the Black authors and authors of color mentioned above envision for themselves forms of transnational identification and belonging that transcend the nation and are rooted in such diasporic experiences as the Black Atlantic and the Black Mediterranean.[13]

Placing such diasporic experiences, rather than an idea of national belonging, at the center of the analysis presented here allows for a continuity to be seen among texts coming from different national, cultural, and linguistic contexts. The reading in Chap. 4 of the memoir by African

---

[12] I consider my writing about race and the processes of racialization to be one way to expose racism, create awareness, and contribute to the critical debate on these issues, and give the deserved attention to the work of Black intellectuals, artists, and artivists in Italy who are reshaping Italian culture. As a "white" woman, I acknowledge that being the subject of racism is not part of my everyday lived experience—although being the subject of sexism is—and therefore I do not claim to be speaking as part of the racialized community but rather as an active and empathetic ally of racialized communities in the fight against racism.

[13] For a theorization of the Black Mediterranean, see, among others, Kelley (2010), Di Maio (2012), Hawthorne (2017), Smythe (2018), Proglio (2019), Proglio et al. (2021), and Hawthorne (2022).

Italian American writer and filmmaker Kym Ragusa, *The Skin Between Us: A Memoir of Race, Beauty, and Belonging* (2006) (later translated into Italian as *La pelle che ci separa*, 2008), vis-à-vis the memoir of Somali Italian writer and activist Igiaba Scego, *La mia casa è dove sono* (My Home is Where I Am) (2010), demonstrates that the presumed whiteness on the basis of which African migrants and their descendants are discriminated against in contemporary Italy was not necessarily considered a characteristic of Italian emigrants in the United States.[14] A comparative analysis of Ethiopian Italian writer and musician Gabriella Ghermandi's novel *Regina di fiori e di perle* (2007) (*Queen of Flowers and Pearls*, 2015), and Ethiopian American writer Maaza Mengiste's latest novel, *The Shadow King* (2019) (later translated into Italian as *Il re ombra*, 2021), recounts the (hi)story of the Italian occupation of Ethiopia and, in the combined perspective the two texts weave together, questions not only Italian colonial rule but also the patriarchal systems that constantly plagued both the society of the colonizers and that of the colonized (although in different ways). Being attentive to how Black Italian writers and artivists engage with the work of other European (and extra-European) Black writers and artists highlights the importance of building a Black European tradition that emphasizes local contexts and transnational trajectories over national identities.[15]

---

[14] Translations of the titles of works are presented in italics (in the case of books) or quotation marks (in the case of chapters) if they are taken from published translations. If the works have not been published in an English translation, titles are the translator's translations and are presented in Roman text without italics or quotation marks.

[15] I would like to provide some examples: in the anthology *Future* (Scego 2019), there are references to Opitz et al. (1992), Kilomba (2008), and in general to the work of, among others, Frantz Fanon and W. E. B. Dubois; Marie Moïse and Mackda Ghebremariam Tesfaù have recently translated Grada Kilomba's *Plantation Memories* into Italian and published it in Italy with the title *Memorie dalla piantagione*; in November 2019, African Italian writers and Associated Experts of Associazione Il Razzismo è una brutta storia Ndack Mbaye and Espérance Hakuzwimana (Ripanti) entertained a conversation on the social role and cultural production of Black Italians in Italy with Chimamanda Ngozi Adichie, who was in Milan to receive the BookCity Special Prize "Africas." At the press conference organized by the publisher Einaudi before the main event, the three writers discussed the condition of Italians of African origins and the work of African Italian authors. During the interview at the main event later, Chimamanda Ngozi Adichie addressed the issue of African Italians and said that "the story of Afroitalians—not only of Afroitalians—the story of Afroeuropeans is invisible" (Adichie 2019, 34:00). I would like to point out that, even if the stories of African Italians are not part of the mainstream narrative in Italy, those stories are not silent; they have been told for over 30 years now, as this book testifies. Black authors and authors of Color have been working for decades to write their counterhistories and reshape cultural imaginaries, and the impact of their work is visible. See also Igiaba Scego's comments in "Chimamanda Ngozi Adichie—Italiani e cittadinanza" (Associazione Il Razzismo è una brutta storia n.d.)

In order to create such a transnational exchange, the importance of translation in association with the idea of movement (as evident from the prefix *trans-*) is crucial in the cultural context of an Italy characterized by migrations and mobilities because it allows for the circulation of texts, ideas, cultural traits, imaginaries, and memories (Polezzi 2020). The translation of Kym Ragusa's *The Skin Between Us* (*La pelle che ci separa*), for instance, far from simply facilitating a transition from one language to another, has facilitated the transition from one cultural context to another and back, making available to the Italian audience a history of their own past of which they are in general not aware—when Italian emigrants were racialized in the United States—and compelling them to question their own whiteness as the principle whereby Black immigrants and their descendants are currently racialized in Italy.[16] At the same time, according to African American translators Barbara Ofosu-Somuah and Candice Whitney, translating a text such as the anthology *Future* into English means translating Blackness from one historical and geopolitical context to another, thus facilitating a conversation between these Italian authors' particular experience of Blackness and the experience of other Black women around the world:

> These narratives, which resonate with aspects of our own experiences of living in Black bodies in the United States, made clear that Black existence and meaning-making, regardless of borders, is a process that is always relational. We believe that people within the African diaspora are connected by navigating and translating how they see themselves and what is claimed for them. (Ofosu-Somuah and Whitney 2020, para. 1).[17]

---

[16] When in 2006 I recommended Ragusa's memoir for translation to the publishing house Nutrimenti (which published it in 2008), the debate on the processes of racialization that Italian emigrants and immigrants have undergone had just begun in Italy. Since then, I have used this text in different classes, where we have discussed constructions of race and gender, colonialism, postcoloniality, and Italian emigration. I have always found that Ragusa's text facilitates the students' repositioning of themselves from a racial standpoint and that students welcome such a questioning process. See Ragusa (2006, 2008).

[17] The translation of *Future* into English is currently underway.

Far from being a mere linguistic process, then, translation "becomes a mode of cultural production, circulation, and consumption, a creative and productive process in its own right" (Polezzi 2020, 26).[18]

Of the four chapters that follow this introduction, Chap. 2, "Italian Postcolonial Literature: An Overview," presents a survey of Italian postcolonial literature from 1990 (the conventional date of its inception) to 2022, through a periodization in four phases. This periodization, rather than rigidly delimiting the different periods, serves to highlight the existence of trajectories and trends that characterize them. The chapter fulfills two main functions: the first is to show the great number and extraordinary variety of writers, works, themes, subjects, genres, and styles that give life to Italian postcolonial literature and to investigate the many ramifications that have developed and transformations that have occurred within this body of literature in the (more than) three decades that separate us from its inception; the second is to present the temporal continuum with the characteristics of the different periods in such a way as to make comprehensible to readers how the texts analyzed in the following chapters are situated in the general context of Italian postcolonial literature, as well as in the specificity of a given period. To this end, in this chapter, I briefly outline the initial steps that marked the birth of Italian postcolonial literature and its consolidation: the first phase (1990–1994), constituted exclusively by migrant writers and characterized mainly by collaborative texts centered on themes such as migration and marginalization, but also by texts revealing processes of racialization and other colonial legacies in contemporary Italy (the latter aspect is addressed in Chap. 4); and the second phase (1994–2000), an in-between period during which collaborative

[18] In this regard, I would like to draw attention to the series Other Voices of Italy: Italian and Transnational Texts in Translation recently established by Rutgers University Press and directed by Eilis Kierans, Alessandro Vettori, and Sandra Waters. The principal aim of the series, according to the mission statement "is to introduce new or past authors—who have until now been marginalized—to an English-speaking readership" and to "highlight contemporary immigrant authors," thus increasing "the appreciation of translation as an art form that enhances the importance of cultural diversity" (the website is still under construction). As a member of the advisory board, I have recommended the translation of Geneviève Makaping's *Traiettorie di Sguardi. E se gli altri foste voi* (2001), which has recently been republished by Rubbettino (2022) and translated by Giovanna Bellesia-Contuzzi and Victoria Offredi Poletto as *Reversing the Gaze: What If the Other Were You?* (forthcoming in 2023).

writing is gradually abandoned, while at the same time the artistic and cultural roles of some writers are corroborated, other important authors emerge, prizes begin to be established, and dedicated journals are founded. After the first two phases are briefly sketched, the most substantial analysis in this chapter is devoted to the third phase (2001–2019), characterized by great complexity and development in multiple directions. Distinctive traits are examined within this phase: themes related to migration become increasingly distant, even though a strong diasporic awareness remains; there is a further shift away from collaborative writing toward linguistic and stylistic experimentation; both first- and second-generation writers articulate oppositional narratives that contribute to the rewriting of Italian colonial history, with the assistance of official and personal archives. An important turning point in this phase is signaled by the arrival on the literary and cultural scene of "second generations."[19] Through their cultural (not only literary) production, they denounce the processes of othering and racialization and other mechanisms that relegate the children of migrants outside of the national body—including the denial of their right to citizenship; they create important points of contact with the second generations of other European (and non-European) countries who, like them, are opposed to the presumed European somatic and cultural norms; they contribute to the formation of imaginaries that disconnect Italianness

---

[19] Maurizio Ambrosini (2004) has pointed out that the expression "second generations" is generic because it encompasses very heterogeneous personal stories and experiences of people who were born in Italy or arrived in Italy at different ages. With regard to the terminology, see Ambrosini (2004, 5–6). For an analysis of the subject of second generations in Italy from a sociological perspective, see Ambrosini and Molina (2004). For a reflection on African Italian second generations, see Andall (2002). I use the expression "second generations" merely as a term of convenience to include those generations that, in sociology, are designated with the number 2 (those born in their parents' country of destination), 1.75 (those who emigrated between 0 and 5 years of age), 1.5 (those who started primary school in the country of origin and completed it in the country of destination), or 1.25 (those who emigrated when between 13 and 17 years of age). I am aware, however, that "second generations" is a very problematic term that disregards the age of arrival (for those who were not born in the destination country), produces temporal immobility (as does the expression "new" Italians) when it is used to refer to all subsequent generations (not necessarily only the second), and homogenizes radically different experiences. This expression is therefore always intended to be read as if it were in quotation marks (to signal my distance from it) throughout the book, although the quotation marks will be implied in nearly all cases. For a deep analysis of the problematics associated with this term, see also Grimaldi (2021).

from biological characteristics and see it instead as increasingly inclusive of diversity, staging in their works what already constitutes a social reality; but they are also critical of their own families' societies of origin, having acquired a certain distance from them.

At the end of the chapter, I outline what to me appears as a fourth phase (2019–present), characterized by the lively presence of a large group of Black[20] and non-white writers, intellectuals, activists, artivists, bloggers, and social media artists (almost exclusively women and non-binary), who are deploying an intersectional methodology to elaborate the first systematic theorization on race and racism articulated in the Italian cultural context and written in the Italian language by Black Italian intellectuals and intellectuals of Color. A significant group of these writers emerged in the extraordinary collection *Future*, edited by Igiaba Scego (2019); others appeared soon after and consolidated their theorizations when, following the brutal killing of George Floyd by the police in Minneapolis in 2020, the Black Lives Matter movement also became more vocal in Italy. Although it is not the first time that issues of race are discussed by postcolonial authors in Italy, the difference in this phase is represented by the fact

---

[20] Here and throughout the book, I have adopted the policy implemented by the *New York Times* and the *Washington Post* in 2020 to capitalize Black and Blackness (Coleman 2020; WashPostPR 2020), as "a recognition and acknowledgment not only of the cultural bonds and historical experiences shared by people of African heritage, but also the shared struggles of the descendants of enslaved people, families who immigrated generations ago and more recent immigrants from Africa, the Caribbean and other corners of the world" (WashPostPR 2020, para. 1). Unlike the *Washington Post* (and like the *New York Times*), I choose not to capitalize white, as it "has long been capitalized by hate groups" (Coleman 2020, para. 18) and "white supremacists have long favored the uppercase style, which in itself is reason to avoid it" (Baquet and Corbett 2020, para. 5). Finally, unlike the *New York Times* (which does not capitalize brown) and the *Washington Post* (which capitalizes Brown in quotes, and otherwise only sparingly), I choose to capitalize Brown—although this term "has generally been used to describe a wide range of cultures" (Coleman 2020, para. 18) and its "designation is seen by many as a catchall to describe people of color of vastly diverse ethnic and cultural backgrounds who are not Black" (WashPostPR 2020, para. 4)—to also acknowledge the oppression and racial discrimination of Brown people in the United States, in Italy, and around the world. I do understand that "'Brown' has been used to describe such a disparate range of people—Latin, Indigenous, Asian, Middle Eastern—that the meaning is often unclear" and I agree that "a more specific description is generally best" (Baquet and Corbett 2020, para. 6). For this reason, I employ this term only when referring to racialized groups (not individuals) in Italy, and capitalize Brown and Brownness as signifiers designating such racialization.

that race issues have become the core of these authors' work and that they produce a systematic theorization starting from their own personal experience and connect it to other studies on race produced (mainly) in the United States and other European countries, thus creating important transnational connections.

As previously mentioned, the survey presented in Chap. 2 is useful for positioning the works examined in the following chapters on a temporal continuum and for contextualizing them. Chapters 3, 4, and 5 abandon the (more or less) chronological presentation to adopt a thematic one. They deploy an intersectional methodology—which places emphasis on the need to consider different categories of oppression (gender, race, color, nationality, class, religion, and sexual orientation, among others) in their simultaneous presence and intersection rather than as separate from each other and simply addable to one another—and focus on representations of gender (Chap. 3) and race (Chap. 4) and on how these categories of oppression are crucial in processes of constructing (especially urban) spaces (Chap. 5). The apparent contradiction of first underlining the need to use an intersectional methodology and then dedicating each chapter to a single axis of differentiation is not in fact a contradiction but rather a deliberate choice of "strategic essentialism" (Spivak 1987). Through this strategy, differences are temporarily downplayed and unity within a group temporarily assumed in order to achieve a specific goal, which in this case is to scrutinize the mechanisms that lie hidden in the dynamics of gender and race/color, and to then relate both to the way in which physical and symbolic spaces are constructed and strengthened through them. At the same time, in the analysis presented in these chapters, such strategical essentialism is interwoven with an intersectional approach, firmly and consistently adopted to analyze the different categories of differentiation in their interrelationship.

Chapter 3, "Gender and Its Intersections," defines intersectionality as a political practice and a methodology and then focuses on the intersection of gender with race and color in Italian postcolonial literature. The chapter examines the continued prevalence in the Italian national imaginary of the entire apparatus of images and stereotypes related to the "Black Venus" (with specific references to three of Carlo Lucarelli's novels) and the oppositional narratives written by contemporary Black women authors such as Igiaba Scego, Isabella Marincola, Shirin Ramzanali Fazel, Gabriella

Ghermandi, Maaza Mengiste, and Ubax Cristina Ali Farah, which inter-rupt and disturb such notably stereotypical and victimizing accounts. The last part of the chapter is devoted to Geneviève Makaping, Christiana de Caldas Brito, Ingy Mubiayi, and Gabriella Kuruvilla, who challenge the notion of universal sisterhood and express the need to consider the differ-ent positioning of women in Italian society and their differential access to agency and empowerment.

Chapter 4, "Defying the Chromatic Norm: Race, Blackness, (In)Visibility, Italianness, Citizenship," is centered on the categories of race and color and analyzes how Blackness has been and still is consid-ered alien to the social, political, cultural, and symbolic space of the Italian nation. To this end, in the first part of the chapter, I again adopt a chronological approach to analyze the ways in which race and Blackness have been represented in Italian postcolonial literature by authors such as Pap Khouma, Salah Methnani, Maria Abbebù Viarengo, Nassera Chohra, Geneviève Makaping, Dagmawi Yimer, Garane Garane, and Cheick Tidiane Gaye, as well as how such representations have gradually constructed a symbolic space in which the national chromatic norm is questioned and, at least partially, redefined. The chapter then examines how such redefinition is possible, thanks in particular to the cultural production of second-generation artists—including writers such as Jadelin Mabiala Gangbo, Ingy Mubiayi, Gabriella Kuruvilla, Ubax Cristina Ali Farah, Laila Wadia, the 11 authors included in the anthology *Future*, Oiza Queens Day Obasuyi, Nadeesha Uyangoda, Antonio Dikele Distefano, and filmmakers such as Fred Kuwornu, Medhin Paolos, Amin Nour, Suranga Deshapriya Katugampala, and Phaim Bhuiyan—who forcefully demand a more inclusive conception of Italianness, along with a reform of the citizenship law. Finally, in the last part of the chapter, Italian Blackness is investigated from a transdiasporic perspective through the writing of Italian African American author Kym Ragusa and Somali Italian author Igiaba Scego, with particular attention paid to the visibil-ity of Black bodies in the Italian communities in the United States and in Italy and to the development of aesthetic practices associated with those bodies.

Chapter 5, "Geographies of Diaspora and New Urban Mappings," con-centrates on an analysis of the relationships between (symbolic and geo-graphical) space and gender, race, articulations of power, and processes of identity construction, highlighting in particular how urban spaces are continually redefined by migratory movements and new communities that settle in cities and implement living practices there. The chapter focuses on the literary production of second-generation writers Igiaba Scego, Ubax Cristina Ali Farah, Jadelin Mabiala Gangbo, and Gabriella Kuruvilla and on the urban countermappings they draw. In their writings, they restructure the conventional spaces assigned to "non-conventional" bodies by the institutions of a state that controls migration flows, excluding such bodies from the physical and symbolic spaces of the national territory or including them only in a limited, differential way.

The global migrations of recent decades have radically changed the composition of the Italian population, which has been migrating around the world for centuries—thus disseminating language, culture, imaginaries, memories—and which, inside national boundaries, is becoming more diverse every day. Starting from the early 1990s, literary representations of the social changes that incoming migrations have produced have been written by migrant and postcolonial authors. These narratives reshape *italianità* through transnational, transcultural, and translingual trajectories and conceive of Italian national literature as taking place across borders and involving different languages and cultures. In order not to weaken this cultural production's power to articulate a political and social critique, however, the transnational and transcultural approaches need to be combined with a postcolonial and decolonial perspective. This synergy of approaches can more forcibly contribute to a decolonization of Italian society and culture and of Italian studies by promoting equity, denouncing the reproduction of colonial mechanisms of marginalization and exclusion in the present, sustaining the reform of the law for the obtainment of citizenship, and radically questioning the very notion of a chromatic norm in contemporary Italy.

In future years, it will be necessary to observe the developments of postcolonial literature to examine what relationship of continuity and discontinuity it will create with "traditional" Italian literature and whether, as time passes, social changes will render the existence of a designated literary space for these texts obsolete. This will also depend on whether Italy will (re)conceive of itself as that multicultural society it has always been since antiquity and will consider the presence of foreigners, and their descendants, as an asset rather than a threat from a social, economic, and cultural point of view. It will also depend on the way in which "traditional" culture and the intellectual elites will deal with these cultural voices, whose texts can no longer be considered "foreign" or "comparative" literature but rather literature that is integral to and representative of Italian national culture.

BIBLIOGRAPHY

Adichie, Chimamanda Ngozi. 2019. Chimamanda Ngozie Adichie a Bookcity 19. Facebook, November 17. https://www.facebook.com/einaudieditore/videos/502532033668914.

Ambrosini, Maurizio. 2004. Il futuro in mezzo a noi. Le seconde generazioni scaturite dall'immigrazione nella società italiana dei prossimi anni. In *Seconde generazioni. Un'introduzione al futuro dell'immigrazione in Italia*, ed. Maurizio Ambrosini and Stefano Molina, 1–53. Turin: Edizioni della Fondazione Giovanni Agnelli.

Ambrosini, Maurizio, and Stefano Molina, eds. 2004. *Seconde generazioni. Un'introduzione al futuro dell'immigrazione in Italia*. Turin: Edizioni della Fondazione Giovanni Agnelli.

Andall, Jacqueline. 2002. Second-Generation Attitude? African-Italians in Milan. *Journal of Ethnic and Migration Studies* 28 (3): 389–407.

Associazione Il Razzismo è una brutta storia. n.d. Chimamanda Ngozi Adichie—Italiani e cittadinanza. http://www.razzismobruttastoria.net/2019/11/18/chimamanda-ngozi-adichie-a-bookcity-milano-2019-afroitaliani-e-cittadinanza/.

Baquet, Dean, and Phil Corbett. 2020. Uppercasing 'Black.' *New York Times*, June 30. https://www.nytco.com/press/uppercasing-black/.

Bazzocchi, Marco A., ed. 2021. *Cento anni di letteratura italiana 1910–2010*. Turin: Einaudi.

Bond, Emma. 2014. Towards a Trans-National Turn in Italian Studies? *Italian Studies* 69 (3): 415–424. https://doi.org/10.1179/0075163414Z.0 0000000080.

Boscolo, Claudia. 2021. Il Nobel per la letteratura a Gurnah accolto con freddezza in Italia. *Valigia Blu*, October 16. https://www.valigiablu.it/premio-nobel-letteratura-gurnah-italia/?fbclid=IwAR3eJfHMi_jmVvmsCTFzgtqa-boK19Bl2uTluXLNeI3KnsnwJb6z7UgCoF8I.

Burdett, Charles, and Loredana Polezzi, eds. 2020. *Transnational Italian Studies*. Liverpool: Liverpool University Press.

Burdett, Charles, Loredana Polezzi, and Barbara Spadaro, eds. 2020. *Transcultural Italies. Mobility, Memory and Translation.* Liverpool: Liverpool University Press.

Caponetto, Rosetta Giuliani. 2021. Fear and Nostalgia in Italian Studies. In *Diversity in Italian Studies*, ed. Siân Gibby and Anthony Julian Tamburri, 45–55. New York: John D. Calandra Italian-American Institute.

Coleman, Nancy. 2020. Why We're Capitalizing Black. *New York Times*, July 5. https://www.nytimes.com/2020/07/05/insider/capitalized-black.html.

Derobertis, Roberto. 2014. La critica italiana tra narrazioni, pratiche sociali e culturali. In *Postcoloniale e revisione dei saperi*, ed. Annalisa Oboe. Special issue, *aut aut* 364 (October–December): 153–159.

Di Maio, Alessandra. 2012. Mediterraneo nero. Le rotte dei migranti nel millennio globale. In *La città cosmopolita. Altre narrazioni*, ed. Giulia De Spuches, 142–163. Palermo: Palumbo Editore.

Donnarumma, Raffaele. 2014. *Ipermodernità. Dove va la narrativa contemporanea.* Bologna: Il Mulino.

Duncan, Derek. 2019. Collaging Cultures: Curating Italian Studies. *Italian Culture* 37 (1): 3–25. https://doi.org/10.1080/01614622.2019.1609211.

El-Tayeb, Fatima. 2011. *European Others: Queering Ethnicity in Postnational Europe.* Minneapolis: University of Minnesota Press.

Gabaccia, Donna. 2000. *Italy's Many Diasporas.* Seattle: University of Washington Press.

Ghermandi, Gabriella. 2007. *Regina di fiori e di perle.* Rome: Donzelli. Trans. Giovanna Bellesia-Contuzzi and Victoria Offredi Poletto as *Queen of Flowers and Pearls: A Novel* (Bloomington: Indiana University Press, 2015).

Gibby, Siân, and Anthony Julian Tamburri, eds. 2021. *Diversity in Italian Studies.* New York: John D. Calandra Italian-American Institute.

Gilroy, Paul. 1993. *The Black Atlantic: Modernity and Double Consciousness.* Cambridge, MA: Harvard University Press.

Grimaldi, Giuseppe. 2021. The Habesha Italians: The Black Mediterranean and the Second-Generation Condition. In *The Black Mediterranean: Bodies, Borders and Citizenship*, ed. Gabriele Proglio, Camilla Hawthorne, P. Ida Danewid, Khalil Saucier, Giuseppe Grimaldi, Angelica Pesarini, Timothy Raeymaekers, Giulia Grechi, and Vivian Gerrand, 233–261. Cham: Palgrave Macmillan.

Hawthorne, Camilla. 2017. In Search of Black Italia. *Transition* 123: 152–174.

———. 2022. *Contesting Race and Citizenship. Youth Politics in the Black Mediterranean.* Ithaca: Cornell University Press.

Hine, Darlene Clark, Trica Danielle Keaton, and Stephen Small, eds. 2009. *Black Europe and the African Diaspora.* Urbana: University of Illinois Press.

Jensen, Lars. 2020. *Postcolonial Europe: Key Words.* London: Routledge.

Jensen, Lars, Julia Suárez-Krabbe, Christian Groes, and Zoran Lee Pecic, eds. 2017. *Postcolonial Europe: Comparative Reflections after the Empires, Crisis in the Nordic Countries and Beyond.* London: Rowman & Littlefield.

Kelley, Robin D.G. 2010. Foreword. In *Black Marxism: The Making of Black Radical Tradition,* by Cedric Robinson, xi–xxvi. Chapel Hill: University of North Carolina Press.

Kilomba, Grada. 2008. *Plantation Memories: Episodes of Everyday Racism.* Münster: Unrast Verlag. Trans. Marie Moïse and Mackda Ghebremariam Tesfaù as *Memorie dalla piantagione. Episodi di razzismo quotidiano* (Alessandria: Edizioni Capovolte, 2021).

Lombardi-Diop, Cristina, and Caterina Romeo, eds. 2012. *Postcolonial Italy: Challenging National Homogeneity.* New York: Palgrave Macmillan.

———. 2014a. Il postcoloniale italiano. Costruzione di un paradigma. In *L'Italia postcoloniale,* ed. Cristina Lombardi-Diop and Caterina Romeo, 1–38. Florence: Le Monnier-Mondadori.

———. 2014b. The Italian Postcolonial: A Manifesto. *Italian Studies* 69 (3): 425–433.

———, eds. 2015a. *Postcolonial Europe.* Special issue of *Postcolonial Studies* 18 (4).

———. 2015b. State of the Union: Survival Blankets and Falling Stars. *Postcolonial Europe,* ed. Cristina Lombardi-Diop and Caterina Romeo. Special issue, *Postcolonial Studies* 18 (4): 337–352.

Makaping, Geneviève. 2001. *Traiettorie di sguardi. E se gli altri foste voi?* Soveria Mannelli: Rubbettino. Republished in 2022 (Soveria Mannelli: Rubbettino). Trans. Giovanna Bellesia-Contuzzi and Victoria Offredi Poletto as *Reversing the Gaze: What If the Other Were You?* (New Brunswick: Rutgers University Press, forthcoming in 2023).

Mengiste, Maaza. 2019. *The Shadow King.* New York: Norton. Trans. Anna Nadotti as *Il re ombra* (Turin: Einaudi, 2021).

Ofosu-Somuah, Barbara, and Candice Whitney. 2020. Translating Italy, Translating Blackness. *Public Books,* October 12. https://www.publicbooks.org/translating-italy-translating-blackness/.

Opitz, May, Katharina Oguntoye, and Dagmar Schultz, eds. 1992. *Showing Our Colors: Afro-German Women Speak Out.* Amherst: The University of Massachusetts Press. Trans. Anne V. Adams, in cooperation with Tina Campt, May Opitz, and Dagmar Schultz. Originally published as *Farbe bekennen: Afro-deutsche Frauen auf den Spuren ihrer Geschichte* (Berlin: Orlanda Frauenverlag, 1986).

Parker, Deborah. 2018. Race and Foreign Languages. *Inside Higher Education,* Inside Higher Education, June 21. https://www.insidehighered.com/views/2018/06/21/paucity-asians-and-other-minorities-teaching-and-studying-italian-and-other-foreign.

Phillip, Nicole, 2018. My Very Personal Taste of Racism Abroad. *New York Times*, October 23. https://www.nytimes.com/2018/10/23/travel/racism-travel-italy-study-abroad.html.

Polezzi, Loredana. 2020. Translation and Transnational Creative Practices in Italian Culture. In *Transnational Italian Studies*, ed. Charles Burdett and Loredana Polezzi, 25–45. Liverpool: Liverpool University Press.

Ponzanesi, Sandra, and Gianmaria Colpani, eds. 2016. *Postcolonial Transitions in Europe: Contexts, Practices and Politics*. London: Rowman & Littlefield.

Proglio, Gabriele. 2019. *Mediterraneo nero. Archivio, memorie, corpi*. Rome: manifestolibri.

Proglio, Gabriele, Camilla Hawthorne, P. Ida Danewid, Khalil Saucier, Giuseppe Grimaldi, Angelica Pesarini, Timothy Raeymaekers, Giulia Grechi, and Vivian Gerrand, eds. 2021. *The Black Mediterranean: Bodies, Borders and Citizenship*. Cham: Palgrave Macmillan.

Purtschert, Patricia, Francesca Falk, and Barbara Lüthi. 2016. Switzerland and 'Colonialism without Colonies': Reflections on the Status of Colonial Outsiders. *Interventions: International Journal of Postcolonial Studies* 18 (2): 286–302.

Puwar, Nirmal. 2004. *Space Invaders: Race, Gender and Bodies out of Place*. Oxford: Berg.

Ragusa, Kym. 2006. *The Skin Between Us: A Memoir of Race, Beauty, and Belonging*. New York: Norton. Trans. Clara Antonucci and Caterina Romeo as *La pelle che ci separa* (Rome: Nutrimenti, 2008).

———. 2008. *La pelle che ci separa*. Trans. Clara Antonucci and Caterina Romeo. Rome: Nutrimenti. Originally published as *The Skin Between Us: A Memoir of Race, Beauty, and Belonging* (New York: Norton, 2006).

Said, Edward W. 1979. *Orientalism*. New York: Vintage Books.

Scarafia, Sara. 2021. La sua Africa in aula: 'Il Nobel Gurnah lo racconto agli studenti.' *La Repubblica*, October 9. https://palermo.repubblica.it/societa/2021/10/09/news/la_sua_africa_in_aula_il_nobel_gurnah_lo_racconto_agli_studenti_-321432094/.

Scego, Igiaba. 2010. *La mia casa è dove sono*. Milan: Rizzoli.

———, ed. 2019. *Future. Il domani narrato dalle voci di oggi*. Florence: Effequ.

———. 2021. L'Africa e il senso di una vittoria: il Nobel per la letteratura a Abdulrazak Gurnah. *La Repubblica*, October 7. https://www.repubblica.it/cultura/2021/10/07/news/l_africa_e_il_senso_di_una_vittoria_il_nobel_per_la_letteratura_a_abdulrazak_gurnah-321258829/.

Simonetti, Gianluigi. 2018. *La letteratura circostante: narrativa e poesia nell'Italia contemporanea*. Bologna: Il Mulino.

Smythe, S.A. 2018. The Black Mediterranean and the Politics of Imagination. *Middle East Report* 286: 3–9.

Spivak, Gayatri Chakravorty. 1987 (1985). Subaltern Studies: Deconstructing Historiography. In *Other Worlds: Essays in Cultural Politics*, 197–221. New York: Methuen.

Tirinanzi De Medici, Carlo. 2018. *Il romanzo italiano contemporaneo. Dalla fine degli anni Settanta a oggi*. Rome: Carocci.

WashPostPR. 2020. The Washington Post Announces Writing Style Changes for Racial and Ethnic Identifiers. *Washington Post PR Blog, Washington Post*, July 29. https://www.washingtonpost.com/pr/2020/07/29/washington-post-announces-writing-style-changes-racial-ethnic-identifiers/.

CHAPTER 2

Italian Postcolonial Literature: An Overview

2.1 Introduction

In the following survey, I examine the important literary and cultural contributions to Italian literature and culture offered by writers who maintain a postcolonial relationship of some kind with Italy, be it direct or indirect.[1] The periodization that I propose here is not intended as a rigid classification, but rather as a loose indication of the different trends and trajectories that have characterized different periods. The dates, therefore, are generally indicated with a certain degree of approximation, the different phases flow into one another, and writers can populate more than one phase. The primary aim of this excursus, which cannot and is not intended to be exhaustive, is to demonstrate the great complexity and variation of the literary panorama examined in this volume. Over time, postcolonial writers have experimented across literary genres, modes of expression, languages, and themes, giving rise to a literary tradition that, to paraphrase Virginia Woolf, is of great importance since masterpieces are never born in isolation: they need predecessors, they need continuity, they need

---

[1] For a conceptualization of and a reflection on the "direct" and "indirect" nature of Italian postcoloniality, see Lombardi-Diop and Romeo (2012, 2015) and Fiore (2012).

© The Author(s), under exclusive license to Springer Nature Switzerland AG 2023
C. Romeo, *Interrupted Narratives and Intersectional Representations in Italian Postcolonial Literature*, Italian and Italian American Studies,
https://doi.org/10.1007/978-3-031-10043-7_2

community. To consider these literary works as a *corpus*—however hetero-geneous it may be—means to empower the counterdiscourse they articu-late and to legitimize the counterhistories they narrate.

In this chapter and in this volume in general, as I point out in Chap. 1, I designate the works produced by migrant and second-gen-eration authors since 1990 as "Italian postcolonial literature." This lit-erature, according to the loose periodization that I propose here, is divided into four principal phases characterized by specific trajectories as well as common practices and tendencies.

For the literary production of the first phase (1990–1994), I use the expression "migration literature" because the authors are often recent immigrants working in collaboration with co-authors. Their narratives deal mostly with issues related to migration and the sense of displacement and uprooting they experience in the society of destination.

The second phase (1994–2000) can in many ways be considered a "transitional phase." The issues at the core of this phase are still often linked to the difficulties experienced by migrants in the society of destina-tion. At the same time, this body of literature begins to have its own cul-tural and social stability through the creation of literary awards and journals devoted to migration literature.

I devote most of my analysis to the third phase (2001–2019), examin-ing the extraordinary diversity of the literary and cultural production of this period. The analysis of the third phase is organized into subsections: here I distinguish between direct and indirect postcolonial literature—which is based on the distinction between "direct" and "indirect" colonial relations and "direct" and "indirect" postcoloniality—conferring on writ-ers whose origins lie in former Italian colonies a privileged status from a historical, linguistic, and cultural perspective. I devote a separate section to Albanian Italian literature, given the particular position Albania occupies in Italian history, both because of its colonial history (however brief) and because the Albanian community constitutes one of the largest migrant groups in contemporary Italy (unlike communities coming from the former colonies in Africa, which are much smaller in comparison) (Centro Studi e Ricerche IDOS 2021).[2]

Because they rewrite colonial history and promote a critical review of it, writers originating from Italian ex-colonies offer a specific contribution to Italian culture. At the same time, their cultural production intersects the oppositional writings and counterhistories of postcolonial writers whose cultures do not originate in countries with a direct colonial relationship with Italy. This intersection produces a systematic critique of the processes of racialization enacted in contemporary societies, which are strongly tied to colonial racism and neo-racist strategies that aim to lead to the exclusion of migrants, refugees, and asylum seekers—and subsequent generations—from the body of the Italian nation and Fortress Europe.

In this chapter, I also formulate, for the first time, the hypothesis that a fourth phase has recently begun (2019–), which is characterized by the production—also for the first time—of race studies in the Italian language by (mainly) Black Italian women and non-binary authors on issues of race, color, gender, sexuality, citizenship exclusion, and racism from an intersectional perspective.

Italian postcolonial literature contributes to the questioning of the Italian cultural and social "norms." The literary production of these writers promotes the dissemination of new decolonizing imaginaries, encouraging deep and meaningful sociocultural change and a new politics of inclusion that extends Italian citizenship to Italians of foreign origins living in Italy today.

---

[2] Out of a total population of 5,013,215 foreign residents in Italy in 2020 (8.5% of the Italian population of 59,257,566), Albanians represented the second largest community, with 410,087 people. Romanians were the largest community, with a population of 1,137,728, followed by Albanians, Moroccans (408,179), Chinese (288,679), and Ukrainians (227,587) (Centro Studi e Ricerche IDOS 2021, 14). As for communities from Italian ex-colonies in Africa, only 2756 residents were from Libya (478), 8580 from Somalia, 7889 from Eritrea, and 6851 from Ethiopia (479).

2.2   THE FIRST PHASE: MIGRATION LITERATURE (1990–1994)[3]

The date generally ascribed to the origin of migration literature—the first phase of Italian postcolonial literature[4]—in Italy is 1990, the year in which three important autobiographical texts were published: *Io, venditore di elefanti* (*I Was an Elephant Salesman*) by Senegalese writer Pap Khouma in collaboration with Oreste Pivetta (Khouma 2006); *Immigrato* (Immigrant) by Tunisian writer Salah Methnani in collaboration with Mario Fortunato (Fortunato and Methnani 2006); and *Chiamatemi Alì* (Call Me Ali) by Moroccan writer Mohamed Bouchane, edited by Carla De Girolamo and Daniele Miccione (Bouchane 1990).[5] The prevailing genre throughout the first half of the 1990s was the collaborative autobiography, which, in the first phase of migration literature, seemed to satisfy

[3] The sections devoted to the first and second phase are rather brief because much has been written about them. In the present chapter, I focus mainly on the complexities of the third phase and on the emergence of the fourth phase.

[4] Due to space limitations, this article will not give poetry, children's literature, and theater the attention they deserve. I limit myself to providing some information and bibliographical notes on these topics. Magazines such as *Caffè*, *Sagarana*, and *El Ghibli* dedicate specific sections to poetry. The same is true of the Eks&Tra, Prize for Migrant Writers. Collections that introduce the poetry of migrant and postcolonial writers include Lecomte (2006, 2011), and Lecomte and Bonaffini (2011). In 2009, Mia Lecomte founded the Society of Women Poets, which includes Prisca Agustoni, Ubax Cristina Ali Farah, Anna Belozorovitch, Livia Bazu, Laure Cambau, Adriana Langtry, Mia Lecomte, Sarah Zuhra Lukanic, Vera Lucia de Oliveira, Helene Paraskeva, Brenda Porster, Begonya Pozo, Barbara Pumhösel, Francisca Paz Rojas, Candelaria Romero, Barbara Serdakowski, Jacqueline Spaccini, and Eva Taylor, foreign poets and Italian poets of foreign origins whose lives are characterized by different forms of migration and who write in Italian (see the website of Compagnia delle poete). For an analysis and a substantial bibliography of migration literature for children, see Luatti (2010a, b). The I Mappamondi (Globes) series from Sinnos Publishing is central with regard to children's literature. Sinnos was founded in 1990 in the Roman prison of Rebibbia and has always promoted a strong social commitment. This series was created for schools in 1991 and encourages students to learn about other places in the world (all authors are either foreigners or the children of foreigners writing about their country of origin) and promotes a mutual understanding between Italians of Italian origins and Italians of foreign origins. The more than 20 volumes in this series include an introductory text by Tullio De Mauro. They also include parallel text translations, accompanying drawings, and a section called "Mappapagine" at the end of each book, with information on the presence of foreign communities in Italy. As an example, see Sibhatu (2012b). For sources on theater, see Hoyet (2006), and especially Mauceri and Niccolai (2015).

[5] For a compelling analysis of the practice of storytelling in autobiographical texts by African authors in Italy, see Lombardi-Diop (2005).

both the authors' desires to recount their impressions of Italy and the curiosity of Italians to learn something about migrants' experiences in their country.[6] Other autobiographies that emerged in this period include *La tana della iena. Storia di un ragazzo palestinese* (The Hyena's Den: Story of a Palestinian Boy) (1991) by Palestinian writer Hassan Itab (written in collaboration with Renato Curcio),[7] *Volevo diventare bianca* (I Wanted to Become White) (1993) by French Sahawari Algerian writer Nassera Chohra (edited by Alessandra Atti Di Sarro), and *Con il vento nei capelli. Vita di una donna palestinese* (1994) (*The Wind in My Hair*, 2007) by Palestinian writer Salwa Salem (in collaboration with Laura Maritano).[8]

The autobiography of Brazilian author Fernanda Farias de Albuquerque, *Princesa* (1994), was also published in the early 1990s and is unique among these works. Created inside Rome's Rebibbia Prison, it is the result of a collaborative effort between Farias de Albuquerque and Maurizio Jannelli, a former member of the Red Brigades serving time in jail. An additional collaborator, Giovanni Tamponi, an incarcerated Sardinian

---

[6] The term "collaborative autobiography" is used here to refer to any kind of autobiography that is the result of a collaboration between a narrator/author and an editor/co-author. Not only is the collaborator's input in these instances necessary because of an inadequate level of linguistic knowledge and competence on the part of the narrator, the collaborator also acts as a cultural mediator, helping with the clarity and readability of the text and aiding the storytellers in establishing contact with the publishing market. Any such collaboration entails a power relationship, which is an integral part of the work's origin and characterizes the work itself (see Romeo 2015). The role of the editor, therefore, cannot be considered transparent, but rather must always be scrutinized. On collaborative texts as possible decolonial practices, see Brioni (2013b).

[7] The publishing house that published *La tana della iena,* Sensibili alle foglie, was founded in 1990 under the directorship of Renato Curcio, an ex-Red Brigadier, with the purpose of promoting activities and publishing texts on different experiences of reclusion. See the website of Sensibili alle foglie.

[8] After the initial phase of migration literature and with the advent of second-generation writers, the need for both linguistic and cultural mediation is replaced by the authorial individual, while the genre of autobiography gives way to that of the novel and the short story. There are, however, some collaborative autobiographies that have been published in more recent years, among which it is worth mentioning Tekle (2005) and Uba (2007). In addition, in the section on direct postcolonial literature, two important collaborative autobiographical texts by Martha Nasibù and Isabella Marincola will be discussed (see Nasibù 2005; Wu Ming 2 and Mohamed 2012).

shepherd, functioned as an intermediary between the two.[9] In a mixture of Portuguese, Italian, and Sardinian, Farias de Albuquerque first recounted her story to Tamponi, detailing her early life in Brazil as Fernando, her transition from male to female, her migration, and her experience as a sex worker right up to her incarceration in Rebibbia for attempted murder. Surrounded by the senseless and unchanging routines of penitentiary life, the co-authors forged their own language and found a way to transcend the narrow confines of their imprisonment by reinventing, through the power of storytelling, the world from which they were banned.[10]

Personal experience is also at the core of several novels written collaboratively with Italian co-authors during those same years, such as *La promessa di Hamadi* (Hamadi's Promise) (1991) and *La memoria di A.* (A.'s Memory) (1995) by Senegalese writer Saidou Moussa Ba (in collaboration with Alessandro Micheletti) and *Pantanella. Canto lungo la*

---

[9] The project "Princesa 20" was started in 2015: it was designed by Ugo Fracassa, directed by Fracassa and Anna Proto Pisani, and funded by the Department of Humanities of the Roma Tre University (with co-financing from the Centre d'Etudes Romanes Aixois [CAER] at Aix-Marseille University). In this extraordinary multimedia project, the text of *Princesa* interacts with other narratives: the eponymous song (lyrics and music) (1996) that Fabrizio De André dedicated to Fernanda Farias de Albuquerque's story; the documentary *Princesa. Incontri irregolari* (Conversi 1994) made for the Anna Amendola series *Storie Vere*, broadcast by RAI in 1994; the documentary *Le strade di Princesa. Ritratto di una trans molto speciale* (Consiglio 1997); and the film *Princesa* by Brazilian director Henrique Goldman (2001). In addition to the complete text of the book, the project made a collection of new materials available online, such as part of the original manuscripts and of the correspondence between the author and the collaborators. The site also contains a collection of critical materials about the text. See the website of Il Progetto Princesa 20. The fact that Fabrizio De André referred to Fernanda Farias de Albuquerque's book in 1996 signals an interesting phenomenon grossly overlooked in Italian academia: that exchanges between "canonical" Italian culture—in this case, music—and the cultural production of migrant and postcolonial authors have taken place in both directions, and major Italian intellectuals have been engaging with the work of migrant and postcolonial writers for decades.

[10] This information is taken from Maurizio Jannelli's introductory notes to *Princesa* (1994), "Brevi note di contesto" (Brief Background Notes), in which he describes the context of their encounter and provides interesting details about how the text reached its final form. There is a striking similarity between the narrative settings in this book and those in Hector Babenco's film *Kiss of the Spider Woman* (1985), based on Manuel Puig's novel *El beso de la mujer araña* (1976). In the film, Valentin Arregui (Raúl Juliá), a political activist, is incarcerated in a South American prison, where he shares a cell with Luis Molina (William Hurt), a flamboyant gay man. Every time Valentin goes back to their cell after being tortured by the police, Luis soothes his wounds through both physical care and storytelling.

strada (Pantanella: A Song Along the Road) (1992), written in Arabic by Tunisian writer and director Mohsen Melliti and translated into Italian by Monica Ruocco.[11]

All of these autobiographical narratives, which shape the first phase of Italian postcolonial literature, present stories about the difficult lives, both individual and collective, of immigrants in Italy, narrated for the first time not *by* Italians but *to* Italians by migrants themselves. The commonplace strategy used by these migrant writers of evoking their countries of origin in their stories serves not only to reinstate the bonds that migration has severed but also to represent the full complexity of their lives before their arrival in Italy. Such complexity comes from having a history, a past, and a dense network of relationships and feelings—in stark contrast to the monolithic perception of undesirability usually projected onto migrants by the host society.

2.3   The Second Phase (1994–2000)

The first phase of Italian migration literature in the early 1990s was characterized by a type of socio-anthropological interest that facilitated the creation of an editorial space and led to the publication of the first collaborative autobiographies. Such interest, however, was accompanied by a marked reluctance on the part of Italian culture and academia to acknowledge these works as literary texts because—as often happens in the case of so-called minority literatures—they were considered too personal and thus insufficiently "universal."

The first phase of migration literature, then, was characterized by a certain homogeneity, as the needs of the new writers were aligned with the demands of the publishing market. In the transitional phase that lasted from 1994 to 2000, this homogeneity gave way to a greater diversity, preparing for a subsequent phase that emerged at the turn of the twenty-first century, characterized by a variety of styles and themes and by a strong criticism of different aspects of Italian culture and society. The writers active in the latter half of the 1990s were still for the most part actual migrants (rather than second-generation authors), and themes closely related to migration as both a material and a psychological experience were still powerfully present in much of their work. Nevertheless, during

---

[11] Mohsen Melliti is also the author of *I bambini delle rose* (1995), his first text written directly in Italian, and director of the film *Io l'altro* (2007).

the same period, a more pronounced attention to stylistic elements became evident in their texts, along with the appearance of a wider range of themes that characterized the writings published in the subsequent decade, especially following the emergence of second-generation writers.

The second half of the 1990s saw the creation of literary competitions and of the earliest magazines specializing in migrant literature, while additional prizes were established and magazines founded in the new millennium. In 1995, the literary competition Eks&Tra was established for migrant writing, with the specific intent to "promote mutual understanding, verify the point to which integration between cultural expressions that can be mutually enriching has been reached or can be reached, discover how fundamental human values are the same everywhere"[12] (Eksetra n.d., para. 2). Its purpose was to give voice and visibility "to those who are often perceived as foreign bodies to be marginalized, ghettoized, or even expelled"[13] (Eksetra n.d.). Over the course of the years, this literary contest facilitated the emergence of writers who went on to dominate the field of postcolonial and migration literature. One of the prizewinners that first year, for example, was the Albanian poet Gëzim Hajdari,[14] who would two years later win the Montale Prize. Another prizewinner was the Brazilian Italian novelist and short story writer Christiana de Caldas Brito for her story "Ana de Jesus" (1995), which subsequently became a cult text in Italian postcolonial literature.[15] The undisputed protagonists of the collection in which this short story appears are immigrant women who suffer isolation and marginalization and whose stories, finally told in their own voices, defy media representations that present them merely as members of the workforce rather than as complex individual subjects. These characters denounce the exploitation meted out to immigrant women, not only by men, but also by Italian women in a way that calls into question the notion of "universal sisterhood" historically cherished by Italian

---

[12] "Promuovere la conoscenza reciproca, verificare fino a che punto è giunta o può giungere l'integrazione tra espressioni culturali che possono mutualmente arricchirsi, scoprire come i valori fondamentali dell'uomo siano ovunque gli stessi." [All translations are the translator's unless noted otherwise].

[13] "a coloro che vengono spesso considerati come corpi estranei da emarginare e ghettizzare o anche da espellere."

[14] See the section below dedicated to Albanian Italian literature.

[15] de Caldas Brito is a prolific writer who later published several books, including the collection of short stories *Qui e là* (2004), the novel *500 temporali* (2006), and the creative writing guide *Viviscrivi. Verso il tuo racconto* (2008).

feminism.[16] As Franca Sinopoli (1998) observes, de Caldas Brito's work is characterized by the kind of stylistic lightness that Italo Calvino hoped could be achieved in twenty-first century literature.[17] This quality results in part from the writer's linguistic experimentation with "portuliano," the mixture of Portuguese and Italian spoken by Brazilian immigrants in Italy, which de Caldas Brito codifies—and thereby authorizes—in her writing.

Other stories that won the Eks&Tra award in 1995 were "Io marocchino con due kappa" (I, a Moroccan with Two Ks) (1995) by Syrian author Yousef Wakkas, written from prison while the author was in an extreme state of marginalization, and "Solo allora, sono certo, potrò capire" (Only Then, I Am Sure, Will I Be Able to Understand) (1995) by Algerian writer Tahar Lamri, which focuses on the impossibility of migrants recuperating their original identities. [18] In 1996, Cape Verdean writer Maria de Lourdes Jesus's *Racordai. Vengo da un'isola di Capo Verde* (Racordai. I Come from One of Cape Verde Islands)—a text in which Italian appears alongside the Portuguese creole typically spoken in Cape Verde—was published in the I Mappamondi (Globes) series.

Important literary prizes continued to be established in the new millennium: among them, in 2005, Daniela Finocchi founded the national literary competition Lingua Madre for foreign women and women of foreign origin who are Italian residents and who write in Italian in order to "deepen the relationship between identity, roots, and 'other' worlds"[19] (Concorso Letterario Nazionale Lingua Madre n.d., para. 2).[20] The contest was created specifically as a "significant example of the interactions that are redrawing the cultural map of the new millennium"[21] (Concorso Letterario Nazionale Lingua Madre n.d., para 3). Lingua Madre also implicitly promoted creative partnerships between Italian women and foreign women insofar as it accepted the submission of collaborative writings.

---

[16] On the notion of "universal sisterhood" challenged by migrant women, see Chap. 3.

[17] Sinopoli's introduction to *Amanda Olinda Azzurra e le altre* (de Caldas Brito 1998) is replaced by a new introductory text by de Caldas Brito in the 2004 edition.

[18] Other notable works from these two authors include Wakkas (2004, 2005, 2007) and Lamri (2006).

[19] "approfondire il rapporto fra identità, radici e mondo 'altro.'"

[20] This contest is sponsored by the Region of Piemonte and the International Book Fair in Turin.

[21] "un esempio significativo delle interazioni che stanno ridisegnando la mappa culturale del nuovo millennio."

The mid-1990s also saw the emergence of the first important literary journals dedicated (almost) exclusively to migrant and postcolonial writing. These continued to develop in the new millennium, highlighting the ways in which forms of artistic expression linked to the representation of immigration were changing. In 1994, the first journal focused entirely on migration literature, *Caffè. Rivista di letteratura multiculturale*, was founded by intellectuals and activists involved in immigration issues and by migrant writers.[22] In 1997, Armando Gnisci created the database BASILI,[23] BAnca dati degli Scrittori Immigrati in Lingua Italiana (Database of Immigrant Authors Writing in Italian), which was accompanied in 2000 by the magazine *Kúmá. Creolizzare l'Europa*, also steered by Gnisci. Another group, Scritti d'Africa, based at the Casa delle Culture in Rome, was also founded in 1997. It included writers such as Ubax Cristina Ali Farah and Jorge Canifa Alves, among others, and was aimed at familiarizing the Italian public with different African cultures mainly through exposure to literary works written by both African authors and Italian authors of African descent.[24] The online magazine *Sagarana*, edited by Brazilian writer Julio Monteiro Martins, was founded in 2000 and hosted by the Sagarana school of creative writing, which, from 2001 onwards, has offered the *Seminari degli Scrittori Migranti* (Migrant Writers Seminars).[25] *El Ghibli. Rivista online di letteratura della migrazione*, the first magazine whose editorial staff was entirely composed of migrant writers (in the broadest sense of the term), under Pap Khouma's editorship, was created in 2003, and other journals focused on migrations flourished in the new

---

[22] See the website of *Caffè. Rivista di letteratura multiculturale*.

[23] The BASILI (BAnca dati degli Scrittori Immigrati in Lingua Italiana) database, once located at http://www.disp.let.uniroma1.it/kuma/kuma.html, was closed from 2014 to 2017. In April 2017, the database, under the new name BASILI&LIMM (BAnca dati degli Scrittori Immigrati in Lingua Italiana e della Letteratura Italiana della Migrazione Mondiale), became accessible again at https://basili-limm.el-ghibli.it/. Armando Gnisci's introduction to this new edition of the database, "Ritorna la banca dati BASILI nella nuova versione BASILI&LIMM. Dal primo BASILI al nuovo BASILI&LIMM," is available at https://basili-limm.el-ghibli.it/, currently under the supervision of Maria Cristina Mauceri, now also includes the work of second generations (originally not included in BASILI).

[24] See the website of Scritti d'Africa.

[25] See the website of *Sagarana*.

millennium.[26] *Scritture migranti. Rivista di scambi interculturali* was founded by members of the Department of Italian Studies at the University of Bologna in 2006 and published by Clueb until 2012 and then by Mucchi Editore starting in 2013. As the website announces, "Over the past ten years, *Scritture Migranti* has been developing critical work on the writings generated by migratory processes, exploring the themes of exile, journey, diaspora and the transcultural movements triggered by the post-colonial condition" (Stem Mucchi Editore 2018). This publication, rooted as it is in the awareness that globalization and transnational migrations (phenomena closely related to decolonization) have radically changed the way people think about culture and about the very concept of "nation," is noted for promoting the methodologies of cultural and postcolonial studies.

The magazine *Trickster. Rivista del Master in Studi Interculturali* was also created in 2006. Published by the University of Padua, it similarly placed the condition of migrants at the center of social and cultural issues in contemporary Italy.[27]

* * *

During the same period, literary work by writers of Eastern European origin also began to appear in Italy. A figure who stands out in this context is Jarmila Očkayová, a Slovak writer who arrived in Italy in 1974 and published three novels in Italian in the late 1990s: *Verrà la vita e avrà i tuoi occhi* (Life Will Come and Will Have Your Eyes) (1995), *L'essenziale è invisibile agli occhi* (What Is Essential Is Invisible to the Eyes) (1997), and

---

[26] See the website of *El Ghibli*. The website *LettERRANZA* is also dedicated to migrant literary production in Italian. In addition to providing a bibliographic database, it includes reviews, interviews, and information on events. I would also like to point out the website of the cultural association Il Gioco degli Specchi: Migranti, Cultura, Società. This association, founded in 2009 and based on a project by the same name, has over the years organized numerous cultural events related to migrations, literature, and cinema, as well as Italian language courses for foreigners.

[27] The journal is no longer being published, but some information is still available at https://logosunipd.wordpress.com/2008/11/18/trickster-la-rivista-del-master-in-studi-interculturali/.

Requiem per tre padri (Requiem for Three Fathers) (1998).[28] These texts are highly introspective first-person narratives, in which the themes of diversity and displacement are linked both to the issue of involuntary migration and to a more deeply existential experience. These novels contain distinctive echoes of psychoanalysis—dream-like narration occurs extensively in the second novel—and the personal and historical dimensions constantly intersect. In *Requiem per tre padri*, for example, which focuses on the Prague Spring and is dedicated to Jan Palach (a Czechoslovakian student who became the symbol of anti-Soviet resistance), historical events are narrated from the intimate perspective of the protagonists.

The late 1990s saw the publication of *La straniera* (The Stranger) (1999) by Iraqi writer Younis Tawfik, who had previously produced numerous Italian translations of Arabic texts and various essays on Muslim culture.[29] In this novel, which was awarded the Grinzane Cavour Prize in 2000, the past that emerges in the protagonists' memories and the influence of Arab traditions come together against the backdrop of contemporary, multicultural Turin. In some ways, *La straniera* could be considered an unconventional migration narrative since the male protagonist ("the Architect") enjoys an elevated social position and an enviable degree of "integration," unlike the characters appearing in narratives written during the initial autobiographical phase of migration literature. The novel, however, does not abandon earlier conventions and stereotypes in its depiction of the female protagonist, Amina. The author oscillates between exoticizing images (reinforced by the image of an orientalized Arab woman on the book cover) and victimized female characters. Amina, unlike the Architect, lives on the margins of society, works as a prostitute, and is sacrificed at the end of the narrative. Such representations reinforce the stereotype that

---

[28] Očkayová is also the author of, among other texts, *Occhio a Pinocchio* (2006), a book that, starting from Carlo Collodi's famous novel *Le avventure di Pinocchio. Storia di un burattino* (1883), reflects on themes that recur in Očkayová's literary production, such as the process of structuring one's identity and sense of belonging, individual and cultural roots, and family relationships.

[29] Younis Tawfik arrived in Italy in 1979 and studied literature and philosophy in Turin. He writes for several national newspapers and teaches Arabic Language and Literature at the University of Genoa. In addition to *La straniera* (1999), Tawfik has published numerous novels, including *La città di Iram* (2002), *Il profugo* (2006), and *La ragazza di Piazza Tahrir* (2012). The first novel, *La straniera*, was made into a film of the same title (Turco 2009).

deprives migrant women of all forms of agency and relegates them to roles such as caregivers and sex workers.

In the same period, Jadelin Mabiala Gangbo, who came to Italy with his family at the age of four from his birthplace of Brazzaville, Congo, appeared on the literary scene. At a time when migration literature was still dominated by first-generation writers, Gangbo was an exception because he grew up and went to school in Italy with Italian as his first language and Italian culture as the dominant one. Gangbo is a pioneering figure, presenting issues and themes incorporated into Italian postcolonial literature only years later. His work is characterized by different approaches to narrative and an experimental writing style. In his first novel, *Verso la notte bakonga* (Toward the Bakonga Night) (1999), Gangbo uses the classical form of the Bildungsroman, which is centered on the existential malaise of the protagonist, Mika, and his desire to find his own path. However, the relationship between the individual and society in this novel is rearticulated around the alienating effect produced by the protagonist's Blackness.[30] The second novel, *Rometta e Giulieo* (2001)—which marks Gangbo's transition to a major publisher—is highly experimental in both its language and its formal structure. To some extent a rewriting of Shakespeare's *Romeo and Juliet,* the novel recounts the romance between a female Italian student and a Chinese pizza deliveryman through a meta-narrative that operates as a continuous reflection on the writing process. Gangbo's use of the Italian language—a mixture of street slang and the language of Shakespeare (including stage directions in the novel)—marks the transition from migrant writers (who mostly write in Italian with the aid of an editor) to a new generation of Italian writers whose familiarity with the language makes it possible to alter the language from within and experiment with it and with literary genres. Such strategies, utterly new in the Italian literary and cultural context, suggest that shifting social conditions require new tools of literary expression and new forms of creativity.

The same type of linguistic experimentation is found in the story "Com'è se giù vuol dire ko?" (What If Down Means KO?) (Gangbo 2005), in which the author exposes the police violence directed at young

---

[30] It is important to note that this novel was published when most second-generation writers had yet to make their appearance on the literary scene. For an analysis of the author's first and third novels, see Chap. 4.

immigrants and Black Italians.[31] The two teenage characters (one is the son of Moroccan immigrants) speak in rap style, mixing Italian street slang and Bolognese dialect, which underlines the "glocal" character of the space they inhabit: local because specifically rooted in the geographical area of Bologna; global because they share the uneasiness of immigrants' children in other urban contexts around the world.[32] The title of Gangbo's most recent novel, *Due volte* (Two Times) (2009), foregrounds the theme of duality, which is central to the life and literary production of immigrant and second-generation writers and, in this novel, is not limited to a binary opposition of Italian/immigrant or Black/white.[33] The protagonists are twin 10-year-old boys who have migrated from Benin and are sent to a children's home run by a religious order after being abandoned by their father. They feel torn between a sense of belonging to their father's culture and a desire to integrate into the new society in which they live, while their difficulties are intensified by the other kinds of hardship experienced by all the socially marginalized children who live in the same institution.

The second phase of Italian postcolonial literature, although brief and transitory, is characterized by a much broader spectrum of authors, genres, themes, and styles than that of the period immediately preceding it, as well as a certain degree of institutionalization through the creation of literary awards and journals devoted exclusively (or almost exclusively) to migration literature. Crucially, this transitional phase marks a growing variety among the narratives produced and the themes developed (including social diversity, processes of racialization, and the complexity of national identity in contemporary Italy), which are profoundly significant at the beginning of the twenty-first century and more relevant than ever in the Italian society and culture of today. These themes become even more prominent in the third phase of Italian postcolonial literature.

---

[31] For a reading of this text in relation to the global hip-hop scene and the cultural production of the second generations, see Clò (2012). See my analysis of the story in relation to urban spaces in Chap. 5.

[32] As I show in Chap. 5, the text contains strong references to the Paris *banlieues* through citations to the film *La Haine* (Kassovitz 1995).

[33] See my analysis of this novel in Chap. 4.

2.4   The Third Phase (2001–2019)

The new millennium, as previously stated, heralds a phase that is both more literary and more discernibly postcolonial. Among the topics that begin to emerge and develop over time during this third phase are the processes of racialization enacted by Italian society both past and present, historical and contemporary racism, the continuity existing between a colonial past and a postcolonial present, the construction of an Italian identity for immigrants and their children, and the difficulty of attaining Italian citizenship for second generations.[34] The literature produced since the beginning of the new millennium (often) presents an oppositional character and is articulated through counterhistories strongly critical of Italy's colonial past and the way in which that legacy informs contemporary postcolonialism. This phase is thus characterized by both the emergence of new writers and a process of consolidation witnessed in the work of those authors already influential within the cultural scene. This section, dedicated to the third phase, is divided into subsections that provide space for several prominent writers from countries that have an indirect postcolonial relationship with Italy; Albanian Italian literature, in light of its complexity and importance to the Italian cultural and literary context; the

---

[34] My periodization differs from scholars such as Maria Grazia Negro (2015), who classifies as "postcolonial literature" only the work produced by authors from the Horn of Africa, which I define in this essay "(direct) postcolonial literature." In her view, a new phase began around 2005, and not at the beginning of the century. This disparity in periodization can be attributed to our differences in definition, which are not simply descriptive but rather based on distinct focuses and priorities. Negro's linguistic analysis is based on the differentiation between writers originating from Italian ex-colonies and those coming from the ex-colonies of other European countries. My study focuses instead on the modes in which colonial mechanisms of the past are brought back to life in the present and therefore considers issues such as processes of racialization and the acquisition of citizenship. Therefore, in my analysis, it is important to consider how authors from the Horn of Africa enter into dialogue with African Italian writers from countries that were once colonized by other European powers. Geneviève Makaping's text *Traiettorie di sguardi* (2001, republished in 2022) (*Reversing the Gaze: What If the Other Were You?*, 2023), to which I return later, provides a specific reflection on the themes of race, gender, and citizenship, as does Igiaba Scego's short story "Salsicce" (2005b). These texts, which in my opinion mark a watershed in Italian literature, are from 2001 and 2003 respectively (although for Scego I use the 2005 edition), and so precede 2005. For this reason, I locate the beginning of the third phase of postcolonial literature at the inception of the twenty-first century. Here and throughout the book, I refer to the 2001 edition of *Traiettorie*; the book was just republished by Rubbettino in Italian (2022) and is about to be published in English translation (forthcoming in 2023).

cultural work of authors more directly linked to Italy's colonial history who come almost exclusively from the Horn of Africa and whose acknowledgment enabled the development of a more directly postcolonial Italian literary and cultural phase[35]; and the advent of second-generation writers who have a direct or indirect postcolonial relationship with Italy.[36]

2.4.1   The Third Phase: Some Prominent Writers (Indirect Postcolonial Literature)

One of the leading figures to emerge on the cultural and literary scene at the beginning of the twenty-first century is writer Julio Monteiro Martins. After publishing numerous books in his home country and teaching creative writing at universities in the United States, Brazil, and Portugal, he arrived in Italy in 1995. He taught literary translation and Portuguese at the University of Pisa for several years. In 2000, he founded the Sagarana School in Lucca, for which he directed the Master's Workshop in fiction writing and, as previously mentioned, edited the online magazine of the same name. A multifaceted author, Monteiro Martins experimented with various genres, including short stories, novels, poems, essays, and plays.[37]

The Algerian writer Amara Lakhous, one of Italy's most internationally renowned postcolonial authors, made his Italian literary debut in 1999 with the novel *Le cimici e il pirata* (The Bedbugs and the Pirate).[38] His breakthrough, however, came in 2006 with the publication of *Scontro di civiltà per un ascensore a Piazza Vittorio* (*Clash of Civilizations Over an Elevator in Piazza Vittorio*, 2013), which was awarded the Flaiano Prize and the Racalmare-Leonardo Sciascia Prize in the same year and which was included in the *Corriere della Sera*'s ranking one of the most widely

---

[35] As we will see later, Italian direct postcolonial literature developed from 1990 onwards and produced important texts prior to 2000. From a temporal perspective, therefore, the first texts of this literature could be included in Sect. 2.2 in the first phase (migration literature), which spans the years 1990 to 1994. I choose to include these texts in Sect. 2.4.3, dedicated entirely to direct postcolonial literature, in order to highlight their valuable contribution in connecting Italian colonial history and contemporaneity.

[36] For a deeper investigation of these topics, see Sect. 4.3.

[37] See Martins (2000, 2003). Other publications by Martins include the novel *Madrelingua* (2005) and another collection of short stories, *L'amore scritto* (2007).

[38] The novel, published in Arabic with parallel text in Italian, was reprinted after the Arab Spring under the title *Un pirata piccolo piccolo* (2011).

read books in Italy.[39] As has been observed, the text is influenced in equal parts by Italian film comedy (*commedia all'italiana*) and Carlo Emilio Gadda's *Quer pasticciaccio brutto de via Merulana* (1957) (*That Awful Mess on the Via Merulana*, 1965), while the autobiographical elements so pervasive in the writings of other migrant authors appear to be absent. Other aspects typical of postcolonial literature are instead present in the novel, such as the multicultural composition of society, linguistic plurality, and narrative polyphony. The characters do not merely provide information to help the investigation of the police commissioner, who must solve a murder that occurred in an apartment building near Piazza Vittorio inhabited by people from around the world, but also offer an analysis of the multicultural society they embody. The text very centrally ironizes the assumption that clashes are inevitable where different cultures coexist. In narrating the events, the use of different registers is accompanied by linguistic and cultural contamination.

Lakhous's fascination with the linguistic plurality that is manifest in Italy through the use of dialects is also present in his third novel, *Divorzio all'islamica a viale Marconi* (2010) (*Divorce Islamic Style in Viale Marconi*, 2013). The novel's protagonist, Christian, is a Sicilian who speaks a version of Italian that is enriched by many expressions and sentence constructions informed by dialect (as seen, for example, in his abundant usage of the preterit tense, the Italian passato remoto) and who is also completely fluent in Arabic. He goes undercover and infiltrates the Muslim community, which is allegedly planning a terrorist attack. If in *Scontro di civiltà* no one, until the time of the murder, ever suspected that "Amedeo the Italian" was actually "Ahmed the immigrant," in this novel Christian's physical appearance and knowledge of Arabic enable him to pass easily as Tunisian: both instances, one the reversal of the other, underscore the fact that immigrants and "normative" Italians are not so different after all.

Lakhous ironically takes up themes such as the incompatibility between cultures and the notion of the Muslim peril obsessively touted following the attacks of September 11, 2001. His subsequent novels, *Contesa per un maialino italianissimo a San Salvario* (2013) (*Dispute over a Very Italian Piglet*, 2014) and *La zingarata della verginella di via Ormea* (2014) (*The*

---

[39] *Scontro di civiltà per un ascensore a Piazza Vittorio* (2006) is the Italian rewriting by Lakhous of a text he had written in Arabic that was published under the title *Come farsi allattare dalla lupa senza che ti morda* (2003). In 2010 *Scontro di civiltà* was made into the eponymous film directed by Isotta Toso (2010).

Prank of the Good Little Virgin of Via Ormea, 2017), are modeled on some of the central aspects of the first two. The city that provides the setting for these novels—as is hinted at in the titles—is Turin, where Lakhous lived from 2011 to 2014, prior to moving to the United States, where he still resides. The urban fabric in which the novels unfold is strongly characterized, as in the earlier books, by the coexistence of different cultures, a consequence of Italy's historic internal migrations and its more recent experiences of transnational migrations.[40] As a whole, these novels show, with a levity that is typical of Lakhous's style, how urban contexts have changed in Italy and how they will continue to change in the future, representing the conflicts that the coexistence of different cultures can trigger, while raising the possibility that such coexistence might unfold peacefully, proving itself to be an enriching factor in various Italian geographical and cultural contexts.[41]

2.4.2   The Third Phase: Albanian Italian Literature

The works of Albanian writers in Italian, one of the most interesting strands in Italian postcolonial literature, deserve a separate discussion. The relationship between Italy and Albania has long-standing roots (at the very least, one must remember the Arbëreshë communities in Southern Italy[42]), going back long before the great waves of migration that began in Albania in 1991 after the collapse of the communist regime. From 1939 to 1943, the two countries maintained a clear colonial relationship that has had a profound impact on Albania's history. Later, at the end of the

---

[40] The same continuity between past internal migrations and contemporary transnational migrations is present in Gabriella Kuruvilla's novel *Milano, fin qui tutto bene* (2012). For a more detailed examination of this topic, see Chap. 5.

[41] Among the many writers I exclude from this survey for reasons of space, I wish to acknowledge Adrian Bravi, an Argentinian of Italian origin. His work is remarkable not only for its literary qualities but also because it represents a new phenomenon within migratory movements toward Italy, namely the return migration of the descendants of Italian emigrants. For writers like Bravi, Italy is in a certain sense their homeland. At the same time, however, these writers often have a relationship of deep estrangement from the country and from the Italian language. Among the books published in Italy by Adrian Bravi are *Restituiscimi il cappotto* (2004), *La pelusa* (2007), *Il riporto* (2011) (finalist for the 2012 Comisso Prize), and *L'albero e la vacca* (2013). On return migration and the way in which "return emigrants" can be inserted into the discourse on the Italian postcolonial due to the double meaning of the word "colony," see Fiore (2012).

[42] On this subject see, among others, Perta (2011) and Liuzzi (2016).

1970s, and especially after the death of Enver Hoxha in 1985, Albania's geographical proximity to Italy enabled the reception of Italian television by Albanian audiences, which provided them with access to the "Western world" in the final years of the communist era's media censorship and information restriction. This opening to the West, with its emphasis on the welfare of the individual subject as opposed to state-sanctioned communities, contributed greatly to shaping Albanians' desire for freedom, for materialism, and eventually for emigration (see King and Mai 2008). Thus, although Italian colonialism in Albania was short-lived, the relationship between the two countries can be considered postcolonial, not only by virtue of the colonial relationship in the past, but also because of a more recent form of cultural colonialism that strongly informed the Albanians' desire to migrate, resulting in a robust flow from Albania to Italy over the past 30 years. Since the images of ships overloaded with immigrants (the *Vlora*, primarily) that began to arrive in 1991 on the coast of Apulia were first imprinted in the collective imaginaries of both Albanians and Italians,[43] the Albanian community has come to constitute the second-largest immigrant group in Italy.[44]

The strong Italian influence on Albanian history and culture is present in the literary output of writers of Albanian origin, some of whom are "transmigrants" (after migrating to Italy, these writers have moved to other countries).[45] An important presence on the literary scene is the Albanian poet Gëzim Hajdari, who left his homeland in 1992 for political reasons and, once in Italy, began writing in Italian.[46] In 1995 he won the Eks&Tra Prize, and in 1997 he was awarded the Montale Prize for an unpublished collection of poetry, the core of which was later published as *Corpo presente* (Body Present) in 1999. In spite of these and other important literary acknowledgments, he has remained somewhat at the margins

---

[43] This can be seen in two documentaries, *La nave dolce* (Vicari 2012) and *Anija la nave* (Sejko 2013).

[44] See note 2 in this chapter.

[45] For a definition of "transmigrant," see Schiller et al. (1995).

[46] Gëzim Hajdari has to his credit the publication of many poetry collections, most of which are in both Italian and Albanian. Among these volumes are *Ombra di cane/Hije qeni* (1993), *Sassi controvento/Gurë kundërerës* (1995), *Antologia della pioggia/Antologjia e shiut* (2000), *Spine nere/Gjëmba të zinj* (2004), *Poema dell'esilio/Poema e mërgimit* (2005), *Peligòrga/Peligorga* (2007), *Poesie scelte 1990–2007* (2008), *Corpo presente/Trup i pranishëm* (2011), *Evviva il canto del gallo nel villaggio comunista/Rroftë kënga e gjelit në fshatin komunist* (2013), and *Poesie scelte 1990–2015* (2015).

of the Italian literary scene. Themes of exile, isolation, and foreignness are central to his poetry, in which images of his native country emerge from memory, together with a past from which he cannot and does not want to break free.

Ron Kubati, who arrived in Italy during the exodus in 1991, has a very pronounced and complex relationship with Italian language and culture. He received his first doctorate in Modern and Contemporary Philosophy at the University of Bari and began his work as a writer in Italian at the same time. He later moved to the United States, where he earned a second doctorate in Italian studies at the University of Chicago.[47] In his first two novels, *Va e non torna* (The No Return Way) (2000) and *M* (2002), autobiographical elements coexist alongside history and literary fiction. If the hopes of a generation struggling with their new life permeate these two novels (centering on the possibilities of migration in the first and the issue of integration into an already heavily multicultural society in the second), such hopes disappear in the gloomy atmosphere of his third novel, *Il buio del mare* (The Darkness of the Sea) (2007). In *La vita dell'eroe* (The Life of the Hero) (2016), Kubati's most recent novel—and the first written in the United States (but still in Italian)—the personal stories of the characters intersect with the history of Albania, especially with the Fascist occupation of Albania from 1939 to 1943, the resistance of the National Liberation Army, and the establishment of Hoxha's communist regime.[48]

Ornela Vorpsi was included among the 35 best European writers in the 2010 anthology *Best European Fiction* (Hemon 2010), the inaugural volume in a series that identifies writers of note from various European countries every year. Vorpsi arrived in Italy in 1991, studied at the Brera Academy of Fine Arts, and then moved to Paris, where she trained as a photographer and visual artist. Vorpsi, whose work has been translated into many languages, originally wrote her novels in Italian and only later shifted to French as her preferred language. She made her debut in Italy in 2005, when she released her first novel, *Il paese dove non si muore mai* (2005) (*The Country Where No One Ever Dies*, 2009), which was written

---

[47] Kubati, who currently lives in New York City, writes in both Italian and English: he wrote his dissertation at the University of Chicago in Italian and English and uses both languages in his academic writing. As for creative writing, Kubati released his latest novel in Italian, *La vita dell'eroe* (The Life of the Hero) (2016), but in the future he may change his language of publication. Thanks to Ron Kubati for providing me with this information in an email exchange in June 2021.

[48] Kubati has recently co-edited a volume on diversity in Italian contemporary literature and culture (Orton et al. 2021).

in Italian, as was the subsequent novel, *La mano che non mordi* (The Hand You Do Not Bite) (2007); both, however, were first published in France in French and only later in Italian.[49] Her writing style, both spare and incisive, is reminiscent of Ágota Kristóf's, and her stories often revolve around female characters, their social positions, and their sexuality. The first novel, *Il paese dove non si muore mai*, takes place in Albania and focuses on power relations between the sexes and the ways in which women's sexuality is socially regulated. Personal stories also merge with official ones in the second novel, *La mano che non mordi*, in which a trip to Sarajevo—a city that is not located in the protagonist's homeland but with which she nevertheless maintains a relationship of proximity and contiguity—brings back memories of the Albania left behind long ago and causes the protagonist to reflect on her own sense of displacement. The 14 stories in *Bevete cacao Van Houten!* (Drink Van Houten Cocoa!) (2010) are animated by the dreams and desires of migration of the protagonists, depicted right at the moment when such desires become reality and their personal stories begin to unfold toward different—sometimes tragic—ends.[50] Vorpsi's latest novel, *Viaggio intorno alla madre* (A Journey Around the Mother) (2015), marks her passage from writing in Italian to writing in French. It is an intimate and courageous work—as her novels often are—that places the protagonist's sexual desire at the center of the narrative, seriously questioning the traditional roles of wives and mothers to which women are still often relegated.

Elvira Dones left Albania in 1988, before the fall of the communist regime, and relocated to Switzerland, where she spent 16 years. From 2004 to 2015, she resided in the United States, first in Washington, DC, and then in California, and worked as a writer, screenwriter, journalist, and documentary filmmaker; she then moved back to the Italian part of Switzerland, the Canton of Ticino, where she currently resides. Her literary production includes six novels published in Italy; the first four written

---

[49] These two novels have received numerous literary prizes: *Il paese dove non si muore mai* was awarded, among others, the Grinzane Cavour Prize for Best Young Author and the Viareggio Prize European Cultures, while *La mano che non mordi* won the Albatros Città di Palestrina prize for travel literature and the Città di Tropea national literary prize. In between the two novels, Vorpsi published *Vetri rosa* (2006).

[50] Vorpsi later also published *Fuorimondo* (2012).

in Albanian and the others, published in 2007 and 2011, in Italian.[51] Her works often focus on societal norms, with special attention paid to the exploitation of women and the social construction of gender. At the center of the novel *Sole bruciato* (Burnt Sun) (2001), for example, is the trafficking of Albanian girls who are brought to Italy at a very young age and are forced to enter the sex trade. Dones has also filmed a documentary on this issue (with Mohamed Soudani) entitled *Cercando Brunilda* (Searching for Brunilda) (Dones and Soudani 2003), a reflection on both the dangers of the journey of undocumented migrants and the condition faced by female victims of sex trafficking.[52] In her novel *Vergine giurata* (2007b) (*Sworn Virgin*, 2014), the events develop partly in northern Albania and partly in the United States, where the protagonist Hana/Mark migrates to begin a new life. The transition occurs not only at a social, cultural, and linguistic level but also at the level of gender identity. Hana's body is placed at the center of the narrative.[53] In order not to submit to her Albanian village's patriarchal rules and marry against her will, she resorts to the ancient law of the Kanun and becomes a "sworn virgin."[54] This social role requires a woman to swear to remain a virgin for life and, in exchange, she is authorized by society to assume a masculine appearance and lead life as a man, with all the privileges that result from this change of status. Yet the transition brings with it all the limitations entailed in the denial of one's original gender identity and one's assumption of another. The motivation to migrate coincides with Hana/Mark's desire to reclaim her earlier identity and to inhabit that earlier sexuality, dismantling the patriarchal laws that her home village would never have allowed her to break.

Anilda Ibrahimi worked as a journalist in Albania until 1994, when she moved first to Switzerland and then, in 1997, to Italy, where she continues

---

[51] *Senza bagagli* (1998), *Sole bruciato* (2001), *Bianco giorno offeso* (2004), and *I mari ovunque* (2007a) were originally written in Albanian, whereas *Vergine giurata* (2007b) and *Piccola guerra perfetta* (2011) were written directly in Italian.

[52] *Cercando Brunilda*, produced by Radiotelevisione Svizzera Italiana (RSI), was a finalist for the 2004 "Ilaria Alpi" Journalism Prize. Also for RSI, Dones and Fulvio Mariani made the documentary *I ngujuar* (*Inchiodato*) (2005) on the blood feud in northern Albania, which in 2005 was awarded the "Fipa d'Argent" in the "Grands Reportages et faits de société" category during the eighteenth Festival International de Programmes Audiovisuels at Biarritz in France.

[53] On the different transitions of Hana's body, see Bond (2018), in particular Chap. 3, and O'Healy and Romeo (2022).

[54] On this issue, Elvira Dones filmed a documentary entitled *Vergini giurate* (2006), which won the award for best documentary at the Baltimore Women's Film Festival in 2007.

to live and work. In her first novel, *Rosso come una sposa* (Red Like a Bride) (2008), which, like her other works, was written directly in Italian, the theme of migration is almost entirely absent and appears only toward the end of the text.[55] Here, the history of Albania—from ancient times through the Fascist and later the Nazi occupation to the communist and post-communist era—is interwoven with the stories of a single family, especially the genealogy of its women, their strengths, and the traditions that govern their lives. Ibrahimi's narration takes on the tone of an epic novel in the style of Helen Barolini's *Umbertina* (1999), which has achieved epic status within Italian American literature and culture.[56] The construction of an official history via personal stories is a constant feature in the works of this author. The setting for her second novel, *L'amore e gli stracci del tempo* (Love and the Scraps of Time) (2009), is still the Balkans, and the personal stories of two families, one Serbian and the other ethnically Albanian from Kosovo, are also interwoven with historical events. In Ibrahimi's third novel, *Non c'è dolcezza* (There Is No Sweetness) (2012), the intimate sphere is privileged, although Albanian history is still present as a backdrop. The deep friendship between the protagonists, Lila and Eleni, as well as their status in Albanian society, their personal and professional desires, and the status of motherhood—attained by one of the women with the help of the other—are all at the core of a narrative in which the rural and urban, the modern and traditional intersect. Ibrahimi's most recent novel, *Il tuo nome è una promessa* (Your Name Is a Promise) (2017), tells the story of a family of German Jews who flee to Albania during the Second World War, showing the fractures that history produces and observing how those who survive must come to terms with its legacy.

[55] This novel has received numerous literary prizes, including the Edoardo Kihlgren Prize, the Corrado Alvaro Prize, and the Città di Penne Literary Prize.

[56] I compare Ibrahimi's novel to Barolini's because, for both, the definition of "epic" is notably different from the conventional meaning. The epic features of these narratives are to be found in the tradition that the women from the two families, at different times and places, create for themselves and for the generations to come, as well as in the daily lives of women who are able to determine the course of their own personal history in conjunction with that of their country. The authors represent women—Albanian and Italian American—with features that go far beyond the stereotypes relegating them to the role of victims of patriarchy. The figure of the grandmother is also a defining one in both novels (Saba in Ibrahimi's novel, and Umbertina in Barolini's eponymous one): not only do the two women embody the origin of a genealogy of women, but they also act as a point of reference for subsequent generations in an era of change and migrations.

2.4.3   The Third Phase: (Direct) Postcolonial Literature[57]

Italian (direct) postcolonial literature refers to the body of texts that is the outcome of Italy's direct postcoloniality: literature written by authors from the Horn of Africa and Libya, places where Italian colonization was extensively present and has thus left lasting effects.[58] From a cultural point of view, there is a "privileged" relationship between a nation and the territories it once colonized. Even though the following writers are from different generations, come from different countries, and have even more different backgrounds, they share a familiarity with the history, culture, and language of Italy, elements that are in various ways derived from the colonial relationships their countries had with Italy. This relationship is represented in the writings of these authors through an explicit meditation on the historical link between Italy and their own countries, the rewriting of official histories, and a reflection on the memorialization of past events in present times. Another important contribution that these authors make to Italian postcolonial literature—in dialogue with writers who are not from former Italian colonies—is a theoretical elaboration on both how the processes of racialization from colonial societies are reproduced in contemporary Italy and how the allocation or non-allocation of citizenship serves to create and implement systems of marginalization. Writers originating from former Italian colonies in Africa do not constitute the greater part of postcolonial writers; however, they have provided, and continue to provide, a major contribution to contemporary Italian culture.

*   *   *

Although the focus in the following pages is on the most acclaimed writers from the Horn of Africa, it is important to also include in this category other writers from former Italian colonies whose narratives are centered

---

[57] The overview that I present here is not meant to be exhaustive. My intention is rather to trace some useful trajectories for understanding how postcolonial literature written by authors originating from former Italian colonies makes an important contribution to Italian culture and to the decolonization of its literary canon and of Italian society. For an extensive overview of authors who have a direct link with Italian colonization, see Negro (2015).

[58] Almost all the literary production I analyze in this section is connected, in different ways, to the Horn of Africa. The only exception is Luciana Capretti, an Italian writer and journalist born in Libya, who wrote about the exodus of Italians from the North African country, among other subjects.

on Italian colonial history, the history of now decolonized former Italian colonies, and/or the postcolonial Italy of the present.[59] Their inclusion in the category "Italian (direct) postcolonial literature" needs to be (and will be) qualified case by case, as will become clear in the explanations that follow.

Erminia Dell'Oro and Luciana Capretti were born and lived in former Italian colonies: Dell'Oro was born and raised in Asmara and moved to Milan in adulthood, always maintaining close contact with Eritrea; Capretti was born in Tripoli and moved to Rome with her family at an early age in 1967. The Dell'Oro novels tell stories of colonial occupation and the eventual abandonment of the colonies (*Asmara addio* [Goodbye Asmara], 1997) and of interracial relations in the Eritrean colony and the destiny to which children born of such unions were condemned (*L'abbandono* [The Abandonment], 1991).[60] In 2016, Dell'Oro published *Il mare davanti. Storia di Tsegehans Weldeslassie* (The Sea in Front: The Story of Tsegehans Weldeslassie), in which she transcribed the experiences of the protagonist, who fled from Eritrea, crossed the Sudanese and Libyan deserts, and then crossed the Mediterranean on one of those precarious vessels that are shipwrecked on a daily basis. In the novel *Ghibli* (2004), Luciana Capretti relies on documents and testimonies to reconstruct "the exodus of twenty thousand" Italians whom Colonel Gaddafi forced to leave Libya, denying them the right to carry their belongings with them or to claim any of their

---

[59] For the reasons already discussed in Lombardi-Diop and Romeo (2012), I am not including here novels with a setting that is in some sense colonial, such as those written by Carlo Lucarelli (*L'ottava vibrazione*, 2008; *Albergo Italia*, 2014; *Il tempo delle iene*, 2015), Andrea Camilleri (*La presa di Macallè*, 2003; *Il nipote del negus*, 2010), and Enrico Brizzi (*L'inattesa piega degli eventi*, 2008), texts that "adopt vividly exoticized colonial settings shrouded in nostalgic and quasi-elegiac atmospheres where their (for the most part male) protagonists reenact major events of colonial history (in Camilleri and Lucarelli), or imagine a different postcolonial future (in Brizzi)" (Lombardi-Diop and Romeo 2012, 9). These texts appear to ensure that the Italian colonial past becomes part of the nation's common knowledge—considering the prominence of the writers. However, the strong presence of sexist and racist elements, the utter lack of a critical view of colonialism, and indeed the exotic and aesthetic fascination with times and places past show that this literature performs no oppositional function but rather reinforces colonial stereotypes. See Triulzi (2012) in this regard, among others. For an analysis of the representations of gender and race in Lucarelli's novels, see Chap. 3.

[60] See also Dell'Oro's novel *La gola del diavolo* (1999), a colonial history told through the eyes of a young girl.

possessions.[61] While these novels are important within the context of Italian postcolonial literature because they portray colonial settings and events that took place during and after colonization and are critical of the Italian colonial enterprise, there is a significant difference in the positions occupied by these two writers as compared with those discussed later in this section. They identify socially as the offspring of white settlers and not of colonized subjects, and the colonies, as noted by Frantz Fanon (1961), constitute a polarized world in which the two parties are in no way complementary, but are in many ways irreconcilable.[62]

Two other Italian authors who deserve to be mentioned here, although for different reasons, are Giulia Caminito and Francesca Melandri, both of whom write novels that highlight the direct connection between their family history and Italian colonialism. In the novel *La grande A* (The Big A) (2016), in which Giulia Caminito is freely inspired by her own family's experiences, little (and later adult) Giada joins her mother in Assab during WWII and finds herself living in the Italian colonist community among fortune-seeking adventurers and domesticated antelopes. Through the narration of personal events, Caminito constructs a narrative that resists exoticizing imaginaries, reveals Italian responsibilities for crimes committed in the colonies, and denounces the system of exploitation implemented there. *Sangue giusto* (Right Blood) (2017) by Francesca Melandri is an

---

[61] Luciana Capretti, a prolific writer and journalist, is also the author of *Tevere* (2014), a novel in which the personal story of the protagonist, Clara Faiola, a woman who disappeared in Rome in 1975 and was never found, moves along trajectories that interweave Italian history with themes of family abuse and mental illness. Capretti also published an essay on Islamic feminism, *La jihad delle donne. Il femminismo islamico nel mondo occidentale* (2017).

[62] To understand the difference between literature written by the descendants of the colonizers and the descendants of the colonized, I recommend a comparative reading of three novels that take place in different countries, presenting the theme of interracial marriage in colonial times and depicting the fate of the children of these unions: Dell'Oro, *L'abbandono* (1991); Shirin Ramzanali Fazel, *Nuvole sull'equatore. Gli italiani dimenticati: Una storia* (2010); and Carla Macoggi, *Kkeywa. Storia di una bimba meticcia* (2011). There is a striking difference in the way in which the three authors endow their female characters with agency (or deprive them of it). Eritrea is the setting in the first case, Somalia in the second, and Ethiopia in the third. Although Dell'Oro is highly critical of the behavior of Italian men in the colony, who often view their African families as belonging to a parenthesis in their lives, the writer also victimizes Selas and deprives her of agency, so that by the end of the narrative she has no choice but to succumb. The fate of the protagonists in the other two novels is less tragic. The different solutions proposed in the three texts can be ascribed partly to the positioning of the three writers. See also Carla Macoggi's *La nemesi della rossa* (2012), in which the protagonist of her earlier novel arrives in Italy and faces racism and discrimination.

especially important novel that fills a gap in Italian literature. It is set in contemporary Rome, but colonial history bursts into the opening of the novel when Colonel Muammar Gaddafi's imminent official visit to Rome is mentioned. Immediately afterward, the protagonist, Ilaria, finds a young Ethiopian man waiting for her at her front door. He claims to be—and in fact is—her nephew, Shimeta Ietmgeta Attilaprofeti, born out of a relationship her father had had years before with a native woman during the colonial occupation of Ethiopia. The novel's plot interweaves the history of Italy's colonial past with events of the postcolonial present, not only through the flesh-and-blood presence of the young Shimeta but also through the story of his journey across the desert, the camps in Libya, and the Mediterranean to arrive at last in Italy, where he is determined to remain by virtue of the fact that he possesses the "right blood" (the reference is clearly to the law for the attribution of Italian citizenship still largely based on the principle of *ius sanguinis*).

A different position is occupied by Meti Birabiro and Maaza Mengiste, authors of the Ethiopian diaspora who live in the United States and write in English. Even if, strictly speaking, they are not part of Italian postcolonial literature (as they do not identify either with the Italian territory or with the Italian language), they contribute to Italian literature through transnational trajectories because their narratives intersect with Italian colonial history and the postcolonial present in complex and powerful ways.[63] In *Blue Daughter of the Red Sea: A Memoir* (2004), Birabiro shares her experience of poverty and deprivation in Ethiopia prior to migrating to Italy, where her diversity triggers processes of othering, and later to the United States. Maaza Mengiste's first novel, *Beneath the Lion's Gaze* (2010), is centered on the Menghistu dictatorship in Ethiopia and establishes lines of continuity with the period of Italian colonialism, which then is at the core of Mengiste's second novel, *The Shadow King* (2019), set almost entirely during the Italian occupation of Ethiopia (1935–1941). Mengiste's second novel is both a counterhistory of Italian colonial enterprise—which radically questions the splendor of Mussolini's colonial empire and reveals instead the incessant resistance of the poorly equipped Ethiopian army and population, who, in the end, defeated the Italian

---

[63] I include these texts here because, as I make clear in Chap. 1 and throughout the book, I am critical of the notion of an Italian literature and culture articulated within national borders and expressed (almost) exclusively in the Italian national language. See also Burdett and Polezzi (2020) and Burdett et al. (2020).

colonizers—and a counter-counterhistory that reinscribes in that counter-history the presence of women, systematically erased, and their bodies, systematically violated in patriarchal Ethiopian society.[64]

Although in a subtler way than other works considered here, these texts also shed light on Italy's colonial past—and the consequences that it has wrought for the colonized countries in the aftermath of their decolonization—and postcolonial present.

*   *   *

Italian (direct) postcolonial literature emerged in the early 1990s at a very early stage of migration literature. An excerpt of Ethiopian Italian writer Maria Abbebù Viarengo's memoir "Andiamo a spasso" (Let's Go for a Stroll) was published in 1990.[65] This brief memoir is unique in that it represents the way the female author's Blackness was perceived in 1960s Turin, during the years of the great internal migration in which Otherness in Northern Italy was primarily embodied by Southern immigrants. But the extraordinary importance of this text lies also in the fact that, along with Ribka Sibhatu's *Aulò* (1993) (*Aulò Aulò! Aulò!*, 2012b) and Shirin Ramzanali Fazel's *Lontano da Mogadiscio* (1994) (*Far from Mogadishu*, 2013), it is one of the first instances in Italian where the history of colonialism is rewritten by the colonized, which initiates the important process of decolonizing history and memory.

In 1993, Ribka Sibhatu published *Aulò. Canto-poesia dell'Eritrea* (*Aulò Aulò! Aulò!*, 2012b) with the facing text in Tigrinya.[66] The title underlines the strong oral component of the narrative (the *aulò*, explains Sibhatu, is a popular genre in Eritrea consisting of a set of verses that are recited or sung on various important occasions, such as weddings and funerals), in which the autobiographical story is combined with the description of Eritrean customs and traditions, as well as with fables, proverbs, and little

---

[64] For an analysis of Mengiste's *The Shadow King*, see Chap. 3.

[65] The full text of the memoir in Italian, from which this excerpt was taken, has never been published, but a longer excerpt was published in English. See Viarengo (1999).

[66] In 2010, Simone Brioni, Ermanno Guida, and Simone Chiscuzzu made the documentary *Aulò* with Ribka Sibhatu, in which she recites some *aulò* while talking about Italian colonialism in Eritrea and how immigration redefines the concept of national and local identity. See Brioni et al. (2012a). On the genesis of this documentary, see Brioni (2013b). Sibhatu's book *Aulò* is also available with parallel texts in English (Sibhatu 2012a).

history lessons.[67] In 2004, Sibhatu published a text very different from her first, *Il cittadino che non c'è* (The Missing Citizen), in which she presents the results of the research she conducted from 1999 to 2001 on how immigrants are represented in the Italian media.[68]

In 1994, Shirin Ramzanali Fazel published *Lontano da Mogadiscio*, an autobiographical text recounting her life in Somalia, her escape to Italy, her many other migrations around the world, and her subsequent return to Italy.[69] These early (direct) postcolonial texts start the important process of condemning the forgetfulness that has enveloped Italian colonial history in Italy. The narrator of *Lontano da Mogadiscio* speaks Italian, which she learned in school during the Italian trusteeship and the first years of independence. Once in Italy, she quickly realizes that such knowledge is not mutual and that Italians do not even know how to locate Somalia on the map, identifying it as a generically backward and primeval Third World country without having any notion of the Italian colonial presence in the country. A revised and expanded bilingual (Italian and English) edition of this text, titled *Lontano da Mogadiscio/Far from Mogadishu*, was released in 2013. The text thus became available to an English-speaking public, marking the growing global interest in the Italian postcolonial.[70] In 2010, Fazel published a new novel, *Nuvole sull'Equatore* (*Clouds over the Equator*, 2014), where the racialization of Africans central to *Lontano da Mogadiscio* returns within a historical context. Through the story of Giulia, a mixed-race child entrusted to the missions during the period of Somalia's governance under Italian trusteeship, Fazel recounts the social stigma to which the children of mixed marriages were subjected.

---

[67] Although in this chapter I primarily discuss works of fiction and autobiographical texts, it seems important to recall the work of historian Ali Mumin Ahad. In 1993, he published the article "I 'peccati storici' del colonialismo in Somalia." See also his article "Corno d'Africa: L'ex-impero italiano" (Ahad 2006).

[68] As mentioned earlier, Sibhatu returns to children's literature in 2012, with the publication of *L'esatto numero delle stelle* (Sibhatu 2012b).

[69] From the same author, see the story "La spiaggia" (Fazel 2007), in which the theme of European neocolonialism in Africa—which makes up the story's background—is combined with that of the exoticization and commodification of Black bodies (in this case of men), but also with that of the gendered power dynamics in relationships. For an analysis of this story, see Chap. 3.

[70] The volume also includes a lengthy bilingual afterword by Simone Brioni, in which Brioni analyzes the importance of Fazel's work within the landscape of Italian postcolonial literature and reconstructs the history of critical essays written about the book. See Brioni (2013a).

The period between 2005 and 2012 witnessed the publication of a number of texts that have made a crucial contribution to the rewriting of Italian colonial history with the aid of both archival research and personal memories. The year 2005 saw the release of two texts that prompt a historical reflection on the role of Italians in the colonial territories and also (in the case of the first) on the way in which the racialization and othering of colonized subjects are reproduced in contemporary Italy. In Garane Garane's *Il latte è buono* (Milk Is Good) (2005), the main character, Gashan, is part of the Somali generation that grew up mythologizing Rome and Italy, the country whose language and culture he has studied and is familiar with. However, the protagonist's encounter with the actual culture once he arrives in Italy as a university student is very different: Gashan immediately realizes that the continuity that he felt between himself and Italians—by virtue of his perfect knowledge of the Italian language and culture and his strong desire to be part of the latter—is not shared by the Italians, who consider him one of the many African immigrants arriving in Italy. The Italians are utterly unaware of the historical relationship between Italy and Somalia, and they perceive Gashan's perfect knowledge of their language with diffidence: if migrants are expected to imitate the linguistic behavior of Italians, this process must always remain incomplete and signal an approximation that can never become total identification (as with Homi Bhabha's notion of "mimicry," expressed in the notorious formula *"almost the same, but not quite"* [Bhabha 1994, 86]).[71]

Martha Nasibù's *Memorie di una principessa etiope* (Memories of an Ethiopian Princess) (2005) articulates a powerful counterhistory of Italian colonialism. Daughter of the *dejatch* (prince) Nasibù Zamanuel, a member of the Ethiopian nobility and one of the most valiant army commanders involved in trying to repel Mussolini's invasion of 1935–1936, Martha Nasibù tells the story of her family before, during, and after the war that reduced Ethiopia to a territory of the Italian Empire. This autobiographical text has great historical value (as evidenced by colonial historian Angelo Del Boca's preface) because it offers insight into the life of the Ethiopian nobility before the Fascist invasion, narrating the story of the conflict and of the Ethiopian defeat—occasioned by the systematic use of mustard gas banned by the Geneva Convention—and concluding with the eight-year exile of Dejatch Nasibù's family to Italy. This text shows a page of history,

---

[71] For a discussion of the concept of "mimicry" in relation to social relationships in postcolonial societies, see Sect. 4.2, in particular note 33.

that of the Ethiopian resistance, that still remains largely unknown to Italians.[72]

In a series of autobiographical stories, Kaha Mohamed Aden's *Fra-intendimenti* (Mis-understandings) (2010) intertwines the history of Somalia—from colonialism through the Italian administration of Somalia and Siad Barre's dictatorship to civil war—with the history of the Somali diaspora and therefore also with her own personal history. The book's 12 chapters contain the author's contemporary reflections on Pavia—her own relationship with the Somali community, the racism of Italians, and the precariousness caused by the lack of citizenship—along with memories of Somalia, particularly of the life she and her family had lived in Mogadishu.[73]

Timira. Romanzo meticcio (Timira: A Mixed-Race Novel) (2012) is another text of great importance, as much for the process that led to its composition as for the original story it tells. The novel is the result of a collaboration between the narrator and protagonist, Isabella Marincola (known in Somalia as Timira Assan), Italian writer Wu Ming 2, and her son, Antar Mohamed (Wu Ming 2 and Mohamed 2012). The text interweaves Wu Ming 2's personal reflections with Isabella Marincola's diary pages, archival documents, letters, memories, stories, and official history. Through Marincola's memories and personal history, important pages of Italy's colonial history, Italy's postcolonial contemporaneity, and Somalia's history (from the end of the Italian trusteeship to the outbreak of civil war in 1991) are significantly rewritten. This project very clearly seeks to anchor personal narratives within a historical context and to make them part of a history constructed from below; above all, it aims to construct a postcolonial counterhistory that rejects colonial imaginaries and exoticizing representations. These are replaced by Somali Italian Isabella Marincola's memories of her unusual and at times complicated life in the Italy of the 1940s and 1950s, when she was involved in various artistic and cinematographic circles. Such memories tell stories that are quite distant from pre-established and stereotyped ideals of Black women. The oppositional nature of this text, combined with the solidly constructed subjectivity of the narrator, makes it all the more problematic that Marincola is

---

[72] As pointed out elsewhere in this chapter and in Chap. 3, Gabriella Ghermandi and Maaza Mengiste have also made invaluable contributions to this process of rewriting the history of the Ethiopian resistance.

[73] Regarding Aden, see also the documentary *La quarta via* (Brioni et al. 2012b). In this lengthy interview, Aden evokes the history of Mogadishu. On the genesis of the documentary, see Brioni (2013b).

excluded from authorial function in the text.[74] This indicates the problematics of power relations in collaborative authorship, particularly when, as in this case, one co-author is a famous white male writer and the narrator is an almost unknown Black woman.

2.4.4 The Third Phase: Igiaba Scego, Ubax Cristina Ali Farah, and Gabriella Ghermandi

The writing of Igiaba Scego, Ubax Cristina Ali Farah,[75] and Gabriella Ghermandi is analyzed in a separate section because of the pivotal place these authors occupy in Italian culture and in the realm of (direct) Italian postcolonial literature. These three writers and/or their families are all originally from the Horn of Africa, but unlike those included in the previous section, they represent the emergence of a second generation at the beginning of the third millennium for whom Italian is (one of) their native language(s) and Italian culture is their culture.[76]

Igiaba Scego was born in Rome to Somali parents who fled the dictatorship of Siad Barre. She entered the Italian literary scene in 2003, when she won the Eks&Tra competition for migrant writers with the short story "Salsicce" (2005b) ("Sausages," 2005b). In the same year, she published her first book, *La nomade che amava Alfred Hitchcock* (The Nomad Who Loved Alfred Hitchcock) (2003), in which the author tells in the first person the story of her mother Kadija and of her nomadic origins. In the

---

[74] The reason given for ousting Isabella Marincola from her co-author role is her death during the drafting of the text, a justification that seems surprisingly weak. On the genesis of the work and the underlying gender relationships, see the analysis of *Timira* in Chap. 3. On the power dynamics of collaborative autobiographies and the ways that authorship is constructed and signaled, see Romeo (2015). On collaborative texts as potentially oppositional in relation to *Timira*, see Brioni (2013b).

[75] When Ali Farah published her second novel, *Il comandante del fiume* (2014) (*The Commander of the River* 2023), she changed the way she writes her first name from Ubax to Ubah (the final *x* in Somali is read with an aspiration). This choice was made in order for her to be consistent with the way she writes the Italian transliteration of her family name, Ali Farah, which in Somali is Cali Faarax. In this new transliteration, then, Ubah Cristina Ali Farah writes the last letter of both her first and last name in Italian in the same way, h, (as it is in Somali also), and signals that they are both pronounced in the same way, with an aspiration. For sentimental reasons, here and elsewhere, I employ the original transliteration. In the bibliography, I use the original transliteration for texts published before 2014. I would like to thank Ubax Cristina Ali Farah for providing me with this explanation in a private email exchange in March 2017.

[76] On the differences between generations 1.25, 1.5, 1.75, and 2, see note 19 in Chap. 1.

story "Salsicce," written in response to the Bossi-Fini law, which requires immigrants to have their fingerprints taken when they apply for a residence permit, the protagonist wonders what it means to be Italian and reflects on the criteria that regulate access to the "privilege" of Italian citizenship. In this story, it is the presumed Italian "somatic norm" (Puwar 2004) that is questioned in a society in which the juxtaposition of Blackness and Italianness is generally considered an oxymoron. Scego's debut novel, *Rhoda* (2004), was released the following year and presents some of the characteristics that would become typical of her narratives, such as story fragmentation that relies on a plurality of narrative voices (almost exclusively female). While the central character constitutes a somewhat stereotypical representation of the immigrant Black woman—a sex worker (albeit out of self-destructive choice rather than necessity) whose sacrifice at the end of the novel appeases the conventions these types of narratives require—the other first- and second-generation Italian Somali women are able to build a positive destiny for themselves through a process of integration in which they maintain strong ties with the Somali diasporic community.

Scego's second novel, *Oltre Babilonia* (2008) (*Beyond Babylon*, 2019), weaves an intricate web of themes that go well beyond migration, bringing together people and places from different parts of the world. The narratives in this novel are built around the history of Somalia—from colonization to decolonization, from the administration of the Italian trusteeship to Siad Barre's dictatorship—as well as that of Argentina and the *desaparecidos*. These threads are woven together, at different times and in different ways, at an Arabic school in Tunis and a contemporary multicultural school in Rome. Although colonial history was almost absent from Scego's previous texts, from this work onward it becomes a constant presence in her writing and in the broader context of her cultural production. In *Oltre Babilonia*, it invades the narrative with an appalling violence: the rape of a Somali woman (and in this case of a man, too) is depicted not only as a physical violation but also as a metaphor for the penetration of the African territories by Italian colonizers.[77] The conservation and dissemination of personal and collective memory are central themes of the novel, the events of which unfold in contexts that are simultaneously transnational and

---

[77] On representations of the territories to be colonized as being akin to women's bodies and on the connection between colonial and erotic imagery, see McClintock (1995). Part of the analysis developed in Chap. 3 is dedicated to this topic.

local. In this novel, as in *Rhoda*, in the short story "Il disegno" (The Drawing) (2010a), and in the memoir *La mia casa è dove sono* (My Home Is Where I Am) (2010b), Rome is a place where many cultures coexist, where the Roman dialect is spoken as much by the children of immigrants as by the children of Romans, and where colonial history is alive at every corner.[78] In *La mia casa è dove sono*, a collection of personal and family memories are intertwined with the history of Somalia. At the same time, each chapter (except the first and last) bears the name of a place in the city of Rome ("Teatro Sistina," "Piazza Santa Maria sopra Minerva," "La stele di Axum," "Stazione Termini," "Trastevere," "Stadio Olimpico") in which the life of the author's family and that of the Somali community intersect with the lives of the native Italian population. The text concludes with a meditation on the fragmentary nature of memory and the need to transmit history and memory to subsequent generations.

The volume *Roma negata* (Rome Denied) (Bianchi and Scego 2014), with text by Scego and photographs by Rino Bianchi, aims to fulfill that need. The author goes in search of places, buildings, and other landmarks that are linked to the history of Italian colonialism, showing these connections to Italians who are oblivious to their own history. Rino Bianchi photographs the descendants of those who once suffered various forms of colonization—either by Italians or by other Europeans—portraying them in these same places in order to emphasize the indissoluble link between the colonial past and the postcolonial present, but also the sense of belonging these subjects have to the city of Rome and, by extension, to Italy and Europe. This link is also the common thread in Scego's eloquently titled novel *Adua* (2015) (*Adua*, 2017) (Adwa in English, which is the name of a city close to where the Italian army was defeated by the Ethiopian army in 1896, marking the first defeat of a European army at the hands of an African one). Here, Scego investigates the relationship between Italians and Somalis during colonial times—in all its ambivalence—and corroborates the idea that official history is grounded in the stories of individuals. The novel alternates between memories of the past (narrated by Adua's father, Zoppe) and stories from the present (narrated by Adua herself) that show how African bodies in Italy were and still are considered alien, even if their history is strongly tied to the history of Italy, as is the case for Somalis. The novel simultaneously brings into view conflicting race and

---

[78] A reworked version of "Il disegno" became the first chapter of Scego's memoir, *La mia casa è dove sono*, which won the 2011 Mondello Prize under the Italian author category.

gender relationships, not only between Italians and immigrants, but also within the Somali community. The narration of Igiaba Scego's latest novel, *La linea del colore* (The Color Line) (2020), alternates between the past of Lafanu Brown, an African American artist who travels to Europe in a *sui generis* Grand Tour in the nineteenth century and establishes her residence in Rome, and the present of Leila, a researcher of African descent who lives in contemporary Rome and studies representations of slavery in art. In this text, which stems from Scego's fascination with and research on the presence of Black people in Europe well in advance of the twentieth century, and which in some ways reads like a nineteenth-century novel, Scego utilizes a transhistorical and transnational approach to female Blackness that connects contemporary Italy to its colonial past and addresses the ways in which the female body has been racialized in Italy, Europe, and the United States.[79]

Ubax Cristina Ali Farah was born in Verona to a Somali father and an Italian mother, moved to Mogadishu at a very young age, fled to Hungary in 1992 with the eruption of the civil war, and finally returned to Italy, moving first to Verona and then, in 1997, to Rome. She has published several short stories in books and journals, including the extraordinary "Rapdipunt" (2004) ("Punt Rap," 2006), loosely inspired by the story of the Comitiva Flaminio, a group of young African Italians who regularly met at Piazzale Flaminio in Rome.[80] The story's title merges "Puntland," the ancient name of Somalia, with "rap," a part of hip-hop culture that has become a vital expression of the condition of marginalization of Black and Brown youth from the urban peripheries. The Somali Italian characters, like the second-generation characters in Scego's works, speak more Roman dialect than standard Italian and live lives that are highly localized and at the same time strongly transnational. The element that seems to unite the group is their feeling of displacement and their identification, sometimes imbued with pride, with their Blackness and African origins. The disorientation that Ali Farah represents masterfully here is, in fact, characteristic of second generations. Although Italy is the country where they were born

---

[79] Igiaba Scego was awarded the Premio Matilde Serao in 2021. She is the fourth winner of this prize, which is granted to female writers whose social commitment in the fields of literature and journalism echo the public engagement of the Neapolitan writer. The three previous awards were given to Antonia Arslan (2017), Azar Nafisi (2018), and Dacia Maraini (2019). This is due recognition of Scego's major role in contemporary Italian culture.

[80] For an analysis of the short story, see the next chapters, in particular Chap. 5. On the genesis and nature of this group of African Italians, see note 26 in Chap. 5.

and raised, they are constantly made to perceive their diversity with respect to more traditional embodiments of Italianness. At the conclusion of the short story, the young protagonists steal an incense plant from the Trastevere Botanical Garden when they discover it is native to Somalia, which makes them feel an unexpected sense of belonging and of being connected to the past.

Ali Farah's debut novel, *Madre piccola* (2007) (*Little Mother*, 2011), is one of the most significant texts in Italian postcolonial literature. Focused on memory and its preservation and transmission, this is the novel of the Somali diaspora *par excellence*. The text contains historical references to Siad Barre's dictatorship and its demise and to the civil war and the diaspora it unleashed, but there are also references to the consequences of Italian colonization and the Italian trusteeship of Somalia. Like the novels of Scego, this is a polyphonic text. Told through the first-person narratives of two cousins, Barni and Domenica Axad, as well as the latter's husband, Taageere, and featuring the presence of a plurality of other characters in their stories, the novel recounts the tale of the Somali community in various parts of the world. Highly poetic and visual, the narrative does not follow a chronological sequence and is never linear. It also presents marked characteristics of oral narration, such as digressions, narrative heterogeneity, direct dialogue with the listener, and strategies to maintain rapt attention. The use of orality, as Ali Farah affirms, comes from the Somali tradition, but it is also an attempt to bring the author closer to the social function that has been lost by writers in the "West." As she asserts, "I consider literature to be a melody of many voices that the writer orchestrates in a functional way in society, in the sense that the writer returns to society what she/he gets from it"[81] (Ali Farah quoted in Comberiati 2007, 66). The imprint of orality is also visible in chapters presented as dialogues with voiceless interlocutors.

The centrality of urban spaces characterizing the story "Rapdipunt" is also a feature in Ali Farah's second novel *Il comandante del fiume* (2014) (*The Commander of the River*, 2023), a text centered on the history of Somalia and the Somali diaspora, in which the city of Rome is the undisputed protagonist. There is a particular concern with war—the trauma that it produces, the way it is inscribed in people's bodies, and the way in

---

[81] "Considero la letteratura come una melodia a più voci che lo scrittore orchestra in maniera funzionale nella società, nel senso che lo scrittore restituisce alla società quello che da lei riceve."

which processes of memorialization are constructed. This novel is a reflection not only on how the civil war ravaged Somalia for decades but also on the devastating effects of Italian colonialism, Fascist racism, and the period of the Italian trusteeship. The difficult process of building an identity for second generations—with a comparative view of the Somali diaspora in Italy and in England—is tied as much to their troublesome relationship with the country of origin as it is to their ambivalent relationship with Italy. The belonging of these young Black Italians in Italy is constantly challenged by the authorities and at the same time sought after and rejected by the subjects in question.[82]

In 2018, Ubax Cristina Ali Farah rewrote Sophocles' *Antigone* for a theatrical performance entitled *Antigone Power*, the winning project of the MigrArti Spettacolo 2018 competition. The performance involves the participation of young migrants and aims to denounce the way in which Italy regulates its incoming migration flows. *La danza dell'orice* (Dance of the Oryx) (2020) is a short text about a young female warrior, Shaqlan, and her difficulties in joining the Somali resistance army to fight against the British because the army, grounded as it is in a history of patriarchy, would prefer to assign her the role of passive and submissive woman. Shaqlan also faces being exoticized by an Italian producer who uses her to construct the colonial imaginary of the castrating African woman. Ali Farah's latest novel, *Le stazioni della luna* (The Stations of the Moon) (2021), is set in Somalia during the Italian Trusteeship Administration.[83] One of the protagonists, Clara, was born and raised in Somalia during the colonial period, and Ebla, the other protagonist, was Clara's wet nurse. They had not seen each other since 1941, when Clara had been repatriated

---

[82] For a reading of space and places in "Rapdipunt" and *Il comandante del fiume*, see Chap. 5.

[83] In 1949 the United Nations decided to grant Italy trusteeship of Somalia (The Trust Territory of Somaliland under Italian administration / Amministrazione fiduciaria italiana della Somalia—AFIS) from 1950 to 1960. Through this legal instrument (the Trusteeship System), Italy made a commitment in front of the international community to lead Somalia toward independence and democracy. However, as historian Antonio Morone argues, this was a new form of colonialism, "a democratic colonialism" ("un colonialismo democratico") that hid "a series of intrinsic contradictions combined with the difficulties of resuming and concluding, within just a decade, the construction of that modern society that in Somalia had always remained, more than elsewhere, at an initial stage" ("una serie di intrinseche contraddizioni insieme alla difficoltà di riprendere e concludere, nell'arco di appena un decennio, la costruzione di quella società moderna che proprio in Somalia era sempre rimasta, più che altrove, a uno stadio iniziale") (2011, x). On this important chapter of Italian colonial history, see Morone (2011).

to Italy with her mother and brother, but their stories became interwoven again in the early 1950s, when Clara decides to return to Somalia as an adult, urged on by her brother, who has started a profitable business there. Ebla, who as a young girl was taught by her father how to read the stars, represents the moral authority of the story. Her past is told in parallel with her present, when she once again meets Clara, who has come back to Somalia to contribute to the life of a country she considers her own. The two women are reunited at a moment when the Somali people are becoming increasingly intolerant of the neocolonial Italian administration, with its marked privilege and internal contradictions, and are mobilizing in support of the growing independence movement.

Italian colonial history and the war in Ethiopia are central to Gabriella Ghermandi's novel *Regina di fiori e di perle* (2007) (*Queen of Flowers and Pearls*, 2015), as they are to all her cultural production. Born in Addis Ababa to an Eritrean Ethiopian mother and an Italian father, Ghermandi moved to her father's hometown, Bologna, after his death in 1979 and now lives and works in the city. Rather than simply being the author of one novel and several short stories,[84] Ghermandi is above all a storyteller and a performer, and more recently also a musician. Her novel revolves around the character of Mahlet, a little girl who is destined by her ancestors to become the *cantora* (storyteller) of her people.[85] The stories that Mahlet hears, both in Ethiopia and in Italy, narrate the Ethiopian resistance to the Fascist invasion of 1935–1936; the racial laws and the consequences that they produced in the African colonies; the use of the deadly gases prohibited by the Geneva Convention by the Italian army to defeat the resistance; and the heroism of noble woman warrior Kebedech Seyoum, who, after her husband's death, took command of his troops, pausing for only two days when she gave birth to their child and then returning to battle. It is through all these personal and private stories that Ghermandi rewrites official history, conferring dignity and authority on

---

[84] Included among the author's many stories are "Il telefono del quartiere" (1999), which won the 1999 Eks&Tra Prize for Migrant Writers; "Quel certo temperamento focoso" (2002), which won Ghermandi her third prize in the same competition in 2001; and "All'ombra dei rami sfacciati, carichi di fiori rosso vermiglio" (2010), a story that was written to be narrated as a performance. The text and some audio clips of the performance are available on Ghermandi's website.

[85] Part of this novel is also a performance by the same title that Ghermandi has staged around Italy and the world, which can be seen on her website.

the Ethiopian people's oral tradition.[86] The novel ends with an adult Mahlet who, after listening to and collecting many historical accounts, begins writing to keep the promise she made to Elder Yacob years before to tell his story and the history of Ethiopia. In the last sentence, the narrator also directly addresses Italian readers, reminding them that the story she is now writing is not only her own but also *theirs*, and thus establishes a strong connection between the Italian colonial past and the pluralized, multicultural present, urging Italians in particular to know their own history beyond national borders.

In recent years, Ghermandi has become a singer in the Atse Tewodros Project, an important musical undertaking that she designed and implemented, which brings together Ethiopian and Italian musicians, restoring an important cultural connection between the two countries that is very different from that of the colonial past. This project holds firm the need not to erase the past or the consequences it has produced, but to know the past in order to overcome it.[87]

All three of the authors under discussion here—Scego, Ali Farah, and Ghermandi—center their texts on memory, both personal and collective, and on the processes of memorialization not only to understand the past but also to create a bridge between that past and a more equitable, inclusive future. This is particularly important within the context of contemporary Italian culture because the collective national identity is constituted by the ways in which events are publicly remembered (or forgotten) and historical memory built.

2.4.5 The Third Phase: Second-Generation Writers and Anthologies

Together with Ingy Mubiayi, an Italian writer of Egyptian Congolese descent, Igiaba Scego edited the volume *Quando nasci è una roulette* (Once You Are Born It Is a Roulette), a book in which seven Italian youths

---

[86] The theme of authority is intertwined with that of authorship in this text. In the acknowledgments at the end of the book, Ghermandi states that she limited herself to collecting stories, which she then included in the text, thus attributing authorship to those individuals who told the stories to her and giving them the authority to speak on behalf of their own Ethiopian people. Thus, Ghermandi promotes a plural, collective authorial mode, in which individuals speak not only for themselves but also for the community.

[87] See the website of the Atse Tewodros Project.

of African descent tell their stories (Mubiayi and Scego 2007).[88] Second-generation communities have a very important role in Italy, not only from a social and political but also from a literary and cultural point of view.[89] Since the beginning of the twenty-first century, they have begun to create new forms of expression, some of which are closely linked to hip-hop[90] and popular culture: these new forms represent a rapidly changing, multicultural Italian society at the same time that they denounce legal mechanisms of exclusion, such as the acquisition of citizenship.[91] A particularly successful example is the anthology titled *Pecore nere* (Black Sheep) (Capitani and Coen 2005), stories by and about second-generation Black and Brown authors written by Igiaba Scego, Laila Wadia, Ingy Mubiayi, and Gabriella Kuruvilla.[92] While the (questionable) title highlights how the skin color of the four authors relegates them to the margins of Italian society, as Clarissa Clò (2012) argues, the fact that they are defined as "black sheep" also means that they are considered part of the family and, by extension, part of the Italian nation.

Although the eight stories included in the collection are very different from one another, they have in common issues and features, such as a harsh criticism of the way the Italian state regulates the flow of migration and the acquisition of citizenship (Scego and Mubiayi); young people's use of slang and dialect and the (difficult) relationship between first and second generations (Scego and Wadia); processes of racialization and the perpetuation of racism (Scego, Mubiayi, and Kuruvilla); and the feeling of belonging and non-belonging to the society in which second generations

---

[88] See also the Facebook page of Rete G2.

[89] The tenth annual Eks&Tra competition, held in 2004, was dedicated to second generations, as was the documentary film *18 Ius soli* (2011) by Fred Kuwornu, an Italian director of Ghanaian origin.

[90] In this regard, see Angelucci (2021).

[91] For a detailed discussion of the law regulating the acquisition of Italian citizenship, see Chap. 4, in particular Sect. 4.3.1.

[92] Of the four women writers included, only Laila Wadia is not a second-generation author (she was born in India to Indian parents and moved to Italy in young adulthood), but her stories included in this collection concern the meeting and clash between the first and second generations. Gabriella Kuruvilla was born in Milan to an Italian mother and an Indian father, while Ingy Mubiayi was born in Cairo to an Egyptian mother and a father from Zaire, emigrating to Italy while still a child. Three of the stories in this anthology were awarded Eks&Tra prizes, including Scego's already mentioned "Salsicce" (in 2003), Mubiayi's "Documenti, prego" (in 2004), and Wadia's "Curry di pollo" (in 2004). See Scego (2005b), Mubiayi (2005), and Wadia (2005).

live.[93] The authors' skillful use of irony often combines with the irreverent manner in which these four women writers treat Italian culture and the language of Dante Alighieri, by which, unlike the first generation, they are no longer intimidated. Through linguistic and stylistic experimentation, second-generation writers often call into question both their culture of origin and the culture in which they are living. This anthology, therefore, has the merit of bringing together literary texts that experiment at the level of content and language, and texts written by Italian women authors who (or whose families) originate elsewhere, do not conform to the Italian chromatic norm of whiteness, and demand that the category of "Italianness" become more flexible to reflect the changes that have taken place and take place every day in Italian society.[94]

[93] In addition to Igiaba Scego, whom we have already dealt with extensively, the other three authors have a very lively presence on the Italian cultural scene. Among their works are Laila Wadia, *Il burattinaio e altre storie extra-italiane* (2004), *Amiche per la pelle* (2007), and *Come diventare italiani in 24 ore* (2010); Viola Chandra (a pseudonym of Gabriella Kuruvilla), *Media chiara e noccioline* (2001); Gabriella Kuruvilla, *È la vita dolcezza* (2008), *Milano, fin qui tutto bene* (2012), and *Maneggiare con cura* (2020a); and edited by Ingy Mubiayi e Igiaba Scego, *Quando nasci è una roulette* (2007). Gabriella Kuruvilla is also editing the publication of a series of collective volumes of stories dedicated to individual cities and regions (entitled *Milano d'autore*, *Roma d'autore*, *Bologna d'autore*, *Monaco d'autore*, *Genova d'autore*, *Calabria d'autore*, *Sicilia d'autore*, and *Romagna d'autore*, all published by Morellini Editore). See Kuruvilla (2014, 2015, 2016a, b, 2017, 2018, 2019, 2020b).

[94] Anthologies of migration and postcolonial literature in Italy deserve a more extensive discussion. Here I limit myself to providing some bibliographic information: from 1995 to 2004, an anthology presenting a selection of texts that were entered into the Eks&Tra Competition was published almost every year. From 1995 to 1999 came *Le voci dell'arcobaleno, Mosaici d'inchiostro, Memorie in valigia, Destini sospesi di volti in cammino*, and *Parole oltre i confini* (see Sangiorgi and Ramberti 1995, 1996, 1997, 1998, 1999); from 2001 to 2002 came *Anime in viaggio. La nuova mappa dei popoli* (2001) and *Il doppio sguardo* (2002); in 2003, two collections were published: *Pace in parole migranti* (2003) and *Impronte. Scritture dal mondo* (2003); in 2004 came *La seconda pelle* (Sangiorgi 2004). A special mention also goes to *Italiani per vocazione* (Scego 2005a). Other anthologies of note include *Allattati dalla lupa* (Gnisci 2005); *Amori bicolori. Racconti* (Capitani and Coen 2008); all of the anthologies from the national literary competition "Lingua Madre," published every year from 2007 to 2021 as *Lingua Madre. Racconti di donne straniere in Italia* (Finocchi 2007–2021). In the United States, two anthologies were published in English, the first one very early on: *Mediterranean Crossroads* (Parati 1999) and *Multicultural Literature in Contemporary Italy* (Orton and Parati 2007).

2.5   The Fourth Phase (2019–)

From September 2019 to April 2021, an extraordinary number of texts were produced that reflect on the different ways in which the Italian national space is constructed around the chromatic norm of whiteness and non-white bodies are either excluded from that space or are differentially included it in. Representations of Blackness as counternarratives to a presumed national normative whiteness are not new to Italian literature: they already appear in the production of migrant writers during the very first phase of Italian postcolonial literature at the beginning of the 1990s, and, with the passing of time, they become increasingly present in the writings of subsequent generations. Consider, by way of example, the extraordinary work of writers such as Igiaba Scego and Ubax Cristina Ali Farah, as well as the importance of texts such as the aforementioned *Pecore nere*. The texts to which I refer in this section, however, are different from the previous ones and can be considered to constitute the beginning of a fourth phase of Italian postcolonial literature.[95] This phase, strongly tied to the failure to reform the law that regulates the acquisition of Italian citizenship and to the expansion of the Black Lives Matter movement in Italy, articulates for the first time a systematic reflection of race studies in the Italian language by Black and non-white intellectuals, artists, and artivists in Italy, which is part of a broader transnational conversation on the intersection of race, color, gender, class, sexuality, and citizenship carried out by women and feminists of color in different European and non-European countries.[96]

The volume that acts as the turning point and opens this fourth phase is *Future. Il domani narrato dalle voci di oggi* (Futures: Tomorrow

---

[95] Geneviève Makaping's *Traiettorie di sguardi. E se gli altri foste voi?* (2001) (*Reversing the Gaze: What If the Other Were You?*, 2023) establishes a highly significant precedent for an analysis of the intersection of gender, race, and color in Italy. This was a rather isolated text when it was first published, however, and was not part of a broader theoretical elaboration.

[96] In this regard, see, for example, the recent collective volume by Akwugo Emejulu and Francesca Sobande, *To Exist is to Resist: Black Feminism in Europe* (2019), in which Black feminist scholars, artists, activists, and artivists reflect from their different national perspectives on how to construct a Black feminist Europe through an intersectional methodology. Italy is not present in the collection, but I am convinced that had it been published one or two years later, one or more of the writers, theoreticians, artists, and artivists analyzed in this section would have been included.

Narrated by the Voices of Today) (2019), edited by Igiaba Scego.[97] It is the first anthology consisting entirely of works by Black Italian women writers of African and Caribbean descent and includes Marie Moïse (of Haitian descent), Djarah Kan (of Ghanaian descent), Angelica Pesarini and Addes Tesfamariam (of Eritrean descent), Ndack Mbaye (of Senegalese descent), Lucia Ghebreghiorges (of Ethiopian descent), Leaticia Ouedraogo (of Burkinabe descent), Leila El Houssi (of Tunisian descent), Alesa Herero (of Cape Verdean descent), Wissal Houbabi (aka Wii) (of Moroccan descent), and Espérance Hakuzwimana Ripanti (of Rwandan descent). Through highly heterogeneous texts and hybrid narrative forms situated between fictional and autobiographical story, between memoir and critical essay, the 11 authors explore the processes of racialization that have involved and still involve their families and themselves, highlighting connections with the colonial past; they analyze the psychological repercussions of racism and the heavy legacy that it leaves on racialized subjects and their descendants; and they show how the internalization of racism—and the rejection of one's Blackness that follows—creates a deep fracture between the first and subsequent generations, who are deprived of their past and their history. This anthology, which refers to the future in its title, is in fact a polyhedric, polyphonic reflection on the past, as well as on the need to know that past in order to be able to construct a different future. Starting from their own personal experiences, the writers articulate a critical theoretical discourse on these issues that gives voice to a collectivity of Black subjects—mostly women—in Italy.

Immediately after their work appeared in *Future,* Espérance Hakuzwimana Ripanti and Djarah Kan—both of whom are writers, public intellectuals, and social media activists—published the memoir *E poi basta. Manifesto di una donna nera italiana* (Enough is Enough: Manifesto of a Black Italian Woman) (Ripanti 2019) and the short story collection *Ladri di denti* (Tooth Thieves) (Kan 2020) respectively. Both titles were published by People, which also published *Corpi estranei* (Foreign Bodies) (2020) by the Nigerian-Italian writer Oiza Queens Day Obasuyi. *E poi basta,* as the subtitle makes clear, is intended as a manifesto in which the author reclaims her own voice to respond to the racism she has been

---

[97] It seems very important to me that Igiaba Scego, a writer and an intellectual who has worked on racism and the legacy of colonialism in Italy for decades now, is the one to lead these writers into a fourth phase.

exposed to throughout her life in Italy. To do this, Ripanti, originally from Rwanda, adopted by white Italian parents, and raised in the province of Brescia, emerges from the invisibility in which she had hidden—achieved through a practiced silence—and creates a new language capable of responding to the language of oppression that permeates Italian society by "inventing words and placing them in a row in order to help others to breathe, to walk with their heads held high" (2019, 11).[98] Djarah Kan's *Ladri di denti* is also centered on the invisibility—and equally the hyper-visibility—of Black bodies in Italian society, on the hypersexualization of Black women, and on the profound psychological fractures that the internalization of racism produces. Through a very direct and often crude style, Kan denounces the pervasive nature of racism, which in Italy is still widely considered a problem foreign to the nation, despite the steadily increasing number of Black Italians who claim that they feel racialized in their everyday lives. The foreignness of Black bodies in the Italian national context and the pervasive toxicity of racism are also the focus of *Corpi estranei*, an essay in which Obasuyi develops a careful analysis to reveal the subtle mechanisms through which racism operates. The systemic nature of racism, in particular the sexist and racist imaginaries associated with Black women's bodies, is the focus of Rwandan-Italian author Marilena Umuhoza Delli's *Negretta. Baci razzisti* (Little Black Girl: Racist Kisses) (2020), a text that starts with personal experiences and elaborates a critique of everyday racism through the use of irony.[99] Nadeesha Uyangoda, an Italian writer of Sri Lankan origin, writes about the microaggressions a person experiences whenever one is *L'unica persona nera nella stanza* (The Only Black Person in the Room) (2021). The author articulates a complex reflection on the multiple ways in which social, cultural, and institutional spaces in Italy are constructed as white and argues that racism is a pervasive element in contemporary Italian society that endures as a legacy of colonialism.[100] Sabrina Efionayi, an Italian writer of Nigerian origins

---

[98] "inventare parole e metterle in fila per aiutare gli altri a respirare, a camminare a testa alta."

[99] In 2016, Umuhoza Delli also published a memoir entitled *Razzismo all'italiana. Cronache di una spia mezzosangue,* in which she denounces structural racism in Italy.

[100] In April 2021, *Zero* was released on Netflix (Randi et al. 2021). It is the first series to have Black Italian protagonists played by Black Italian actors. *Zero* is based on the novel *Non ho mai avuto la mia età* (2018b) by Antonio Dikele Distefano, an Italian writer of Angolan origin, who is also the author of four other novels (Distefano 2015, 2016, 2017, 2018a). The series *Zero* is briefly discussed in Chap. 4.

who had already published three novels under the pseudonym Sabrynex (2016a, b, 2017), writes a powerful memoir (disguised as a novel) titled *Addio, a domani* (Goodbye, I'll See You Tomorrow) (2022) about being raised by two mothers, one Nigerian and one Italian, between different languages and different cultures.

The texts under consideration here, of which further analysis is presented in Chap. 4, articulate a new phase in Italian postcolonial literature because they constitute a complex and unprecedented theoretical production on race and processes of racialization by Black and non-white women and non-binary subjects. Here, the direct postcolonial relationship with Italy loses importance because the connection between contemporary racism and Italian colonial history is highlighted by all the Black and Brown writers, independent of their origin.[101] These authors—writers, intellectuals, activists, artivists—reestablish the lost connection between Italian colonial history and contemporary postcolonialism; they denounce the structural racism in Italian society that manifests itself through acts that are, however innocuous they may appear to be, the foundation of everyday microaggressions; they underline the need to analyze racism and sexism wherever and whenever they intersect; and they render visible the internalization of racism, the psychological violence it entails, and the fracture that such internalization creates between second generations and their own cultures of origin. These authors do not merely denounce a status quo; rather, they articulate a collective response to structural racism and sexism, indicating trajectories that allow for a different future to be imagined.

2.6   Conclusion

The overview and periodization I have presented in this chapter aim to underscore the importance of postcolonial Italian literature to Italian culture and to examine the extraordinary complexity of such literature, which in the past three decades has traced many different paths, experimented with many new forms, proposed many new themes, and boldly contributed to decolonizing Italian society and culture.

---

[101] It is interesting to note, however, that in the stories that appear in *Future* by Angelica Pesarini and Lucia Ghebreghiorges, Italian authors of Eritrean and Ethiopian origin, respectively, the Italian colonial past makes an explicit appearance in the form of correspondence discovered in an archive or of personal memories that reemerge.

During the initial phase of this literary production, which developed in the first half of the 1990s, autobiographical narratives prevail, arising from migrants' need to tell their own stories in the first person, primarily in response to the ways in which they were being represented by legal texts and the media. This need was combined with the curiosity of Italian readers who wished to hear direct testimonies about aspects of a social reality that was almost unknown to them. This phase, which also involved the participation of small and medium-sized publishing companies, was characterized by a certain uniformity with regard to the types of writers who emerged (recent immigrants who needed the help of cultural and linguistic mediators to write and publish their texts), the motivations for writing (the need for self-definition and the desire to acquire authority through authorship), and the kind of narratives being produced (autobiographies and novels with a strong autobiographical component).

This phase was followed by a defining period in the second half of the 1990s, which saw a marked shift away from co-authorial collaboration and first–person testimonies (considered by the critical establishment to be of little more than socio-anthropological interest) to the production of more distinctly literary texts by the beginning of the new millennium. The greater mastery of language and familiarity with Italian society acquired by the writers active during this phase made the figure of the mediator obsolete, and even the narratives had substantial differences compared with the previous period. While still often focused on issues of migration (because the writers were mostly first-generation), they were in fact starting to concentrate on the more intimate social sphere, on identity and existential explorations. The texts produced during this phase, brought out mostly by small publishers, represented a wide variety of writing subjects (ranging from the occasional writer to the intellectual), literary genres (with a preponderance of novels, short stories, and poems), and themes. In this period of widespread experimentation, anthologies, journals, and competitions specifically dedicated to the literatures and cultures of migration began to emerge. All of this demonstrates that in this transitional phase, there was a growing awareness that Italian migration literature was not a passing phenomenon but rather the initial manifestation of a form of cultural expression that was becoming part of the broader Italian culture and that, because of this, it demanded proper attention, for which specific spaces had to be developed to facilitate its growth and expansion.

The twenty-first century ushered in a new stage of literary diversity—a third phase—in Italian postcolonial literature. Within this heterogeneity, new trends have emerged that have shared characteristics and include more distinctly literary texts. Among these, it is important to highlight the work of authors who read processes of racialization and contemporary racism in continuity with state and colonial racism, thus showing how the colonial systems of power find new incarnations in contemporary Italy. In this phase there is, furthermore, a cultural consolidation of Italian direct postcolonial literature, that is, literature produced by authors from countries and regions with which Italy maintained a direct colonial relationship—such as Albania and the Horn of Africa—and that have therefore undergone Italian influence from both a linguistic and a cultural point of view. This literature demands a reconsideration of how Italian history has been written and historical memory handed down, while at the same time it offers new perspectives on contemporary Italian society and culture and suggests the need for a comparative, transnational analysis of postcolonial literatures in Europe and around the world. Emerging parallel to this in Italy is the literature of second generations, written by (*de iure* or de facto) Italian citizens who come from non-Italian families and construct their own sense of identity at the intersection of their communities of origin, Italian society, and phenomena linked to the globalization of trade and culture. Since they are familiar with the Italian language and Italian culture, these authors promote linguistic hybridization by including street language, the languages of origin of their families, Italian dialects, and multimedia languages in their texts. They also "hybridize" literary genres, mixing together "high" and "low" culture, and literary forms from the countries of both their origin and their destination in search of forms of expression that give voice to changing social and cultural conditions.

Finally, a fourth phase in Italian postcolonial literature has only very recently begun, initiated by Black authors and authors of Color whose work promotes a deeper awareness of the structural racism present in Italian culture and society and a wider knowledge of the global history of racism, as well as the first systematic production of race studies in Italian. It is of great importance to monitor this new phase as it develops, to observe the connections these authors establish with other Black writers, artists, and artivists throughout Europe, and to celebrate their contribution to a transnational theorization on race and processes of racialization that, at the same time, takes into account the specificity of the racial history of Italy.

BIBLIOGRAPHY

Aden, Kaha Mohamed. 2010. *Fra-intendimenti*. Rome: Nottetempo.

Ahad, Ali Mumin. 1993. I 'peccati storici' del colonialismo in Somalia. *Democazia e Diritto* 33 (4): 217–250.

———. 2006. Corno d'Africa. L'ex-impero italiano. In *Nuovo Planetario Italiano. Geografia e antologia della letteratura della migrazione in Italia e in Europa*, ed. Armando Gnisci, 241–293. Troina: Città Aperta.

Ali Farah, Ubax Cristina. 2004. Rapdipunt. In *La letteratura postcoloniale italiana. Dalla letteratura d'immigrazione all'incontro con l'altro*, ed. Tiziana Morosetti, 127–130. Vol. 4 of *Quaderni del '900*. Pisa: Istituti Editoriali e Poligrafici Internazionali. Trans. Giovanna Bellesia-Contuzzi and Victoria Offredi Poletto as "Punt Rap," *Metamorphoses* 14 (1–2, Spring-Fall 2006): 276–280.

Ali Farah, Ubax Cristina. 2007. *Madre piccola*. Rome: Frassinelli. Republished in 2022 (Rome: 66thand2nd). Trans. Giovanna Bellesia-Contuzzi and Victoria Offredi Poletto as *Little Mother* (Bloomington: Indiana University Press, 2011).

Ali Farah, Ubah Cristina. 2014. *Il comandande del fiume*. Rome: 66thand2nd. Trans. Hope Campbell Gustafson as *The Commander of the River* (Bloomington: Indiana University Press, forthcoming in 2023).

Ali Farah, Ubah Cristina. 2020. *La danza dell'orice*. Milan: Juxta Press.

Ali Farah, Ubah Cristina. 2021. *Le stazioni della luna*. Rome: 66thand2nd.

Angelucci, Margherita. 2021. A New Way of Being Italian Through the Lens of Hip Hop. *Journal of Intercultural Studies* 42 (2): 177–193.

Anime in viaggio. La nuova mappa dei popoli. 2001. Rome: Adnkronos.

Babenco, Hector, dir. 1985. *Kiss of the Spider Woman*. USA and Brazil: David Weisman.

Barolini, Helen. 1999. *Umbertina*. New York: The Feminist Press. First published 1979.

Bhabha, Homi K. 1994. *The Location of Culture*. London: Routledge.

Bianchi, Rino, and Igiaba Scego. 2014. *Roma negata. Percorsi postcoloniali nella città*. Rome: Ediesse.

Birabiro, Meti. 2004. *Blue Daughter of the Red Sea: A Memoir*. Madison: The University of Wisconsin Press.

Bond, Emma. 2018. *Writing Migration through the Body*. Cham: Palgrave Macmillan.

Bouchane, Mohamed. 1990. *Chiamatemi Alì. Un anno a Milano nella vita di un clandestino venuto dal Marocco*, ed. Carla De Girolamo and Daniele Miccione. Milan: Leonardo.

Bravi, Adrian. 2004. *Restituiscimi il cappotto*. Ravenna: Fernandel.

———. 2007. *La pelusa*. Rome: Nottetempo. Trans. Patience Haggin as *Dust* (Victoria, TX: Dalkey Archive, 2017).

———. 2011. *Il riporto*. Rome: Nottetempo. Trans. Richard Dixon as *The Combover* (New York: Frisch, 2013).

———. 2013. *L'albero e la vacca*. Milan: Feltrinelli.

Brioni, Simone. 2013a. 'A Dialogue that Knows No Border between Nationality, Race or Culture': Themes, Impact and the Critical Reception of *Far from Mogadishu*. In *Lontano da Mogadiscio/Far from Mogadishu*, ed. Shirin Ramzanali Fazel, 354–381. Milan: Laurana Editore.

———. 2013b. Pratiche 'meticce': narrare il colonialismo italiano 'a più mani'. In *Postcoloniale italiano. Tra letteratura e storia*, ed. Franca Sinopoli, 89–119. Rome: Novalogos.

Brioni, Simone, Ermanno Guida, and Graziano Chiscuzzu, dirs. 2012a. *Aulò: Roma postcoloniale*. Italy: Kimerafilm. Available with Ribka Sibhatu, *Aulò! Aulò! Aulò! Poesie di nostalgia, d'esilio e d'amore / Aulò! Aulò! Aulò! Poems of Nostalgia, Exile and Love*. Italy: Kimerafilm, 2012.

———, dirs. 2012b. *La quarta via*. Italy: Kimerafilm. Available with Simone Brioni, ed., *Somalitalia: Quattro vie per Mogadiscio / Somalitalia: Four Roads to Mogadishu*. Italy: Kimerafilm, 2012.

Brizzi, Enrico. 2008. *L'inattesa piega degli eventi*. Milan: Baldini Castoldi Dalai.

Burdett, Charles, and Loredana Polezzi, eds. 2020. *Transnational Italian Studies*. Liverpool: Liverpool University Press.

Burdett, Charles, Loredana Polezzi, and Barbara Spadaro, eds. 2020. *Transcultural Italies. Mobility, Memory and Translation*. Liverpool: Liverpool University Press.

Camilleri, Andrea. 2003. *La presa di Macallè*. Palermo: Sellerio.

———. 2010. *Il nipote del negus*. Palermo: Sellerio.

Caminito, Giulia. 2016. *La grande A*. Florence: Giunti.

Capitani, Flavia, and Emanuele Coen, eds. 2005. *Pecore nere*. Rome-Bari: Laterza.

———, eds. 2008. *Amori bicolori. Racconti*. Rome-Bari: Laterza.

Capretti, Luciana. 2004. *Ghibli*. Milan: Rizzoli.

———. 2014. *Tevere*. Venice: Marsilio.

———. 2017. *La jihad delle donne. Il femminismo islamico nel mondo occidentale*. Rome: Salerno Editrice.

Centro Studi e Ricerche IDOS. 2021. *Dossier Statistico Immigrazione 2021*. Rome: Edizioni IDOS.

Chandra, Viola. 2001. *Media chiara e noccioline*. Rome: DeriveApprodi.

Chohra, Nassera. 1993. *Volevo diventare bianca*. In collaboration with Alessandra Atti di Sarro. Rome: Edizioni e/o.

Clò, Clarissa. 2012. Hip Pop Italian Style: The Postcolonial Imagination of Second-Generation Authors in Italy. In *Postcolonial Italy: Challenging National Homogeneity*, ed. Cristina Lombardi-Diop and Caterina Romeo, 275–291. New York: Palgrave Macmillan.

Collodi, Carlo. 1883. *Le avventure di Pinocchio. Storia di un burattino.* Florence: Felice Paggi.

Comberiati, Daniele. 2007. *La quarta sponda. Scrittrici in viaggio dall'Africa coloniale all'Italia di oggi.* Rome: Pigreco.

Concorso Letterario Nazionale Lingua Madre. n.d. Bando. https://concorsolinguamadre.it/bando/.

Consiglio, Stefano, dir. 1997. *Le strade di Princesa. Ritratto di una trans molto speciale.* Italy: RAI.

Conversi, Carlo, dir. 1994. *Princesa. Incontri irregolari.* Italy: RAI.

de Caldas Brito, Christiana. 1995. Ana de Jesus. In *Le voci dell'arcobaleno,* ed. Roberta Sangiorgi and Alessandro Ramberti, 59–61. Santarcangelo di Romagna: Fara Editore. Reprinted in *Amanda Olinda Azzurra e le altre,* by Christiana de Caldas Brito. Rome: Lilith Edizioni, 1998.

———. 1998. *Amanda Olinda Azzurra e le altre.* Rome: Lilith Edizioni. Second edition. Salerno-Milan: Oèdipus edizioni, 2004.

———. 2004. *Qui e là.* Isernia: Cosmo Iannone Editore.

———. 2006. *500 temporali.* Isernia: Cosmo Iannone Editore.

———. 2008. *Viviscrivi. Verso il tuo racconto.* San Giovanni in Persiceto: Eks&Tra.

de Lourdes Jesus, Maria. 1996. *Racordai. Vengo da un'isola di Capo Verde.* Rome: Sinnos.

Dell'Oro, Erminia. 1991. *L'abbandono. Una storia eritrea.* Turin: Einaudi.

———. 1997. *Asmara addio.* Milan: Baldini&Castoldi.

———. 1999. *La gola del diavolo.* Milan: Feltrinelli.

———. 2016. *Il mare davanti. Storia di Tsegehans Weldeslassie.* Milan: Piemme.

Distefano, Antonio Dikele. 2015. *Fuori piove, dentro pure, passo a prenderti?* Milan: Mondadori.

———. 2016. *Prima o poi ci abbracceremo.* Milan: Mondadori.

———. 2017. *Chi sta male non lo dice.* Milan: Mondadori.

———. 2018a. *Bozze. Prima e seconda parte.* Milan: Mondadori.

———. 2018b. *Non ho mai avuto la mia età.* Milan: Mondadori.

Dones, Elvira. 1998. *Senza bagagli.* Nardò: Besa.

———. 2001. *Sole bruciato.* Milan: Feltrinelli.

———. 2004. *Bianco giorno offeso.* Novara: Interlinea.

———, dir. 2006. *Vergini giurate.* Italy: Radiotelevisione Svizzera Italiana-Dones Media.

———. 2007a. *I mari ovunque.* Novara: Interlinea.

———. 2007b. *Vergine giurata.* Milan: Feltrinelli. Trans. Clarissa Botsford as *Sworn Virgin* (High Wycombe: And Old Stories, 2014).

———. 2011. *Piccola guerra perfetta.* Turin: Einaudi.

Dones, Elvira, and Mohamed Soudani, dirs. 2003. *Cercando Brunilda.* Bern: Radiotelevisione Svizzera Italiana.

Dones, Elvira, and Fulvio Mariani, dirs. 2005. *I ngujuar (Inchiodato)*. Bern: Radiotelevisione Svizzera Italiana.

Efionayi, Sabrina. 2022. *Addio, a domani*. Turin: Einaudi.

Eksetra. n.d. Concorso. Eks&Tra. http://www.eksetra.net/concorso-eksetra/.

Emejulu, Akwugo, and Francesca Sobande, eds. 2019. *To Exist is to Resist: Black Feminism in Europe*. London: Pluto Press.

Fanon, Frantz. 1961. *Les damnés de la terre*. Paris: Éditions François Maspero. Trans. Richard Philcox as *The Wretched of the Earth* (New York: Grove Press, 2004).

Farias de Albuquerque, Fernanda, and Maurizio Jannelli. 1994. *Princesa*. Rome: Sensibili alle foglie.

Fazel, Shirin Ramzanali. 1994. *Lontano da Mogadiscio*. Rome: Datanews.

———. 2007. La spiaggia. *Scritture migranti* 1: 9–14.

———. 2010. *Nuvole sull'equatore. Gli italiani dimenticati: Una storia*. Cuneo: Nerosubianco. Trans. Shirin Ramzanali Fazel as *Clouds over the Equator: The Forgotten Italians* (United Kingdom: CreateSpace Independent Publishing Platform, 2014).

———. 2013. *Lontano da Mogadiscio/Far from Mogadishu*. Milan: Laurana Editore.

Finocchi, Daniela, ed. 2007–2021. *Lingua Madre. Racconti di donne straniere in Italia*. Vol. 15. Turin: SEB 27.

Fiore, Teresa. 2012. The Emigrant Post-'Colonia' in Contemporary Immigrant Italy. In *Postcolonial Italy: Challenging National Homogeneity*, ed. Cristina Lombardi-Diop and Caterina Romeo, 71–82. New York: Palgrave Macmillan.

Fortunato, Mario, and Salah Methnani. 2006. *Immigrato*. Milan: Bompiani. First published 1990 (Rome: Theoria).

Gadda, Carlo Emilio. 1957. *Quer pasticciaccio brutto de via Merulana*. Milan: Garzanti. Trans. William Weaver as *That Awful Mess on the Via Merulana* (New York: G. Braziller, 1965).

Gangbo, Jadelin Mabiala. 1999. *Verso la notte bakonga*. Fossa: Portofranco.

———. 2001. *Rometta e Giulieo*. Milan: Feltrinelli.

———. 2005. Com'è se giù vuol dire ko? In *Italiani per vocazione*, ed. Igiaba Scego, 137–185. Fiesole: Cadmo.

———. 2009. *Due volte*. Rome: Edizioni e/o.

Garane, Garane. 2005. *Il latte è buono*. Isernia: Cosmo Iannone Editore.

Ghermandi, Gabriella. 1999. Il telefono del quartiere. In *Parole oltre i confini*, ed. Roberta Sangiorgi and Alessandro Ramberti, 73–82. Santarcangelo di Romagna: Fara Editore.

———. 2002. Quel certo temperamento focoso. In *Il doppio sguardo. Culture allo specchio*, 23–39. Rome: Adnkronos.

———. 2007. *Regina di fiori e di perle*. Rome: Donzelli. Trans. Giovanna Bellesia-Contuzzi and Victoria Offredi Poletto as *Queen of Flowers and Pearls: A Novel* (Bloomington: Indiana University Press, 2015).

———. 2010. All'ombra dei rami sfacciati, carichi di fiori rosso vermiglio. In *Roma d'Abissinia. Cronache dai resti dell'Impero: Asmara, Mogadiscio, Addis Abeba*, ed. Daniele Comberiati, 59–72. Cuneo: Nerosubianco.

Gnisci, Armando, ed. 2005. *Allattati dalla lupa*. Rome: Sinnos.

Goldman, Henrique, dir. 2001. *Princesa*. Italy and Great Britain: Parallax-BIM.

Hajdari, Gëzim. 1993. *Ombra di cane/Hije qeni*. Frosinone: Dismisuratesti.

———. 1995. *Sassi controvento/Gurë kundërerës*. Milan: Laboratorio delle Arti.

———. 1999. *Corpo presente*. Tirana: Shtëpia Botuese "Dritero".

———. 2000. *Antologia della pioggia/Antologjia e shiut*. Rimini: Fara.

———. 2004. *Spine nere/Gjëmba të zinj*. Nardò: Besa.

———. 2005. *Poema dell'esilio/Poema e mërgimit*. Rimini: Fara.

———. 2007. *Peligòrga/Peligorga*. Nardò: Besa.

———. 2008. *Poesie scelte 1990–2007*. Nardò: Besa.

———. 2011. *Corpo presente/Trup i pranishëm*. Nardò: Besa.

———. 2013. *Evviva il canto del gallo nel villaggio comunista/Rroftë kënga e gjelit në fshatin komunist*. Nardò: Besa.

———. 2015. *Poesie scelte 1990–2015*. Nardò: Besa.

Hemon, Aleksandar, ed. 2010. *Best European Fiction*. Chicago: Dalkey Archive Press.

Hoyet, Marie-José. 2006. Voci afroitaliane in scena. Per una prima ricognizione. In *Nuovo Planetario Italiano. Geografia e antologia della letteratura della migrazione in Italia e in Europa*, ed. Armando Gnisci, 499–517. Troina: Città aperta.

Ibrahimi, Anilda. 2008. *Rosso come una sposa*. Turin: Einaudi.

———. 2009. *L'amore e gli stracci del tempo*. Turin: Einaudi.

———. 2012. *Non c'è dolcezza*. Turin: Einaudi.

———. 2017. *Il tuo nome è una promessa*. Turin: Einaudi.

Il doppio sguardo. Culture allo specchio. 2002. Rome: Adnkronos.

Impronte. Scritture dal mondo. 2003. Nardò: Besa.

Itab, Hassan. 1991. *La tana della iena. Storia di un ragazzo palestinese*, ed. Renato Curcio. Rome: Sensibili alle foglie.

Jannelli, Maurizio. 1994. *Brevi note di contesto*. In *Princesa*, by Fernanda Farias de Albuquerque and Maurizio Jannelli, 7–10. Rome: Sensibili alle foglie.

Kan, Djarah. 2020. *Ladri di denti*. Gallarate: People.

Kassovitz, Mathieu, dir. 1995. *La Haine*. Paris: Les Productions Lazennec. Released in English as *Hate*.

Khouma, Pap. 2006. *Io, venditore di elefanti. Una vita per forza tra Dakar, Parigi e Milano*, ed. Oreste Pivetta. Milan: Baldini Castoldi Dalai. First published 1990 (Milan: CDE). Trans. Rebecca Hopkins as *I Was an Elephant Salesman: Adventures between Dakar, Paris, and Milan* (Bloomington: Indiana University Press, 2010).

King, Russell, and Nicola Mai. 2008. *Out of Albania: From Crisis Migration to Social Inclusion in Italy*. Oxford: Berghahn Books.

Kubati, Ron. 2000. *Va e non torna*. Nardò: Besa.

———. 2002. *M. Romanzo*. Nardò: Besa.

———. 2007. *Il buio del mare*. Florence: Giunti.

———. 2016. *La vita dell'eroe*. Nardò: Besa.

Kuruvilla, Gabriella. 2008. *È la vita dolcezza*. Milan: Baldini&Castoldi.

———. 2012. *Milano, fin qui tutto bene*. Rome-Bari: Laterza.

———, ed. 2014. *Milano d'autore*. Milan: Morellini Editore.

———, ed. 2015. *Roma d'autore*. Milan: Morellini Editore.

———, ed. 2016a. *Bologna d'autore*. Milan: Morellini Editore.

———, ed. 2016b. *Monaco d'autore*. Milan: Morellini Editore.

———, ed. 2017. *Genova d'autore*. Milan: Morellini Editore.

———, ed. 2018. *Calabria d'autore*. Milan: Morellini Editore.

———, ed. 2019. *Sicilia d'autore*. Milan: Morellini Editore.

———. 2020a. *Maneggiare con cura*. Milan: Morellini Editore.

———, ed. 2020b. *Romagna d'autore*. Milan: Morellini Editore.

Kuwornu, Fred Kudjo, dir. 2011. *18 Ius soli*. Italy and USA: Struggle Filmworks.

Lakhous, Amara. 1999. *Le cimici e il pirata*. Trans. Francesco Leggio. Rome: Arlem.

———. 2003. *Come farsi allattare dalla lupa senza che ti morda*. Algiers: Edizioni Al-ikhtilaf.

———. 2006. *Scontro di civiltà per un ascensore a Piazza Vittorio*. Rome: Edizioni e/o. Trans. Ann Goldstein as *Clash of Civilizations Over an Elevator in Piazza Vittorio* (New York: Europa Editions, 2008).

———. 2010. *Divorzio all'islamica a viale Marconi*. Rome: Edizioni e/o. Trans. Ann Goldstein as *Divorce Islamic style* (New York: Europa Editions, 2012).

———. 2011. *Un pirata piccolo piccolo*. Trans. Francesco Leggio. Rome.

———. 2013. *Contesa per un maialino italianissimo a San Salvario*. Rome: Edizioni e/o. Trans. Ann Goldstein as *Dispute Over a Very Italian Piglet* (New York: Europa Editions, 2014).

———. 2014. *La zingarata della verginella di via Ormea*. Rome: Edizioni e/o. Trans. Antony Shugaar as *The Prank of the Good Little Virgin of Via Ormea* (New York: Europa Editions, 2016).

Lamri, Tahar. 1995. Solo allora, sono certo, potrò capire. In *Le voci dell'arcobaleno*, ed. Roberta Sangiorgi and Alessandro Ramberti, 43–58. Santarcangelo di Romagna: Fara Editore.

———. 2006. *I sessanta nomi dell'amore*. Santarcangelo di Romagna: Fara Editore.

Lecomte, Mia, ed. 2006. *Ai confini del verso. Poesia della migrazione in italiano*. Florence: Le Lettere.

———, ed. 2011. *Sempre ai confini del verso. Dispatri poetici in italiano*. Paris: Chemins de tr@verse.

Lecomte, Mia, and Luigi Bonaffini, eds. 2011. *A New Map: The Poetry of Migrant Writers in Italy*. Ottawa: Legas.

Liuzzi, Antonella. 2016. Old and New Minorities: The Case of Arbëreshë Communities and Albanian Immigrants in Southern Italy. *Migration Letters* 13 (2): 258–268.

Lombardi-Diop, Cristina. 2005. Selling/Storytelling: African Autobiographies in Italy. In *Italian Colonialism: Legacy and Memory*, ed. Jacqueline Andall and Derek Duncan, 217–238. Bern: Peter Lang.

Lombardi-Diop, Cristina, and Caterina Romeo. 2012. Paradigms of Postcoloniality in Contemporary Italy. In *Postcolonial Italy: Challenging National Homogeneity*, ed. Cristina Lombardi-Diop and Caterina Romeo, 1–29. New York: Palgrave Macmillan.

———. 2015. *Postcolonial Europe*. Special issue of *Postcolonial Studies* 18 (4).

Luatti, Lorenzo. 2010a. *E noi? Il "posto" degli scrittori migranti nella narrativa per ragazzi*. Rome: Sinnos.

———. 2010b. La 'nuova' letteratura migrante per ragazzi: somiglianze e differenze con quella rivolta agli adulti. *El Ghibli* 7 (30). https://archivio.el-ghibli.org/index.php%3Fid=1&issue=07_30&section=6&index_pos=13.html.

Lucarelli, Carlo. 2008. *L'ottava vibrazione*. Turin: Einaudi.

———. 2014. *Albergo Italia*. Turin: Einaudi.

———. 2015. *Il tempo delle iene*. Turin: Einaudi.

Macoggi, Carla. 2011. *Kkeywa. Storia di una bimba meticcia*. Rome: Sensibili alle foglie.

———. 2012. *La nemesi della rossa*. Rome: Sensibili alle foglie.

Makaping, Geneviève. 2001. *Traiettorie di sguardi. E se gli "altri" foste voi?* Soveria Mannelli: Rubbettino. Republished in 2022 (Soveria Mannelli: Rubbettino). Trans. Giovanna Bellesia-Contuzzi and Vittoria Offredi Poletto as *Reversing the Gaze: What If the Other Were You?* (New Brunswick: Rutgers University Press, forthcoming in 2023).

Martins, Julio Monteiro. 2000. *Racconti italiani*. Nardò: Besa.

———. 2003. *La passione del vuoto*. Nardò: Besa.

———. 2005. *Madrelingua*. Nardò: Besa.

———. 2007. *L'amore scritto. Frammenti di narrativa e brevi racconti sulle più svariate forme in cui si presenta l'amore*. Nardò: Besa.

Mauceri, Maria Cristina, and Marta Niccolai. 2015. *Nuovo scenario italiano. Stranieri e italiani nel teatro contemporaneo*. Rome: Edizioni Ensemble.

McClintock, Anne. 1995. *Imperial Leather: Race, Gender and Sexuality in the Colonial Contest*. New York: Routledge.

Melandri, Francesca. 2017. *Sangue giusto*. Milan: Rizzoli.

Melliti, Mohsen. 1992. *Pantanella. Canto lungo la strada*. Trans. Monica Ruocco. Rome: Edizioni Lavoro.

———. 1995. *I bambini delle rose*. Rome: Edizioni Lavoro.

———, dir. 2007. *Io l'altro*. Italy: Tree Pictures.

Mengiste, Maaza. 2010. *Beneath the Lion's Gaze*. New York: Norton.

———. 2019. *The Shadow King*. New York: Norton.

Morone, Antonio Maria. 2011. L'ultima colonia. In *Come l'Italia è tornata in Africa 1950–1960.* Rome-Bari: Laterza.

Moussa Ba, Saidou. 1991. *La promessa di Hamadi.* Novara: De Agostini.

———. 1995. *La memoria di A.* In collaboration with Alessandro Micheletti. Turin: Ega Editore.

Mubiayi, Ingy. 2005. Documenti, prego. In *Pecore nere,* ed. Flavia Capitani and Emanuele Coen, 97–107. Rome-Bari: Laterza.

Mubiayi, Ingy, and Igiaba Scego, eds. 2007. *Quando nasci è una roulette. Giovani figli di migranti si raccontano.* Milan: Terre di mezzo.

Nasibù, Martha. 2005. *Memorie di una principessa etiope.* Vicenza: Neri Pozza.

Negro, Maria Grazia. 2015. *Il mondo, il grido, la parola. La questione linguistica nella letteratura postcoloniale italiana.* Rome: Franco Cesati Editore.

O'Healy, Áine, and Caterina Romeo. 2022. Narrating the Transnational Trajectories and Transgender Performances of the Sworn Virgin. *The Italianist* 42 (2): 1–21. https://doi.org/10.1080/02614340.2022.2042086.

Obasuyi, Oiza Queens Day. 2020. *Corpi estranei.* Gallarate: People.

Očkayová, Jarmila. 1995. *Verrà la vita e avrà i tuoi occhi.* Milan: Baldini&Castoldi.

———. 1997. *L'essenziale è invisibile agli occhi.* Milan: Baldini&Castoldi.

———. 1998. *Requiem per tre padri.* Milan: Baldini&Castoldi.

———. 2006. *Occhio a Pinocchio.* Isernia: Cosmo Iannone Editore.

Orton, Marie, and Graziella Parati, eds. 2007. *Multicultural Literature in Contemporary Italy.* Madison, WI: Fairleigh Dickinson University Press.

Orton, Marie, Graziella Parati, and Ron Kubati, eds. 2021. *Contemporary Italian Diversity in Critical and Fictional Narratives.* Vancouver: Farleigh Dickinson University Press.

Pace in parole migranti. 2003. Nardò: Besa.

Parati, Graziella. 1999. *Mediterranean Crossroads: Migration Literature in Italy.* Madison, WI: Fairleigh Dickinson University Press.

Perta, Carmen. 2011. The Albanian Dialects of Southern Italy: A Tenuous Survival. *International Journal of the Sociology of Language* 210 (2011): 127–137.

Puig, Manuel. 1976. *El beso de la mujer araña.* Barcelona: Seix Barral.

Puwar, Nirmal. 2004. *Space Invaders: Race, Gender and Bodies out of Place.* Oxford: Berg.

Randi, Paola, Ivan Silvestrini, Margherita Ferri, and Mohamed Hossameldin, dirs. 2021. *Zero.* Italy: Fabula Pictures and Red Joint Film. Released on Netflix April 21, 2021.

Ripanti, Espérance Hakuzwimana. 2019. *E poi basta. Manifesto di una donna nera italiana.* Gallarate: People.

Romeo, Caterina. 2015. Meccanismi di censura e rapporti di potere nelle autobiografie collaborative. *Between* 5 (9): 1–28.

Sabrynex. 2016a. *Over. Un'overdose di te.* Milan: Rizzoli.

———. 2016b. *Over 2. Camminiamo nel vento.* Milan: BUR.

———. 2017. #*TBT. Indietro non si torna*. Milan: BUR.

Salem, Salwa. 1994. *Con il vento nei capelli. Vita di una donna palestinese*. In collaboration with Laura Maritano. Florence: Giunti. Trans. Yvonne Freccero as *The Wind in My Hair* (Northampton, MA: Interlink Books, 2007).

Sangiorgi, Roberta, ed. 2004. *La seconda pelle*. San Giovanni in Persiceto: Eks&Tra.

Sangiorgi, Roberta, and Alessandro Ramberti, eds. 1995. *Le voci dell'arcobaleno*. Santarcangelo di Romagna: Fara Editore.

———, eds. 1996. *Mosaici d'inchiostro*. Santarcangelo di Romagna: Fara Editore.

———, eds. 1997. *Memorie in valigia*. Santarcangelo di Romagna: Fara Editore.

———, eds. 1998. *Destini sospesi di volti in cammino*. Santarcangelo di Romagna: Fara Editore.

———, eds. 1999. *Parole oltre i confini*. Santarcangelo di Romagna: Fara Editore.

Scego, Igiaba. 2003. *La nomade che amava Alfred Hitchcock*. Rome: Sinnos.

———. 2004. *Rhoda*. Rome: Sinnos.

———, ed. 2005a. *Italiani per vocazione*. Fiesole: Cadmo.

———. 2005b. "Salsicce." In *Pecore Nere*, ed. Flavia Capitani and Emanuele Coen, 23–36. Rome-Bari: Laterza. Trans. Giovanna Bellesia-Contuzzi and Victoria Offredi Poletto as "Sausages," *Metamorphoses: The Journal of the Five College Faculty Seminar on Literary Translation* 13 (2, Fall 2005): 214–225.

———. 2008. *Oltre Babilonia*. Rome: Donzelli. Trans. Aaron Robertson as *Beyond Babylon* (San Francisco: Two Lines Press, 2019).

———. 2010a. Il disegno. In *Roma d'Abissinia. Cronache dai resti dell'Impero: Asmara, Mogadiscio, Addis Abeba*, ed. Daniele Comberiati, 23–40. Cuneo: Nerosubianco.

———. 2010b. *La mia casa è dove sono*. Milan: Rizzoli.

———. 2015. *Adua*. Florence: Giunti. Trans. Jamie Richards as *Adua* (New York: New Vessel Press, 2017).

———, ed. 2019. *Future. Il domani narrato dalle voci di oggi*. Florence: Effequ.

———. 2020. *La linea del colore*. Milan: Bompiani.

Schiller, Nina Glick, Linda Basch, and Cristina Szanton Blanc. 1995. From Immigrant to Transmigrant: Theorizing Transnational Migration. *Anthropological Quarterly* 68 (1): 48–63.

Scritture Migranti. Rivista di Scambi Interculturali. 2018. Stem Mucchi Editore. https://www.mucchieditore.it/index.php?option=com_virtuemart&view=productdetails&virtuemart_product_id=2010&virtuemart_category_id=23.

Sejko, Roland, dir. 2013. *Anija la nave*. Italy: Luce Cinecittà.

Sibhatu, Ribka. 1993. *Aulò. Canto-poesia dall'Eritrea*. Rome: Sinnos.

———. 2004. *Il cittadino che non c'è. L'immigrazione nei media italiani*. Rome: EDUP.

———. 2012a. *Aulò! Aulò! Aulò! Poesie di nostalgia, d'esilio e d'amore / Aulò! Aulò! Aulò! Poems of Nostalgia, Exile and Love*. Introduction by Graziella Parati. Trans. Andre Naffis-Sahely. Rome: Kimerafilm.

———. 2012b. *L'esatto numero delle stelle e altre fiabe dall'altopiano eritreo.* Illustrated by Luca De Luise. Rome: Sinnos.

Sinopoli, Franca. 1998. Introduzione. In *Amanda Olinda Azzurra e le altre*, by Christiana de Caldas Brito, 7–9. Rome: Lilith Edizioni.

Tawfik, Younis. 1999. *La straniera.* Milan: Bompiani.

———. 2002. *La città di Iram.* Milan: Bompiani.

———. 2006. *Il profugo.* Milan: Bompiani.

———. 2012. *La ragazza di Piazza Tahrir.* Siena: Barbera Editore.

Tekle, Feven Abreha. 2005. *Libera. L'odissea di una donna Eritrea in fuga dalla guerra.* In collaboration with Raffaele Masto. Milan: Sperling & Kupfer.

Toso, Isotta, dir. 2010. *Scontro di civiltà per un ascensore a Piazza Vittorio.* Italy: Emme in collaboration with Rai Cinema.

Triulzi, Alessandro. 2012. Hidden Faces, Hidden Histories: Contrasting Voices of Postcolonial Italy. In *Postcolonial Italy: Challenging National Homogeneity*, ed. Cristina Lombardi-Diop and Caterina Romeo, 103–113. New York: Palgrave Macmillan.

Turco, Marco, dir. 2009. *La Straniera.* Italy: CG Home Video.

Uba, Wendy. 2007. *Il mio nome è Wendy.* In collaboration with Paola Monzini. Rome-Bari: Laterza.

Umuhoza, Marilena Delli. 2016. *Razzismo all'italiana. Cronache di una spia mez-zosangue.* Rome: Aracne.

———. 2020. *Negretta. Baci razzisti.* Rome: Red Star Press.

Uyangoda, Nadeesha. 2021. *L'unica persona nera nella stanza.* Rome: 66thand2nd.

Viarengo, Maria Abbebù. 1990. Andiamo a spasso? *Linea d'Ombra* 54: 74–76.

———. 1999. "'Scirscir N'Demna?' (Let's Go for a Stroll)." Trans. Anasuya Sanyal. In *Mediterranean Crossroads: Migration Literature in Italy*, ed. Graziella Parati, 69–78. Madison, NJ: Fairleigh Dickinson University Press.

Vicari, Daniele, dir. 2012. *La nave dolce.* Italy: Microcinema.

Vorpsi, Ornela. 2005. *Il paese dove non si muore mai.* Turin: Einaudi, 2005. Trans. Robert Elsie and Janice Mathie-Heck as *The Country Where No One Ever Dies* (Champaign, IL: Dalkey Archive Press, 2009).

———. 2006. *Vetri rosa.* Rome: Nottetempo.

———. 2007. *La mano che non mordi.* Turin: Einaudi.

———. 2010. *Bevete cacao Van Houten!* Turin: Einaudi.

———. 2012. *Fuorimondo.* Turin: Einaudi.

———. 2015. *Viaggio intorno alla madre.* Rome: Nottetempo.

Wadia, Laila. 2004. *Il burattinaio e altre storie extra-italiane.* Isernia: Cosmo Iannone Editore.

———. 2005. Curry di pollo. In *Pecore nere*, ed. Flavia Capitani and Emanuele Coen, 39–52. Rome-Bari: Laterza. Trans. Monica Hanna as "Chicken Curry." In *Other Italies/Italy's Others*, ed. by Thalia Pandiri. Special issue, *Metamorphoses: The Journal of the Five College Faculty Seminar on Literary Translation* 14 (1–2, Spring and Fall 2006): 150–157.

———. 2007. *Amiche per la pelle*. Rome: Edizioni e/o.

———. 2010. *Come diventare italiani in 24 ore*. Siena: Barbera Edizioni.

Wakkas, Yousef. 1995. Io marocchino con due kappa. In *Le voci dell'arcobaleno*, ed. Roberta Sangiorgi and Alessandro Ramberti, 105–142. Santarcangelo di Romagna: Fara Editore.

———. 2004. *Terra mobile*. Isernia: Cosmo Iannone Editore.

———. 2005. *La talpa nel soffitto. Racconti metropolitani*. Bologna: Edizioni dell'Arco.

———. 2007. *L'uomo parlante*. Bologna: Edizioni dell'Arco.

Wu Ming 2, and Antar Mohamed. 2012. *Timira. Romanzo meticcio*. Turin: Einaudi.

CHAPTER 3

Gender and Its Intersections

*I argue that race, gender and class are not distinct realms of
experience, existing in splendid isolation from each other. ...
Rather, they come into existence* in and through *relation to each other—
if in contradictory and conflictual ways.*
—Anne McClintock, *Imperial Leather*

3.1 INTRODUCTION

In April 2013, the prime minister of Italy at the time, Enrico Letta,
appointed Cécile Kashetu Kyenge, a naturalized Italian citizen originally
from the Democratic Republic of Congo, as minister of integration. This
appointment was destined to create new spaces—and an equal amount of
resistance—in the national imaginary, since Kyenge was not only the first
Black *person* to join an Italian government but also the first Black *woman*
to do so. Barack Obama's election as president of the United States in
2008 had shown how the actors of Italian culture and politics were unpre-
pared to articulate a discourse on race and Blackness, or even to use those
terms appropriately. The Italian prime minister at the time, Silvio
Berlusconi, notoriously acknowledged Obama's victory by referring to

© The Author(s), under exclusive license to Springer Nature
Switzerland AG 2023
C. Romeo, *Interrupted Narratives and Intersectional
Representations in Italian Postcolonial Literature*, Italian and Italian
American Studies,
https://doi.org/10.1007/978-3-031-10043-7_3

him as "young, handsome, and tanned."[1] Kyenge's appointment as a minister in Letta's government five years later not only highlighted once again the total inadequacy of the cultural debate on race and color in Italy but also showed the limitations of the debate on gender and, even more so, on the intersection between these three categories of oppression. The lack of comments about the minister's "tan" on this occasion signals two important points that are connected to the minister's color and gender. While Obama's racial identity, as Cristina Lombardi-Diop argues, had been mocked in an attempt to erase it, demonstrating how "the power of the State cannot possibly be embodied in a black body which, by definition, the state power seeks to exclude" (Lombardi-Diop 2012b, 175), the same process of erasure could not even be attempted in Kyenge's case. Unlike Obama, both the minister's parents are Black, her features are more markedly African, and she was born in Africa (and is thus one of the immigrants whom many would like to send back "home"); her Blackness, therefore, cannot be assimilated to a "simple tan," and neither can it be erased. Moreover, in a nation as strongly heteropatriarchal as Italy, where power is embodied by white masculinity (usually also heterosexual, wealthy, Catholic, and of advanced age), the fact that the minister was not only Black but also a woman aroused skepticism in some people regarding her intellectual and political abilities. The intersection between race/color and gender rendered the minister not only alien but completely unassimilable to the body of the nation and its political institutions.

During her term of office, Minister Kyenge was subjected to serious racial slurs, including from the senator of the Lega Nord (Northern League) Roberto Calderoli.[2] This appalling event, which did not arouse

---

[1] For a discussion on the erasure of Barack Obama's racial identity through Silvio Berlusconi's infamous "joke," see Lombardi-Diop (2012b), Petrovich Njegosh and Scacchi (2012), and Giuliani and Lombardi-Diop (2013). Regarding Obama's election and the significance of the way in which the event was perceived, refer to the introductory section in Chap. 4.

[2] In July 2013, Calderoli, at the time vice-president of the Senate, likened Minister Kyenge's features to those of an orangutan. In September 2015, the Senate granted authorization to prosecute the senator for defamation against former minister Kyenge but rejected the Court of Bergamo's request to prosecute for the offense of incitement to racial hatred (Fantauzzi 2015b). However, in November 2015, the Court of Bergamo lodged an appeal with the Constitutional Court to overturn the decision by the Senate (Fantauzzi 2015a), and the appeal was upheld. In January 2019, Roberto Calderoli was sentenced at first instance to one year and six months of imprisonment for defamation by the Court of Bergamo, which recognized racial aggravation (ANSA 2019).

the outrage it should have in the Italian political world, did, however, provoke a reaction from a large part of civil society. Artivist Karima 2G (Annie Karima Gehnyei), a Black rapper, singer, songwriter, and beat-maker born in Liberia and raised in Italy, dedicated the first single from her first album, *2G*, titled "Orangutan," to the event (Karima 2G 2014). As the video for the song opens, a reporter announces the details on a news broadcast in English, and immediately afterward Karima 2G sings: "2G / Second generation / Citizen right who represent the nation." Superimposed over images of an orangutan walking, climbing, and eating in its natural habitat are cartoon-style drawings, including, for example, a shower of bananas.[3] In addition to inviting Senator Calderoli to become part of her zoo ("I love animals, bears and wolves / Mr. Calderoli come and sit in my zoo"), Karima 2G links racism to other forms of exploitation and violence.[4] She does not limit her denunciation to Calderoli's insults to Kyenge but inscribes that episode in a broader context of discrimination against Blacks and of the exploitation of their labor (both the song and the video refer explicitly to the exploitation of Black women's domestic labor in Western societies). The rapper also combines video images showing instances of racial tension, including a speech by Martin Luther King, Black students dancing in front of soldiers holding guns in South Africa, and Black people being beaten in the street by police in an unidentified location. She thus emphasizes the fact that to understand the nature of racism and how it transforms itself at different moments in history and in different geopolitical contexts, it is necessary not only to understand its local dimension but also to see the existing connections between the various forms of racism through a transnational and intersectional analysis.[5]

In addition to the serious episodes of overt, violent racism against Minister Kyenge, the inadequacy of the debate on the intersection between race, color, and gender has become evident in other episodes—on the surface less serious and certainly less violent—that have shown how racism and sexism are structural elements throughout Italian culture and society.

---

[3] Black athletes have had bananas hurled at them at various sporting venues in Italy, and Minister Kyenge suffered the same fate at the Partito Democratico (Democratic Party) festival in Cervia in the summer of 2013 (*Il Sole 24 Ore* 2013).

[4] For example, the rapper denounces rape as an expression of violence rather than "passion" (disputing the "crime of passion" motivation that is still too frequently adopted by the Italian media when discussing femicide).

[5] For an analysis of Karima 2G's work, see Taronna (2016) and Fabbri (2021).

They therefore end up emerging even in contexts where the intention is not at all discriminatory. For the May 5, 2013, episode of the television program *In mezz'ora*, for instance, which is hosted by "left-wing" journalist Lucia Annunziata, who is noted for being mindful of women's issues, Annunziata had invited newly appointed Minister Kyenge to appear with the clear intention of welcoming her into the symbolic space of Italian national institutions, to confer her visibility, and to counter the racism that the minister would be facing. However, the question with which Annunziata started the interview—about Kyenge's large family and her 38 siblings in Africa—was deeply ethnoanthropological in nature and would, undoubtedly, never have been asked of a white female minister, and perhaps not even of a Black male minister (Kyenge 2013).[6] The attitude of the journalist, who obviously had no racist intention—indeed, quite the opposite—showed clearly how Africa remains a continent represented by images of othering, backwardness, and tribalism, and how Blackness is still difficult to assimilate to Italian institutions, especially if it intersects with the female gender. Annunziata must have realized that the presence of this Black woman in her capacity as a minister would provoke strong emotions, and she must have felt the need to relocate her in a space where the audience—and perhaps she herself—could imagine her without feeling a sense of unease and total estrangement: the domestic space (as opposed to the institutional space) of her homeland and family of origin (as opposed to the Italian/European one).

This lengthy reflection on Kyenge's appointment and on the way in which the minister was received in the Italian institutional space serves as an introduction to the concept of intersectionality and the importance, on both a theoretical and a methodological level, of using such an approach for a social and cultural analysis of differences and discriminations. Annunziata's interview with Kyenge highlights how, even though the journalist does not assume a sexist stance, she still shows the pervasiveness, in her imaginary as well as that of the nation, of a structural racism tied to the Italian colonial imaginary of Africa.

In order to promote a gendered reading of Italian postcolonial literature, an intersectional perspective is required that does not isolate the "gender" category as the only difference but instead considers that global transnational migrations, which have resulted in many non-white women coming to Italy, encourage a rethinking and rearticulation of gender

---

[6] For a critical reading of this interview, see Scego (2013).

discourses that take into account the various positions that indigenous women, immigrant women, and second-generation women occupy on Italian soil. The writers presented in this chapter interrupt the traditional narratives that construct the Italian literary, cultural, and institutional space as a distinctly white, male, space—in which Minister Kyenge is considered a "space invader"[7]—thereby redefining the symbolic spaces of representation and contributing to the construction of new (trans)national imaginaries.

3.2   Intersectionality: A Definition

The term "intersectionality" indicates a theoretical and methodological approach that affirms the need to intersect categories of oppression, rather than considering them separately or simply adding them to one another. The practice of intersectionality began well before 1989, the year when the term was coined by Kimberlé Crenshaw, and dates back to the Black American feminism of the late 1960s and early 1970s. In 1851, however, more than a century before the Combahee River Collective Statement asserted that "the major systems of oppression are interlocking" and defined Black feminism as "the logical political movement to combat the manifold and simultaneous oppressions that all women of color face" (Combahee River Collective 1977, para. 1), Sojourner Truth (1851) delivered a speech that would go down in history with the title "Ain't I a Woman?" at the Women's Rights Convention in Akron, Ohio. In her speech, the former slave and abolitionist observed that in the speech that Black women were de facto excluded from the category of "women," to which she firmly demanded to be included. The foundational concept of Sojourner Truth's speech was taken up again years later by the Black American feminists American feminists Hull et al. (1982), who already in the title of the collection they edited observed that "all the women are white and all the Blacks are men" unless otherwise specified.[8] This demonstrates that considering categories of oppression as monoliths without internal differentiation actually means examining only the group in the

---

[7] Nirmal Puwar's analysis (2004) of bodies considered to be "space invaders" (because they do not conform to the somatic norm of a given place) specifically takes into account the institutional space of the British Parliament.

[8] I refer here to the title of the well-known book *All the Women Are White, All the Blacks Are Men, But Some of Us Are Brave*, a collective volume that, in 1982, systematically addressed the issue of the invisibility of Black women in historical, social, cultural, and political contexts.

most privileged position within that given category (hence the white women in the "women" group of the "gender" category, and the Black men in the "Black" group of the "race/color" category). The intersectional approach emphasizes the heterogeneity that must be taken into account when speaking about women and the fact that not all women have historically shared the same oppression, which, therefore, cannot constitute the common ground for a relationship of (presumed) universal sisterhood.[9]

Since the 1970s, Black feminists have been emphasizing that the history of Black women in the United States was profoundly different from that of white women, who were the true beneficiaries of the slavery system in terms of social advancement. Middle-class white women in the North used the anti-slavery campaigns to practice politics and attain visibility for the feminist campaigns that would follow; white women (mostly) in the South often became complicit in the system of slavery because the oppression of Black women, as well as of Black men, placed them above people more marginalized than they were, allowing them the opportunity for social advancement, however moderate that advancement may have been.[10] Inevitably, the ramifications of these historically consolidated positions and interactions have informed the relationships between white and Black women in contemporary settings. The power relationships that were formed during the period of slavery, as Audre Lorde observed, were still well rooted and visible in the structure of American feminism at the end of the 1970s. At the Second Sex Conference, held in New York in September 1979, to which Lorde had been invited to participate, the African Caribbean American poet highlighted that the conference clearly showed that Black feminists were systematically marginalized by white feminists: whereas the latter were invited to discuss such topics as the dominant culture that imposed silence on women, the relationship between heterosexuality and power, and the development of feminist theory, Lorde was part of a session where Black and lesbian feminists were asked to share their personal experience (as if they could not also contribute to the larger debate). Their inclusion in the conference, however, was only illusory, Lorde (1984) stressed,

---

[9] For a critique of the concept of sisterhood articulated in the context of African American feminism, see, among others, hooks (1984; in particular, Chap. 4, "Sisterhood: Political Solidarity among Women").

[10] In this regard, see the work of Angela Davis and bell hooks, in particular, Davis (1981) and hooks (1981, 1984).

in that the reification of Blackness and lesbianism through the creation of a special space reserved for Black and lesbian intellectuals by hegemonic feminists—white, heterosexual, middle-class—excluded in substance what it formally showed it included.[11]

The practice of considering the differences within the various categories of oppression and of intersecting (and combining) such differences had already spread within African American, Chicana, and postcolonial feminism by the time Kimberlé Crenshaw (1989) coined the term "intersectionality" in a reflection on three legal cases. Crenshaw's reflection demonstrates that intersectionality is not a purely theoretical issue and that the lack of intersectional practice has real and concrete consequences for people's material lives. One of the well-known cases the legal scholar examines is *DeGraffenreid v. General Motors:* in 1976, five Black women filed a claim for damages caused by General Motors, from which they had been fired according to the principle of seniority—"last hired, first fired" (Crenshaw 1989). In their view, this principle perpetuated the effects of past discrimination against Black women, who, unlike white women and Black men, had not been hired by General Motors prior to the enactment of the Civil Rights Act of 1964. For this reason, they would have been unable to accrue greater seniority than other groups and were therefore destined to be laid off first if the need arose to reduce the company's workforce.

These women asked the court to admit "Black women" as a category of discrimination that considered the *simultaneous* oppression of race and gender. Without acknowledging the intersection of oppressions, Black women could not in fact assert their rights: if they had filed a lawsuit on the basis of gender discrimination, they would not have been able to accuse General Motors of not hiring them prior to 1964 because they were women (General Motors had hired *white* women prior to 1964); if they had filed a lawsuit on the basis of racial discrimination, they would not have been able to accuse General Motors of not hiring them prior to 1964 because they were Black (General Motors had hired Black *men* prior to 1964). The court refused to admit the classification of a new "minority"—that of African American women—characterized by two categories

---

[11] Lorde's essay was first published in the groundbreaking anthology *This Bridge Called My Back: Writings by Radical Women of Color,* edited by Cherríe Moraga and Gloria Anzaldúa (1981). Moraga and Anzaldúa use the term "women of color" to refer to Black women, other women of the "Third World," and "minority" women in the United States (including, among others, Chicana, Asian American, and Native American women).

of discrimination (rather than only one), and thus no such lawsuit could be filed. By refusing to consider the categories of race and gender in their simultaneity and intersectionality, the court had effectively relegated these African American women to a space of invisibility, if not total inexistence. This lawsuit—a legal proceeding concerning the work and daily life of the women involved and, therefore, not a theoretical line of reasoning isolated from reality—demonstrated how Black women risk becoming invisible not only in a cultural context, but also in the social, political, and economic contexts upon which their survival depend.[12]

Intersectionality is one of the most significant political, theoretical, and methodological contributions made by Black feminists and feminists of color, as it focuses on the differences in oppression that individual subjects and different groups of women experience and on the need to analyze gender discrimination in its simultaneity with other types of oppression. Speaking of race or gender without adopting an intersectional perspective limits the breadth and depth of analysis. This is the approach that I deploy in this chapter to analyze contemporary representations of Black women by Italian male authors, which are still pervaded by the imaginary of the Black Venus. Such texts are contrasted with self-representations by Black Italian female authors who are rewriting and reinscribing the bodies of Black women in Italian literature and culture, interrupting and boldly questioning conventional narratives based on colonial imaginaries.

3.3   Colonial Imaginaries: Black Venuses

Aethiopia. Appunti per una canzonetta (Aethiopia: Notes for a Popular Song) (2000a),[13] a diary that Ennio Flaiano kept from November 1935 to May 1936 during the Ethiopian campaign, begins with a list of places and dates. It then presents two undated notes that, to a certain extent, serve as an epigraph to *Appunti* (while the long list of notes that follows—which are, in contrast, dated—constitute the text of the diary). In the first of these notes—"The colonies are made with the Bible in hand, but not through the inspiration from the words written in it" (Flaiano 2000a,

---

[12] For a deeper analysis of intersectionality, see also Crenshaw (1991), McCall (2005), Davis (2008), Carbin and Edenheim (2013), and Marchetti (2013). See also Crenshaw's Ted Talk (2016).

[13] This notebook, written before *Tempo di uccidere* (*A Time to Kill*), was published as an appendix to the novel. See Flaiano (2000a, b).

289)[14]—the author inscribes the colonial enterprise in the long tradition of Western imperialism and colonialism, which have historically hidden the true economic and political motivations for invading territories and subjugating populations behind the presumed need to "convert the infidels." From 1700 onward, as Colette Guillaumin contends (1972, 1995, 2006), religion yielded to science, which gradually became the fulcrum of the interpretive paradigm of reality. It is therefore the naturalization of the category of race—and thus the idea that the differences determining the living conditions of people are "natural"—that justifies the civilizing mission (the colonizers no longer bring just the salvation of the soul; they also bring the civilization perceived to be lacking in the colonized populations) (see also Ribeiro Corossacz 2012). As Flaiano observes, however, the work of conversion and civilization is nothing but a pretext for justifying imperialist conquest.

The second note—"The influence of popular songs on colonial recruitment. At the base of every expansion, sexual desire"[15] (Flaiano 2000a, 289)—demonstrates how the process of constructing a white Italian masculinity through the satisfaction of erotic-exotic fantasies is at the core of the colonial enterprise. This signals the need to analyze the sexual politics that the Italian government, first Liberal and then Fascist, implemented in the colonies. As scholars such as Ann Laura Stoler (1991, 1996) and Anne McClintock (1995) have argued, in colonial contexts, the imaginary associated with the penetration of mysterious and unknown territories was indissolubly linked to the desire to penetrate the bodies of indigenous women, considered equally mysterious and unknown.[16] The Italian (male) national identity was in the process of being shaped when the colonial enterprise commenced: just as the process of national unification was completed (between 1861 and 1870), Assab Bay was acquired

[14] "Le colonie si fanno con la Bibbia alla mano, ma non ispirandosi a ciò che vi è scritto." [All translations are the translator's unless noted otherwise].

[15] "Influenza delle canzonette sull'arruolamento coloniale. Alla base di ogni espansione, il desiderio sessuale."

[16] The film *Venus noire* (*Black Venus*) (2010), by the Tunisian French director Abdellatif Kechiche, represents in a very effective way the morbid interest that Black women's bodies aroused in Europe, both erotically and scientifically. This film tells the story of Saartjie Baartman, a South African woman who was exhibited under the name "Hottentot Venus" in freak shows in various cities in England and France in the early nineteenth century. After she died—as the film shows—parts of her body, including her brain and genitals, were displayed at the Musée de l'Homme in Paris. Only in 2002 were Baartman's remains returned to South Africa, at the request of Nelson Mandela's government.

by the Rubattino Shipping Company (in 1869), and Eritrea became the first Italian colony (in 1890). The construction of such identity, therefore, was also based on the ability of Italian males to dominate colonial territories and their populations through sexual politics, which, in fact, allowed the Italian colonizers to exploit the bodies of Black women through practices of prostitution and *madamato*.[17] In order to render the responsibility for such exploitation less visible and to shift attention away from the systematic physical and psychological violence perpetrated in the colonies, Black women were represented as hypersexualized and excessive in their own sexual desire.[18] It is in antithesis to Black women's bodies, then, that the Italian national identity was constructed and established as masculine, white, and Catholic.[19]

From the 1990s onward, a proliferation of studies has been produced within the international academic arena on the manner in which the sexual politics implemented in the colonies actually reinforced the construction of European national identities.[20] In Italy, such studies have developed only in more recent times: in particular, scholars—especially female scholars—have focused their attention on the way in which Black women's

---

[17] The term *madamato* indicated a relationship of colonial concubinage formalized by a sort of marital contract between a male Italian citizen—very often a soldier—and a local woman in Eritrea (and later in Somalia and Ethiopia). Although this arrangement bound both parties to specific rights and duties, Italian men often interpreted it as an opportunity to have free access to sexual intercourse and domestic work. Regarding *madamato*, see Campassi (1987), Barrera (1996), Sòrgoni (1998), Iyob (2005), and Stefani (2007).

[18] To understand the processes by which Black women in the colonies were hypersexualized, refer to bell hooks's work (1981) on the relationship between white women and Black women during slavery and on the male domination exercised through systematic sexual violence, which was partly justified by the presumed excessive sexuality of Black women.

[19] In this regard see, among others, Stefani (2007), Giuliani and Lombardi-Diop (2013), and Giuliani (2015).

[20] For an analysis of sexual politics in the colonies; relationships of domination based on race, gender, and sexuality; and the importance of these dynamics for the construction of European national identities, see, among others, Stoler (1991, 1996, 2002), McClintock (1995), McClintock et al. (1996), and Wekker (2016). For an analysis of these elements in the Italian context, see, among others, Campassi (1987), Barrera (1996, 2002a, b, 2003, 2004), Lombardi-Diop (1999, 2012a, b), and Ponzanesi (2012). For an analysis of the Hottentot Venus, and in particular of the figure and history of Saartjie Baartman, see Crais and Scully (2009). For an analysis of the "Black Venus" in the Italian colonies and for the ways in which such colonial imaginaries survive in contemporary representations, see in particular Campassi and Sega (1983), Sòrgoni (1995, 1998, 2002), Ponzanesi (2005), and Sabelli (2010).

bodies became the catalysts for sexual desire and how the affirmation of masculinity is indissolubly linked to the imposition of colonial domination. In the colonial context, Black women embodied the ultimate otherness, in terms of both gender and race. Their bodies stimulated the erotic fantasies of Italian males in the colonies, promising satisfaction of their forbidden, uncontrollable sexual desires, which were incompatible with the type of sexuality considered acceptable within traditional middle-class families in Italy. These "Black Venuses"—who, like the unexplored territories into which the colonizers ventured, were perceived to be primordial and mysterious in nature—exerted a powerful attraction, but at the same time aroused a deep fear.[21]

The colonial imaginary of the Black Venus remains widespread in Italy today. It circulates both in representations that re-elaborate the colonial period and in those set in contemporary postcolonial contexts. Such an imaginary is, for example, powerfully deployed in Carlo Lucarelli's novels that feature colonial settings. Here, the attitude toward Italian colonial history is only weakly critical, while the atmospheres are highly exoticized and the colonial sexual politics are not questioned in the least; on the contrary, the symbolic devices evoked and reproposed are exceptionally traditional and colonial. Aicha and Ualla, the two African women who open the novels *L'ottava vibrazione* (The Eighth Vibration) (2008) and *Albergo Italia* (Hotel Italy) (2014), for instance, are constructed on the basis of the most traditional of colonial fantasies and are reduced to pure sexuality within casual interracial relationships with Italian men.[22] The power of such an imaginary is evidenced by the fact that both women appear at the beginning of the two novels, just as Flaiano's comment—"At the base of

[21] McClintock (1995, 25–28) analyzes the ambivalent image of the colonized woman, who arouses a strong sexual attraction in European men but who can also assume fearsome guises. McClintock examines a painting by Jan van der Straet (dated 1575) that depicts the discovery of America as an erotic encounter between Amerigo Vespucci and a naked woman, a symbol of the feminized American continent. While the scene of the encounter is placed in the foreground and represents the conquest (symbolized by the upright male figure) of the virgin territory (symbolized by the woman in a passive pose that evokes sexual and territorial submission), in the background some women are depicted roasting a man's leg, presumably to eat it. According to the author, this painting expresses the feeling of male power inherent in the imperial enterprise as much as the sense of anxiety that the European male felt about indigenous women in the colonies, perceived as attractive and threatening at the same time.

[22] For an analysis of the intersections of gender, race, and class in Lucarelli's *L'ottava vibrazione* (2008) and in Wu Ming 2 and Antar Mohamed's *Timira* (2012), see Sabelli (2013).

every expansion, sexual desire"—is placed at the beginning of *Appunti* (2000a, 289).

These two characters, Aicha and Ualla, both portrayed as animalistic, have no other narrative function than to provoke the sexual desire of the colonizers. Their sexuality—and by extension the sexuality of all Black women—is constructed as excessive: Aicha and Ualla persuade two reluctant Italian men to have sexual intercourse with them at the very beginning of each of the novels. Such construction is conducive to allowing the colonizers to absolve themselves of responsibility for their systematic exploitation and sexual violence. In the first novel, Aicha sets a trap for first-class colonial clerk Vittorio Cappa when he goes to the warehouse: she presents herself naked to him, and he ends up surrendering to her "seduction," despite the stifling heat. In the second novel, light infantryman Corbetta Pasquale, on guard at the military depot, is reluctant to give in to Ualla's temptation because he is afraid he will be punished if he is caught, but he too ends up yielding to the woman's persistence. In this type of representation, the interracial relationships actually consolidate and strengthen the boundaries of race and nationality, corroborating from the very beginning the existing nexus—as suggested in Flaiano's *Appunti*—between sexual power and colonialism. This perpetuates the image of the colonial space as "the ideal space for the recovery and realization of full masculinity"[23] (Stefani 2007, 29). These scenes, positioned as they are at the opening of the two novels, reaffirm from the very beginning the parallelism that exists between the penetration of the colonial territories to be conquered and the penetration of the bodies (mainly, but not exclusively) of Black women to be dominated/domesticated.

Such parallelism is further emphasized in *L'ottava vibrazione*: nothing is known about Aicha, including the place from which she presumably originates, "a village without a name that, had it been marked on the maps of the Italian Military Geographic Institute, would have been at the center of a pale ochre area on which is written, in faint characters, 'little known area'" (Lucarelli 2008, 13). Aicha does not speak, and when she does, she expresses herself in an incomprehensible language (as does Mariam in Flaiano's *Tempo di uccidere* (2000b) [*A Time to Kill*, 1992]). Depriving this woman of her voice is a narrative device to ensure that her story is told by others, which in fact occurs at the end of the first chapter in a section entitled "La storia di Aicha, la cagna nera" (The Story of Aicha, the Black

---

[23] "lo spazio ideale per il recupero e la realizzazione della piena mascolinità."

Bitch). This section is only a page and a half long, which suggests that in relation to this woman—and, metonymically, all Black women in the colonies—there is not much to say. Aicha is seen only through Italian men's eyes: a mysterious woman, deprived of history and endowed with an "exotic" beauty, whom these men cast as an instinctive and primordial being who walks around naked and in constant search of sexual satisfaction. The association between Aicha and nature (the second term of the binary opposition culture/nature, which is symmetrical to that of colonizer/colonized) and her hypersexualization emphasize the animality and the subhuman nature imposed upon colonized women, something affirmed by the nickname "the Black bitch" Aisha is given (Lucarelli 2008, 13).

The character Ualla in *Albergo Italia* is outlined in a less two-dimensional way than that of Aicha: the imaginary of the Black Venus is in this case evoked in both its erotic and its threatening aspect.[24] Unlike Aicha, Ualla is conscious of the power her sexuality confers on her, and she uses it to achieve her own ends. The statement that opens the novel—"Ualla, in Tigrinya, means 'monella'"[25] (Lucarelli 2014, 3)—is followed by a scene in which Ualla seduces the light infantryman Corbetta Pasquale, on guard at the military depot in Arkiko, near Massawa, thus distracting him from his duty and allowing a local gang to steal the ammunition stored in the depot. The imaginary that this first scene nurtures is not only the strongly erotic one evoked by the uncontrollable, shameless sexuality of the Black Venus—so Black that the soldier does not see Ualla coming in the dark of night until she smiles and her presence is revealed by the whiteness of her teeth—but also the transgressive one linked to the image

[24] See note 21 in this chapter.

[25] "Ualla, in tigrigna, vuol dire 'monella.'" "Uala" in Tigrinya means "unreliable," "with no ethics," and can be translated as "monella" (I would like to thank Ribka Sihbatu for explaining the meaning of the word to me and for telling me the correct pronunciation, which for obvious reasons I cannot reproduce in writing). *Monella* roughly translates as "naughty little girl," "imp," "street urchin." Ualla's character also appears in the subsequent novel, another colonial thriller set in Eritrea, entitled *Il tempo delle iene* (The Time of the Hyenas) (Lucarelli 2015). Here, Ualla makes only a fleeting appearance: toward the end of the novel, she has sexual intercourse in the street with ex-lieutenant Debaudo—whom she seduces partly because she is a "monella" and partly because she needs money so she can go away for a while—at the end of which she disappears from the scene and the narrative. As in the previous novel, Ualla is characterized here by her "indecent gaze" ("sguardo indecente") (Lucarelli 2015, 120).

of a child, a "monella," to be precise. This reminds readers (albeit, presumably, unintentionally) that Black girls were often sold or given to white men in the colonies while they were still children. On the one hand, Lucarelli evokes the infantilizing process described by Frantz Fanon (1952), according to which the state of nature in which the colonized presumably live is equated to the simplicity of children who are not yet endowed with the complexity they would derive from their cultural development in a "civilized" society. On the other, this evocation of the world of childhood through the term "monella" seems intended to confer an aura of playfulness to the scene in order to dissimulate the systematic violence of the colonizers against African women and girls. But this evocation produces the effect of reminding readers that moral principles, so firm at home, were often set aside in the colonies on the grounds of cultural differences and of the perceived otherness of Africans.[26] As Isabella Marincola's father, who had served in the Italian army in Somalia, expresses it: "When it suits us, we disregard our mission of civilization, perhaps using the

---

[26] In this regard, see Gianni Bisiach's well-known interview with journalist Indro Montanelli (1969) on the program *L'ora della verità*. Speaking of when he was a soldier in Eritrea, Montanelli recounts, with a certain satisfaction, that he had a 12-year-old "wife," a Bilen girl whom he had bought from her father. During the program, the well-known journalist explains how in Africa marrying at the age of 12 was the norm (interestingly, in this regard Italians were eager to respect the presumed African customs and traditions). The intervention in the studio during the interview by feminist activist Elvira Banotti clearly embarrasses Montanelli. Banotti maintains that it is false that girls in Eritrea married so young, points out to Montanelli that such an act would not even be conceivable with an Italian girl, and states that this type of union was nothing more than colonial oppression and sexual violence perpetrated on the body of a little girl (Montanelli 1969). There is a reference to these events in Indro Montanelli's life in the novel *Timira* (Wu Ming 2 and Mohamed 2012; see the discussion later in this chapter, specifically in Sect. 3.4). After receiving a visit from Indro Montanelli in his studio on Via Margutta while Isabella Marincola was posing nude, Bulgarian sculptor Assen Peikov declared, "They say that in Africa he had a child wife and that he loved her" ("Dicono che in Africa avesse una moglie bambina e che le abbia voluto bene") (Wu Ming 2 and Mohamed 2012, 172). What is most noteworthy is that Marincola identifies in that visit by Montanelli the only occasion in her life in which she felt treated like a monkey: the journalist proposed putting a banana in the model's hand, asking her then if she liked peanuts (171).

traditions of the place as an excuse and being careful not to try to correct them"[27] (Wu Ming 2 and Mohamed 2012, 50).[28]

Unlike Aicha, Ualla also embodies the other aspect associated with the imaginary of the Black Venus, namely, the threat of the unknown (associated with the fear of cannibalism).[29] When, toward the end of the novel *Albergo Italia* (Lucarelli 2014), Ualla once more meets the soldier she had "seduced" earlier, who is now the warden of the prison in which she is held, she tries to seduce him again in order to escape before realizing that he will not be tempted this time because he does not want to incur further punishment. At this, she kills him without remorse, just as, indeed, an animal would do.

Although Ualla's character is constructed in a slightly less two-dimensional way than Aicha's, the representation of Black women in the African colonies remains profoundly stereotyped and conventional, in line with the spirit of Lucarelli's novels, which, despite their intention to be critical of the Italian colonial enterprise, are nonetheless imbued with a sexism and exoticism through which the colonial past is evoked as a period of adventure ("the Italian Far West," as Lucarelli himself maintains) (Baricco 2008) and of conquest, both of territory and of the women of

---

[27] "quando ci fa comodo la nostra missione di civiltà ce la mettiamo sotto i tacchi, magari prendendo come scusa le tradizioni del posto e guardandoci bene dal provare a correggerle."

[28] It is worth noting that this particular aspect of Italy's colonial history—namely, the one connected to sexual politics in the colonies and to the systematic rape of African girls—appears in Luciana Capretti's novel *Tevere* (2014), which, unlike her other novel *Ghibli* (2004) mentioned in the previous chapter, focuses on a story and themes unrelated to colonialism. However, the protagonist's father, who in the past was a ruthless, violent Fascist militant, remembers the colonization period as the most sexually gratifying of his life: "They took them young, extremely young. He had bought one, her father had given her to him as a wife. She was 12 years old, she did not look at him, she did not dare, she remained there naked for him, as long as he wanted, just as he wanted. His life for il Duce had been also this, yes. Not even at the brothel with the most expert girls he would have felt this good as he did between those Black child thighs" ("Giovani le prendevano, giovanissime. Lui ne aveva comprata una, il padre gliela aveva data come moglie, aveva dodici anni, non lo guardava, non osava, rimaneva lì nuda per lui, fin quando lui voleva, come lui voleva. La sua vita per il Duce era stata anche questo, sì. Neanche al bordello con le ragazze più esperte sarebbe stato mai così bene come fra quelle cosce nere bambine") (Capretti 2014, 97).

[29] See note 21 in this chapter.

Africa.[30] These novels, as also argued in the previous chapter, do not over-turn but rather reinforce the colonial stereotypes of race and gender that still so firmly pervade the Italian national imaginary and do not enact any postcolonial resistance.[31] Representations in which Black women are reduced to pure sexuality and racialized, as in Lucarelli's colonial novels, "constitute an archive of images and attitudes that have been naturalized, domesticated, and internalized as 'common sense' in a culture where the historical experience of colonialism is to a large extent disavowed" (O'Healy 2012, 205).[32] Lucarelli constructs the characters of African women according to stereotypical colonial imaginaries—hypersexualized, instinctual, animalistic, voiceless women with no history—that titillate the erotic fantasies of the male audience and reinforce the exoticizing

---

[30] I find the gender dynamics of this book problematic not only in terms of the fictionalized representations in the text but also in how the novel was written. In the afterword, entitled "La fortuna degli scrittori" (Writers' Good Fortune), Lucarelli (2008) admits that the archival and bibliographic materials he used were provided to him by a woman he had met for the first time at a book signing. On that occasion, she had heard that he was working on the draft of a novel set in Eritrea during the period of the defeat of Adwa, and she had offered to do some research on the subject and provide him with any documents that might be useful. The material she collected over time, by Lucarelli's own admission, proved to be invaluable: he had decided to devote a long period to study and research, but once he had opened the envelopes the woman had sent him, he realized that everything he needed was already there. To this "marvellous librarian" ("meravigliosa bibliotecaria") (Lucarelli 2008, 454), Patrizia Pastore by name, is given what seems to be very meager thanks. Lucarelli includes the research donated to him by Pastore in a list of fortuitous if unexpected occurrences that sometimes happen to writers and provides no details about the material he had received, thus disregarding the librarian's competence and minimizing her active role in and contribution to the novel.

[31] See, in this regard, Triulzi (2012). Alessandro Triulzi compares texts that recount the history of colonialism and postcolonial migrations, observing the profound differences existing between texts that enact a postcolonial resistance and those that do not. As examples of texts that recount Italian colonialism in a fictionalized, adventurous way, Triulzi cites *L'ottava vibrazione* (2008) by Lucarelli and the graphic novel series *Volto Nascosto* (Hidden Face) (2007–2008) by Gianfranco Manfredi, which he analyzes by comparing them with the novel *Regina di fiori e di perle* (2007) (*Queen of Flowers and Pearls: A Novel*, 2015) by Gabriella Ghermandi and the documentary film *Come un uomo sulla terra* (*Like a Man on Earth*) (2008), by Andrea Segre, Dagmawi Yimer, and Riccardo Biadene.

[32] O'Healy's comment does not refer to Lucarelli's novels.

imaginaries aimed at transforming brutal and systematic oppression into a masculinity-enforcing adventure.

Gabriella Ghermandi's rewriting of the colonial period in her novel *Regina di fiori e di perle* (2007) (*Queen of Flowers and Pearls: A Novel*, 2015) depicts Ethiopia's occupation by Mussolini's army (1935–1936) and the Ethiopians' strong resistance during the entire five years of occupation (1936–1941) from a profoundly different perspective. Unlike Lucarelli, Ghermandi constructs a counterhistory of Italian colonialism through a plural, choral, and postcolonial narrative (see Triulzi 2012). The narrative is entrusted mainly to female characters, including the protagonist Mahlet, who serves as a catalyst for the stories when she is young and then as the storyteller of the Ethiopian people when she grows up. The female characters that populate Ghermandi's novel are not represented according to colonial stereotypes: they are neither prostitutes nor madams, their stories are not written to serve the colonizers, and the way in which the narrative is constructed—namely, through the voices of a plurality of protagonists—shows how Ghermandi's project is to narrate a story from below that deeply modifies the official history of colonialism. The Black Venus imaginary has no place in this novel: the interracial relationship at the beginning of the novel between Yacob's sister, Amarech, and an Italian soldier, Daniel, is based on a substantive equality between the Ethiopian woman and the Italian man, who decides to change allegiance to the Ethiopian resistance because he is revolted by the horrors perpetrated by Fascist colonialism.

The stories Mahlet gathers from different people and perspectives are populated by women such as Empress Taytu, who fought with her own army alongside her husband, Emperor Menelik, destroying the Italian army at Adwa; Kebedech Seyoum, a courageous resistance fighter who, upon the death of her husband, took command of his army and fought with her newborn baby on her back; the mother of the lady of the tortoises, who joined the resistance after Graziani had the population of Addis Ababa massacred in retaliation for the attempt on his life by opposition forces. This same woman is the protagonist in a scene that, as Cristina Lombardi-Diop (2007) observes, reverses the lake scene in Flaiano's *Tempo di uccidere* (2000b), in which the lieutenant for the first time sees Mariam—a character deprived of voice and agency, whom he kills at a later point.[33] The analogous scene in the story told to Mahlet by the lady of the tortoise in *Regina di fiori e di perle* has an entirely different outcome: here, to protect Kebedech Seyoum's son and thus the future of the nation, the female protagonist of the narrative shoots and kills the Italian soldier who, disarmed, is heading toward the child.[34] The resistance of the Ethiopian population, of which we know very little from the official Italian history, constitutes the pivot of the narrative that Ghermandi and Mahlet construct from the individual narratives of people who played a part in and/or conserved a memory of that resistance.

Maaza Mengiste's *The Shadow King* (2019b), a historical novel that tells the story of the occupation of Ethiopia by drawing on Ethiopian oral history, pursues a similar purpose and contributes to the creation of powerful anticolonial imaginaries. In the author's note at the end of the novel as well as in a powerful interview (2020), Mengiste states that *The Shadow King* commenced as a project through which she wanted to fill in the gaps of history and contribute to formulating a counternarrative to the Italian occupation of Ethiopia. According to the story she had heard as a child, which remains a constituent part of the Ethiopian collective imaginary, resistance fighters never allowed Mussolini's Empire to prosper: they resisted for five years with their outdated weapons until they defeated the powerful Italian army. The resistance, the novel's narrator states, actually began with words, with Ethiopians altering Mussolini's name, a sign of calculated disrespect for him and his authority: "Mussoloni: the deliberate mispronunciation has spread across the country, started by those who did not know better and continued by those who do" (Mengiste 2019b, 132).

---

[33] I have always found it significant that some critical texts about Flaiano's novel state that the lieutenant kills the woman (who, he will discover later, is called Mariam) by accident. Mariam is *wounded* by the lieutenant accidentally but is then killed by him in cold blood. The motivation that the lieutenant gives to himself and to readers is that he wants to spare the woman from suffering—as in the case of wounded animals that are put down—since she has no chance of survival, or so he claims. However, it is clear from the narrative that if he went to seek help, the lieutenant would have to reveal his own presence at the scene and attempt to explain the events, which could be dangerous for him. Therefore, killing the woman under the pretext that her wound is too serious for her to survive seems to be the option that benefits the lieutenant most and allows him to feel comfortable in his conscience. Or so he thinks. In fact, as I note in Chap. 4, this murder—a metaphor for the horrors of colonialism—haunts the lieutenant until he leaves Africa and, the novel suggests, afterward as well.

[34] For an analysis of the relationship of continuity existing between Ghermandi's novel and Flaiano's *Tempo di uccidere* (2000b), see Lombardi-Diop (2007), Derobertis (2009), and Benvenuti (2011–2012, 2012).

While this counternarrative of resistance has been and still is powerful in the Ethiopian imaginary, the author embarks on the more deeply challenging process of rewriting such a counterhistory from a gendered perspective: Mengiste, like Ghermandi, highlights the crucial role of Ethiopian women in the anticolonial resistance against the Italians, but, unlike Ghermandi, she denounces the Ethiopian patriarchal social system that oppressed and violated them. This process required that Mengiste excavate stories that had been consistently removed from both the colonial narrative in history books and the anticolonial counternarrative of Ethiopian oral history:

> As a child, you hear these stories of heroism. These men were poorly equipped with old guns, charging a very highly weaponized European army and winning. While doing research, I started thinking about the myths and legends of war, and I realized that if Italy had its propaganda machine, then I also had to accept the fact that Ethiopia had its mythologies about this war. I realized I needed to break apart the myths and legends and propaganda and look deeper. (Mengiste 2019a, para. 5)

Such a complex process implied deconstructing the binary colonizer/colonized and interrogating the homogeneity of the "colonized" category (and, to a certain extent, that of the "colonizer," too). It certainly meant questioning the narrative of the splendor of the Fascist Empire, but it also meant interrogating the heroism of the Ethiopian men who had fought and defeated that empire, the memorialization of whose victory was constructed through the systematic erasure of women—of their lives, their courage, their traumas. Mengiste's reflection, in turn, led her to look deeper into the role of women *before* the war and into the gender politics of Ethiopian society, and to show how the annihilation of women was part of a masculinity construction process grounded in the continuity between the authority to control women and the authority to maintain possession of and control over the land. Such awareness led Mengiste to question the heroism of Ethiopian leaders and to uncover the fact that Ethiopian women had been violated not only by the Italian colonizers. As Mengiste shows, the systematic violation of Black women in the colonies was conducive to the creation and consolidation of both Italian and Ethiopian masculinity. In order to write this counternarrative, Mengiste realized, she needed to listen carefully to the voices of women, the subaltern subjects who refused to remain silent, although trapped in the space articulated between colonialism and nationalism (Spivak 1988).

The Shadow King unfolds during the Italian occupation of Ethiopia—with the exception of the prologue and epilogue, which are set in 1974, when the Ethiopian Empire and its Emperor, Haile Selassie, are about to be overthrown by the Soviet-backed socialist rule of the Derg. The novel opens in the train station of Addis Ababa in 1974, where the female protagonist, Hirut, has arrived from her faraway village with a metal box, which she has been guarding for Italian military photographer Ettore Navarra since the end of the occupation and of which she is now impatient to rid herself. She knows that meeting Navarra will force her to remember the war and all its violence. To this end, in this first scene she grounds her narrative in her family history ("I am Hirut, she reminds herself, daughter of Getey and Fasil, born on a blessed day of harvest, beloved wife and loving mother, a soldier" [Mengiste 2019b, 5]) and inscribes her presence in a female genealogy of Ethiopian warriors (which includes "some of the greatest fighters Ethiopia had ever known, women named Aster, Nardos, Abedech, Tsedale, Aziza, Hanna, Meaza, Aynadis, Debru, Yodit, Ililta, Abeba, Kidist, Belaynesh, Meskerem, Nunu, Tigist, Tsehai, Beza, Saba, and a woman simply called the cook" [4]).

The history of Ethiopia and the story of Hirut are told in the present tense (not as a remembrance, then). It is the end of 1935 and Hirut lives and works as a maid in the house of Kidane and Aster after her parents die. When Mussolini's intentions to invade Ethiopia become clear, Kidane, who is an officer in Emperor Haile Selassie's army, begins to travel across the country to recruit the most valiant soldiers and organize the resistance. Once the war begins, the women, led by Aster, demand to take up roles beyond preparing food, healing the wounded, and burying the dead, but Aster's request is rejected by Kidane. This, however, changes after Hirut devises a plan to save Ethiopia following the emperor's escape to England: disguising a peasant named Minim (which, significantly, means "nothing") as the emperor and making him appear in the battlefields to boost the morale of the Ethiopian population and troops. When Hirut's plan proves successful, she acquires authoritativeness and Kidane, although reluctant, is forced to allow Hirut and Aster to take up arms.

The complex and sophisticated architecture of *The Shadow King* weaves together multiple narrative threads that mesh personal stories with official history. The macronarrative of the novel conceals a multitude of micronarratives—with a refined psychological analysis of the characters centered on their insecurities and fears—that expose the two different armies as being representative of national societies that are not homogeneous but rather traversed by deep inner fractures. Ettore Navarra—the Italian soldier sent to Ethiopia with a camera to document the Italian victories there (and, when such victories do not occur, to visually construct a grandiosity of the Fascist Empire that was never a reality)—finds himself interrogating his own sense of belonging to the Italian nation when the racial laws are implemented in Italy, his Jewish family is deported to a concentration camp, and he himself is forced to live in constant fear of being reported by his superior officer, Colonel Carlo Fucelli. The Ethiopian society is also represented as fractured along different lines. While the novel is extremely critical of colonialism and its brutality and shows the deep trauma it created in Ethiopia (and also, in very different ways, in the Italian army), the most powerful operation at play in this novel lies in the process of exposing the rigidly patriarchal structures of Ethiopian society and the ways in which the heroism of men was constructed on the constant erasure and annihilation of women. By centering on the roles of women, Mengiste is able to question the roles of male leaders in Ethiopian society: consecrated by history as national heroes, in reality they asserted their masculinity through the exercise of their patriarchal power and a systematic sexual violation of women's bodies, thus sacrificing their own daughters and the daughters of Ethiopia. The scenes in which a solitary Emperor Selassie is haunted by the presence of his late daughter, Zenebework—who had been forced to marry the hereditary prince of the eastern Tigray Province, Dejazmach Haile Selassie Gugsa, at the age of 15 and who had constantly complained of her husband and his family's mistreatments until she had suddenly died at the age of 17—are among the most powerful in the novel. When the emperor's advisers had urged him not to retaliate against his son-in-law for political reasons, they had pointed out that "girls die from many causes: childbirth, illness, disease, *men*" (Mengiste 2019b, 131; emphasis is mine). The destructiveness of patriarchy—so deeply ingrained in Ethiopian society that it is here equated to a natural event— systematically deprives women of agency and attempts to annihilate them.

Through her deployment of an intersectional perspective, Maaza Mengiste suggests that the colonizer/colonized dichotomy is insufficient if history is told through women's point of view and denounces the violation of women's bodies by both Italian and Ethiopian men. In order for subaltern women to speak and have their voices heard, the colonialism/nationalism dichotomy that entraps and silences them must be deconstructed. As Mengiste reminds the reader, history in Ethiopia has been a male-dominated business, not because men have been the only actors in it, but because they have been the only ones to tell the story, to be allowed to remember and to construct a national memory that has constantly erased the presence and the strength of women. Such history, Mengiste states in the author's note at the end of the novel, should be retold by women in order to narrate a counterhistory not only to the violence of the Italian occupation but also to the patriarchy in Ethiopian society.

Ghermandi's and Mengiste's novels are centered on women's resilience and resistance and show two different articulations of anticolonial counternarratives from a gendered perspective. Their texts do not reproduce exoticizing and hypersexualized stereotypes: women are not subjected to a process of compulsory victimization, nor are they perfidious cannibals and calculators. Both authors' representations disturb and rewrite consolidated narratives that reduce Black women in the colonies to pure sexuality and animality, deprive them of agency, and render them purely functional to the history of conquest and domination authored by the Italian colonizers. Mengiste's intersectional perspective, moreover, deconstructs the colonizer/colonized binary and highlights how the role of Ethiopian women entailed not only fighting a war of liberation from Fascist colonialism alongside men but also strongly questioning Ethiopian masculinity and opposing Ethiopian patriarchy.

3.4   Postcolonial Imaginaries: Counternarratives

The imaginary of the Black Venus constructed during the colonial period remains powerful in contemporary times and is constantly associated with the bodies of Black women in widespread culture—for example, in advertising, especially of food products[35]—as much as in Italian literature and

---

[35] For the ways in which Black women's bodies are often used in commercials for food products to (also) evoke sexual desire—wherein food consumption is associated with sexual consumption—see Fabbri (2021). Fabbri analyzes, among others, the "Release the beast" advertising campaign for Magnum ice cream, which evokes women's animality even more than the Italian campaign "Libera il tuo istinto," ("Release your instinct"), in which an image of ice cream is associated with the photograph of a face that is half non-white woman and half tiger (there are other images in the same campaign that associate the face of a white, blonde woman with that of a lioness); the advertisement for Universal coffee, in which Black women's bodies are lying on coffee beans that are the same color as they are; and the 2015 Lavazza calendar with photographs by Steve McCurry that features the caption "The Earth Defenders" and shows several Black women in "traditional" clothing in a presumably African setting, thus reinforcing not only the idea of parallel consumption of a food product and a woman's body but also the colonial nexus between the Black woman's body and unknown territory (both to be penetrated).

films.[36] In such representations, which can take place either in reconstructed colonial contexts (such as the novels by Lucarelli examined in the previous section) or in present postcolonial contexts (such as the texts analyzed in this section and the next), the image of the Black woman continues to be associated with an untamed, excessive sexuality, domination over which is considered necessary for the establishment and strengthening of Italian masculinity. The imaginary of the Black Venus also remains prevalent in Italian culture in incarnations of the domestic worker and the sex worker. Such an imaginary is sometimes present in the texts of migrant and postcolonial authors, who, to a certain degree, have interiorized these representations and at times deploy them in their writing. More frequently, however, postcolonial writers introduce a critical perspective, as is the case with Geneviève Makaping (2001, 30) and Kaha Mohamed Aden (2010, 13), who, in recounting being approached in the street by men who treated them as prostitutes only because they were Black, denounce the ongoing association of Black women's bodies with sexual openness.

Igiaba Scego develops a similar critique in her short story "Identità" (Identity) (2008) and in her first novel, *Rhoda* (2004). In "Identità," the Black Venus is evoked in an article by the hard-hitting journalist Milena Morri. In the article, Black women in Italy who have romantic relationships with white men are portrayed as the new madams (conscious of their "privilege" and thus servile, submissive, and compliant). The protagonist Fatou, of Somali origin and born and raised in Rome, certainly does not identify with such an imaginary. She is in a relationship with Valerio, born in Rome and raised in Mogadishu. In the short story, the Black Venus is not only evoked but appears in the flesh in a photograph that the protagonist one day finds hanging in her apartment. Valerio found the photo at his father's house, and since it portrays a woman who comes from the city of Brava, Fatou's family's hometown, he hangs it in their home to "honor" his girlfriend and her sister, Nura, who has just arrived from Manchester. In this story, the author intersects, in an apparently light way, highly complex issues, such as the perception of interracial relationships in Italian society, the difficult relationships of diasporic subjects with their family of

---

[36] For an analysis of the way in which the imaginary of the Black Venus persists, implicitly or explicitly, in Italian films, see especially the work of Áine O'Healy and Rosetta Giuliani Caponetto, in particular, O'Healy (2009, 2012) and Caponetto (2012, 2013).

origin, and the insularity of Somali diasporic communities. The story of Black Venuses, particularly of the madams, is narrated by the author with a few essential but harsh brushstrokes and, above all, from *their* point of view. Through the synecdochical use of the term "vagina," which identifies these women with their genitalia, the narrative, blunt and ruthless, leaves no room for make-believe romanticisms, exoticisms, or dreams of love:

> That woman had come from the past. She was a madam of Italian colonialism, a Somali woman who during Fascism had been, like so many others, the official lover of an Italian man. An almost wife. The madam would wash the Italian man's clothes, then iron them, prepare his meals, massage his smelly feet; then at night the madam would take off all her clothes, lie next to him, and let him enter her vagina. Every night the vagina would await the Italian man's penis. The Italian man didn't always worry about being nice to the madam. He would enter her without cleaning the mud off his shoes, without washing his armpits, without caring about his alcohol breath. The vagina wanted to fall in love with that penis, but she found it difficult. So why did she accept all this? The poor vagina no longer knew why. At first, other vaginas had told her that it was all very nice. That Italian men showered their madams with gifts. "You become a lady, you're respected, you have so many clothes." But the vaginas weren't telling their sisters the whole truth. It was all completely different. All of it! The vaginas were afraid to be pitied. They wanted to be envied, not pitied. So, in order to survive, they invented stories where love had the white skin of the invaders.[37] (Scego 2008, 27–28)

[37] "Quella donna era venuta dal passato. Era una madama del colonialismo italiano, una donna somala che durante il fascismo era stata come tante l'amante ufficiale di un italiano. Una quasi moglie. La madama lavava i vestiti dell'italiano, poi li stirava, preparava il suo cibo, massaggiava i suoi piedi maleodoranti, poi la notte la madama si toglieva tutti i vestiti, si sdraiava accanto a lui e lo faceva entrare nella sua vagina. Ogni notte la vagina aspettava il pene dell'italiano. Non sempre l'italiano si preoccupava di essere carino con la madama. Entrava dentro senza pulirsi le scarpe dal fango, senza lavarsi le ascelle, senza curarsi del suo alito alcolico. La vagina voleva innamorarsi di quel pene, ma le risultava difficile. Allora perché ci stava? Non lo sapeva più la povera vagina. All'inizio le avevano detto altre vagine che era tutto molto bello. Che gli italiani colmavano le loro madame di regali. 'Diventi una signora, sei rispettata, hai tante stoffe.' Ma le vagine non raccontavano tutta la verità alle loro sorelle. La faccenda era tutta diversa. Tutta quanta! Le vagine avevano paura di essere compatite. Volevano essere invidiate loro, non compiante. Allora per sopravvivere si inventavano storie dove l'amore aveva la pelle bianca degli invasori."

In addition to the imaginary created by Italian men about Somali women (in the colonial past and in the postcolonial present), Scego presents the imaginary created about Somali women by Somali men in diasporic contexts. Nura's visit to her sister Fatou seems to be aimed at arranging her marriage to one of the many Somali men residing in Manchester—of whom Nura has brought many photographs—who are "hungry for … a Somali woman"[38] (Scego 2008, 16). At the end of the story, Fatou meticulously and systematically destroys the photo of the madam, the article written about her and Valerio by Milena Morri, and the photos of the potential Somali suitors. Through this gesture, Fatou refuses to adhere both to the historical imaginary of the colonial madam and to the postcolonial imaginary of the idealized neo-madam presented in the article; at the same time, she also rejects an uncritical attachment to Somali tradition and to the conventional role to which the Somali community in diaspora would like to confine her. By preventing others from telling her story, Fatou performs an important act of self-affirmation and self-determination, which enables the subaltern to speak.[39] This places her in a relationship of discontinuity with the colonial past and with the fantasies associated with it, as well as with Somali diasporic nationalism and with the limitation of her subjectivity that it aims to impose.

The issue of gender in Scego's novel *Rhoda* (2004) emerges from the female protagonists, who are represented as diverse, complex personalities who entertain articulated relationships among themselves and with the surrounding urban and social environment. Already in this first novel, Scego experiments with a choral narrative, in which every chapter is named after—and narrated in rotation by—one of the protagonists: Rhoda and Aisha, sisters who escaped from Somalia and settled in Rome; their aunt Barni, who welcomed them in the Eternal City and took care of them; and Pino, who volunteers for an association that brings comfort to sex workers in the streets of Naples. The Black Venus in this novel appears in the embodiment of the sex worker: this is the path that Rhoda has taken, surrendering to the pressures of an Italian society that perceives pure sexuality in her Black body. The young woman becomes a sex worker in Naples,

---

[38] "fame di donna … somala."

[39] The explicit reference here is to Gayatri Chakravorty Spivak's essay "Can the Subaltern Speak?" (1988).

contracts AIDS, and, when her death is imminent, returns to Mogadishu to end her days in her homeland.[40]

Also present in this novel is the figure who, in migratory contexts, occupies an opposite, specular position with respect to the sex worker,[41] namely, that of the domestic worker (a figure also linked to the colonial imaginary of the indigenous maid). Here Scego, however, goes beyond colonial imaginaries by creating less conflictive characters such as Aisha, who feels part of the multiracial society that for some time now has populated the city of Rome. While the narrative sacrifices Rhoda, it simultaneously suggests that salvation for these diasporic Black women can be achieved by their collaborating among themselves and with local women (and men), and by their establishing a strong presence in the city, which will allow them to emerge from the invisibility of the domestic space.[42] Scego thus denounces the stereotyped way in which Black women are perceived in Italy—as bodies to be exploited, in terms of either sexual work or domestic labor—but she also suggests that these women need to assume responsibility for the social changes that their presence in Italy is generating, thereby regaining the agency to them the capacity of agency of which colonial representations have historically deprived them.[43]

The protagonist's agency is the pivot of the novel *Timira* (Wu Ming 2 and Mohamed 2012), a complex and utterly unconventional autobiographical narrative, which takes shape in the collaboration between Isabella Marincola (a Somali Italian woman and the sister of the Black partisan Giorgio Marincola,[44] who later takes the name of Timira Assan), her son (Antar Mohamed), and the writer Wu Ming 2. The novel, centered on

---

[40] Rhoda tells her story from the grave; her voice reaches readers post mortem.

[41] For an analysis of the positions that migrant women occupy in destination societies and the fact that the roles of sex workers and domestic helpers are not in opposing positions, but rather embedded in the same continuum, see the last section in this chapter.

[42] In this regard, see Sect. 5.2.

[43] For a deeper analysis of the novel *Rhoda* and the relationships that the female characters of the novel have with the surrounding space, see Sect. 5.2.

[44] In the summer of 2020, a station on Line C of the Rome Metro then under construction, already named Amba Aradam/Ipponio, was renamed after Giorgio Marincola, "the Black partisan" killed at age 21 by Nazi troops in 1945. This name change, proposed and approved during the period of protests sparked by the Black Lives Matter movement (also) in Italy, has a strong symbolic value. It promotes a process of memorialization that does not celebrate the name of one of the most infamous battles fought by the Fascist army during the occupation of Ethiopia in 1936—won thanks to the use of chemical weapons even on the civilian population—but instead remembers the valor and courage of the Somali Italian partisan. See Einash (2020).

Isabella Marincola's life and reminiscences, presents continuous intersections between history and memory, as well as letters, diaries, photographs, and documents from official and private archives. The result is a hybrid text, part memoir, part historical novel, which from the beginning emphasizes the impossibility of telling a story that is *entirely* true (the book's epigraph states, "This is a true story... / including the parts that are not"[45]), thus questioning the objectivity of both the individual stories and the official history. Narrated by the voice of Isabella Marincola, the novel reconstructs several chapters of Italian history (colonialism, Italian culture and society profoundly permeated by colonialism, and immigration in contemporary Italy) and of Somali history (Isabella Marincola had returned to live in Mogadishu in the 1960s and remained there until 1992, when she was repatriated to Italy thanks to her Italian citizenship following the outbreak of the civil war).

Giorgio and Isabella were born in Somalia to an Italian soldier and a Somali woman and, at a very young age, were taken away from their mother, Ashkiro Hassan, by their father, Giuseppe Marincola, and relocated to Italy, where they were raised as Italian children in his (already existing) family. While in Italy, little Isabella's racial difference was perceived with a certain interest because it metonymically identified her with the colonial "adventure" and with the "civilizing mission" ("they were enthusiastic about this 'beautiful Abyssinian' who spoke Italian and curtsied"[46] [Wu Ming 2 and Mohamed 2012, 169]); at the same time, such difference marked her in an indelible way, rendering her unassimilable ("but they were very careful not to invite me for a snack with their daughters"[47] [169]). When she later grew up, this chromatic difference became an irresistible erotic attraction for men, because in their imaginary her Black body promised "easy and wild sex, as hot as an equatorial night"[48] [128]). Isabella became a model, was drawn by artists, became an actress (including in Giuseppe De Santis's [1949] film *Riso amaro*), but her body was barely perceived beyond the exotic-erotic imaginary associated with the Black Venus in the conformist Italy of the 1940s and 1950s. Italians did not know how to decode the body of a Black woman who not only spoke Italian perfectly but could translate from Greek and Latin, and was independent, resourceful, and an actress.

---

[45] "Questa è una storia vera ... / comprese le parti che non lo sono." This epigraph, as Simone Brioni states (2013, 103), is taken from John Landis's film *Burke & Hare* (2010).

[46] "Erano entusiasti di questa 'bella abissina' che parlava italiano e faceva la riverenza."

[47] "ma si guardavano bene dall'invitarmi per una merenda con le figliole."

[48] "sesso facile, selvaggio e caldo come una notte equatoriale."

Therefore, they sometimes considered her a kind of savage on whom Italy had successfully performed its extraordinary civilizing mission (through her inclusion in an Italian family and the Italian school system); at other times, they associated her with an African princess, so that the noble title could mitigate her phenotypic traits and everything that was associated with them (hypersexuality, natural state, subhuman condition) (Wu Ming 2 and Mohamed 2012, 205). Marincola's comment about what was written on the note accompanying the roses offered to her by the professor for whom she worked ("For Princess Makonnen"[49] [204]) reveals another facet of the colonial imaginary of the Black Venus, according to which the relationships that white men could have with Black women were almost exclusively relationships of domestic and/or sexual exploitation. In order for a romantic relationship to be conceivable, it was necessary for the Black woman in question to be assimilated with a presumed nobility of blood (even if, as Marincola asserts, in Somalia there never was a royal family and therefore there were no princesses [204]) and identified with an "exoticism" from *One Thousand and One Nights* that cloaked everything with a hot and sensual aura. Marincola also reveals the orientalist vision infused in the message she received, in which, through a homogenizing imperialist approach, historical and geographical specificities of different populations are drawn together solely by their alterity with respect to the West:

> Furthermore, Princess Makonnen was Ethiopian, not Somali: a difference that to the good Manlio must have seemed minuscule, but that in reality was no small matter. For Somalis, Ethiopia is a cumbersome neighbor, always ready to encroach, to invade, to impose an empire. I cared little about the relations between the two populations; nevertheless, I found it deranged that an admirer would expect to flatter me by giving me the name of the quintessential "beautiful African princess," someone with no connection to me. What would a Polish lady think if a German philanderer offered her flowers with the inscription "For the Czarina of Russia"?[50] (Wu Ming 2 and Mohamed 2012, 205)

---

[49] "Per la principessa Makonnen."

[50] "Per di più, la principessa Makonnen era etiope, non somala: una differenza che al buon Manlio doveva essere sembrata minuscola, ma che in realtà non era di poco conto. Per i somali, l'Etiopia è un vicino ingombrante, sempre pronto a sconfinare, a invadere, a imporre un impero. A me poco importava dei rapporti tra i due popoli, ciò nondimeno trovavo demenziale che un corteggiatore pretendesse di adularmi affibbiandomi il nome della 'bella principessa africana' per antonomasia, una tizia con la quale non avevo nulla a che vedere. Cosa penserebbe una signorina polacca, se un cascamorto tedesco le offrisse dei fiori, con dedica scritta: 'Per la zarina di Russia'?"

Orientalism is not only based on a stratification of representations that over time has consolidated imaginaries beyond which any subsequent representation becomes difficult, but it roots these imaginaries in a homogenizing view of the colonized, constructed as the Other, in which any geopolitical difference is insignificant in the eyes of the colonizers. Through the parallel created between Somalia and Ethiopia on the one hand and Poland and Russia on the other, the narrator-protagonist emphasizes how a distinct geopolitical identity, recognized for European states, is instead denied to African nations, all of which are indifferently considered merely colonial possessions.

Isabella Marincola rebels against the stereotyped colonial representation to which Italian society wants to reduce her. Such representation, as Barbara Ehrenreich and Arlie Russell Hochschild (2003a) argue, is reproposed in contemporary postcolonial societies in the continuum that connects the role of domestic workers to that of sex workers.[51] The protagonist refuses to do housework because her father's wife, Flora Virdis, has always relegated her to "being a servant girl"[52] and, at the same time, "deemed [her] a slut by nature and by necessity"[53] (Wu Ming 2 and Mohamed 2012, 206). Isabella does not identify with either of these roles, which reflect the imaginaries associated with Black women during colonialism. At the same time, the difference that had always marked her had caused her to become extremely critical of the middle-class, self-righteous, and hypocritical morality common in post-war Italy. When a man accosts her in the street to request sexual services, Isabella wonders, "Was it really more dignified for me to drag myself home with no heel and miss dinner, than to hustle the first man who came along? What if they had told me the story that way just for the sake of complicating my life?"[54] (191). Conforming to certain moral principles, Isabella Marincola observes here, is easier if they are associated with the social privilege of whiteness and financial well-being. The narrator, instead, claims the possibility of considering sex for payment an entrepreneurial activity rendered possible by her body's beauty and difference—which render her desirable in the eyes of Italian men—an activity that has nothing to do with her "nature" but

[51] See also the last section in this chapter.

[52] "fare la servetta."

[53] "la credeva mignotta per natura e per necessità."

[54] "Davvero era più dignitoso trascinarmi a casa senza un tacco e saltare la cena, piuttosto che fare una marchetta col primo venuto? Non è che magari me l'avevano raccontata così, solo per il gusto di complicarmi la vita?"

rather with the awareness of being able to utilize her body to consolidate her independence from a colonialist and patriarchal system.

Timira is a postcolonial text that narrates a counterhistory opposed to sexist and racist colonial imaginaries through the voice of a Somali Italian woman who, starting from her own personal memories, gives an account of Italian and Somali societies and of the relationships that have existed between them for almost a century. In such a visibly oppositional text, which foregrounds Isabella Marincola's strong subjectivity, the decision to exclude the narrator from the authorial role (which instead comprises Wu Ming 2 and Isabella's son, Antar Mohamed, who had been the connection between his mother and the writer) is particularly problematic. Wu Ming 2 is aware of the necessity to question the collaborative writing process, on which he reflects in the four "Lettere intermittenti" (Intermittent Letters) (a prelude, two interludes, and a postlude). In particular, in "Interludio. Lettera intermittente n. 2" (Interlude: Intermittent Letter No. 2) (Wu Ming 2 and Mohamed 2012, 158–60), he records, with great honesty, the contrast between the narrator's desire to understand what form her own narrative would take and the vagueness of his intentions in this regard. At first, he does not appear to want to acknowledge that within collaborative writing the power relations that are established tend to reproduce colonial-type relationships in which, as Gayatri Spivak puts it, the constant risk is that the act of *darstellen* ("represent," in the sense of portray) will, in fact, turn into *vertreten* ("represent," in the sense of speak on behalf of).[55] Isabella, according to what can be inferred from "Lettera intermittente n. 2" (Intermittent Letter No. 2), is not at all convinced about Wu Ming 2's decision to transform her narrative into a novel; and yet, after her death, this is the form that the collaborative text takes, that of a *Romanzo meticcio* (Mixed-Race Novel). Interestingly, the term "mixed-race" here seems to have the function of reinforcing the presence of the narrator's subjectivity at the very moment when she is deprived of her authorial role; it is almost as if the mixed race and hybridity of the narrator-protagonist could

---

[55] Emphasizing the ambiguity that can arise from the fact that the verbs *darstellen* ("represent" in the artistic sense, portray) and *vertreten* ("represent" in the political sense, act in representation of a subject or a group) are translated in English (and in Italian) with the same verb ("represent"), Spivak warns against the danger that "First World" intellectuals ventriloquize the discourse articulated by "Third World" subjects, rendering their own position transparent, and thus neutral. See Spivak (1988, 1999) and D'Ottavio (2012). Keeping in mind the difference between *darstellen* and *vertreten* is necessary when analyzing collaborative writing.

be extended to the novel itself, and, in this way, could serve as a denunciation of colonialism. In "Lettera intermittente n. 3" (Intermittent Letter No. 3), Wu Ming 2's reflection on the constant danger of deploying colonial attitudes that were thought to be permanently set aside also besieges the process of constructing the text. Wu Ming 2 acknowledges that if he had been the only one to make decisions, and if Marincola and her son had not opposed it, he would probably have reproduced a colonial relationship in the organization of the text, which would have been thus configured:

> *If we had done it my way, paying heed to my fixations and fears, today we would have three talk show figures on the page:*
>
> 1. *the old granny, only good for remembering and repairing the past;*
> 2. *the woman who bears a life testimony and the man of experience who interprets it;*
> 3. *the dark-skinned outcast who can tell his story only by donning the costume of the "poor negro," to then borrow the voice of a white-skinned ventriloquist.*[56]
> (Wu Ming 2 and Mohamed 2012, 344)

Wu Ming 2 is deeply aware of the danger of colonial-type subjugation and of the possible transformation of *darstellen* into *vertreten*. The manner in which the authorial role was assigned, however, reflects a lack of awareness and inclusion of gender issues on his part (as well as on Antar Mohamed's): if the authorship of the colonized "other" is safeguarded and Antar Mohamed is inserted as the second co-author (through his participation in the writing of the text after his mother's death), what is left of the Black woman on the cover is her face and her name in the title, *Timira*. She has thus become the object of the writing within a text whose form was decided between males (one the son of colonizers, the other of the colonized). After reading a narrative that highlights the pride and fierce spirit of the narrator-protagonist—which had led her to carve out roles that were utterly unconventional in both Italian and Somali society

---

[56] "*Se avessimo fatto a modo mio, dando ascolto alle mie fisime e alle mie paure, oggi avremmo sulla pagina tre figurine da talk show:*

1. *la vecchia nonnina, buona solo per rammentare e rammendare il passato;*
2. *la donna che porta una testimonianza di vita e l'uomo esperto che la interpreta;*
3. *l'emarginato di pelle scura che può raccontare la sua storia solo indossando il costume del «povero negro», per poi farsi prestare la voce da un ventriloquo di pelle bianca.*"

and that were certainly not conceived for women like her—readers cannot help but wonder whether Isabella Marincola would have supported such an operation, one that in part relegates her to the margins of her own story.

The imaginary of the Black Venus also appears prominently in Igiaba Scego's novel *Adua* (2015) (*Adua*, 2017), an oppositional narrative that already in its title suggests a strong connection with Italian colonial history.[57] The novel is set during the period of Fascist colonization (in Magalo and Mogadishu, in Rome, and in Addis Ababa), in the 1970s (in Somalia and in Rome), and finally in contemporary Rome, and renders visible the deep connection existing in Italy (and, by extension, in other European countries) between the colonialism of the past and the postcoloniality of the present. The novel frequently alludes to the way in which erotic fantasies informed the colonial imaginaries of the past—both in its references to Fascist colonialism and in its descriptions of the environment of Roman cinema in the 1970s—and pervade the postcolonial imaginaries of the present. During the period preceding the conquest of Ethiopia, Zoppe, Adua's father, worked in Rome as a translator for the Fascist government and then returned to Ethiopia as part of Count Anselmi's entourage. During his service, it became apparent to him that, in the fascist imaginary, Black women were reduced to bodies to be dominated, domesticated, and penetrated. When Zoppe was incarcerated in Rome, the warden Beppe, in order to humiliate and terrorize him, masturbated over a photograph that depicted Zoppe's younger sister Ayan when she was still a child, reminding Zoppe that his sister, as a Black woman in the colonies, was constantly at risk of being violated by soldiers. When Zoppe was later released to follow Count Anselmi to Addis Ababa, as soon as they arrived in the city a young man in the count's entourage asked Zoppe to procure an Abyssinian woman for him for his own sexual pleasure, making explicit reference to the colonial postcards that were circulated in Italy to titillate Italian males' erotic imaginary and attract men to the colonies (Scego 2017, 89–92).

---

[57] The Battle of Adwa (Adua in Italian) in 1896, in which the Ethiopian army under the leadership of Negus Menelik II defeated the Italian army led by General Oreste Barattieri, marks not only the greatest defeat of the Italian army but also of any European army in Africa. Through this victory, Ethiopia was able to maintain its independence until the invasion by the Fascist army in 1935–1936.

Later, in the 1970s, Adua is taken to Rome at the age of 17 and delivered to director Arturo Sposetti and his wife, Sissi, to be introduced into the world of pornographic films (Adua is unaware of this plan: she believes she will study acting in Rome and dreams of becoming a great actress). An explicit reference to *madamato* (colonial concubinage) appears here, when Sissi tells Adua "during the African campaign my father bought a wife from where you're from"[58] (Scego 2017, 113). In general, however, there are few references in the text to the dynamics of exploitation of Black women in the colonial period. Instead, the story of Adua and her participation in the genre of exotic-erotic film that was so popular in Italy in the 1970s[59] is studded with episodes that show how, with respect to Black women, the erotic fantasies of Italians were still firmly rooted in colonial imaginaries, even decades after that historical period. The novel also refers to traditional gender roles in Somalia, which govern the subordinate relationship Adua and her sister, Malika, have with their father, Zoppe: he forces his daughters, whom he wants to be obedient and submissive, to undergo infibulation. Although relations among women are left in the background and are not explored in depth, there are frequent references to how different things can be when women take care of other women. Adua and Malika's mother, Asha the Rash,[60] would never have allowed Zoppe to infibulate their daughters if she had been alive (Scego 2017, 84). Adua wonders how her existence would have differed if her dear friend Lul—who returns to Somalia after the war ends but who remains close to her through her advice and affection—had been there to support her in her young age (Scego 2017, 151–54). As in her first novel, *Rhoda*, Scego here shows how affiliations among Somali women of the diaspora (as well as among other diasporic women) can create a space of female agency, which might otherwise be thwarted by the patriarchal rules of their own communities.

A partial redefinition of this patriarchal society—structured in a diasporic context where individuals' ties to their society of origin and their social roles in the new contexts profoundly change—is also visible in the kind of relationship that Adua entertains in Rome with her husband,

---

[58] "durante la campagna d'Africa aveva comprato una moglie dalle tue parti" (Scego 2015, 119).

[59] On this subject, see Caponetto (2012).

[60] A more appropriate and closer translation of "Asha la Temeraria" from the original Italian text would be "Asha the Fearless."

"Titanic" (this nickname, as Adua explains, is given to recent immigrants who have survived shipwrecks [Scego 2017, 21]). An unusual gender dynamic and a partial reversal of roles are introduced in the novel when Adua, who is a middle-aged woman, admits to having married a young man who had just arrived from Lampedusa, as so many of the women from her country do, conducting what the protagonist does not hesitate to describe as a "trade"[61] (Scego 2017, 23). This type of arrangement is entered into between Somali women who had arrived in Italy in the 1970s—and therefore enjoy relative financial well-being—and young men who have just landed and who are consequently far from their loved ones and without means of sustenance. While it is true that this arrangement tends to keep the women anchored to domestic roles ("They kiss us and we sew their holey socks"[62] [Scego 2017, 23]), at the same time Scego emphasizes how these women, along with affection, also seek sexual satisfaction with the young men. Migratory movements can trigger profound changes in gender roles within diasporic communities: in the case of Adua's "trade," for instance, the roles of those who request and those who offer sexual services are reversed. Even though the relationship between Adua and Titanic cannot be described as a true commodification of the male body, the two maintain a relationship characterized by emotional and erotic practices shaped within the migratory context resulting from the decade-long colonial relationship between Italy and Somalia.

True commodification of the male body in a neocolonial context is at the core of Shirin Ramzanali Fazel's short story "La spiaggia" (The Beach) (2007), centered around the phenomenon of sexual tourism. The narrative point of view, in the first person, is that of a woman who early one morning takes her dog for a walk on a "tropical" beach—which here serves as topos of sex tourism in neocolonial contexts—in a country of the Global South not further identified.[63] The lack of a precise geographical reference pertains to the idea that the dynamics of neocolonial exploitation that the woman witnesses could take place on any beach in any country of the Global South. The narrator, presumably a local resident, observes from the outside the dynamics that develop between the other two social groups present in the story: on the one hand, the female tourists, women

---

[61] "compravendita" (Scego 2015, 68).

[62] "Loro ci baciano e noi gli cuciamo i calzini bucati" (Scego 2015, 68).

[63] Rebecca Hopkins (2007) states that "La spiaggia" is set in Kenya, but that information is not present in the text, where, significantly, no indication of place is provided.

of a rather advanced age who come to these places from "First World" countries in search of a "simulation of sexual and romantic love" (Ehrenreich and Hochschild 2003a, 4); on the other, men who provide services to them, as hotel waiters, Masai street vendors, and, especially, "beach boys," young men who offer them sexual satisfaction and an illusion of love. In exchange for their services, these young men receive financial compensation that usually entails a more complex transaction than the (immediate) type characterizing female prostitution; such complexity is necessary to keep in place the illusion of love, which is an integral part of the deal. In these kinds of relationships, the transaction—a practice the narrator claims to have witnessed many times—often entails the woman buying a house for her partner or buying other assets that will enable the local young man to start a business. This house or business will presumably be enjoyed by the two together in a manner to be determined. Such expectations, however, will be systematically disregarded in the future, the narrator maintains. This type of relationship is based on gender roles that are reversed from the traditional dynamics of sex tourism; however, it still constitutes a neocolonial practice that reenacts the dynamics of colonial domination and erotic fantasies to be satisfied by "exotic" bodies in "exotic" places—Anne McClintock's "porno-tropics" (1995). In these new figurations, the parallel between territorial and sexual penetration requires an intersectional perspective that combines the category of age with those of gender, race, social class, and geopolitical positioning. The women in Fazel's narrative are depicted as vulnerable and thus susceptible to seduction by the young local males, who employ their bodies as assets to acquire financial security. The impartiality of the narrator's gaze in this short story is thought-provoking: she shows empathy toward all the parties involved, inasmuch as they are embedded in a mechanism that they cannot actually control, even though they do not realize their complicity. Indeed, the beach boys and the elderly women "pursue one another in an absurd circle of socio-economic dependency that the story suggests has been created by something larger than these individuals" (Hopkins 2007, 19–20). The story shows social dynamics that are the result of globalization and that reproduce, at times in inverted form, ancient colonial relationships imbued with erotic fantasies, colonial memories, and processes of exoticization both of places and of their inhabitants.

3.5   *ALLE FRAUEN WERDEN SCHWESTER?*[64]
RELATIONSHIPS OF POWER
AND (FAILED) SISTERHOOD AMONG WOMEN

In the poem "Sisterhood," which opens *African Women and Feminism: Reflecting on the Politics of Sisterhood*, a volume edited by Oyèrónké Oyĕwùmi (2003) investigating the "politics of sisterhood," the feminist poet and theorist Nkiru Nzegwu (2003b) paints a domestic scene that eloquently illustrates the blindness of white feminists in the face of the privilege that whiteness confers on them and to the various oppressions that, for many women, intersect those of gender. In the poem, a white woman gives lessons in feminism to her Black housekeeper while the latter is cleaning the floor on her hands and knees, following her employer's instructions. The notion of "sisterhood," which appears in the title, at the end of the poem turns into "sisterarchy," the oppression by women in hegemonic positions of other women in subordinate positions:

> white sister told me
> all women are one
> united in de face
> of chau'vism
> (pa'don my engilis)
>
> I smiled
>
> pa...paa
> pa..tri..archy is the cross
> women carry, she charged
> we must unite
> to fight it
> with all our might.

---

[64] This title—"Will All Women Become Sisters?"—contains a clear reference to "Ode to Joy" from Ludwig van Beethoven's Ninth Symphony, composed using the text of the ode of the same name written by Friedrich von Schiller (*An die Freude*). This hymn, which has become the anthem of the European Union, expresses the hope for a society in which "*Alle Menschen Werden Brüder*," that is, where all men (in the sense of human beings) will become brothers. In the transposition of the verse in the hymn, with the questioning intonation to indicate doubt, I intend to convey a certain skepticism about the possibility of creating a society, or a global women's movement, characterized by universal sisterhood.

...

I looked up
from my chore
on the kitchen floor
where, new found sister
had ordered me to be
on knees

to scrub the floor clean
for the pittance she paid:
on knees
to scrub the floor clean
for sisterarchy.⁶⁵ (Nzegwu 2003b, 7–8)

The language in this poem marks the gap between the two women, which exists in part because the "white sister" has a perfect command of English that enables her to tell "quixotic tales / of male 'xploitation" (Nzegwu 2003b, 7), while the speaker has limited language skills ("pa'don my engilis") (Nzegwu 2003b, 7). However, it is not the domestic worker's limited knowledge of English that makes what she is listening to incomprehensible but rather the deep gap between the sisterhood her employer is discussing and the obvious disparity in the two women's access to power, of which the mistress of the house is so clearly oblivious. Such disparity is also articulated spatially, with the white woman on her feet and the Black woman on her knees. The poem illustrates the contradiction inherent in the fact that white women in the "First World" often relegate Black women to the domestic space that they themselves have been able to abandon (at least in part) thanks to the feminist battles fought since the end of the 1960s. And it is precisely about this feminist ideology and the need for all women to fight against patriarchy that the white woman wants to educate the Black immigrant woman while she orders her to kneel and scrub the floor, unwilling to question the contradiction inherent in such dynamic.

⁶⁵While the term "patriarchy" indicates the oppression of daughters by fathers, and by extension, of women by men, "sisterarchy" refers instead to the oppression of subaltern women by women in positions of power. For further discussion on the notions of "sisterhood" and "sisterarchy," see Nzegwu (2003a) and Oyěwùmi (2003).

The concept of universal sisterhood, still so strong in Italian feminism, is also radically challenged by the Cameroonian Italian writer Geneviève Makaping, who, in following the work of bell hooks, raises the issue of the relationship between white and Black feminists[66]:

> I wonder then if it is possible to speak of panfeminism. Why on earth should the "First World" woman and I, together, take joint action against male power, hers and mine, if I am already disadvantaged to begin with, because of her white privilege? A privilege that Western women are not always critically aware of.[67] (Makaping 2001, 56)

Audre Lorde, in 1979, raised the issue of white privilege and of the way in which an intersectional analysis (which in this case took into consideration gender, race, and class) made it possible to highlight the disparity existing between women based on adequate considerations about who does and who does not perform domestic work. To not consider the privileges that derive from whiteness and social class, Lorde maintained, produces and corroborates a racist feminism:

> If white American feminist theory need not deal with the differences between us, and the resulting difference in our oppressions, then how do you deal with the fact that the women who clean your houses and tend your children while you attend conferences on feminist theory are, for the most part, poor women and women of Color? What is the theory behind racist feminism? (1984, 112)

bell hooks, with the due differences, addresses this question by underlining the continuity of the white woman/Black woman dichotomy from the period of slavery to the present, since the domestic work of Black women remains exploitative and keyed to the social advancement of white women

---

[66] The intersection between race and gender and the relationship between white and Black women are central issues in all of hooks's work. For some of the early texts that were turning points in these theorizations, see hooks (1984, 1989, 1990).

[67] "Mi chiedo quindi se sia possibile parlare di un panfemminismo. In nome di che cosa la donna del 'Primo mondo' ed io dovremmo, insieme, intraprendere delle azioni comuni contro il potere del maschio, suo e mio, se io parto già svantaggiata, visto il privilegio della sua bianchezza? Un privilegio di cui le donne occidentali non sempre hanno consapevolezza critica."

and their families and is displayed as a tangible sign of material well-being (see hooks 1981).[68]

Contemporary transnational migrations impose a reflection on the privilege of white women and on the fact that they hold neocolonial relations with the immigrant women who perform caregiving and domestic work in their homes. The laws of the markets and those that regulate the flow of migration in (not only) Western societies have ensured and continue to ensure that migrant women have relatively easy access to employment as domestic workers and "caregivers"—a global, transnational version of Woolf's "angel in the house"—and to the sex market as prostitutes and sex workers—its demonic, hypersexualized opposite. According to Barbara Ehrenreich and Arlie Russell Hochschild, the allocation of these social roles to immigrant women does not indicate opposing fields of meaning, because these professions are all positioned on the same continuum and aimed at providing different forms of love (and its surrogates) that, as the two scholars assert, seem to have become insufficient in "First World" countries (2003a, 4–5).

The issue of the relationship between white and non-white women, especially in the context of the globalization of care work, is addressed by writers such as Christiana de Caldas Brito, Ingy Mubiayi, and Gabriella Kuruvilla. Their three short stories, "Ana de Jesus" (de Caldas Brito 1995) ("Ana of Jesus" 1999), "Documenti, prego" (Documents, Please) (Mubiayi 2005), and "Colf" (Housekeeper) (Kuruvilla 2008), respectively, denounce the profound social differences existing between the women in the texts. The short story by de Caldas Brito is a monologue in which Ana, a Brazilian maid, rehearses the conversation in which she intends to announce to her employer that she has decided to return to Brazil. The responses from her employer that Ana imagines and the anxiety she feels about having to make this announcement expose the subservient relationship that Ana has with her employer. Ana's fear of being accused of ingratitude demonstrates that the neocolonial exploitation of transnational care workers is disguised, de facto, as a relationship in which "First World" women "save" "Third World" women by offering them a job, the income from which will allow them to provide for their own

[68] Francesca Decimo (2006) maintains that the models of femininity and female productivity in the third millennium have changed. In contrast to what hooks claims, social prestige no longer derives from displaying "servitude" as a sign of economic well-being but from hiding it and thus appropriating domestic workers' labor. Through this dissimulation, women can show that they can perfectly reconcile the work outside the home with their domestic work and social life.

children in their country of origin. In neocolonial settings, this revives the rhetoric of the "civilizing mission" of the colonial era.

The short story "Documenti, prego" by Ingy Mubiayi (2005), which is narrated with irony and (apparent) levity by a Black migrant cleaning lady's daughter, also addresses the issue of Black female workers' exploitation by white female employers who often consider themselves to be benefactors. This text implicitly leads to important considerations about the fact that access to the public sphere for Italian women, a right fought for vigorously by Italian feminists in the 1970s, has not occurred as the result of the redistribution of domestic work and care work within the family—in a strongly patriarchal country such as Italy, where housework and care work remain principally the domain of women—but rather of hiring immigrant women who often carry out those tasks that allow Italian women to work outside their homes.[69]

The color differences between non-white women and the importance of social class as a discriminating element are at the core of Gabriella Kuruvilla's short story "Colf" (2008), which raises the issue of race and color in a very different way from that of the previously mentioned authors. The first encounter between the protagonist, a single Indian mother who works as a cleaning lady, and her Black African employer is problematically structured around the Indian woman imagining her own refusal to enter into a sisterly relationship with the African woman based on the fact that both are not white. The South Asian woman considers her Brownness racially superior to her employer's Blackness and is therefore outraged by the position of subordination she is called upon to occupy:

> We are different: you were slaves, we servants. The idea of serving a slave does not entice me. This game of roles is not amusing.
>
> And please do not treat me like a sister, considering that I am supposed to clean your toilet and make it sparkle.[70] (Kuruvilla 2008, 71)

---

[69] Foundational texts presenting a feminist analysis of care work at the time of globalization are Anderson (2000), Parreñas (2001), and Ehrenreich and Hochschild (2003b). For a racial and postcolonial analysis of the relationship between Italian women and immigrant women who perform care work and domestic work in Italy, see especially the pioneering work of Jacqueline Andall (1992, 2000), as well as Ghidei Biidu and Hagos (2010) and Marchetti (2011). On the relationship between white and Black women and between white feminism and immigrant women in contemporary Italy, see Pojmann (2006), Merrill (2006), and Marchetti et al. (2021).

[70] "Siamo diverse: voi eravate schiave, noi serve. L'idea di servire una schiava non mi alletta. Non è divertente questo gioco delle parti. E non trattarmi, ti prego, come una sorella. Dato che io dovrei pulire il tuo cesso per renderlo luccicante."

Kuruvilla's story highlights not only how important it is to consider sexism and racism as interdependent, but also how the white/Black binary is extremely reductive in analyzing processes of racialization. In the text, for example, the color white is absent, and the relationship that the story prefigures is between two non-white women. The Indian woman (a homodiegetic narrator) does not recognize herself in the Blackness of the African woman and feels superior to her. The Black African woman, however, belongs to a wealthier social class and is thus in the position of exploiting the work of the South Asian woman, who, on the other hand, is exoticized by her Italian neighbors, who have reduced India to an esoteric place, the spirituality of which they mix—or rather confuse—with that of Tibet and Jamaica.

While de Caldas Brito, Mubiayi, and Kuruvilla condemn the racism perpetrated against Black women by other women, Ubax Cristina Ali Farah denounces the sexism perpetrated against Black women by Black men, thus showing that people who are subject to forms of racism are not at all immune from sexism, and vice versa. In the short story "Rapdipunt" (2004), for instance, Ali Farah deplores the sexism enacted by the boys of the Piazzale Flaminio group in Rome, specifically those of Somali origins.[71] The observations of the young narrator-protagonist, who also embodies the moral authority of the story, are particularly useful for highlighting the sexism expressed within the group, composed entirely of racialized Black youths, almost all of whom are male. Through their catcalling of white girls and boasts about only marrying women from their countries of origin, the boys in the group overturn (and thus do not deconstruct but perpetuate) the colonial imaginary of the female body, reducing white girls to sexual objects and Black girls to incarnations of an "African" tradition and culture. Ali Farah also condemns the dynamics of gender exploitation within a Black community such as the Italian Somali community: the boys in the group do not attend school and do not work but live off what their mothers earn by working as domestic laborers and caregivers. In the dedication in the English translation of the story (which does not appear in the Italian version), the author writes:

This monologue is dedicated to the mothers of these young men.

---

[71] For a more detailed analysis of this story, see Chap. 5.

They arrived with the first waves of immigrants in the Sixties and Seventies. They were forced, out of necessity, to work as maids while their children grew up in institutional care.(Ali Farah 2006, 276)[72]

Through the reference to the first migrant waves that reached Italy from the former colonies along the Horn of Africa in the 1960s and 1970s, Ali Farah also implicitly denounces Italian colonialism and the exploitation of colonized subjects both during colonialism and in neocolonial and postcolonial contexts, such as that of contemporary Italy, in which the relationships of colonial hegemony find new incarnations and articulations.

In the novel *Il comandante del fiume* (Ali Farah 2014) (*The Commander of the River* 2023), the protagonist's mother, Zahra, does not show any faith in blood relationships as such or in the traditional family structure. Her critical attitude extends to diasporic Somali communities in Rome and around the world. Such communities tend to reproduce in an identical—and perhaps even a more rigid—way the clan structure of Somali society, which, as readers discover in the narrative, has created a very deep wound in Zahra's family.[73] The desire of such communities to remain "authentic" generates falsehood and hypocrisy and produces a (self-)ghettoization of Somali communities around the world. For all these reasons, Zahra chooses to form a family by choice that includes her son, Yabar, her friend Rosa and Rosa's daughter, Sissi, and that is based not on blood relations but on affection, complicity, and common principles. The author thus highlights how the diaspora profoundly changes connections and relationships within communities, as well as how such changes can engender new social structures in which affiliations—chosen rather than imposed—contribute to disrupting traditional social hierarchies and building new systems of transnational alliances.

---

[72] Originally, the dedication was included in the first Italian draft of the story, written by Ubax Cristina Ali Farah as a monologue for the actress Cristina Deregibus, which was staged at the Vascello Theater in Rome in February 2005 during the Festival Autori per Roma—short plays directed by Pierpaolo Palladino. For reasons the author does not recall, however, the dedication disappeared when the short story was published (in Italian), to later reappear in the published English translation. My thanks to Ubax Cristina Ali Farah for providing me with this information in an email conversation on July 9, 2015.

[73] Regarding Ubax Cristina Ali Farah's criticism of the clan structure of Somali society and the way in which it is reproduced in diasporic Somali communities, see the analysis of *Il comandante del fiume* in Chap. 5.

3.6   Conclusion

Colonial-style gender representations are still firmly rooted in contemporary Italian imaginary. An examination of such representations requires an intersectional analysis of the categories of gender, race, and color centered on the notion that gender and race do not exist as categories isolated from each other but are, as McClintock (1995, 4–5) asserts in the epigraph to this chapter, put into effect through their interrelationship.

Such an analysis enables an identification of the ways in which the colonial imaginary of the Black Venus survives and thrives in contemporary Italy, as well as an examination of how the counternarratives of postcolonial writers subvert these imaginaries and represent Black women of the present and the past outside the trite stereotypes of gender, race, and color, which confine them to the invisibility of domestic work or the invisibility/hypervisibility of sexual work. The counterstories analyzed in this chapter have an opposing function with respect to the colonialism and sexism/racism perpetrated in the colonies. The rare cases in which it is Black men who are hypersexualized show how, if the gendered perspective is reversed, the entire system of exploitation changes: it still has a colonial matrix, but it is redefined in a global capitalist context.

The postcolonial authors whom I have examined in this chapter are critical of the concept of universal sisterhood, which is so central to white feminism, and instead ask that white women consider the privilege that they enjoy, which has historically put them in a position of domination over Black women from the colonies, as was the case during the colonial period, and that today puts them in a position of domination, although of a different kind, as employers of "global women" (Ehrenreich and Hochschild 2003b) in contemporary postcolonial societies. At the same time, these postcolonial authors promote systems of collaboration among women based on mutual support. Through a critique of the sexism in their countries of origin, in the communities of origin in the destination countries, and in the society at large in the countries of arrival, these authors interrupt traditional narratives that reduce the subaltern to silence through the creation of complex female characters, women who are versatile, multifaceted, critical, and endowed with agency, who construct new social structures through various forms of affiliation with other women.

BIBLIOGRAPHY

Aden, Kaha Mohamed. 2010. *Fra-intendimenti*. Rome: Nottetempo.

Ali Farah, Ubax Cristina. 2004. Rapdipunt. In *La letteratura postcoloniale italiana. Dalla letteratura d'immigrazione all'incontro con l'altro*, ed. Tiziana Morosetti, 127–130. Vol. 4 of *Quaderni del '900*. Pisa: Istituti Editoriali e Poligrafici Internazionali.

———. 2006. Punt Rap. In *Other Italies/Italy's Others*, ed. Thalia Pandiri. Special issue, *Metamorphoses: The Journal of the Five College Faculty Seminar on Literary Translation* 14 (1–2, Spring–Fall): 276–280.

Ali Farah, Ubah Cristina. 2014. *Il comandante del fiume*. Rome: 66thand2nd. Trans. Hope Campbell Gustafson as *The Commander of the River* (Bloomington: Indiana University Press, forthcoming in 2023).

Andall, Jacqueline. 1992. Women Migrant Workers in Italy. *Women's Studies International Forum* 15 (1): 41–48.

———. 2000. *Gender, Migration and Domestic Service: The Politics of Black Women in Italy*. Aldershot: Ashgate.

Anderson, Bridget. 2000. *Doing the Dirty Work? The Global Politics of Domestic Labour*. London: Zed Books.

ANSA. 2019. Calderoli condannato per gli insulti a Kyenge. *ANSA.it*, January 14. https://www.ansa.it/lombardia/notizie/2019/01/14/condanna-calderoli-per-insulti-a-kyenge_08d010b1-3ea6-40fb-85f8-9d0378914350.html.

Baricco, Alessandro. 2008. Carlo Lucarelli e il Far West dell'Italia coloniale. *L'ottava vibrazione* raccontata a Baricco. *Cultura 2.0*, April 2. http://cultura.blogosfere.it/2008/04/carlo-lucarelli-e-il-far-west-dellitalia-coloniale-lottava-vibrazione-raccontata-a-baricco.html/. Site discontinued.

Barrera, Giulia. 1996. *Dangerous Liaisons: Colonial Concubinage in Eritrea, 1890–1941*, Doctoral Dissertation. Evanston, IL: Program of African Studies, Northwestern University.

———. 2002a. *Colonial Affairs: Italian Men, Eritrean Women and the Construction of Racial Hierarchies in Colonial Eritrea (1885–1941)*. Evanston, IL: Northwestern University.

———. 2002b. Patrilinearità, razza e identità: l'educazione degli italo-eritrei durante il colonialismo italiano (1885–1934). *Quaderni storici* 37 (109 (1)): 21–53.

———. 2003. Mussolini's Colonial Race Laws and State-Settler Relations in Africa Orientale Italiana (1935–41). *Journal of Modern Italian Studies* 8 (3): 425–443.

———. 2004. Sex, Citizenship and the State. The Construction of the Public and Private Spheres in Colonial Eritrea. In *Gender, Family and Sexuality: The Private Sphere in Italy (1860–1945)*, ed. Perry Willson, 157–172. Basingstoke: Palgrave Macmillan.

Benvenuti, Giuliana. 2011–2012. Da Flaiano a Ghermandi: riscritture postcoloniali. In *Coloniale e Postcoloniale nella letteratura italiana degli anni 2000*, ed.

Silvia Contarini, Giuliana Pias, and Lucia Quaquarelli. Special double issue, *Narrativa* 33–34: 311–321.

———. 2012. *Il romanzo neostorico italiano. Storia, memoria, narrazione.* Rome: Carocci.

Brioni, Simone. 2013. Pratiche "meticce": narrare il colonialismo italiano "a più mani". In *Postocoloniale italiano. Tra letteratura e storia*, ed. Franca Sinopoli, 89–119. Rome: Novalogos.

de Caldas Brito, Christiana. 1995. Ana de Jesus. In *Le voci dell'arcobaleno*, ed. Roberta Sangiorgi and Alessandro Ramberti, 59–61. Santarcangelo di Romagna: Fara Editore. Trans. Rodolfo A. Franconi and Graziella Parati as "Ana de Jesus". In *Mediterranean Crossroads: Migration Literature in Italy*, ed. Graziella Parati, 162–164 (Madison: Fairleigh Dickinson University Press, 1999).

Campassi, Gabriella. 1987. Il madamato in Africa Orientale. Relazioni tra italiani e indigene come forma di aggressione coloniale. *Miscellanea di storia delle esplorazioni* 12: 219–258.

Campassi, Gabriella, and Maria Teresa Sega. 1983. Uomo bianco, donna nera. L'immagine della donna nella fotografia coloniale. *Rivista di Storia e critica della fotografia* 4 (5): 54–62.

Caponetto, Rosetta Giuliani. 2012. Blaxploitation Italian Style: Exhuming and Consuming the Colonial Black Venus in 1970s Cinema in Italy. In *Postcolonial Italy: Challenging National Homogeneity*, ed. Cristina Lombardi-Diop and Caterina Romeo, 191–203. New York: Palgrave Macmillan.

———. 2013. Zeudi Araya, Ines Pellegrini e il cinema italiano di seduzione coloniale. In *L'Africa in Italia. Per una controstoria postcoloniale del cinema italiano*, ed. Leonardo De Franceschi, 109–123. Rome: Aracne.

Capretti, Luciana. 2004. *Ghibli*. Milan: Rizzoli.

———. 2014. *Tevere*. Venice: Marsilio.

Carbin, Maria, and Sara Edenheim. 2013. The Intersectional Turn in Feminist Theory: A Dream of a Common Language? *European Journal of Women's Studies* 20 (3): 233–248.

Combahee River Collective. 1977. *The Combahee River Collective Statement*. April. http://circuitous.org/scraps/combahee.html.

Crais, Clifton, and Pamela Scully. 2009. *Sara Baartman and the Hottentot Venus: A Ghost Story and a Biography*. Princeton: Princeton University Press.

Crenshaw, Kimberlé. 1989. Demarginalizing the Intersection of Race and Sex: A Black Feminist Critique of Antidiscrimination Doctrine, Feminist Theory and Antiracist Politics. *University of Chicago Legal Forum* 1989 (1): 139–67, article 8. https://chicagounbound.uchicago.edu/uclf/vol1989/iss1/8/.

———. 1991. Mapping the Margins: Intersectionality, Identity Politics and Violence against Women of Color. *Stanford Law Review* 43 (6): 1241–1299.

———. 2016. *The Urgency of Intersectionality*. TED video. https://www.ted.com/talks/kimberle_crenshaw_the_urgency_of_intersectionality/up-next.

D'Ottavio, Angela. 2012. Subalterna. Ai margini del femminismo. In *Femministe a parole. Grovigli da districare*, ed. Sabrina Marchetti, Jamila M.H. Mascat, and Vincenza Perilli, 11–14. Rome: Ediesse.

Davis, Angela Y. 1981. *Women, Race and Class*. New York: Random House.

Davis, Kathy. 2008. Intersectionality as Buzzword: A Sociology of Science Perspective on What Makes a Feminist Theory Successful. *Feminist Theory* 9 (10): 67–85.

De Santis, Giuseppe, dir. 1949. *Riso amaro*. Italy: Lux Film. Released in English as *Bitter Rice*.

Decimo, Francesca. 2006. Le migranti, le reti, la mobilità. Sguardi dislocati di ricerca sociale. In *Altri femminismi. Corpi. Culture. Lavoro*, ed. Teresa Bertilotti, Cristina Galasso, Alessandra Gissi, and Francesca Lagorio, 85–100. Rome: manifestolibri.

Derobertis, Roberto. 2009. Per la critica di una modernità maschile e coloniale italiana. Note su *Tempo di uccidere* di Ennio Flaiano e *Regina di fiori e di perle* di Gabriella Ghermandi. In *Moderno e modernità: la letteratura italiana, Atti del XII Congresso Nazionale dell'Associazione degli Italianisti, Roma 17–20 settembre 2008*. Rome: Sapienza Università di Roma. https://www.italianisti.it/pubblicazioni/atti-di-congresso/moderno-e-modernita-la-letteratura-italiana/Derobertis%20Roberto.pdf.

Ehrenreich, Barbara, and Arlie Russell Hochschild. 2003a. Introduction. In *Global Woman: Nannies, Maids, and Sex Workers in the New Economy*, ed. Barbara Ehrenreich and Arlie Russell Hochschild, 1–14. New York: Holt.

———. 2003b. *Global Woman: Nannies, Maids, and Sex Workers in the New Economy*. New York: Holt.

Einash, Ismail. 2020. Il partigiano nero alla fermata della metropolitana. *Internazionale*, August 29. https://www.internazionale.it/notizie/ismail-einashe/2020/08/29/marincola-roma-metropolitana.

Fabbri, Giulia. 2021. *Sguardi (post)coloniali. Razza, genere e politiche della visualità*. Verona: ombre corte.

Fanon, Frantz. 1952. *Peau noire, masques blancs*. Paris: Les Éditions du Seuil. Trans. Richard Philcox as *Black Skin, White Masks* (New York: Grove Press, 1967).

Fantauzzi, Paolo. 2015a. Insulti alla Kyenge, Calderoli (di nuovo) a rischio processo per razzismo. *L'Espresso*, November 26. https://espresso.repubblica.it/palazzo/2015/11/26/news/insulti-alla-kyenge-calderoli-di-nuovo-a-rischio-processo-per-razzismo-1.241118.

———. 2015b. 'Kyenge pare un orango,' il Pd salva Calderoli. Per il Senato non c'è discriminazione razziale. *L'Espresso*, September 16. https://espresso.repubblica.it/palazzo/2015/09/16/news/kyenge-pare-un-orango-il-pd-salva-calderoli-per-il-senato-non-c-e-discriminazione-razziale-1.229691.

Fazel, Shirin Ramzanali. 2007. La spiaggia. *Scritture migranti* 1: 9–14.

Flaiano, Ennio. 2000a. Aethiopia. Appunti per una canzonetta. In *Tempo di uccidere*, 287–313. Milan: BUR.

———. 2000b. *Tempo di uccidere*. Milan: BUR. First published 1947 (Milan: Longanesi). Trans. Stuart Hood as *A Time to Kill* (London: Quartet Books, 1992).

Ghermandi, Gabriella. 2007. *Regina di fiori e di perle*. Rome: Donzelli. Trans. Giovanna Bellesia-Contuzzi and Victoria Offredi Poletto as *Queen of Flowers and Pearls: A Novel* (Bloomington: Indiana University Press, 2015).

Ghidei Biidu, Domenica, and Elisabetta Hagos. 2010. Io Noi Voi. Intervista a donne della diaspora eritrea nell'Italia postcoloniale. In *Brava gente. Memoria e rappresentazioni del colonialismo italiano*, ed. Sabrina Marchetti and Barbara De Vivo. Special issue, *Zapruder. Storie in movimento* 23 (September–December): 144–152.

Giuliani, Gaia, ed. 2015. *Il colore della nazione*. Florence: Le Monnier-Mondadori.

Giuliani, Gaia, and Cristina Lombardi-Diop. 2013. *Bianco e nero. Storia dell'identità razziale degli italiani*. Florence: Le Monnier-Mondadori.

Guillaumin, Colette. 1972. *L'idéologie raciste. Gènese et langage actuel*. Paris: Mouton.

———. 1995. *Racism, Sexism, Power and Ideology*. London: Routledge.

———. 2006. Il corpo costruito, ed. Renate Siebert, with a postscript by Roberta Sassatelli. *Studi culturali* 3 (2): 307–341.

hooks, bell. 1981. *Ain't I a Woman: Black Women and Feminism*. Cambridge, MA: South End Press.

———. 1984. *Feminist Theory: From Margin to Center*. Cambridge, MA: South End Press.

———. 1989. *Talking Back: Thinking Feminist, Thinking Black*. Boston: South End Press.

———. 1990. *Yearning: Race, Gender, and Cultural Politics*. Boston: South End Press.

Hopkins, Rebecca. 2007. Transnational Global Culture in 'La spiaggia' by Shirin Ramzanali Fazel. *Scritture migranti* 1: 15–23.

Hull, Gloria T., Patricia Bell-Scott, and Barbara Smith, eds. 1982. *All the Women Are White, All the Blacks Are Men, But Some of Us Are Brave*. New York: The Feminist Press.

Il Sole 24 Ore. 2013. A Cervia lancio di banane contro la ministra Kyenge. July 27. http://www.ilsole24ore.com/art/notizie/2013-07-27/cervia-lancio-banane-contro-100016.shtml?uuid=AbRwgvHI.

Iyob, Ruth. 2005. Madamismo and Beyond: The Construction of Eritrean Women. In *Italian Colonialism*, ed. Ruth Ben-Ghiat and Mia Fuller, 233–244. New York: Palgrave Macmillan.

Karima 2G. 2014. Orangutan. First single of *2G*. Soupu Music. Video. https://www.youtube.com/watch?v=EKQOltcexX0.

Kechiche, Abdellatif, dir. 2010. *Venus Noire*. France: MK2 Productions. Released in English as *Black Venus*.

Kuruvilla, Gabriella. 2008. *È la vita, dolcezza.* Milan: Baldini Castoldi Dalai.

Kyenge, Cécile. 2013. Cecile Kyenge—*In mezz'ora* del 05/05/2013. Interview by Lucia Annunziata. Rai3, May 5. https://www.rai.it/dl/RaiTV/programmi/media/ContentItem-f7830543-375f-4844-aa20-7bc48685e163.html.

Landis, John, dir. 2010. *Burke & Hare.* Ealing Studios.

Lombardi-Diop, Cristina. 1999. Madre della nazione: una donna italiana nell'Eritrea coloniale. In *Africa Italia. Due continenti si avvicinano,* ed. Sante Matteo and Stefano Bellucci, 117–136. Santarcangelo di Romagna: Fara.

———. 2007. Tempo di sanare. Afterword to *Regina di fiori e di perle,* by Gabriella Ghermandi, 257–264. Rome: Donzelli.

———. 2012a. Igiene, pulizia, bellezza e razza. La 'bianchezza' nella cultura italiana dal Fascismo al dopoguerra. In *Parlare di razza. La lingua del colore tra Italia e Stati Uniti,* ed. Tatiana Petrovich Njegosh and Anna Scacchi, 78–96. Verona: ombre corte.

———. 2012b. Postracial/Postcolonial Italy. In *Postcolonial Italy: Challenging National Homogeneity,* ed. Cristina Lombardi-Diop and Caterina Romeo, 175–190. New York: Palgrave Macmillan.

Lorde, Audre. 1984. The Master's Tools Will Never Dismantle the Master's House. In *Sister Outsider: Essays and Speeches by Audre Lorde,* 110–113. Freedom, CA: The Crossing Press.

Lucarelli, Carlo. 2008. *L'ottava vibrazione.* Turin: Einaudi.

———. 2014. *Albergo Italia.* Turin: Einaudi.

———. 2015. *Il tempo delle iene.* Turin: Einaudi.

Makaping, Geneviève. 2001. *Traiettorie di sguardi. E se gli "altri" foste voi?* Soveria Mannelli: Rubbettino. Republished in 2022 (Soveria Mannelli: Rubbettino). Trans. Giovanna Bellesia-Contuzzi and Vittoria Offredi Poletto as *Reversing the Gaze: What If the Other Were You?* (New Brunswick: Rutgers University Press, forthcoming in 2023).

Manfredi, Gianfranco. 2007–2008. *Volto Nascosto.* Vol. 14. Milan: Sergio Bonelli Editore.

Marchetti, Sabrina. 2011. *Le ragazze di Asmara. Lavoro domestico e migrazione postcoloniale.* Rome: Ediesse.

———. 2013. Intersezionalità. In *Le etiche della diversità culturale,* ed. Caterina Botti, 133–148. Florence: Le Lettere.

Marchetti, Sabrina, Daniela Cherubini, and Giulia Garofalo Geymonat, eds. 2021. *Global Domestic Workers: Intersectional Inequalities and Struggles for Rights.* Bristol: Bristol University Press.

McCall, Leslie. 2005. The Complexity of Intersectionality. *Signs* 30 (3): 1771–1800.

McClintock, Anne. 1995. *Imperial Leather: Race, Gender and Sexuality in the Colonial Contest.* New York: Routledge.

McClintock, Anne, Aamir Mufti, and Ella Shohat, eds. 1996. *Dangerous Liaisons: Gender, Nation, and Postcolonial Perspectives*. Minneapolis: University of Minnesota Press.

Mengiste, Maaza. 2019a. Breaking Apart the Myths of War. Interview by Alden Mudge. BookPage, October. https://bookpage.com/interviews/24444-maaza-mengiste-fiction#.YNaAT-gzaUk.

———. 2019b. *The Shadow King*. Edinburgh: Canongate.

———. 2020. Book Club: A Conversation On 'The Shadow King' With Author Maaza Mengiste. By Greta Johnsen. *WBEZ Chicago*, September 11. https://www.wbez.org/stories/a-conversation-about-the-shadow-king-with-maaza-mengiste/bc01683c-c9e6-46a9-98b5-22a1cc11e851.

Merrill, Heather. 2006. *An Alliance of Women: Immigration and the Politics of Race*. Minneapolis: University of Minnesota Press.

Montanelli, Indro. 1969. Interview by Gianni Bisiach. *L'ora della verità*. YouTube video. https://www.youtube.com/watch?v=PYgSwluzYxs.

Moraga, Cherríe, and Gloria Anzaldúa, eds. 1981. *This Bridge Called My Back: Writings by Radical Women of Color*. New York: Kitchen Table/Women of Color Press.

Mubiayi, Ingy. 2005. Documenti, prego. In *Pecore nere*, ed. Flavia Capitani and Emanuele Coen, 97–107. Rome-Bari: Laterza.

Nzegwu, Nkiru. 2003a. O Africa: Gender Imperialism in Academia. In *African Women and Feminism: Reflecting on the Politics of Sisterhood*, ed. Oyèrónké Oyěwùmi, 99–157. Trenton: Africa World Press.

———. 2003b. Sisterhood. In *African Women and Feminism: Reflecting on the Politics of Sisterhood*, ed. Oyèrónké Oyěwùmi, 7–8. Trenton: Africa World Press.

O'Healy, Áine. 2009. '[Non] è una somala': Deconstructing African Femininity in Italian Film. *The Italianist* 29 (2): 175–198.

———. 2012. Screening Intimacy and Racial Difference in Postcolonial Italy. In *Postcolonial Italy: Challenging National Homogeneity*, ed. Cristina Lombardi-Diop and Caterina Romeo, 205–220. New York: Palgrave Macmillan.

Oyěwùmi, Oyèrónké, ed. 2003. *African Women and Feminism: Reflecting on the Politics of Sisterhood*. Trenton: Africa World Press.

Parreñas, Rhacel Salazar. 2001. *Servants of Globalization: Women, Migration, and Domestic Work*. Stanford, CA: Stanford University Press.

Petrovich Njegosh, Tatiana, and Anna Scacchi, eds. 2012. *Parlare di razza. La lingua del colore tra Italia e Stati Uniti*. Verona: ombre corte.

Pojmann, Wendy. 2006. *Immigrant Women and Feminism in Italy*. Aldershot: Ashgate.

Ponzanesi, Sandra. 2005. Beyond the Black Venus: Colonial Sexual Politics and Contemporary Visual Practices. In *Italian Colonialism: Legacy and Memory*, ed. Jacqueline Andall and Derek Duncan, 165–189. Bern: Peter Lang.

———. 2012. The Color of Love: Madamismo and Interracial Relationships in the Italian Colonies. *Research in African Literatures* 43 (2): 155–172.

Puwar, Nirmal. 2004. *Space Invaders: Race, Gender and Bodies Out of Place.* Oxford: Berg.

Ribeiro Corossacz, Valeria. 2012. Razza. Come liberarsene? In *Femministe a parole. Grovigli da districare,* ed. Sabrina Marchetti, Jamila M.H. Mascat, and Vincenza Perilli, 237–241. Rome: Ediesse.

Sabelli, Sonia. 2010. L'eredità del colonialismo nelle rappresentazioni contemporanee del corpo femminile nero. In *Brava gente. Memoria e rappresentazioni del colonialismo,* ed. Elena Petricola and Andrea Tappi. Special issue, *Zapruder. Storie in movimento* 23 (September–December): 106–115.

———. 2013. Quale razza? Genere, classe e colore in 'Timira' e 'L'ottava vibrazione.' In *La sottile linea bianca. Intersezioni di razza, genere e classe nell'Italia postcoloniale,* ed. Gaia Giuliani. Special issue, *Studi culturali* 10 (2): 286–293.

Scego, Igiaba. 2004. *Rhoda.* Sinnos: Rome.

———. 2008. Identità. In *Amori bicolori. Racconti,* ed. Flavia Capitani and Emanuele Coen, 3–33. Rome-Bari: Laterza.

———. 2013. Annunziata vs Kyenge: le peggiori domande di sempre. *globalist.it,* May 6. https://www.globalist.it/news/2016/05/08/annunziata-vs-kyenge-le-peggiori-domande-di-sempre-43762.html.

———. 2015. *Adua.* Florence: Giunti. Trans. Jamie Richards as *Adua* (New York: New Vessel Press, 2017).

———. 2017. *Adua.* Trans. Jamie Richards. New York: New Vessel Press. Originally published as *Adua* (Florence: Giunti, 2015).

Segre, Andrea, Dagmawi Yimer, and Riccardo Biadene, dirs. 2008. *Come un uomo sulla terra.* Italy: Archivio delle Memorie Migranti e Asinitas-ZaLab. Released in English as *Like a Man on Earth.*

Sòrgoni, Barbara. 1995. La Venere Ottentotta. Un'invenzione antropologica per 'la difesa della razza'. *Il Mondo* 3 (2): 366–375.

———. 1998. *Parole e corpi. Antropologia, discorso giuridico e politiche sessuali interrazziali nella colonia Eritrea (1890–1941).* Naples: Liguori.

———. 2002. Racist Discourses and Practices in the Italian Empire Under Fascism. In *The Politics of Recognizing Difference: Multiculturalism Italian-Style,* ed. Ralph Grillo and Jeff Pratt, 41–58. Aldershot: Ashgate.

Spivak, Gayatri Chakravorty. 1988. Can the Subaltern Speak? In *Marxism and the Interpretation of Culture,* ed. Cary Nelson and Lawrence Grossberg, 271–313. Basingstoke: Macmillan Education.

———. 1999. *A Critique of Postcolonial Reason: Toward a History of the Vanishing Present.* Cambridge, MA: Harvard University Press.

Stefani, Giulietta. 2007. *Colonia per maschi. Italiani in Africa Orientale: una storia di genere.* Verona: ombre corte.

Stoler, Ann Laura. 1991. Carnal Knowledge and Imperial Power: Gender, Race, and Morality in Colonial Asia. In *Gender at the Crossroads of Knowledge: Feminist Anthropology in the Postmodern Era*, ed. Micaela di Leonardo, 51–101. Berkeley: University of California Press.

———. 1996. Making Empire Respectable: The Politics of Race and Sexual Morality in Twentieth-Century Colonial Cultures. In *Dangerous Liaisons: Gender, Nation, and Postcolonial Perspectives*, ed. Anne McClintock, Aamir Mufti, and Ella Shohat, 344–373. Minneapolis: University of Minnesota Press.

———. 2002. *Carnal Knowledge and Imperial Power: Race and the Intimate in Colonial Rule*. Berkeley: University of California Press.

Taronna, Annarita. 2016. *Black Englishes. Pratiche linguistiche transfrontaliere Italia-USA*. Verona: ombre corte.

Triulzi, Alessandro. 2012. Hidden Faces, Hidden Histories: Contrasting Voices of Postcolonial Italy. In *Postcolonial Italy: Challenging National Homogeneity*, ed. Cristina Lombardi-Diop and Caterina Romeo, 103–113. New York: Palgrave Macmillan.

Truth, Sojourner. 1851. Ain't I a Woman? Speech presented at the Women's Rights Convention, Akron, Ohio, July 29. https://www.thesojournertruth-project.com/.

Wekker, Gloria. 2016. *White Innocence. Paradoxes of Colonialism and Race*. Durham, NC: Duke University Press.

Wu Ming 2, and Antar Mohamed. 2012. *Timira. Romanzo meticcio*. Turin: Einaudi.

CHAPTER 4

Defying the Chromatic Norm: Race, Blackness, (In)Visibility, Italianness, Citizenship

Your story doesn't matter, nor does who you are. If you are colored, you are different.
—Maria Abbebù Viarengo, "Scirscir N'Demna?"

Sissi and I cannot be equals for a whole series of reasons, but there is one that is more important than the others and this reason is that I am Black, born of two Black parents, while Sissi is white, and has golden curls and gray-green eyes.
—Ubah Cristina Ali Farah, *Il comandante del fiume*

I had that feeling, all too familiar, of wanting to climb out of my skin, to be invisible.
—Kym Ragusa, *The Skin Between Us*

4.1 INTRODUCTION

With the election of Donald J. Trump in 2016, it became immediately clear that the "postracial" society invoked following Barack Obama's 2008 victory had been nothing more than an illusion. Claims that Obama's election had put an end to the long-running issue of

© The Author(s), under exclusive license to Springer Nature Switzerland AG 2023
C. Romeo, *Interrupted Narratives and Intersectional Representations in Italian Postcolonial Literature*, Italian and Italian American Studies,
https://doi.org/10.1007/978-3-031-10043-7_4

race—after all, if a Black man could be elected president, how could anyone maintain that there was still race-based inequality?—and that the United States had now become a postracial society were challenged by just as many claims that the election of a Black president was not enough to set aside centuries of slavery and racism in American history.[1] Tim Wise, for instance, judged the election of Obama not as proof that racism had been defeated but rather as a sign that racism had changed shape, "from Racism 1.0 to Racism 2.0, an insidious upgrade that allows millions of whites to cling to racist stereotypes about people of color generally, while nonetheless carving out exceptions for those who, like Obama, make us comfortable by seeming so 'different' from what we view as a much less desirable norm" (2010, 15). Eduardo Bonilla-Silva considered Obama's election an expression of the "new racism" that has characterized the United States since the 1960s (2014, 257). Within this framework, selected "minorities" have been chosen over time for social ascension and their representatives have been elected, which has allowed for the idea that American democracy enjoys excellent health, while most of the "minorities" have, in fact, been consigned to the margins of the social fabric.

Trump's election—described by many as a "whitelash"[2]—made clear (if there were still the need) that the racial question had not subsided and that the presence of the first Black president in the White House had actually increased the anger of reactionary white people who for eight years had felt deprived of their power and who, through the election of Trump, had seemingly regained that power. As was repeatedly observed, in many cases "Make America Great Again" was simply code for "Make America White Again."[3] All this shows that if the category of race is set aside in the

---

[1] On this issue see, among others, Wise (2010) and Bonilla-Silva (2014). See also Dawson and Bobo (2009), Love and Tosolt (2010), and Clayton and Welch (2016).

[2] Among them, Van Jones, who states, "This was a whitelash against a changing country. It was a whitelash against a Black president, in part" (quoted in Andrews 2016, para. 13).

[3] In this regard, see the fine article by Toni Morrison (2016) "Making America White Again." This article is part of a series published in the November 21, 2016, issue of *The New Yorker*—a few days after Trump's election—entitled "Aftermath: Sixteen Writers on Trump's America," which offers a reflection on the subject through the voices of 16 different writers. See also Blow (2016).

political, social, and cultural analysis of a country when racialism—and all the discriminatory practices that are based on it—persists, then that analysis risks ignoring the fact that considerations based on race, which may seem to have disappeared, have in fact only evaporated and may be ready to reappear at any moment.[4]

The expression "racial evaporation," coined by David Theo Goldberg (2006, 342), evokes the presence of something that has momentarily become invisible—as in the pretense of postraciality causing the category of race to disappear from the theoretical debate—while actually remaining present and pervasive. Such presence, like the presence of steam, saturates the air, rendering it heavy and unbreathable. There remains, moreover, a constant threat that race, subjected to new pressures deriving from social tensions, could undergo further change of state and once again become visible and tangible. Even if today the term "race" (usually) indicates a category of oppression, a social construct that transforms itself through history and changes shape in different geopolitical contexts,[5] for centuries it was considered a biological factor, which is what authorized the process of racializing the "other." In Europe, this process was also structured in the encounter with the Black populations of the colonies. After the Second World War, an analysis of the racialization enacted in Europe mostly concerned the Shoah—setting aside the racialization of Black Africans in colonial possessions. Such racial inferiority constructed in the colonies, however, historically constitutes one of the foundations on which individual European nation states, and Europe as a whole, have shaped their identity.

To analyze this process, the category of "race" alone is insufficient and must be intersected with the category of "color,"[6] which is crucial for a

---

[4] Regarding the concept of "racial evaporation," see Goldberg (2006, 2009).

[5] Instead of the expression "social construction," Matthew Jacobson uses "social fiction" (1998, 11) to further emphasize that race is not a biological—and therefore natural—category, but rather a social—and therefore cultural—construction.

[6] For an analysis of whiteness as a category on which the process of constructing European identity is founded, see, among others, Gilroy (1987), Balibar (1991, 2004), Goldberg (2006, 2009), Mohanram (2007), Hine et al. (2009), El-Tayeb (2011), Lombardi-Diop and Romeo (2015b), and Wekker (2016).

discourse analysis of the racialization processes in the United States and South Africa, for instance, but also for an understanding of the racial history of Europe that developed in the colonies. Colonial history, however, by virtue of the "externality" (Goldberg 2006, 332) that has characterized it—the fact, that is, that colonialism developed in territories outside Europe—has been relegated to the margins of European history and has usually been considered a non-European phenomenon. Over time, this externality has enabled the systematic removal of colonial history and memory in Europe, as well as of the racialization processes implemented in the colonies. Toni Morrison observes that, since racial history in the United States developed *within* the country, the category of color is indispensable for analyzing the mechanisms that define racial identities: "Unlike any nation in Europe, the United States holds whiteness as the unifying force. Here, for many people, the definition of 'Americanness' is color" (2016, para. 1). Taking this into consideration, I argue that the category of color as it intersects with that of race in an analysis of European countries is less visible because it has been historically understudied: "as emerging European whiteness studies have shown, the continent's racial paradigms differ from the U.S. context, in which whiteness studies originate, in a number of ways that still need to be fully explored" (El-Tayeb 2011, xiv). However, the examination of the category of color is no less indispensable in Europe than it is in the United States. An analysis based solely on race in Europe allows for the examination of the great European racial crimes, such as the extermination of "communists, homosexuals, gypsies, and Ashkenazi Jews" in Nazi concentration camps and the ethnic cleansing carried out during the Balkan Wars (Griffin and Braidotti 2002, 227), but leaves out the crimes of colonialism, in which color plays a fundamental role. The cancellation of the intersection between race and color from the critical theoretical debate, therefore, and its substitution by the category of ethnicity, in Italy as in the rest of Europe, risks erasing some pivotal elements for analyzing European colonial history, whose "externality" has often favored processes of obscurity, marginalization, improper burial, and evaporation (Goldberg 2006, 2009).[7]

---

[7] On the concept of improper burial see in particular Kilomba (2008) and the first chapter of Goldberg (2009), appropriately entitled "Buried, Alive."

The novel *A Time to Kill* by Ennio Flaiano novel *Tempo di uccidere* (2000) (*A Time to Kill*) (1992) is an apt literary metaphor for such processes. Improper burial, which both Goldberg (2006) and Grada Kilomba (2008) use in a metaphorical sense,[8] is a real-life obsession of the lieutenant, the novel's protagonist. He fears that the odor of Mariam's corpse, which he buried in haste and thus without the necessary precautions, could end up revealing the murder he has committed. Toward the end of the novel, the lieutenant confesses his crimes to a fellow soldier, who absolves him and reassures him about the possible consequences of his actions because nothing that the lieutenant has done has been discovered or denounced and what has been done in Africa will remain in Africa.[9] Like the lieutenant, Europeans intended to confine their colonial misdeeds to Africa by virtue of the fact that that chapter of national history had unfolded elsewhere. But Flaiano, with extraordinary foresight, does not appear to be convinced of the possibility that this externality can permanently guarantee that such events will be forgotten and erased. In the final scene of the novel, just as he is about to board the ship that will take him back to Italy, free to resume his life where he left off before going to Africa, the lieutenant notices a smell that is at first sweet, and then, immediately afterward, nauseating (this is not the first time that a nauseating smell is detected in the novel). The lieutenant is unable to comprehend

---

[8] Goldberg argues that "For Europeans, race is not, or really is no longer. European racial denial concerns wanting race in the wake of World War II categorically to implode, to erase itself. This is a wishful evaporation never quite enacted, never satisfied. A desire at once frustrated and displaced, racist implications always lingering and diffuse, silenced but assumed, always already returned and haunting, buried but alive" (2006, 334). Portuguese and West African artivist and intellectual Grada Kilomba argues that the ghost of slavery lingers in the history of the present, that the improper burial of race signals repression of the collective trauma caused by the crimes of slavery and colonialism from the conscious sphere, and that everyday acts of racism bring back that past, causing the trauma to resurface (2008, 137).

[9] "'It seems to me pointless to talk of crimes since no one is looking for me.' 'Yes,' he replied, 'quite pointless.' 'If no one is looking for me,' I insisted, 'we can go.' 'Without another thought,' he replied. 'Our neighbours are too busy with their own crimes to worry about ours.'" (Flaiano 1992, 270). ("'Mi sembra inutile parlare di delitti visto che nessuno mi cerca.' 'Sì' rispose 'proprio inutile.' 'Se nessuno mi cerca', insistei 'possiamo andarcene.' 'Tranquillamente' rispose. 'Il prossimo è troppo occupato coi propri delitti per accorgersi dei nostri'" [Flaiano 2000, 284–85].)

where the stench is coming from—perhaps it is his interlocutor's cheap hair pomade; perhaps it is the sickly sweet smelling flowers that are rotting all around the harbor—but it surrounds him and, indeed, precedes him.[10] Thus, Flaiano suggests that the colonizers will not be allowed to leave their "adventure" behind and that the consequences of their actions will follow them to Italy, or perhaps even precede them.

As Flaiano intuits, the fact that colonialism took place outside the borders of Europe has not made it any less of a European phenomenon, and its consequences have profoundly influenced the political, economic, and social history of the ex-colonies, as well as the new configurations of contemporary Europe, which for several decades now has been one of the principal destinations for global transnational migrants from former colonized countries. Understanding the continuity existing between European colonial history and the postcolonial condition of Italy and other European countries allows us to consider contemporary manifestations of racism as a colonial legacy. Such manifestations cannot simplistically and reductively be ascribed to the growing intolerance of European citizens toward economic migrants, refugees, and asylum seekers, disregarding the fact that contemporary transnational migrations are one of the historical consequences of colonialism and that intolerance is one of the effects produced by the colonial policies that constructed European whiteness in opposition to the Blackness of the colonized. For this reason, now just as then, Blackness and Europeanness are considered two mutually exclusive terms. To understand and analyze contemporary manifestations of racism and the processes of racialization in Europe thus requires the category of color and the characteristic of "visibility" to be retained and prioritized so that the connection with colonial history is made evident.

In the Italian context, Goldberg's evaporation metaphor is particularly useful for analyzing the country's current sociopolitical climate and the way in which race and Blackness have long been excluded from critical theoretical debate. The consequence of this exclusion is that episodes of racist violence have been—and often still are—represented by the media and in the culture at large as isolated outbursts, exceptions to the general rule of civility and social cohesiveness. Acknowledging the fact that colonialism as it was historically enacted in Italy and throughout Europe has been repressed as a matter of course—and at times as a matter of policy—allows for a reading of the ongoing manifestations of racism not as a series of sporadic,

---

[10] On the nauseating smells in *A Time to Kill* as a metaphor for the rottenness of the colonial system, see Brunetti (2010) and Fracassa (2012).

unconnected events but rather as the product of a common, colonial-style matrix: in other words, to connect Italy's colonial past with its postcolonial present. The prefix "post" in the terms "postcolonial" and "postracial," as Cristina Lombardi-Diop argues, signals the yearned-for and (presumably) accomplished liberation from something unseemly (e.g., colonialism and racialization), and removes both colonialism and the discourse on race from Italian history and from present-day Italian culture (see Lombardi-Diop 2012b, 2014; Lombardi-Diop, in Giuliani and Lombardi-Diop 2013, 67–116). Blatant episodes of racism in recent Italian history and the way in which they have been reported by the media show that Italy has not processed the fact that colonialism and racism are foundational to its national identity or that the notion of Italy in the collective imaginary has always been and remains associated with a white space within which Black bodies are not recognized as having a legitimate existence. Such episodes include: the killing of Jerry Masslo in Villa Literno (1989); the massacre in Castel Volturno of immigrants Julius Francis Kwame Antwi, Eric Affun Yeboa, and Christopher Adams from Ghana, Ababa El Hadji and Samuel Kwako from Togo, and Alex Jeemes from Liberia (2008); the shooting of two African immigrants in the streets of Rosarno and the subsequent riots (2010)[11]; the brutal murders of Abdul Salam Guibre in Milan (2008), Samb Modou and Diop Mor in Florence (2011), Emmanuel Chidi Nnamdi in Fermo (2016), Idy Diene in Florence (2018), Willy Monteiro Duarte in Colleferro, near Rome (2020); the shooting in the streets of Macerata of Jennifer Otioto, Gideon Azeke, Mahamadou Toure, Wilson Kofi, Festus Omagbon, and Omar Fadera (2018)[12]; and countless occasions of racist chants directed at numerous African Italian athletes over the years.

The strategies commonly used to make the categories of race and color disappear from the critical theoretical debate fluctuate between evaporation—in which episodes of racism are minimized or labeled as something else (whether that be ignorance, exasperation, or madness)—and making the discourse on race coincide with other discourses, such as immigration, citizenship, clandestinity, religion, or, more generally, "cultural

---

[11] Regarding the events in Rosarno, see Nicola Angrisano's video *Il tempo delle arance* (2010), Andrea Segre's documentary *Il sangue verde* (2010), and Jonas Carpignano's film *Mediterranea* (2015).

[12] After Willy Monteiro Duarte was murdered by Marco and Gabriele Bianchi in Colleferro in September 2020, the association Il Razzismo è una brutta storia (Racism is a nasty thing) published an article titled "L'Italia e i suoi George Floyd," in which a long list of Black people brutally murdered in Italy for racist reasons is presented (Associazione Il Razzismo è una brutta storia 2020).

differences." "Racism without races," a new incarnation of colonial racism that is spreading in contemporary postcolonial Europe, is "a racism whose dominant theme is not biological heredity but the insurmountability of cultural differences, a racism which, at first sight, does not postulate the superiority of certain groups or peoples in relation to others but 'only' the harmfulness of abolishing frontiers, the incompatibility of life-styles and traditions" (Balibar 1991, 21). As Étienne Balibar argues, "neo-racism" (1991, 17) is a characteristic of the decolonization era, a period in which the dichotomy between the ex-colonizers and the ex-colonized is articulated on European soil and therefore functions to create mechanisms of differential inclusion and social marginalization in European states that have become the destination of transnational global migrants. A shift occurs, therefore, from "classic racism," which postulates the existence of a hierarchy of different races with different biological characteristics (with the white race at the top), to what Pierre-André Taguieff (1999) terms "differentialist racism," which is based instead on the irreducible difference and irreconcilability of groups that are the bearers of different cultures and that follow different religions.

Contemporary postcolonial Italy is connected to other European countries in part because of the hegemonic power it attaches to whiteness—a whiteness that was codified (also) during the colonial period and that remains persistent in current debates about migrants, refugees, and asylum seekers. Unlike with most other European nations, however, such hegemony has been undermined by Italy's history of emigration, which has seen Italians relegated to a subaltern position, whether during the century of mass emigration spanning 1876–1976 or in response to the strong intranational migration from Southern Italy to the North or in relation to the "new mobilities" of the twenty-first century.[13] The resulting subalternity

---

[13] Starting in 2013, the migration balance has reversed, and outward migrations have again surpassed inward migrations. The term "new mobilities" is usually employed to refer to the outward migrations that, since the beginning of the third millennium, have again characterized the history of Italy. The term "mobility" is used instead of "migration" or "emigration" to highlight the different nature of these flows as compared with those of the past. The "newly mobile" (nuovi mobili) are generally characterized by a high(er) level of education and of digitization, which allows them to maintain closer contact with their country of origin. They are also aided by low-cost air travel (Tirabassi and del Pra' 2014). According to the *Rapporto italiani nel mondo 2021* (Fondazione Migrantes 2021), outward mobility from Italy has increased by 82% since 2006. The motivations for this massive outflow of people are not, however, strictly economic, but instead reflect a more general dissatisfaction, especially among the younger population, which is in search of a less provincial lifestyle in a more meritocratic and less homophobic, sexist, and gerontocratic society.

severely undermined the hegemonic position that Italy attempted to assert through colonialism, which, in turn, weakened Italy's position in the international arena and continues to weaken it today in the context of the European Union.[14] These relationships of hegemony and subalternity, deeply connected to migratory movements, have historically been crucial to the formation of an Italian national identity (see, among many others, Gabaccia 2000; Labanca 2002b; Guglielmo and Salerno 2003; Guglielmo 2003; Lombardi-Diop and Romeo 2012, 2014; Petrovich Njegosh and Scacchi 2012; Giuliani and Lombardi-Diop 2013; Aru and Deplano 2013; Giuliani 2015; Ben-Ghiat and Hom 2016; Tintori 2016; Grechi and Gravano 2016; Bordin and Bosco 2017; Fiore 2017; Ricatti 2018).

Studies on race and processes of racialization in Italy started to develop systematically in the 1990s.[15] Initially, this field of studies produced three lines of research that originated from three different trajectories of analysis: (1) studies on Fascist racism and anti-Semitism, both at home and in the colonies, and on the processes of racialization that derive from them[16]; (2) studies on the historical racialization of the North and the South that created a hierarchy between the two regions, with the North occupying

---

[14] Boaventura de Sousa Santos's (2002) theorization of Portuguese "minor" colonialism, which makes the dichotomies "hegemonic/subaltern" and "self/other" inadequate for reading the country's colonial history and the postcoloniality of the present, can be applied to Italy as well, with noted differences. While Italians had a hegemonic role in the colonies, their history of emigration and the peripheral position of Southern Italy with respect to Northern Italy and Europe repeatedly placed them in a position of subalternity. This produced a "minor" colonialism, in which Italy had a hegemonic position with respect to its colonial subjects but a subaltern one with respect to British and French colonial empires. Similar to Santos's (2002) claim about Portugal's status among European powers, this places Italy in a semi-peripheral position in the contemporary European context. In this regard, see also Lombardi-Diop and Romeo (2015b).

[15] For a rather comprehensive survey of critical race studies about the Italian context produced in Italy in 1990–2020, see Fabbri (2021), specifically Chap. 2.

[16] This line of research was inaugurated in Italy with the volume edited by the Centro Furio Jesi, *La menzogna della razza. Documenti e immagini del razzismo e dell'antisemitismo fascista* (The Lie About Race: Documents and Images of Fascist Racism and Anti-Semitism) (1994), which includes an analysis of race and racism extending beyond anti-Semitic persecution to colonial racism, devoting particular attention to visual sources that illustrate well the extent of Fascist racism. For an analysis of racism and anti-Semitism in Italy and in the colonies, see Burgio and Casali (1996), Burgio (1998, 1999, 2001), Sòrgoni (1998), Rivera (2003, 2009), Bonavita et al. (2005), Stefani (2007), Cassata (2008), De Napoli (2009), Poidimani (2009), Curcio and Mellino (2012), Giuliani and Lombardi-Diop (2013), Lombardi-Diop and Romeo (2012, 2014), Giuliani (2015), Grechi and Gravano (2016), and Bordin and Bosco (2017).

the position of superiority[17]; and (3) studies on the (presumed) whiteness of Italian emigrants in the United States—as well as in South America and Australia—and on the way in which Italian Americans have been (and are still) considered in terms of race and color.[18] While these three lines developed from distinct trajectories, in the decades since the end of the twentieth century they have given rise to a field of studies that emphasizes the correlation between colonialism, inward and outward transnational migrations, intranational migrations, and, more recently, new mobilities.[19] What

[17] This second line of research began in Italy with the publication of Vito Teti's *La razza maledetta. Origini del pregiudizio antimeridionale* (The Damned Race: Origins of the Anti-Southern Prejudice) (1993), in which the author traces the construction of the subalternity of Southern Italy's inhabitants to the biologist theories on race developed by positivist scholars such as Alfredo Niceforo, Giuseppe Sergi, and Cesare Lombroso, who theorized, in different ways, the existence of two distinct Italian races: the Northern and the Southern. On the racialization of the inhabitants of Southern Italy, especially in relation to other phenomena such as migrations, the construction of national identity, and connections among the other societies of the Global South, see, among others, Verdicchio (1997), Schneider (1998), Burgio (1999), Moe (2002), Cazzato (2008), Brunetti and Derobertis (2014), Derobertis (2012), Giuliani and Lombardi-Diop (2013), and Pesole (2015).

[18] This debate is part of a broader discussion on the process of whitening different immigrant communities during and after the Great Migration (in this regard, see, among others, Roediger [1991] and Jacobson [1998]). Concerning the debate on the whiteness of Italian immigrants in the United States, see, among others, Vecoli (1995), Guglielmo (2003), Guglielmo and Salerno (2003), and Lombardi-Diop (2015). These scholars have analyzed how in the United States Italians were white from a legal standpoint but were often not considered such in everyday life. These shades of whiteness (what Matthew Jacobson [1998] calls "whiteness of a different color") were derived from the intersection of race and color with political, economic, social, and cultural factors that were then transposed on and transformed into overtly racial characteristics. On the ambivalence with which Italian emigrants in the United States were perceived in terms of race and color, see, among others, the memoiristic essay by DeSalvo "Color: White/Complexion: Dark" (2003). Here the writer, in analyzing her grandmother's naturalization documents, notes how the clerk at the Immigration and Naturalization Office had registered not only her grandmother's skin color (white) but also her complexion (dark), even though her grandmother's complexion was actually fair. DeSalvo's reflection centers on the way in which the (legally sanctioned) whiteness of Italians was continually "darkened" by other factors such as, in this case, social class (Italians who emigrated to the United States were predominantly Southerners and peasants, and for this reason their complexion was always associated with the dark complexion of those who work in the fields). Another very significant text in this regard is Kym Ragusa's memoir (2006, 2008a), which is discussed later in this chapter.

[19] Among the studies that have linked Italian colonialism, emigration, and immigration, see Verdicchio (1997), Gabaccia (2000), Labanca (2002a, 2002b), Choate (2008), Lombardi-Diop and Romeo (2012, 2014), Derobertis (2012), and Fiore (2012, 2014, 2017).

emerges from these newer, more coordinated analyses is that these various migratory movements repositioned Italians in terms of their hegemony/subalternity differently during different historical periods and in different geopolitical contexts, and that this profoundly influenced the process whereby the national identity of Italy was formed and consolidated, including the way in which Italians were perceived (and perceived themselves) from a racial perspective. In the past decade, for instance, Robert Viscusi (2010) has used postcolonial terminology to examine Italian American culture in terms of the double subalternity Italian emigrants in the United States have experienced in relation to both their country of origin and their country of destination; Cristina Lombardi-Diop (2015) has extended the methodology of postcolonial studies to Italian American studies to analyze how the whiteness of Italians took shape and was consolidated on both sides of the Atlantic through racial opposition to Black populations in the African colonies and through a process of progressive "whitening" of Italian Americans in the United States; and Teresa Fiore (2017) has linked the cultural production of Italian emigration to that of immigration by extrapolating common themes and aesthetics in literary, musical, and film texts that are far apart in terms of both geography and chronology.

4.2   Between Invisibility and Hypervisibility

Even though the categories of race and Blackness are still very much absent from the Italian cultural debate and incidents that reveal processes of racialization are often considered episodic and unconnected, the evaporation of race has become increasingly difficult to sustain in contemporary Italy due to the work of Black Italian writers, intellectuals, directors, artists, and artivists, who have been representing Italian Blackness with ever greater frequency and complexity since the 1990s, thus making it more visible not only in the context of literature and the arts but also in that of culture at large.

In the works I examine in this chapter, the discourse on race and color goes well beyond the binaries of white/Black and racist/racialized, just as it goes well beyond episodes of blatant racism. Racism is revealed as a systemic structure that is all the more insidious the less visible it is—and all the more dangerous the more it lurks in seemingly harmless and benevolent attitudes (such as orientalization, exoticization, do-goodism, and tolerance). In their representations, Black Italians have opened a breach in the Italian imaginary that has historically associated Italians with whiteness, with an absence of color and, as Alessandro Portelli (2003) has argued, with "normality."[20]

Sarah Ahmed (2007) contends that the whiteness of a given space is constructed through the reiteration of the same kind of bodies in that space (see also Nirmal Puwar's "somatic norm," 2004), a reiteration that occurs at a phenomenological and not discursive level (i.e., through the recurrent way in which white bodies manifest themselves and not through a linguistic act that permits or forbids their presence).[21] What both Ahmed and Puwar observe in their analyses of non-segregated spaces is that the prohibition against certain bodies occupying certain spaces is not explicitly formulated as a verbal ban but is instead enforced through implication, through the repeated presence of exclusively white subjects in those spaces. The fact that the ban is not verbalized confers transparency and normative status to whiteness. To claim that a place is not characterized by any color means to refuse to see that such a space is de facto marked by the color white, and that that color instantiates and authorizes privilege. Such strategy has been employed over time by Italian publishers, along with academics and members of the media, who have constructed the national literary and cultural space as white by reiterating whiteness as the norm. When at the beginning of the 1990s (predominantly) African Italian postcolonial writers began to mark such symbolic space with their Blackness, resistance to this "intrusion" was often enacted through the delegitimization of their writing

[20] The association of whiteness with an absence of color and with "normality" is not just an Italian phenomenon. As critical whiteness studies showed in the early 1990s (beginning in the United States), whiteness has been considered an absence of color, a neutral, natural, invisible category, the norm, which, as such, does not require critical theoretical discussion. Some of the texts from the 1990s that have provided the coordinates for the discourse on whiteness and the decentralization of white culture are those by Roediger (1991), Morrison (1993), Frankenberg (1993), and Dyer (1997).

[21] Along with Grada Kilomba (2008), Sarah Ahmed (2007) uses her own experience as a non-white academic in a European university to explain how the normative color of a space is constructed. Ahmed observes that everyone notices when non-white academics enter a room, which highlights how the academic space is still strongly characterized by whiteness (2007, 157). Grada Kilomba recounts her experience of being the only Black student in the Psychology Department at the Freie Universität in Berlin, as well as the only Black faculty member in her department later on, and one of only a few in the entire university (2008, 35).

(which was recognized as having sociological but not "universal" literary value).[22] Undeterred, migrant and second-generation writers have "tak[en] the floor"[23] (Khouma 1995, 115) by questioning and deconstructing the somatic norm in the symbolic space of Italian literature and culture, interrupting traditional hegemonic narratives, and articulating new ones that take into account the transformed social and cultural structures of Italy.

In 1990, three texts were published that are widely regarded as having launched Italian migration and postcolonial literature: *Io venditore di elefanti* (*I Was an Elephant Salesman*) by the Senegalese writer Pap Khouma ([1990] 2006), *Chiamatemi Alì* (Call Me Ali) by the Moroccan author Mohamed Bouchane (1990), and *Immigrato* (Immigrant) by the Tunisian writer and journalist Salah Methnani (Fortunato and Methnani [1990] 2006). In each of them, the central theme is the social marginalization of immigrants tied to their illegal status.[24] The subjects of race and color appear in these texts in different ways that denote not only the different subjectivity of the three authors but also the different racial self-perception of the protagonists and the perception that Italians, as well as other immigrants, have of them based on their degree of divergence from the chromatic norm.

In the new introduction to the 2006 edition of *Io venditore di elefanti*, editor Oreste Pivetta provides a brief reflection on the subject of racism:

> In the end Pap pointed out to me that we had never used the word racism.
> I do not know whether I did it by chance or whether his story was such that
> it ruled out resorting to something that might have seemed a bit ideological:
> the fact is that we had left it to the story itself to say everything and to teach
> us to distinguish between the good and the bad, the generous and the cruel,

---

[22] According to Alessandro Portelli, the fact that Salah Methnani's *Immigrato*, written in collaboration with Mario Fortunato (2006), was composed as a novel but accepted for publication as an autobiography demonstrates the unofficially sanctioned position that "an immigrant cannot give us anything but the undeveloped material of experience and is not entitled to reelaborate it imaginatively" ("un immigrato non po[ssa] darci altro che la materia non elaborata dell'esperienza e non [abbia] diritto a rielaborarla immaginativamente") (Portelli 2000, 78). All translations are the translator's unless noted otherwise.

[23] "preso la parola."

[24] In this regard, see Chap. 2.

between the arrogant policeman who confiscates your goods and the police-man who can be understanding.[25] (Pivetta 2006, 8)

Inspired to a significant degree by Khouma, this retrospective reflection by Pivetta shows the need to analyze how and why racism is often per-ceived as a voluntary act rather than as a pervasive, structural social prin-ciple. If, however, racism is considered systemic, then it is easier to understand how, in binaries such as good/bad, generous/cruel, under-standing/arrogant, it can lurk in the first as well as the second term. Although the racialization of Senegalese and other Black Africans in Italy in the 1980s is not confronted directly in the book, the issue of the social invisibility of Blacks—denounced by Ralph Ellison (1952) in *Invisible Man*—is constantly interwoven with the excessive visibility that derives from their divergence from the presumed chromatic norm ("a Black man in Rimini or Riccione is always out of place"[26] [Khouma 2006, 33]). The text also shows forms of racism that are enacted through the stereotyping and essentializing of Senegalese immigrants. This occurs particularly in the scenes in which a policeman asks the narrator to break-dance and in which some potential customers ask him to show them his genitalia, the latter a process that recalls the hypersexualization of Black bodies—in this case of men—in the colonies. Khouma's writing arises precisely in response to the social invisibility/hypervisibility of Black immigrants in 1980s Italy and to their exclusion from the symbolic space of self-definition.

Because both author and protagonist in *Chiamatemi Alì* are North African, and thus experience racism differently from sub-Saharan Africans,[27] Bouchane's articulation adds another layer of complexity to the issue. The discrimination experienced by himself and other North Africans at the hands of Italians is often diminished or ignored by the protagonist because the same discriminatory system places North Africans in a superior posi-tion in regard to sub-Saharan Africans (the issue of racialization of

---

[25] "Alla fine Pap mi fece notare che non avevamo mai usato la parola razzismo. Non so se mi fosse venuto per caso o se il suo racconto fosse tale da escludere il ricorso a qualcosa che sarebbe potuto sembrare un po' ideologico: sta di fatto che avevamo lasciato alla storia in sé il compito di dire tutto e di insegnarci a distinguere tra il buono e il cattivo, il generoso e il crudele, tra il vigile arrogante che sequestra la merce e il poliziotto che sa donare comprensione."

[26] "un nero a Rimini oppure a Riccione è sempre fuori posto."

[27] The issue of the racialization of sub-Saharan immigrants by North African immigrants is discussed later in this chapter.

sub-Saharan immigrants by North African immigrants is discussed further below). As Bouchane himself states several times in the text, he experienced "ignorance, rudeness, but not racism"[28] (1990, 157). Alessandro Portelli observes that racism is often justified by claiming ignorance: "Ignorance, indeed, is the most common way of explaining away racist attitudes in youth culture .... Th[e] combination of denial, paternalism, and 'innocence' in Italy makes possible things that would be unthinkable elsewhere" (2003, 34–35). This is in keeping with Audre Lorde's claim, made at the Second Sex Conference in New York in 1979, that ignorance is not and cannot be considered innocent, that the mechanism of blaming the oppressed for the ignorance of the oppressors is an age-old tool used to induce the oppressed to continue focusing on the well-being of the oppressors rather than on their own.[29]

In his collaborative autobiography *Immigrato*, Salah Methnani intersects the issue of racism toward immigrants with that of intranational racism (Fortunato and Methnani 2006). The author recounts the journey he takes through Italy, from Sicily in the south to Turin, Milan, and Padua in the north, offering unique perspectives on the relationships of continuity that exist between Southern Italy, where Methnani makes landfall, and the Global South that he embodies (despite himself) in the eyes of the West and the Global North. The text takes shape around the disillusionment of those who have looked to the West and the Global North as sites of increased opportunity and financial well-being but who have, upon arriving, found themselves facing exclusion and racism. The author's journey to different regions of the country leads him to observe the deep division that exists between the South and the North. In Sicily, there are numerous occasions when people from the area identify their own subalternity with that of migrants, complaining about the backwardness of the South, which has a high rate of youth emigration (Fortunato and Methnani 2006, 16), and recalling that the intranational migrations from the South to the

---

[28] "ignoranza, maleducazione, ma non razzismo."

[29] In this lecture, Audre Lorde harshly criticizes white feminists and the fact that they ask to be educated by Black feminists about racism: "Women of today are still being called upon to stretch across the gap of male ignorance and to educate men as to our existence and our needs. This is an old and primary tool of all oppressors to keep the oppressed occupied with the master's concerns. Now we hear that it is the task of women of Color to educate white women—in the face of tremendous resistance—as to our existence, our differences, our relative roles in our joint survival. This is a diversion of energies and a tragic repetition of racist patriarchal thought" (1984, 113).

North have been and continue to be a constant trait of the country's history (21). Although the proximity between the different Souths sometimes produces at least a partial identification between Southerners and immigrants, what is actually established, more so than solidarity, is a paternalistic attitude on the part of the former. Not surprisingly, it is an attitude expressed through colonial processes of inferiorization and infantilization. The "Mamma Bar" (47) in Naples, which derives its name from the owner's desire to be considered a mother to immigrants, is reminiscent of the character Mamma Africa in Jonas Carpignano's film *Mediterranea* (2015), who also wants to be identified as a mother to the immigrants who pick oranges in the Rosarno groves in Calabria, feeding them and teaching them good table manners, as if they were her children.

The issue of the proximity of Southern Italian and North African populations, as well as of the racialization of both by Northern Italians, is at the core of the documentary *Soltanto il mare* (*Nothing But the Sea*) by Yimer et al. (2011). The geopolitical position of the island of Lampedusa—off the coast of Sicily and closer to Africa than to Italy—is even more peripheral than that of Southern Italy. In the interviews that Dagmawi Yimer conducts with the inhabitants of the island, it becomes evident that the proximity between Lampedusans and Africans is not only geographical but also rooted in a condition of common subalternity, often reiterated in the interviewees' comments ("We are Turks too"[30] [Yimer et al. 2011]). On the other hand, as Áine O'Healy (2015) observes, of the three groups present on the island (i.e., Lampedusans, tourists, and migrants), the Lampedusans find themselves in a subaltern position with respect to the Italian tourists, whose nationality they share, but in a hegemonic position with respect to the migrants, whose sense of precariousness they share (albeit in a decidedly weaker way). One of the interviewees in the documentary expresses rage regarding the marginal position the Lampedusans occupy with respect to the North of the nation, both on a geopolitical level ("On the map we are Italians, but we are not Italians. We are Lampedusans, or rather, we are North Africans"[31] [Yimer et al. 2011])

---

[30] "Nu autri simu puru turchi" (Sicilian dialect). The term "Turks" (turchi) is here used to refer to all the dark-skinned people arriving from the other side of the Mediterranean.

[31] "Nella carta risultiamo italiani, ma noi non siamo italiani. Noi siamo lampedusani, anzi, siamo nordafricani."

and on a racial level ("They can't stand us, and can stand you even less"[32] [Yimer et al. 2011]), referring to the way in which Northern Italians consider the chromatic difference of both Southerners and immigrants to be deviant from the norm of whiteness. The same interviewee makes it clear that the rhetoric of crisis that for years has accompanied the arrival of migrants on the Lampedusan coast is functional to shifting attention away from the subaltern status of the South in general and of the island in particular.

The texts of Khouma, Bouchane, and Methnani also recall some of the more subtle mechanisms of colonial racism enacted upon non-white immigrants by Italians, such as the frequent infantilizing behavior theorized by Frantz Fanon (1952) and mentioned earlier, as well as the fact that in the "mimicry" process, as theorized by Homi Bhabha, similarity must always remain imperfect and incomplete (*"almost the same, but not quite"*[33] [Bhabha 1994, 86; italics in the original]). Significant in this sense is the linguistic behavior of the protagonists, along with that of other immigrants, who speak Italian to Italians because they know that they are expected to make themselves understood (*"the same"*), but who make an effort to do so in a faltering manner, even though they have perfect command of Italian (*"but not quite"*), because they know that excessive identification between themselves and Italians would be viewed with suspicion and consequently would lead to hostility. The migrants in Methnani's story, for example, accept the infantilization process to which they are subjected because they know that this makes their presence less threatening in the eyes of Italians (the street vendors selling lighters say "mila lire" even though they know well that in Italian 1000 is "mille," not "mila," and therefore it should be "mille lire" [Fortunato and Methnani 2006, 114]).

In the novel *Il latte è buono* (Milk is Good) by Garane Garane (2005), the main character Gashan also understands the need for his mimicry to remain always imperfect and unfinished—a fact he gleans as soon as he

---

[32] "Non ci possono vedere a noi, figuriamoci a voi." The Lampedusan man is here being interviewed by Dagmawi Yimer: by "you" in "can stand you even less" he means non-white migrants in general.

[33] This expression—*"almost the same, but not quite"*—is widely regarded as one of Bhabha's signatures. Of interest in this regard is Pap Khouma's remark about Mario Balotelli: "Balotelli is the neighbor whose face looks strange and whose perfect accent from up there [Northern Italy] is disturbing" ("Balotelli è il vicino di casa la cui faccia sembra strana e il suo perfetto accento di lassù disturba") (2010, 26).

arrives in Italy. When he lands at Rome's Fiumicino Airport from Somalia, his excessive proximity to Italianness (he presents a Somali passport written in Italian, and he speaks impeccable Italian) is immediately considered suspicious. The fear his presence elicits is that excessive similarity accompanied by spatial contiguity (such as coexistence on Italian national soil) will blur the firm borderlines that mark the physical, social, and political difference between Italians and "immigrants," and that this process will, over the long term, deprive Italians of their privileges "of blood."

The processes of racialization in contemporary Italy as a legacy of Italian colonialism are at the center of Maria Abbebù Viarengo's memoir *Andiamo a spasso?* (1990) ("Scirscir N'Demna? [Let's Go for a Stroll]," 1999), of which only excerpts were published both in Italian and in English. In this text, the author recounts how her chromatic difference was perceived in Turin at the end of the 1960s, when she and her sister, daughters of a Turinese man and an Ethiopian woman, moved to Turin at the bidding of their father. At the time, immigration to Turin (in the northern region of Piedmont) came mainly from Southern Italy, and Southerners were perceived as radically different and marginalized (Viarengo 1990).[34] The Piedmontese, who feel their regional identity more strongly than their national one, at times consider Abbebù Viarengo more similar to them than Southern Italians, since she speaks Piedmontese perfectly, having learned it from her father ("Madam, you understand the Piedmontese dialect, and you speak it as well. You are better than our Southern Italians"[35] [Viarengo 1999, 78][36]). At other times, however, the author is made to feel that her Blackness is the only characteristic noticed by Italians ("Your story doesn't matter, nor does who you are. If you are colored, you are different" [Viarengo 1999, 71]). Unsurprisingly, this produces in her a sense of alienation.

Blackness is also the pivot around which Nassera Chohra's autobiography, *Volevo diventare bianca* (I Wanted to Become White) (1993),

---

[34] For a filmic representation of this marginalization, see *Rocco e i suoi fratelli* (Visconti 1960).

[35] "Oh … madamin, ma chila a lu capis il piemunteis, e lu parla co. Chila, a le mei che i nustri napuli" (Viarengo 1999, 70). These words are uttered in Piedomontese dialect by a non-identified speaker who designates Southern Italians as "napuli" (Naples) and classifies people from the South as Neapolitans. In this process of otherization and orientalization of Southern Italians, the speaker does not acknowledge the existence of the part of Italy that lies south of Naples and implies that the South is an indistinct territory with no specific characteristics and differences.

[36] This quotation and the next one are taken from the English translation of a long passage from the memoir that was published in English but not in the Italian original.

revolves. As the title suggests, the text addresses the construction of race and color and their intersections with other categories such as gender, social class, and religion.[37] In the opening chapter, in which the author discovers her own Blackness as a child because a little girl with whom she is playing calls her "n*****"[38] (Chohra 1993, 11), the color difference is associated with colonial and ethnocentric images in which the colonized are depicted as living in a state "close to nature," thus rendering them incapable of the type of ordering and organization "civilization" requires.[39] The text maps the space constructed on the (post)colonial center/periphery dichotomy and stages a continuous dislocation that takes place among the suburbs of Marseille, the Sahara and Sahrawi community to which the protagonist's family belongs, the space of the (post)colonial metropole of Paris, and finally Italy, where the author moves as a young adult and eventually writes her memoir. When Chohra leaves the marginalized space she was inhabiting in Paris and moves to Italy, she distances herself from both her culture of origin (Algerian Sahrawi) and her adopted culture (French). This move enables her to enter a privileged social space, both on a textual and a linguistic level (through rejection of the postcolonial language, French, and adoption of Italian) and on a practical level (through her marriage to an Italian man and her life in Italy). After narrating her attempts at passing throughout the book, the author reaches a degree of social whitening that leads her to unexpectedly assert that "white and Black are nothing other than shades"[40] (133) and to describe a Senegalese street vendor ("a poor boy as Black as ebony"[41] [132]) as genetically inclined to commerce ("He must be Senegalese, I thought. They have this trade in their blood."[42] [132]).[43]

---

[37] I limit myself to a brief analysis of Blackness in Chohra's text because I have already examined it in the article "Il colore bianco" (The Color White). See Romeo (2006).

[38] "negra."

[39] On the relationship between the binaries order/disorder and white/Black in Chohra's text, see Parati (1997). For an interesting reading of Chohra's autobiography, see also Parati (2005). For a parallel between Chohra's text and African American literature, see Portelli (2000).

[40] "bianco e nero non sono altro che sfumature."

[41] "un povero ragazzo nero come l'ebano."

[42] "Deve essere senegalese, pensai. Loro questo mestiere ce l'hanno nel sangue."

[43] Chohra's racialization of the Senegalese immigrant is probably the result of a combination of the privileged social position that the author attains in Italy and the widespread racialization of sub-Saharan Africans by North Africans that I have previously noted.

Traiettorie di sguardi. E se gli "altri" foste voi? (2001) (*Reversing the Gaze: What If the Other Were You?*, 2023) by Geneviève Makaping is unique in the context of twenty-first century Italian literature and culture, not only because it overturns an outmoded approach to ethnographic observation in which African populations are constituted as the object of observation rather than as the discursive subject, but also because it signals the beginning of a theoretical reflection on structural racism and the inter-section between race and gender on the part of Black Italian intellectu-als.[44] Notably, Makaping uses her personal story—which starts in Cameroon prior to her escape from that country and then turns to the difficulties and the daily encounters with racism in France and later Italy—to reflect on the ways in which colonial racism has influenced the subjec-tivity construction process in the colonized and on the persistence of such influences in the social structures of postcolonial Europe. The uniqueness of this text lies in the fact that Makaping is among the first Black Italian female writers and intellectuals to denounce the structural nature of racism in Italian society—and in contemporary postcolonial societies more gener-ally—and to critically reflect on such issues in an intersectional perspective, while emphasizing the need to create greater awareness about the perva-siveness of racism ("Certainly the masses who make use of racist apartheid terms are not always aware of it, and so they should not be blamed either, but they should certainly be educated"[45] [Makaping 2001, 39]).

The fact that, unlike violent, blatant racism, structural racism often occurs unintentionally and unconsciously does not make it any less violent or dangerous; rather, its latent, subterranean nature makes it that much more insidious, as when the processes of racialization emphasize racial

---

[44] I decided to place the analysis of Makaping in this chapter, rather than in Chap. 3, where it would also fit, because as I state in Chap. 2, *Traiettorie di sguardi* represents a watershed in Italian postcolonial literature precisely because of the way in which it reflects on the pro-cesses of racialization in Italy. It is this text, according to the periodization that I propose, that started the third phase of Italian postcolonial literature, a stage in which counternarra-tives strongly critical of racism in colonial times and processes of racialization in the postco-lonial present appear and are developed by first- and (especially) second-generation Black Italian writers whose families originated in countries that have not necessarily had a direct colonial relationship with Italy. In this regard, see note 34 in Chap. 2. For an analysis of Makaping's text, see also Romeo (2006, 2012) and Sabelli (2010). In addition, see Elia Moutamid's documentary film about Geneviève Makaping written in collaboration with Simone Brioni, *Maka* (Moutamid 2022).

[45] "Certamente la massa che fa uso di termini razzisti dell'apartheid non sempre ne è cons-apevole, e quindi non va neanche colpevolizzata, ma sicuramente va educata."

hierarchies by implicitly marking spaces with the color of normative bodies. All this has deep and lasting repercussions at the psychological level, often causing, as Fanon (1952) argues, formerly colonized subjects to internalize a sense of inferiority and a desire to resemble their colonizers. In Black subjects, this produces mechanisms of self-hatred and a rejection of their Blackness ("Among us, to say that a person was beautiful, rich, good, well-educated and the best that could be said about him, it was enough to say that he was white .... If one of us emigrated and made even a small fortune, we would say: 'c'est notre blanc,' he's our white man."[46] [Makaping 2001, 8]). Makaping states that in Cameroon shades of color are deeply meaningful: "For the girls whose parents were asked for their hand in marriage, the lighter the color of their complexion, the higher their price as brides"[47] (8). Understanding that the discourse on racialization cannot be limited to the binary white/Black, Makaping employs a strategy to counteract the negativity attributed to Blackness not through reversal but through deconstruction and resignification of commonly used expressions such as "man of color" and "extracommunitarian"[48] (31). This process is based on the repositioning of colonized subjects and on their self-assertion ("I want to be the one to say what I sould be called"[49] [31]), so that they can rename and redefine themselves ("I am not a 'woman of color.' I am a 'Negra.'"[50] [38]). Articulating her own voice from the margin—the reference is to *Elogio del margine* (In Praise of the Margin) by bell hooks (1998)[51]—Makaping also wonders which language she can use to articulate and narrate counterstories that produce oppositional imaginaries with respect to the colonial one. In this, she echoes Ngũgĩ Wa Thiong'o (1986), who contends that the process of decolonizing imaginaries imposes the abandonment of the colonizers' language and the return of local languages.

In constructing her individual subjectivity and reclaiming her own voice, Makaping interrogates the power white women have exerted over

---

[46] "Fra di noi, per dire che una persona era bella, ricca, buona, ben educata e quanto di meglio si potesse affermare su di lei, bastava dire che era un bianco .... Se uno di noi emigrava e faceva fortuna anche minima, dicevamo: 'c'est notre blanc', è il nostro bianco."

[47] "per le ragazze ai cui genitori si andava a chieder la mano, più il colore della carnagione era chiara [sic], più saliva il loro prezzo come spose."

[48] "uomo di colore" and "extracomunitario."

[49] "Voglio essere io a dire come mi chiamo."

[50] "Io non sono una 'donna di colore.' Sono una Negra."

[51] This publication collects some of bell hooks's essays translated into Italian.

Black women from the time of colonialism and slavery to the postcolonial present, seriously questioning the concept of "panfeminism" (2001, 54). The methodological approach adopted by Makaping is intersectional, at a time when such methodology was almost non-existent in Italy. Starting from race, color, and gender, the author gradually intersects other categories, including that of citizenship, and she structures her own subjectivity through processes of identification and disidentification:

> And then the we: we extracommunitarians—we extracommunitarian women—we Africans—we sub-Saharan Africans—we Negroes—we Negro women—we Cameroonians and we Cameroonian women, until arriving at we Bamileke—we Bamileke women and finally me, an immigrant Bamileke woman, who is all these women together and who has formally renounced her citizenship of origin to assume Italian citizenship.[52] (2001, 49)

The process of constructing one's individual subjectivity is complex and requires constant negotiation at both the personal and social levels since, as Makaping highlights, subjects take shape at the intersection of different categories of oppression that act simultaneously.

In the second part of the text, Makaping presents an ethnographic study conducted through participant observation. Starting from a series of personal experiences she uses as case studies, she identifies and denounces what she calls "little acts of everyday racism"[53] (Makaping 2001, 49). The intention here is to overturn the ethnocentric perspective of the (ex-)colonizers and to show how racism is pervasive in Italian society—even the racism of those who consider themselves immune to it. Makaping uses the methodology adopted in 1984 by Philomena Essed (1990),[54] which emphasizes the importance of analyzing cultural, institutional, and individual racism, but also of identifying another type of racism, what she calls "everyday racism," that is, the more latent structural racism that is not usually identified as such by white researchers (who have historically

---

[52] "E poi il noi: noi extracomunitari—noi extracomunitari donne—noi africani—noi africani sub-sahariani—noi negri—noi donne negre—noi camerunesi e noi camerunesi donne, fino ad arrivare a noi Bamiléké—a noi donne Bamiléké ed infine a me, donna bamiléké immigrata, che è tutte queste donne insieme e che ha formalmente rinunciato alla cittadinanza di origine per assumere quella italiana."

[53] "piccoli atti di razzismo quotidiano."

[54] Essed's text was published in Dutch in 1984. Part of it was later reworked into *Understanding Everyday Racism* (Essed 1991).

constituted and still constitute the majority of researchers) and therefore is not examined. In her research, Essed interviews women from Suriname in the Netherlands and African American women in the United States, while Makaping starts from her own personal experience. Such a methodology, rooted in her personal observation as a Black woman, creates a rupture with more traditional and historically racialized research practices which only consider legitimate the observations of white researchers. The kind of research that scholars such as Essed and Makaping conduct situates Black women in the position of subjects who are producers of epistemologies—a role from which they have, historically, been rigorously excluded—starting from their personal experiences and their theorizing on the basis of those experiences. By denouncing acts of daily racism, the two scholars develop and enact a survival strategy for non-white women in contexts where white privilege is as prevalent as it is invisible. The knowledge that these women produce constitutes a public archive which is necessary for the formation and consolidation of Black subjectivities that, starting from their individual stories of opposition, reshape the official history by articulating new perspectives.[55]

The issue of the intersection between Blackness and Italianness—and the process of structuring subjectivities that such a combination proposes—is also explicitly addressed by Pap Khouma in the article "Io, nero italiano e la mia vita ad ostacoli" (Me, Black Italian and My Obstacle Life), which appeared in *la Repubblica* at the end of 2009. There, the author lists a series of episodes in which his Blackness is considered incompatible with his Italian citizenship, even when that citizenship is sanctioned by identity documents issued by the Italian state. Recalling that W. E. B. DuBois starts *The Souls of Black Folk* with an essay in which he wonders whether it is possible to be both Black and American, Alessandro Portelli (2010) notes that, at the beginning of the twenty-first century in Italy, it is necessary to wonder whether it is possible to be both Black and Italian. This is what Pap Khouma questions in his book *Noi italiani neri. Storie di ordinario razzismo* (We Black Italians: Stories of Ordinary Racism) (2010), observing the generalized resistance to including in the body of the nation those who have characteristics that do not conform to the Italian

---

[55] On Black women's need for personal narratives as a survival strategy, their oppositional role with respect to dominant narratives, and the importance of personal archives, see Eggers (2005) and Kilomba (2008), who theorize race and Blackness in the German social and cultural context.

chromatic norm. In this text, in which Khouma examines systematically minimized episodes of daily racism and analyzes topics ranging from race relations on soccer fields to the contribution of Black soldiers during the Second World War, there is a strong denunciation of state racism as it is articulated through discriminatory legislation that acts to institutionalize fear. Khouma states:

> But if true integration requires a shift in consciousness, it is also true that politics can give a push in this direction, can indicate a route, in some way educate, if I may use the term. It is serious, then, that the threats for Italians who are different come from people with institutional positions who have powerful tools to exacerbate the frustration of people already frightened by the social changes generated by the presence of millions of immigrants who have arrived over a few years, from every part of the world.[56] (2010, 155)

What the institutions are defending (in the above excerpt) is the principle underlying the "racial state" (Goldberg 2002), that is, the presumed racial homogeneity of the population upon which the modern nation state is predicated. However, in the context of a postcolonial contemporaneity characterized by transnational migrations, it becomes necessary to reconfigure the very concept of nation and of citizenship based on shared biological characteristics in order to conceive of national formulations derived from mobility and heterogeneity.

Cheick Tidiane Gaye's *Prendi quello che vuoi ma lasciami la mia pelle nera* (Take What You Want But Leave Me My Black Skin) (2013) is a reflection—written in the form of a letter to a friend—on the way in which the racial difference of migrants is perceived in Italy. The author denounces the racial harassments that he and other immigrants from Africa are forced to endure, at the same time reminding Italians that their history has been characterized by intranational racism and by mass emigrations.

The narratives analyzed so far are all by migrant authors who examine the way in which (their) Blackness is and has been perceived in Italy, denounce acts of individual and state racism, and highlight the processes

---

[56] "Ma se la vera integrazione richiede un mutamento delle coscienze, è anche vero che la politica può dare una spinta in tal senso, può indicare una rotta, in qualche modo educare, se posso usare il termine. È grave allora che le minacce per gli italiani diversi vengano da persone con incarichi istituzionali e che dispongono di strumenti potenti per inasprire la frustrazione di gente già di per sé spaventata dai cambiamenti sociali generati dalla presenza di milioni di immigrati arrivati in pochi anni, da ogni parte del mondo."

of racialization taking place in Italian society in regard to migrants. In the following sections, the analysis shifts to address the cultural work of so-called "second generations." These authors, regardless of whether they have or do not have Italian citizenship, consider themselves Italian by virtue of the fact that they were born and/or grew up in Italy and share language, culture, education, and everyday practices with other Italians. Despite this, they still must contend with the fact that the children of migration are often considered non-Italian because of their distance from the national chromatic norm and are thus kept at the margins of society, a process institutionalized in the attribution of citizenship in Italy, for instance, which still privileges the right of blood (*ius sanguinis*). In these writers' cultural productions, the categories of race, Blackness, and gender intersect with that of citizenship to represent a country that is becoming increasingly plural, diversified, and heterogeneous.

4.3 Different Shades of Italianness: Blackness and Citizenship in the Narratives of Second-Generation Authors

4.3.1 Literature

The year 2017 saw an extraordinary mobilization in support of reforming the citizenship law in Italy. Associations such as L'Italia sono anch'io (I Am Italy Too), Rete G2 (G2 [Second generation] Network), and Italiani senza cittadinanza (Italians Without Citizenship) joined forces with university professors and associations of teachers from schools of all types and levels to ensure that the process for the final approval of the law would be completed in the Senate following approval in the Chamber of Deputies on October 13, 2015.[57] The new law, based on the principle of moderated *ius soli*, that is, *ius soli* (the acquisition of citizenship on the basis of one's country of birth) combined with *ius culturae* (the acquisition of

---

[57] Currently, the acquisition of Italian citizenship is regulated by Law No. 91, enacted on February 5, 1992. The fact that the principal mechanism whereby Italian citizenship is acquired is still based on the principle of *ius sanguinis*, or blood lineage, has the paradoxical effect of making it easier for the children of emigrants (who might have no knowledge of Italy, its language, or its culture) to acquire citizenship than it is for the children of immigrants who (were born and) live in Italy. Regarding the process of acquiring Italian citizenship, see Farnesina and Ministero degli Affari Esteri e della Cooperazione Internazionale (2021).

citizenship on the basis of one's country of education), would have facilitated the acquisition of citizenship for second generations by replacing the current law, which is based mainly on the principle of *ius sanguinis* (the acquisition of citizenship on the basis of biological descent).[58]

The fact that this bill had to undergo such an arduous approval process—and that, ultimately, it was not presented for debate in the Senate before the end of the parliamentary term and was therefore never adopted—highlights that granting citizenship to the children of immigrants is still a highly controversial issue in Italy that meets with strong resistance. Such resistance escalates due to the fact that the issue of the citizenship law is often wielded by political parties of the right and extreme right, such as the Lega, Fratelli d'Italia, and Forza Italia, and by the newspapers associated with them to stoke fears about the danger of migrant "invasion" and the "proliferation of Islamic terrorism."[59] Such propaganda fuels a growing sense of insecurity and precariousness in the weakest segments of the Italian population and in those most affected by economic crises, thus creating social division.

The government that took office in March 2018, presided over by Giuseppe Conte and supported by a coalition composed of a majority of the Lega and Movimento 5 Stelle parties, worked to reinforce those divisions, introducing new restrictive measures for acquiring Italian citizenship through Decree Law No. 113/2018 (the infamous security laws "Decreti sicurezza"), which also introduced the possibility of revoking citizenship in the event of a conviction for some serious crimes (although not for citizens of "Italian blood"). This produced an extremely racist and xenophobic climate in which Black and non-white people in Italy felt

---

[58] The principle of *ius soli temperato* (here translated as "moderated *ius soli*") as it was formulated in the proposed law, still imposes certain conditions on the granting of citizenship to second generations (i.e., at least one parent must have a residence permit, and citizenship is not acquired automatically but must be requested), unlike the principle of *ius soli*, which establishes that anyone born in a given country automatically acquires citizenship at birth (as in the United States, for example). *Ius culturae* extends the right to apply for Italian citizenship to children who arrived in Italy before their twelfth birthday and who have attended the Italian school system for at least five consecutive years. Even taking these requirements into consideration, the principle of acquiring Italian citizenship under the new law would have combined a sense of geographical and cultural belonging absent from the current law. For the full text of the law, see Cittadinanza italiana (2021).

[59] In this regard see, among others, De Lorenzo (2017).

deeply threatened.[60] The COVID-19 pandemic, which began in March 2020, deflected attention away from the necessity of approving a new citizenship law. Such process, however, cannot be postponed any longer because the future of Italian society depends on it. If people born and raised in Italy continue to be excluded from the national body, social conflicts will only grow more frequent and more troubled.

The issues of citizenship and of the intersection between Blackness and Italianness are very much present in the cultural production of second generations in Italy. Because of this, their contributions mark a significant and innovative shift, promoting as they do the spread of postnational imaginaries, aesthetic practices, and identities that not only radically challenge the idea of national culture as it has been conceived until very recently but also enact the profound changes that have taken place and that take place daily in contemporary Italian society as a result of transnational global migrations. Second-generation authors fill the category of "Italianness" with new meanings, both in terms of individual and collective identities and in terms of a cultural production that is reflective of those identities; they rewrite the history of Italian colonialism; they reconnect the widespread racism of contemporary Italy to Italian colonial history; they represent—in literature, music, film, series, news media, social media—the children of immigrants and the way in which they are rooted in Italian soil; they question the basis upon which Italian citizenship is granted; they mobilize to support reforming the citizenship law; and—most importantly—they are critical not only of their culture of destination but also of their culture of origin, from which, in certain ways, they have distanced themselves.

As has been noted elsewhere, the cultural production of second generations in Italy started to develop at the beginning of the twenty-first century. One notable exception is Jadelin Mabiala Gangbo, a second-generation writer of Congolese origin who began his career when second generations were barely visible and the debate about their presence was limited to

[60] The climate was similar in the months preceding the elections of March 4, 2018. During that election campaign, Matteo Salvini, leader of the Lega, inflamed the emotions of Italians with extremely xenophobic and racist messages. On February 3, 2018, in Macerata, the far-right militant Luca Traini shot and wounded Jennifer Otioto, Gideon Azeke, Mahamadou Toure, Wilson Kofi, Festus Omagbon, and Omar Fadera, six sub-Saharan immigrants. On March 5, 2018, in Florence, Roberto Pirrone left his home with suicidal intentions but then turned his gun and fired six shots at Idy Diene, a Senegalese street vendor who had lived in Italy for more than 20 years. Both these crimes were racially motivated.

critical inquiry of a sociological nature. In his writing, particularly in the more autobiographical narratives, the social exclusion of Black Italians and the violence against them intersects with more intimate reflections. The type of narrative that Gangbo produces is unique for the time, both in the broader context of Italian literature and in the narrower context of the postcolonial literature that was developing through the work of migrant writers, whose relationship with the Italian language, culture, and society is very different from his. Gangbo's first novel, *Verso la notte bakonga* (Toward the Bakonga Night) (1999), for instance, includes an early scene in which an entire public school elementary class—and by extension the whole Italian educational system—is unable to decode the protagonist's Black body and even less to welcome him into the school community he has just joined:

> "Children, this is your new school mate; she will take part in your activities for the rest of the year. She comes from Africa; do you know Africa?" The children nodded enthusiastically. "Her name is Mirka."
>
> "No, his name is Mika; he's a boy," chimed in Giuliano, shyly in the doorway. The principal laughed. "We'll have to get used to it." The teacher laughed too. So did the children.
>
> I didn't like them at all.
>
> None of them was Black like me.[61] (Gangbo 1999, 10)

If Mika's Black child's body is illegible, as he grows up it becomes at once hypervisible (his diversity always draws curious and/or hostile looks, and at times he is even the target of racist violence) and socially invisible, as was also the case with his brother Beriù, who had died in prison without any mention of the incident being made in the media. Not surprisingly, this leads Mika to internalize his somatic difference as a negative characteristic and, as a result, to implement strategies of invisibility: he often stays confined in his apartment and, when he shows himself to the world, he does

---

[61] "'Bambini, questa è la vostra nuova compagna, parteciperà alle vostre attività per il resto dell'anno. Viene dall'Africa, conoscete l'Africa?' I bambini annuirono entusiasti. 'Si chiama Mirka.'

'No, si chiama Mika, è un maschio' intervenne Giuliano sottile sulla soglia. La responsabile rise: 'Ci dovremo abituare.' Rise anche la maestra. Anche i bimbi.

Non mi piacevano affatto.

Nessuno di loro era nero come me."

so at great speed, tearing along on his skateboard, so that the eyes of strangers do not have time to decode the image they see. Gangbo's Bildungsroman, in which the protagonist becomes an adult *and* a writer, is centered on how this second-generation boy of the African diaspora constructs his own subjectivity. Mika knows that society considers him too Black to be assimilable to Italianness; at the same time, his strong local identity ensures that he is not considered African either ("'But, you're not a real Negro ...'—she seemed disappointed—"... In fact, you seem like a perfect Bolognese to me."[62] [Gangbo 1999, 42]).

In Gangbo's most recent novel, *Due volte* (Two Times) (2009), the social exclusion experienced by the twin protagonists, Daniel (the narrator) and David, is tied not only to their somatic difference but also to the fact that they live outside the core unit of Italian society—the family—and grow up in an institution with other children and adults who, for various reasons, live at the margins of society.[63] The unassimilability of Black bodies into the Italian national identity is presented at the very beginning of the novel through the synecdochical reference to hair, a central issue for Africans of the diaspora. The nuns at the institution want to cut off the two boys' dreadlocks because, they say, they give them a feminine appearance (as they did Mika in *Verso la notte bakonga*, who is in fact mistaken for a girl). For Daniel and David, however, their dreadlocks represent their only remaining connection to their father's Rastafarian community. Although the two boys are constantly subjected to racial abuse at the institution ("they call me Kunta Kinte or Filthy Slave, or they say, Dirty n*****, get to work!"[64] [Gangbo 2009, 8]),[65] they show a deep attachment to their Blackness, which they consider a distinctive trait that upholds their connection to their father, to his teachings, to Africa, and to all other Rastafarians the world over. Moreover, they are convinced that their Blackness will one day enable them to reach a state of enlightenment and

---

[62] "Be', non sei un vero negro ..." sembrò delusa "... Anzi mi sembri un perfetto bolognese."

[63] For a compelling reading of this novel and, more generally, of Jadelin Mabiala Gangbo's literary production, see Pezzarossa (2014).

[64] "a me mi chiamano Kunta Kinte o Lurido Schiavo, o dicono, Sporco n****, lavora!"

[65] Kunta Kinte is the protagonist of the television mini-series *Roots*, based on Alex Haley's novel, which in 1978 brought the history of American slavery into the homes of Italians for the first time. In her memoir *La mia casa è dove sono*, Igiaba Scego (2010) also states she was called "Kunta Kinte" at school (see Sect. 4.4 and note 134 in this chapter).

higher consciousness. For both boys, the activation of their "Black heart" symbolizes reaching a nearly metaphysical state. Daniel explains to his brother what has happened to him:

> Did it really get activated?
> At school.
> That's good news. So what did it feel like?
> You feel a beating in a place you don't know.
> Where?
> I don't know.
> In the chest?
> It's indecipherable. But it's as if at a certain point you rest and someone helps you to say in a perfect way the things you would like to say. You don't struggle at all. You use the right words, everything comes out as clean as can be, and afterward you too feel clean, even those who are listening to you look at you cleanly.[66] (Gangbo 2009, 181)

The idea that this metaphysical state is characterized by "cleanliness" is especially significant in a context in which processes of racialization are being enacted. As Cristina Lombardi-Diop argues, the issue of hygiene in the Fascist colonial era is functional to the construction of the Italian whiteness associated with it (as opposed to the Blackness associated with uncleanliness). Such associations are still present in the collective Italian imaginary. When, after the Second World War, race became unmentionable, these associations were conveyed through advertising campaigns for skin care products and laundry detergent (see Lombardi-Diop 2012a, b,

---

[66] "Ti si è attivato veramente?
A scuola.
È una bella notizia.
E cosa hai provato?
Senti un battito in un punto che non conosci.
Dove?
Non lo so.
Nel petto?
È indecifrabile. Però è come se a un certo punto tu ti riposi e qualcuno ti aiuta a dire in modo perfetto le cose che vorresti dire. Non fai nessuna fatica. Usi le parole giuste, tutto ti esce pulito come non mai, e dopo anche tu ti senti pulito, anche quelli che ti ascoltano ti guardano puliti."

2014).[67] Daniel's words seem to suggest that the boys' Blackness can become socially acceptable only if it rises to a higher state (i.e., through activation of the Black heart) associated with cleanliness (keyed here to whiteness).

The metaphysical quest the two young boys set out on is also part of a complex process of growth that involves the construction of their subjectivities. As part of this process, they must negotiate a whole host of issues: their father's abandoning them; Blackness in a society constructed as homogeneously white; the sometimes difficult, sometimes violent, sometimes tender relationships with the other youths and children in the institution; and the complicated relationships with the adult world, including the nuns, the teachers at school, the adults in the institution, other children's families, and the family that wants to adopt them. The point of view of an 11-year-old boy bestows upon the narrative an innocent and ingenuous gaze. The future that the two protagonists dream about for themselves is as illogical as it is romantic—Daniel dreams of becoming a "leaf tamer"[68]; David, together with the Camorrista Pasquale, wants to change the world through poetry.[69] The present they are living is idealized to a degree, featuring as it does intense emotion and first loves, but it is also starkly realistic, marred by the violence that some of the people around them have suffered—either within their families or, more broadly, within the societies of origin—a violence they tend to reenact by directing it toward the weakest in the institution.[70] Somatic difference in this novel is interwoven with many other differences and is combined with a deep psychological investigation, creating a narrative that is as disenchanted as it is innocent, a fact that emphasizes how difficult growing up is for children

---

[67] On the use of hygiene policies to also racialize the Roma, Sinti, and Caminanti peoples, and on the fact that their presumed lack of cleanliness is considered a biological threat to the integrity of the Italian national body, see Clough Marinaro (2014).

[68] "domatore di foglie." No explanation is offered in the text in reference to this expression. I imagine that the boy is referring to the city administration workers who use leaf blowers to gather fallen leaves for removal.

[69] David and Pasquale want to wage "the war of words" ("la guerra di parole") (Gangbo 2009, 159) by writing poems on the walls, thus causing people who walk by them to reflect.

[70] An analysis of Gangbo's short story "Com'è se giù vuol dire ko?" (What If Down Means KO?) (2005) is included in the next chapter because, although the text focuses on the ways in which Blackness is socially constructed, paying particular attention to the reactions it provokes from institutions, the story also proposes an interesting remapping of urban spaces.

who occupy marginal social spaces—which, in turn, is a reminder about what is at stake whenever pathways to citizenship are up for debate.

As is evident from the title, Italian citizenship is the focus of Ingy Mubiayi's short story "Documenti, prego" (Documents, Please) (2005b), included in the collection *Pecore nere* (Black Sheep) (Capitani and Coen 2005). In this story, the author depicts the precariousness of the characters' process of identity construction by creating a series of binary oppositions that are then constantly deconstructed. Mubiayi also uses irony to mock Italians who identify with the high culture of their country and are convinced that such identification cannot be shared by those whose roots are not planted deeply in that culture. The story opens with:

> "We need to help Abdel Hamid prepare the documents," an imperious voice rises from the kitchen …. At that moment I don't grasp the profound meaning of that sentence, also because I'm concentrating on the theme song of the legendary Chief Inspector Derrick: the most inhumane television series that we have ever watched. We are completely spellbound by that way of communicating the death of a family member to the relatives: face to face at less than two centimeters apart, reaction of the relatives: none. When they are particularly close, such as father and son, "Ah, please leave me alone; this is an uncontainable pain for me" is more than sufficient. Never a tear.[71] (Mubiayi 2005b, 97)

The issue of citizenship is introduced in the incipit of the story and developed through a constant repositioning that destabilizes the Italian/immigrant binary. Mubiayi (2005b) plays with Italian readers and induces ambivalence in them by creating narrative situations in which they feel by turns distant from and complicit with the immigrant protagonists. The title ("Documents, please") and the opening line of dialogue ("We need to help Abdel Hamid prepare the documents" [Mubiayi 2005b, 97]) inscribe from the very beginning the presence of migrants in the Italian legal system, suggesting an irreconcilable distance

---

[71] "'Dobbiamo aiutare Abdel Hamid a preparare i documenti,' si leva imperiosa una voce dai fornelli […]. Lì per lì non colgo il senso profondo di quella frase, anche perché sono concentrata sulla sigla del mitico Ispettore Capo Derrick: la serie televisiva più inumana che abbiamo mai seguito. Ci ha completamente stregati quel modo di comunicare ai familiari la morte di un congiunto: faccia a faccia a meno di due centimetri, reazione dei parenti nulla. Quando sono particolarmente prossimi, tipo padre e figlio, è più che sufficiente un 'Ah, vi prego di lasciarmi solo, è una pena incontenibile per me.' Mai una lacrima."

between Italian readers and the protagonist and narrator, who is Egyptian on her mother's side and from an unspecified African country on her father's, together with her family. The element of otherness is introduced through the Arab name of the person who needs assistance—Abdel Hamid—and the mention of needing to prepare citizenship application documents. The Italian/immigrant binary, however, is immediately destabilized a few sentences later, when the author creates a sense of "Mediterranean" complicity by introducing the most common stereotypes about Germany—the presumed coldness of the people, their lack of humanity, and, later in the text, the grayness of the sky. By creating ambivalence, Mubiayi encourages readers not to let themselves be seduced by the simplistic Italian/immigrant binary, suggesting instead that there is need for a continuous repositioning that, even if it causes a sense of disorientation, induces readers to consider their own positionality as changeable and temporary.

The alliance between immigrants and natives, however, is also only ever temporary. Immediately after this relationship is established, in fact, the protagonist describes the sense of physical discomfort that pervades her at the mere thought of having to once again undertake the lengthy process of applying for citizenship. Italian society is here identified with the world of bureaucracy—in the story, comparable to Dante Alighieri's *Inferno*—in which the individual identity of migrants is erased, only to be replaced by a collective one characterized by undesirability. This, too, though, is almost immediately overturned when Italian culture reappears—this time in one of its most powerful and popular incarnations, pasta—reestablishing an alliance, however brief, between Italians and migrants. It is important to note in this context that "high" culture and the "glorious" Italian past are treated with a certain detachment, even with evident irony. The author refers to Dante, regarded as the father of the Italian language, comparing her own voyage and that of her family's to obtain Italian citizenship with the one that Dante takes in the afterlife (on the prefecture door the narrator has written the words "Abandon all hope ye who enter here") (Mubiayi 2005b, 107). While on the one hand Dante's presence emphasizes the cultural hierarchy separating Italians from immigrants, on the other it suggests that the Italian language is synonymous with the uninspired, unsophisticated language of bureaucracy. The story concludes with another pointed mockery of Italy's past when the narrator describes the expression depicted on her brother's face as "unworthy of a poet, a saint, or a navigator"[72] (107).[73] Although the members of this family have legally become Italian citizens, the author ironically notes that their otherness is and will remain inscribed on their faces: citizenship will grant them the opportunity to become "new Italians" but they will never be able to gain access to the past that makes Italy one of the pillars of Western culture and civilization. Mubiayi, though, seems to be suggesting, through the use of irony particularly, that the presumed purity and homogeneity of Italian identity is constantly being challenged by subjects who redefine the somatic, chromatic, cultural, and linguistic norm of Italianness, and that this norm is progressively moving toward a plurality in which being directly connected to the nation's past will be only *one* of the ways of being Italian.

In Mubiayi's short story "Concorso" (Competition) (2005a), also included in the anthology *Pecore nere*, the protagonist Hayat—who is Italian, Black, and Muslim—questions her chances of winning a competition for employment in the police force, knowing that, in Italy, her somatic, cultural, and religious characteristics are more frequently associated with those who break the law than with those who uphold it. Yet, at the end of the story, Hayat sends her application, which suggests the possibility of a shift taking place in the not too distant future within the collective imaginary of Italian institutions and, by way of those institutions, in that of the Italian population.

Gabriella Kuruvilla's two short stories included in *Pecore nere* (2005a, b) both examine in racial and postcolonial terms the author's problematic relationship with her own past, which she has inherited from her father. In "Ruben" (2005b) ("Ruben" 2018), Kuruvilla narrates the first meeting between her parents:

> My mother was white, Italian, with brown hair and green eyes. My father was Black, Indian, with black hair and black eyes. Monochrome. The only white thing about him were some spots on his face, around his chin—

---

[72] "indegna di un poeta, di un santo o di un navigatore."

[73] These words are instantly recognizable within the context of popular Italian culture, even though they have mostly lost their connection to the context in which they were first pronounced. Benito Mussolini referred to Italians as a population "of poets, artists, heroes, saints, thinkers, scientists, navigators, and transmigrants" ("di poeti, di artisti, di eroi, di santi, di pensatori, di scienziati, di navigatori, di trasmigratori") in his famous speech of October 2, 1935, in which he announced the invasion of Ethiopia (see Rochat 1973). These words are carved on the four facades of the Palazzo della Civiltà Italiana in Rome's EUR neighborhood. See also the reflection on symbols of Fascism in Sect. 5.2.

vitiligo, due to stress. His encounter with the West had stamped small white spots on his skin. An unusual form of integration.[74] (2018, 438–39)

Her father's stress-induced vitiligo reminds the reader of the mysterious and sudden skin whitening of Saleem Sinai, the protagonist of Salman Rushdie's novel *Midnight's Children* (1980), in the aftermath of India's independence. This whitening, both for Sinai and for Kuruvilla's father, functions as a metaphor for their desire to resemble and to blend in with the hegemonic subjects, to wear a white mask in order to hide one's Black (or Brown) skin.[75] Through this process of mimicry, Kuruvilla's father symbolically seeks invisibility, adherence to a somatic norm that his body cannot guarantee him, a conformity that protects him from the racial discrimination that he has always had to face in Italy.

If familiarity with the culture of destination allows second-generation authors an ironic detachment—as in the case of Mubiayi's relationship to Italian "high" culture—irony is also often used by second-generation authors to articulate a criticism from within their own cultures of origin. In the continuous deconstruction of binaries that Mubiayi operates in "Documenti, prego," for example, the author refuses to consider Italians as exclusively racist and immigrants as exclusively racialized. The protagonist and narrator of that story notes the racism of which immigrants are victims, while at the same time denouncing with irony the racism of which they are perpetrators:

We were ... clandestine immigrants! But no one used this term at the time and no one spoke of extracommunitarians either. People used the term n*****s, just like that. And my mother never put up with it. When she insulted us she would say "You're n*****s just like your father." A worse

---

[74] "Lei bianca, italiana, capelli castani e occhi verdi. Lui nero, indiano, capelli e occhi neri. Monocromo. Di bianco aveva solo delle macchie sul viso, intorno al mento. Vitiligine. Da stress. L'incontro con l'Occidente aveva impresso sulla sua pelle piccole chiazze chiare. Una strana forma di integrazione." (Kuruvilla 2005b, 84)

[75] See Fanon (1952). As Grada Kilomba (2008, 16–23) points out, masking not only serves as a metaphor for the desire on the part of the colonized to have a different skin color, it was also a practical tool (albeit in the form of a different kind of mask) used on sugarcane and cocoa plantations to prevent African slaves from eating what they harvested. Such masks, of which Kilomba reproduces a photo, consisted of a bit that was placed within the mouth between the tongue and the jaw and secured behind the head with strings. The practical effect that this mask produced was the impossibility of speaking; it thus becomes a metaphor also for the reduction to silence of the slaves on the plantation.

insult didn't exist. Considering that my father had abandoned us to make
the good life of a refugee in France ... My mother was Arab and there was
no way, map in hand, to make her accept that Egypt is in Africa, so she too
is African, like the n*****s. At that point, she would invoke racial differences to support her thinking and on that I had fewer arguments.[76] (Mubiayi
2005b, 110)

The author's deconstruction here of both the white/Black and racist/
racialized binaries effectively criticizes not only the society of destination
but also the society of origin.

In Ubax Cristina Ali Farah's novel *Il comandante del fiume* (2014)
(*The Commander of the River* 2023), the diasporic Somali community in
London has retained only a superficial attachment to their traditions,
underneath which hides the second generations' desire to integrate into
British society and erase their differences from the British youth. To
eliminate such differences, however, these young men must contravene
the rules dictated by their families of origin. The cousins of the protagonist, Yabar, who has just arrived in London from Rome, first go to the
mosque to pray in order to please their parents and be accepted by the
community, then lay down their tunics, skullcaps, and prayer beads and
let loose in nightclubs, drinking alcohol (which they conceal in Coca
Cola paper cups), only to solemnly swear to their parents, once they have
returned home, that they behaved like good Muslims while out (see Ali
Farah 2014).

The Indian parents of 16-year-old Anandita, the narrator of the short
story "Curry di pollo" ("Chicken Curry") by Laila Wadia (2005a), are
depicted in a caricatural way as nostalgically attached to the past, to the
village from which they come, to the culinary habits of their country of
origin, and to its aesthetic canons (e.g., coconut oil to make hair shiny, no
tattoos, no piercings). In Wadia's short story "Karnevale" (2005b),

---

[76] "noi eravamo ... clandestini! Ma allora non si usava questo termine e non si parlava nem-
meno di extracomunitari. Si utilizzava il termine negri, tout court. E mia madre questa non
l'ha mai mandata giù. Lei quando ci insultava ci diceva 'Siete proprio dei negri come vostro
padre.' Peggiore insulto non esisteva. Visto che mio padre ci aveva abbandonati per fare la
bella vita di rifugiato in Francia. ... Mia madre lei era araba e non c'era verso, cartina alla
mano, di farle accettare che l'Egitto è in Africa quindi anche lei è africana, come i negri.
Allora invocava le differenze razziali a sostegno del suo pensiero e su quello avevo meno
argomenti."

attachment to tradition is staged through little rituals—such as the purchase of precooked Indian dishes at the supermarket—which make clear how weak this attachment has become, if it even exists at all. Like the way her neighbors' apartment looks in the short story "Colf" (Housekeeper)—eliciting a sense from the narrator that she is "in a Bombay souvenir store, of the most blatantly touristic kind"[77] (Kuruvilla 2008, 67)—the presence of Indian products in Italian supermarket chains induces reflections on multiculturalism. On its surface, that Indian products are sold in Italian stores appears to promote the idea of the peaceful coexistence and cohabitation of different cultures in a given society; in point of fact, though, this actually tends—as these two authors point out—to exoticize sociocultural differences and transform them into consumer goods while not questioning the ability (or the lack thereof) to renegotiate power relations among the various cultures that coexist in a given social context.

While Italy is becoming an increasingly diversified country, the subject of interracial couples is appearing more and more frequently in the literature of the second generations, as well as in films by Italian directors and in television series aired in prime time on national networks.[78] This subject is at the center of the collection of stories entitled *Amori bicolori* (Bicolor Love) (Capitani and Coen 2008). In the short stories "Identità" (Identity) (2008) by Igiaba Scego and "Nascita" (Birth) (2008) by Ingy Mubiayi, the authors highlight the symbolic weight that mixed marriages carry in Italy, often depicted as unions between two civilizations, or two worlds, rather than simply between two individuals. Added to this is the fact that the position of Black women as partners or wives of white men seems to require constant legitimization. The protagonist of "Identità," Fatou, who is Somali Italian, finds herself imprisoned between the exoticizing images Italian media has constructed of her, the colonial past—which one day appears in the apartment she shares with her (white Italian) partner in the form of a photograph of a madam with bare breasts[79]—and the traditional roles for Somali women invoked by her sister Nura.[80] Through the

---

[77] "in un negozio di souvenir di Bombay, di quelli più smaccatamente turistici."

[78] On representations of interracial couples in Italian cinema, see in particular O'Healy (2012, 2014) and Caponetto (2012, 2013, 2014). On interracial couples in recent TV series broadcast on Rai 1, see Sect. 4.3.2 on film and television series.

[79] For an explanation of the institution of "madamato," see note 17 in Chap. 3.

[80] For an analysis of this story, see Chap. 3.

reference to the "sheep poster"[81] (Scego 2008, 31)[82]—a poster that was part of a campaign launched in 2007 in Switzerland by the right-wing party Schweizerische Volkspartei (SVP), which gave rise to a very controversial debate on race and racism—Scego prompts a reflection on contemporary racism as part of the colonial legacy that unites Italy with other European countries (including those that did not have a colonial history) that share with Italy a postcolonial condition.[83]

In Ingy Mubiayi's story "Nascita" (2008), which revolves around the absence of the writer/narrator's father, the birth of a new generation makes relationships with the past urgent and the awareness of one's skin color ever present (just as with Kuruvilla's "Ruben" [2005b] ["Ruben" 2018]). The awareness of being different is increasingly marked with the arrival of the next generation, and with it, for Black women, the fear of being rejected once their children internalize the notion they encounter daily that the color difference they have inherited from one or both of their parents confers no socially or culturally positive value.[84]

Igiaba Scego (2009) analyzed the subject of Italian Blackness from a historical point of view in a radio program entitled *Black Italians*, in which she presented the lives of contemporary Black Italians who have had a significant impact on the country's culture and history. Scego selected personalities who have distinguished themselves in various areas, including sports

---

[81] "manifesto delle pecore."

[82] The expression "sheep poster"—which is in English in the original—is taken from Michel (2015, 410). In that article, Michel analyzes the reaction of different political forces to this poster, which features a cartoon with three white sheep kicking a black sheep out of a space marked by the Swiss flag. The message on the poster reads "Sicherheit schaffen," which means "Achieve security"—a play on words between *schaffen*, which means "achieve," and *Schafe(n)*, which means "sheep." Through a combination of visual and textual images, this poster once again represents migrants from Africa, and non-white people in general, on Swiss (and, by extension, European) soil as dangerous and undesirable. For an analysis of the way in which Switzerland's postcolonialism can be compared to that of other European countries, see Lombardi-Diop and Romeo (2015a, b).

[83] On Switzerland's postcolonial status, even in the absence of a colonial history, see Purtschert et al. (2012, 2016).

[84] Shame about one's skin color and origins, which Alessandro Portelli (2000) identifies as a recurring feature in African American literature and which he also traces in the autobiography of Nassera Chohra, is also present in African Italian literature. For example, in a scene from *Il cittadino che non c'è* (The Citizen Who Does Not Exist) by Ribka Sibhatu, the author tells of the time when her daughter, in kindergarten at the time, was teased about the color of her skin by her classmates and had, in response, stopped drawing herself as brown and had begun instead to draw herself as pink (2004, 23).

(such as Egyptian Italian track and field star Ashraf Saber and Congolese Italian boxer Leone Jacovacci), politics (Congolese Italian parliamentarian Jean Leonard Touadi and Somali Italian partisan Giorgio Marincola), cinema (Beninese Italian actress Esther Elisha), music (Somali Italian singer Saba Anglana), and urban culture (the group of youths known by the name of "Comitiva Flaminio" or "Flaminio Maphia," who also appear in Ubax Cristina Ali Farah's short story "Rapdiput" (2004) ("Punt Rap" 2006) and her novel *Il comandante del fiume* (2014) (*The Commander of the River* 2023).[85] By gathering such heterogeneous personalities under the heading of a single narrative, Scego shows the historical significance of Black Italians and the valuable cultural contributions they have made and continue to make, challenging the presumed chromatic homogeneity of Italianness not only in the present but also in the past.

As noted in Chap. 2, 2019 marks the beginning of a new phase of Italian postcolonial literature characterized by the production of critical race studies focused on the intersection of race, gender, and color. The text that inaugurates this phase is the anthology *Future. Il domani narrato dalle voci di oggi* (Futures: Tomorrow Narrated by the Voices of Today) (2019), edited by Igiaba Scego, the first anthology of Black Italian writers of African and Caribbean origin, which includes Marie Moïse (of Haitian descent), Djarah Kan (of Ghanaian descent), Angelica Pesarini and Addes Tesfamariam (of Eritrean descent), Ndack Mbaye (of Senegalese descent), Lucia Ghebreghiorges (of Ethiopian descent), Leaticia Ouedraogo (of Burkinabe descent), Leila El Houssi (of Tunisian descent), Alesa Herero (of Cape Verdean descent), Wissal Houbabi (aka Wii) (of Moroccan descent), and Espérance Hakuzwimana Ripanti (of Rwandan descent).[86]

---

[85] On Comitiva Flaminio's presence in the works of Ubax Cristina Ali Farah, see Sect. 5.2. See note 26 in Chap. 5 on Comitiva Flaminio.

[86] Following Djarah Kan in the essay "Non chiamatemi afroitaliana" (2020b), I use here and elsewhere the expression "African Italians" and "of African descent" only when I refer to a plurality of people, to a group, a community. As Kan observes, the term African American, from which the term African Italian is derived, refers to an African origin that is unspecified because it cannot be retraced. African Italian writers' origins, however, are known and must be acknowledged in order to understand and to highlight the many differences inherent in the term "African" (as Kan is keen to point up, Africa is a continent, not a country). Camilla Hawthorne makes a similar statement in her preface to *Future*, in which she suggests that "a single 'Afro-Italianness' does not exist," but is instead "a multiplicity of experiences that converge around a series of shared subjectivities and struggles" ("non esiste una singola 'afroitalianità', ma una molteplicità di esperienze che convergono intorno a una serie di soggettività e lotte condivise") (2019, 26–27).

The tone of this anthology is profoundly different from that of the other landmark anthology discussed in Chap. 2, *Pecore nere* (Black Sheep) (2005), a collection of stories by Black and non-white female writers of African and South Asian descent.[87] Whereas *Pecore nere* suggests that because the presumed homogeneity of Italianness is already under constant interrogation by subjects who do not conform to the somatic, chromatic, and cultural norms of Italianness, racial difference in the future will no longer determine the principle of belonging (or not belonging) to the nation, *Future* is informed by the deep and abiding disappointment felt after the Italian parliament failed to act to reform the current citizenship law, which, in turn, ignited more frequent episodes of racist violence.

The curator of the collection, Igiaba Scego, considers this book her *J'accuse*: she accuses her country of not being able to pass a new citizenship law that would link second generations' sense of belonging not only to their everyday experiences and practices (e.g., their participation in the educational system and their use of the national language and of local dialects), but also, first and foremost, to their legal status as Italian citizens. Still, in the final sentence of her editor's note, Scego claims that the anthology is "also a love hymn for a future that we want to be different"[88] (2019, 17).

In her preface, Camilla Hawthorne (2019), who is of Italian and African American origins, underlines that the short stories/memoirs/essays in *Future* are part of the work and mobilization of young Italians around such categories as Italian Blackness as it connects to European Blackness. If, as Fatima El-Tayeb contends, "black studies scholars increasingly argue that diasporic thinking beyond the national paradigm is a necessary prerequisite for an inclusive black subjectivity, that is, one that does not create its own internal Others," (2011, 44), the authors in *Future* have envisioned for themselves forms of transnational identification and belonging that transcend the nation and are rooted in such diasporic experiences as the Black Atlantic and the Black Mediterranean.[89] Hawthorne's reference to the groundbreaking collection *Showing Our Colors: Afro-German Women Speak Out* (Opitz et al. 1992), which was first published in German

---

[87] In the Italian cultural debate on race, there is no distinction between the categories of Black and Brown.

[88] "questo libro è un *J'accuse*. Ma anche un inno d'amore per un futuro che desideriamo diverso."

[89] On the notion of the Black Atlantic, see Gilroy (1993). On the notion of the Black Mediterranean, see Proglio et al. (2021).

in 1986 and for the first time collected theoretical texts on racism and sexism by German women of African descent, underlines the importance of articulating a specifically European discourse on Blackness and on the processes of racialization in Europe, thus decentering the United States from the production of racial theory and opposing the location of racism outside Europe.

Future is a heterogeneous collection in terms of both the authors' origins and the narratives they produce. The majority of these texts are memoiristic essays, combining personal experience with deep theoretical and critical analysis focused on the intersection of racism and sexism. As the title *Future* suggests, the collection is centered on the axis of temporality. Against a futurity constructed according to a linear and teleological conception of time that leads to a modernity historically considered inaccessible to Black people, this collection proposes that such inaccessibility can be contrasted through the acquisition of knowledge of the past, at both a personal and a historical level. The anthology renders the connection between colonialism and contemporary racism visible in a nation that has systematically erased colonial memory, and at the same time questions and denormalizes whiteness and exposes white privilege.

Following Fanon (1952), some of the texts reflect on the internalization of racism that deeply informs the lives of Black people (specifically in Europe in this case). In Leaticia Ouedraogo's short memoir "Nassan Tenga" (which means "Europe" in the Mooré language of Burkina Faso), the racism perpetrated daily against the protagonist's father has annihilated in him any vision of a possible future in Italy, which has resulted in an inability to use the future tense when he speaks Italian, even though he has retained such ability in his native Mooré language:

Fucking n***** was said to Dad for the first time at age thirty, Dirty n***** to me at age eleven, maybe just after I got off the plane that was taking me with my mom to the promised land, where we could be reunited with that fucking n***** father of mine ... But as for Mathys, N*****, and then stupid N*****, and then ugly N***** was first said by his classmates in first grade, at age six.[90] (Ouedraogo 2019, 99)

[90] "N**** di merda a papà per la prima volta è toccato a trent'anni, Sporca n**** a me a undici anni, forse appena uscita dall'aereo che mi portava con la mamma nella terra promessa, dove avremmo potuto ricongiungerci proprio a quel n**** di merda di mio padre ... A Mathys invece N****, e poi N**** scemo, e poi N**** brutto, lo hanno detto per la prima volta i suoi compagni di classe in prima elementare, a sei anni."

The disabling psychological consequences of racism are scrutinized in both "Nassan Tenga" and Marie Moïse's "Abbiamo pianto un fiume di risate" (We Have Cried a River of Laughter) (2019), both short Fanonian memoirs in which the authors also examine the legacy left to subsequent generations by Black people traumatized by racism. From childhood, Moïse's light skin, her apparent adherence to the hegemonic white norm, and the distance from her father while growing up all contributed to her being nearly oblivious to her Black Haitian heritage. Such erasure, however, had caused her, just like her father, to develop what she calls the "Haitian syndrome," a condition connected to her family's denial of their history and heritage as a result of their internalization of racism.

In her fictional short story "Il mio nome" (My Name), Djarah Kan explores the importance of one's family history and heritage by underlining the power of naming as an act of (self-)determination and (self-)assertion, in contrast with such violent practices as the imposition of masters' names onto African American slaves and, in contemporary times, the adoption of names from the country of arrival as a strategy of "passing" for migrants who have internalized the presumed inferiority of their cultures of origin. The narrator is deeply critical of her parents' determination to create an utterly negative narrative of their past and to sever their connections with their country of origin, which she recognizes as a form of internalized racism that in turn produces a deep fracture in the relationship second generations have with their family histories.

At the core of several narratives is the important role of archives, both personal and public, in the process of building a collective memory from below that combines but also contrasts with official processes of memorialization. Lucia Ghebreghiorges's short story "Zeta" (Zed), for example, examines the issue of interracial families through the lens of Afrofuturism[91]: the protagonist's memories reemerge, unrequested, when her virtual assistant, Zeta, presents her with photos from her past, including one in which she appears with her adoptive parents outside of Addis Ababa's orphanage.

The centrality of private and family archives—stories, memories, objects, and photographs—to the creation of counternarratives is further underlined when a public archive makes its appearance in Angelica Pesarini's "Non s'intravede speranza alcuna" (No Hope in Sight) (2019). Here, the author, who is conducting archival research in Asmara on forgotten and abused children during the Italian occupation, is able to

---

[91] For an Afrofuturistic reading of Ghebreghiorges's short story, see Fabbri 2020.

reconstruct the story of two mixed-race children, Maddalena and Gabriele, through official documents, but also to illuminate what those documents in fact silence thanks to stories she has heard from her grandmother. Thus Pesarini utilizes both private and public archives to shed light on colonial racism and on its many complex implications in determining individual as well as collective destinies; at the same time, these archives allow for the recovery of fragments that contribute to the shaping of a counterhistory not yet fully narrated (and, in parts, not narrated at all).

Such a counterhistory also recounts the trauma inherited by the descendants of people who have suffered racism in its many forms. As Alesa Herero notes in "Eppure c'era odore di pioggia" (And Yet It Smelled Like Rain) (2019b), quoting Grada Kilomba, the descendants of slaves have no direct memory of slavery, but they are nevertheless haunted by the memory of loss. This idea surfaces in "Nassan Tenga," when Ouedraogo claims that her generation's first step in overcoming their traumatized parents' silence was their own refusal to remain silent, which she shared with a community of Black youths, ranging in age from 18 to 25, with similar histories and problematic family heritages.

Future opens up an elaboration of race studies without precedent in Italy. It is joined by other groundbreaking texts, such as Espérance Hakuzwimana Ripanti's memoir *E poi basta. Manifesto di una donna nera italiana* (Enough is Enough: Manifesto of a Black Italian Woman) (2019), Djarah Kan's short story collection *Ladri di denti* (Tooth Thieves) (2020a), and Nigerian Italian writer Oiza Queens Day Obasuyi's essays in *Corpi estranei* (Foreign Bodies) (2020).[92] The publication of these texts so close together (along with Igiaba Scego's novel *La linea del colore* [The Color Line] and Marilena Delli Umuhoza's autobiographical text *Negretta. Baci razzisti* [Little Black Girl: Racist Kisses], both published in 2020, and later in 2022 of Sabrina Efionayi's *Addio, a domani*), marks a very important moment in Italian culture. Representations of Blackness as counternarrative to the presumed national normative whiteness are not new in the literary landscape of Italy. As this chapter has already shown,

---

[92] These three texts were published by the People Publishing House, which was established in 2018 by former Democratic Party parliamentarian Pippo Civati together with writers Stefano Catone and Francesco Foti and which has a strong focus on contemporary social issues in Italy, particularly immigration, inequalities, and racism. In 2018, People also published *Lettera agli italiani come me* by Elizabeth Arquinigo Pardo, in which the Peruvian Italian author reflects on the tragic consequences that Salvini's security decrees produced for second-generation people like her.

they appear in the work of migrant writers during the very first phase of postcolonial literature in the early 1990s and become increasingly present in the writings of subsequent generations (consider, by way of example only, the extraordinary work of Igiaba Scego and Ubax Cristina Ali Farah, and the importance of Geneviève Makaping's *Traiettorie di sguardi. E se gli altri foste voi?* (2001) (*Reversing the Gaze: What If the Other Were You?*, 2023), discussed earlier in this chapter, and, later on, the work of Liberian Italian beatmaker Karima 2G). However, what distinguishes this most recent phase is that all these texts are published within a short period of time and they present a more specifically theoretical reflection on the intersection between racism and sexism.

Nadeesha Uyangoda's collection of theoretical and memoiristic essays *L'unica persona nera nella stanza* (The Only Black Person in the Room) (2021) also revolves around the ways in which social, cultural, and institutional spaces in Italy are constructed on the implicit norm of whiteness. Uyangoda joins the chorus of voices of second-generation associations, artists, activists, and artivists who have denounced the lack of reform of the citizenship law, which, because it still centers on the principle of *ius sanguinis* (right of blood), reinforces the idea that Italianness and Blackness are mutually exclusive. Such institutional racism corroborates the discriminatory structures on which Italian society is based and reveals the subtle mechanisms of "everyday racism" (Essed 1990, 1991): the exclusion of Black people from the category of "Italianness," their invisibility in the media and in institutions in terms of representation and representativeness, and the absence of Black subjects in the literary canon. All this, according to Uyangoda, has produced and continues to produce a strong limitation of imaginaries, which in turn generates a chronic lack of self-esteem: "When you grow up with the impression that the only character that vaguely resembles you is destined to be marginal, it is difficult to believe that reality is very far from fiction"[93] (2021, 17).

Uyangoda explains the use of terms from the Anglo-American debate on race, racism, and processes of racialization (e.g., BLM, BAME, colorism, tokenism, minority myth, visible minorities) still used infrequently in the Italian debate, which continues to lag significantly on these issues.

---

[93] "quando cresci con l'impressione che l'unico personaggio che ti somiglia vagamente è destinato a essere marginale, è difficile credere che la realtà sia molto lontana dalla finzione."

Uyangoda also criticizes the frequent invocation of a presumed "anti-Italian racism"[94] (2021, 129), showing that there is no such thing as reverse racism, nor can the binary white/Black simply be reversed, because that binary is tied to a history that for centuries has seen the systematic discrimination of Blacks by whites (and not vice versa). Uyangoda also denounces the use of terms such as n***** and of racist practices such as blackface (100), regularly enacted on television and sometimes even in public institutions, and advocates for the right of Black people and people of color to self-definition and self-representation.

"Italy is an integral part of a structurally racist reality,"[95] argues Oiza Queens Day Obasuyi (2020, 140), corroborating Achille Mbembe's assertion that "racism is not an accident; it is an ecosystem"[96] (quoted in Obasuyi 2020, 137). The racist structure of Italian society was formed and then reinforced in the colonial era when the newly formed Italian nation was constructing its identity through policies that opposed Italian (and European) whiteness to the Blackness of those being colonized. In this way, whiteness was established as the "somatic norm" (Puwar 2004) in Italy, and consequently, Blackness and Italianness (or even Europeanness) were—and are still—considered mutually exclusive categories. On whiteness as the norm, Obasuyi quotes Alesa Herero, one of the authors whose work appears in *Future*, who argues that "whiteness is a system, it is this imperious structure based on capitalism, racism, patriarchy, classism, and deeply internalized colonial and paternalistic dynamics. For centuries, it has represented the norm against which everything else is viewed as different"[97] (Obasuyi 2020, 48–49; Herero 2019a, n.p.).

The connection between colonial history and contemporary postcolonialism, however, is often disregarded in a society that struggles to confront its colonial past. Race and color as categories of oppression are still largely absent from the cultural debate and critical discourse in Italy, just as the continuity existing between the colonial imaginary of the Black Venus and the hypersexualization of Black women in contemporary Italy is systematically obscured. This absence means that episodes of racist

---

[94] "razzismo antitaliano."

[95] "L'Italia è parte integrante di una realtà strutturalmente razzista."

[96] "Le racisme n'est pas un accident, c'est un écosystème."

[97] "la bianchezza è un sistema, è questa struttura imperiosa fondata su capitalismo, razzismo, patriarcato, classismo e dinamiche coloniali e paternaliste profondamente interiorizzate. Da secoli rappresenta la norma a partire dalla quale tutto il resto è diverso".

violence are still seen as events that happen routinely in other countries but not in Italy, except for isolated cases. Acknowledging the process of colonial suppression as it has been historically enacted in Italy, and in general in many European countries, allows for a reading of the ongoing manifestations of racism not as sporadic events, but as originating from a shared colonial matrix.

The authors analyzed above warn readers that racism is expressed not only through verbal or physical violent acts but also through seemingly innocuous and benevolent daily attitudes that reveal its systemic nature. Among these, the writers mention mechanisms that at times display anti-racist intentions or merely stage seeming opposition to racism but that, in fact, reaffirm discrimination: the "White Saviour Complex" (in English in the original) similar to the colonial "civilizing mission"[98] that often animates humanitarian organizations (Obasuyi 2020, 47); "tokenism" (in English in the original), that is, allowing a single subject or a limited number of non-normative subjects to access a physical and/or symbolic space constructed as white in order to avoid being accused of racism/sexism (Obasuyi 2020, 113; Uyangoda 2021, 99)[99]; "wannabe anti-racism,"[100] that is, the attitude of people who believe they are anti-racist simply because they claim not to see color or make occasional gestures that respect "minorities" (Ripanti 2019, 161); and "performative anti-racism,"[101] that is, adopting behaviors that stage anti-discriminatory strategies so as to be considered anti-racist, while in fact such strategies only act on the surface and do not actually oppose racism in any significant way (Obasuyi 2020, 135).

Self-definition and self-representation are powerful practices for African people and people of African descent to engage in to counter the social invisibility they regularly face and to represent their own history beyond stereotypes. As Djarah Kan argues, stories about Africa are considered interesting only if they provide a representation of Africa that is acceptable to the "First World," namely, the primitive, exoticizing Africa of *The Lion*

---

[98] "missione civilizzatrice."

[99] As seen in the introduction to this chapter, Eduardo Bonilla-Silva explains this mechanism in the context of Barack Obama's election.

[100] "antirazzismo *wannabe.*"

[101] "antirazzismo performativo."

King (2020a, 107–14) or the Africa of total misery and deprivation associated in the Italian imaginary with "Biafran children" (108). If, according to this line of thinking, Black bodies do not conform to such representations, they are not worthy of being represented, and thus they become socially invisible (while, at the same time, they are constantly epidermically hypervisible). Subjects who have internalized the undesirability of their somatic difference protect themselves by trying to become invisible and retreating into silence ("Neither Dad nor Mom had answers for me. Least of all did my teachers. I retreated into an increasingly more rarefied silence"[102] [Ouedraogo 2019, 111]) or by adopting dissimulation (the protagonist of Kan's short story "Gli ultimi giorni di agosto" [The Final Days of August] draws herself as a blonde child with blue eyes [2020a, 9–54]). The desire to become invisible is overturned in these texts by authors dedicated to transforming their Blackness into a proud affirmation, and in the case of Ripanti, into a manifesto.[103]

Many of the authors discussed here have played an active role when the Black Lives Matter movement spread to Italy following the killing of George Floyd in Minneapolis on May 25, 2020. Young Black activists in Italy promoted a general mobilization that took place both in Italian squares and on the internet. As Angelica Pesarini argues, however, it is necessary to acknowledge the fact that the mobilization in Italy occurred only after the latest of countless acts of institutionalized racist violence in the United States, as if to underline once again that racism is an American

---

[102] "Né papà né mamma avevano risposte per me. Tantomeno gli insegnanti. Io mi chiudevo in un silenzio sempre più rarefatto."

[103] A (relatively) widespread debate about Black Italianness has developed in the past decade on social media. These digital spaces have facilitated the articulation of a newly constituted virtual community that includes African Italians residing in different parts of the peninsula; at the same time, these spaces have allowed their members to make connections with other Europeans of African descent. More recently, Black Italian authors and activists have employed podcasts to enhance the debate on race and processes of racialization. See, for instance, *Sulla razza* (Fernando et al. 2021), *Blackcoffee* (Tekle and Maréchal 2020–21), *Tell Me Mama* (Scego and Elisha 2021), *The Chronicles of a Black Italian Woman* (Djumpah 2020–), and *Storia del mio nome. La storia incredibile e vera di Sabrina Efionayi* (Efionayi 2022–). See also *Calabria Mondo* (a podcast produced by Radio NoBorders and hosted by Alessandra Menniti and Wanees Mousa [2020–2021] that focuses on the intersection of different subalternities in Northern and Southern Italy).

phenomenon, alien to Italian institutions or everyday life.[104] Pesarini notes, for instance, that no mobilization followed the brutal assassination of Soumalia Sacko, a union member and farm laborer in the Gioia Tauro Plain in Calabria originally from Mali, who was shot and killed on June 2, 2018, because he and two co-workers had broken into a factory to retrieve scrap metal they intended to use to construct a shack in the San Ferdinando ghetto (Pesarini 2020). In a published epistolary exchange between Pesarini and Camilla Hawthorne, Pesarini specifies that the term "Black Italians" homogenizes a group of subjects who have different degrees of privileges within Italian society (Hawthorne and Pesarini 2020a, b). She goes on to say that the first form of racism that must be thwarted in present-day Italy is the norm that regulates the attribution of citizenship through *ius sanguinis* and that the anti-racist struggle is not separate from the migrant issue, the exploitation of African laborers in agricultural work, the physical and psychological violence perpetrated in repatriation centers, or the militarization of the Mediterranean.

All these writers assert in different ways—in continuity with what Makaping claimed at the beginning of the twenty-first century—that racism is systemic in contemporary Italian society, pervaded as it is by the legacy of colonialism, which saw European states (Italy among them) build their sense of national identity on the racialization and inferiorization of the Other in the colonies. Far from being innocuous statements,

---

[104] The fact that racism has always been considered an issue that is foreign to Italian history and contemporaneity also became evident during the European Soccer Championship in 2021. When, at the beginning of the tournament, the players on other teams took a knee as a sign of solidarity with the Black Lives Matter movement, the Italian players, who did not have a position on the matter, remained standing. Then, when the entire Welsh team took a knee before the start of the Italy–Wales match, five Italian players (Rafael Tolói, Matteo Pessina, Emerson Palmieri dos Santos, Federico Bernardeschi, and Andrea Belotti) knelt while the others remained standing. When the Italian team was asked to take a unanimous position regarding this symbolic gesture, it was decided that the Italian national team would not take a knee unless the opposing team did; in that case, the Italian players would kneel *as a sign of solidarity with the opposing team* (and *not* as a sign of solidarity with the victims of racism in Italy and elsewhere). The Italian team, therefore, knelt before the semifinal against Belgium and before the final against England (both the opposing teams had announced prior to the matches they would be taking a knee). What this says, both to the international community and to those who have experienced racism in Italy, is that the Italian national soccer team, one of the nation's most powerful symbols, considers Italy to be a country unaffected by racism, a country in which solidarity, when it is shown, is extended only to those who oppose racism in other nations and not to those who oppose it and/or who have been subjected to it in Italy. In this regard, see Nidi (2021) and *adnkronos* (2021).

comments such as "You speak Italian well" or questions such as "Where are you *really* from?" when addressed to Black and non-white Italians should be viewed as daily microaggressions, in that they point out the incompatibility between Blackness and Italianness and reaffirm the exclusion of Black bodies from the Italian national space. In the texts examined in this section, literature often intersects with activism to give substance to the first significant theoretical reflection on race by Black and non-white feminist intellectuals in Italy who form part of a broad transnational conversation that includes women of color in Europe and in many other parts of the world. These authors—writers, intellectuals, activists, and artivists—restore the lost connection between Italian colonial history and contemporary postcolonialism; they denounce the structural racism in Italian society manifested through acts that are seemingly innocuous; they underline the need to analyze racism and sexism in their intersections; and they render visible the internalization of racism, the psychological violence that it involves, and the fracture that such internalization creates between the second generations and their cultures of origin. These authors do not simply denounce a status quo; they articulate a collective response to structural racism and sexism, indicating trajectories that allow for the imagining of a different future.

4.3.2   Film and Television Series[105]

The past decade has witnessed significant developments in terms of the contribution second generations have made to film and documentary production in Italy. Directors have advocated for citizenship reform; they have represented the intersection between Blackness and Italianness as not only conceivable but already real; they have investigated the strong sense of ambivalence attending second-generation Black Italians as they grow up; they have reread Italian colonial history in the postcolonial cities of the present; and they have represented an Italian society that becomes more diverse every day.

---

[105] The overview that I present here is far from comprehensive. In this section, I limit myself to discussing few films and television series that, because of the themes they consider, are in dialogue with the literary texts examined so far and hereafter. For a comprehensive analysis of the production of films and television series by second generations in Italy, see De Franceschi (2018). For a complex analysis of Italian transnational cinema, see, among others, O'Healy (2019).

The documentary that paved the way in this regard, focusing on the need for a new citizenship law in contemporary Italy is *18 Ius soli* (18 Right of the Soil) (2011) by Ghanaian Italian director Fred Kudjo Kuwornu (2011),[106] winner of the Premio Mutti—AMM in 2009. This documentary offers a reflection on the plural identities of second generations in Italy and on the practical and symbolic value of obtaining citizenship. The director interviews 15 second-generation Italians who explain the difficulties they experience in their daily lives because they are not legally recognized as Italian citizens and who share the psychological effects this institutionalized rejection has on them. From the very beginning, the documentary presents a clear picture (and soundtrack) of the great heterogeneity that migrations have contributed to the already heterogeneous composition of the Italian nation.[107] When the interviewees state their families' place of origin and the place in which they now live, their regional accents immediately reveal how rooted they are in Italy. The documentary opens with the words of the former president of the Italian Republic, Giorgio Napolitano, who emphasizes the great contribution that second-generation people have made and continue to make to Italy. It then cuts to the racist insults repeatedly directed at soccer player Mario Balotelli in various Italian stadiums, which highlight the presumed impossibility of the intersection between Blackness and Italianness. By allowing second-generation subjects to speak to the complexity of their lives while also showing them performing everyday activities at ease in their surroundings, Kuwornu's narrative constructs an important counter

---

[106] Kuwornu also directed the important documentary *Blaxploitalian: 100 Years of Blackness in Italian Cinema* (2016a) on the presence of Black actors, authors, and filmmakers (African or of African descent) during the first century of Italian cinema. *Blaxploitalian* is based on Leonardo De Franceschi's (2013) pioneering work. See also the conversation between Fred Kuwornu and Camilla Hawthorne on diversity in Italian cinema (Kuwornu 2016b).

[107] At the end of the twentieth century, the immigrant population in Italy was among the most diversified in Europe, coming from Eastern Europe, Mediterranean and sub-Saharan Africa, Central-South and East Asia (especially China), and Central and South America (see Grillo and Pratt 2002). For an analysis of the "minorities" that have always lived in Italy and the more recent "minorities" associated with contemporary migratory movements, see, among others, Campani (2008).

representation with respect to the dehumanizing narrative presented by numbers and statistics.[108]

The second half of the documentary focuses more specifically on the legal consequences suffered by people born and/or raised in Italy who are excluded from Italian citizenship. While these people are minors, for instance, not having Italian citizenship—and therefore not having an Italian passport—means not being able to take part in activities in which their fellow students can and do participate (they cannot go on school trips to other countries, nor can they participate in national-level sporting competitions). Their status becomes much more complicated once they come of age: at that point, they have exactly one year to apply for citizenship (until the day before they turn 19). Since the process of obtaining citizenship can take years, however, they need a residence permit to be allowed to legally remain in the country where they (were born and) have always lived. As is evident from many interviewees' comments, this is perceived as a symbolic rejection that produces a strong sense of alienation. The words of the interviewees are reinforced by the rap song "Sono nato qui" (I Was Born Here) (2011) by Valentino Ag, who sings "It's still strange / to hear me speak Roman ... like you I was raised on pasta with butter and parmesan."[109]

The documentary *Asmarina* (2015) by Alan Maglio and Medhin Paolos (Paolos is an Italian of Eritrean origin) recounts the life of the Eritrean Ethiopian community in Milan through the voices of interviewees and photographs found in official, personal, and family archives, all of which presents a much-needed reflection on the long history that ties Italy to Eritrea. Such history includes colonialism, past and present migrations

---

[108] The protagonists of the documentary, with a certain irony, present situations that expose the absurdity of being Italian without being legally recognized as a citizen. The Nigerian Italian rapper and actor Valentino Agunu (aka Valentino Ag), for example, observes how his thick Roman accent is not noticed when he speaks with strangers because the Blackness of his skin produces a visual effect that inhibits the ability to consider other elements that clearly signal his Italianness. When a white Italian woman told him that he spoke Italian well, the rapper replied, "So do you." Valentino Agunu is also the lead performer in the television movie *Le nozze di Laura* (*Laura's Wedding*), by Pupi Avati (2015), which aired on December 7, 2015, on Rai 2 during prime time. At the center of the film is the love story between Laura, a Calabrian girl from a very well-to-do family, and Karimu, a student from Chad who works as an orange picker in Calabria, and all the difficulties the two must face in a country that is still deeply afraid of diversity.

[109] "ancora fa strano / sentirmi parlare romano ... come te son cresciuto a pasta burro e parmigiano."

of Eritreans to Italy, and the life of the Eritrean community in present-day Milan. Many of the interviewees say that there has never been a true debate on the colonial history that has so firmly connected the destinies of Eritrea and Italy. The official history, presented in the documentary by engineer Franco De' Molinari (president of the Associazione Nazionale Reduci e Rimpatriati d'Africa—ANRRA; National Association for Veterans and Refugees of Africa), who praises the architectural and engineering works of Italians in the "colonia primigenia,"[110] is contradicted by the counterstories of the Eritreans interviewed, who on several occasions denounce the brutality of the Italian colonization, including the use by the Italian army of gas prohibited by the Geneva Convention of 1928, and repeatedly state that Italians know very little about this history. Among the people interviewed in the documentary is Erminia Dell'Oro, a well-known writer and the daughter of Italians in Eritrea, who relocated to Italy at the end of the 1950s.[111] Dell'Oro, who was 20 years old at the time, recounts that Italians did not know where Asmara was when she mentioned being born there.

Maglio and Paolos's work can be read, in a certain sense, in continuity with that of Lalla Golderer and Vito Scifo—both interviewed in *Asmarina*—who in 1985 published a photography book entitled *Stranieri a Milano. Volti di una nuova immigrazione* (Strangers in Milan: Faces of a New Immigration), in which various migrant communities, the Eritrean community in particular, were portrayed. These interviews, as Golderer affirms, made clear that not only were these communities present in the city but also that they were very well organized: they were not in Milan to survive but rather to contribute in significant and meaningful ways to the city's life. Expanding on this observation, Maglio and Paolos include footage of the international festival of Eritrean people, organized by the Eritrean People's Liberation Front, which was held annually in Bologna from 1973 to 1991—and which is almost entirely unknown in the Italian culture at large, despite the fact that every year about 15,000 to 20,000 Eritreans belonging to different diasporic communities in Europe and outside Europe would attend the festival, staying in the city for weeks,

---

[110] Colonia "primigenia" o "primogenita" (which literally means, "the first to be generated, first born") was the name given to Eritrea by the Italians, who thus highlighted the importance of Ethiopia as their first colony.

[111] On Erminia dell'Oro's work, see Sect. 2.4.3.

thus also providing an important economic contribution to Bologna and to the country (Maglio and Paolos 2015).

Many aspects of colonial history emerge from the words of the interviewees: the presumed "civilizing mission" (with the construction of schools and roads, for instance); the brutality of the Fascist regime; and the fate of mixed-race children, who were often not acknowledged by their fathers (who had other families in Italy) and who were also rejected by the local community. Such is the story of Michele Lettenze, interviewed in the documentary, who was repatriated to Italy in 1963 and who has lived in Milan ever since. As some of the men in the community say in the opening scenes of the documentary, Lettenze is the living archive of their community. And it is he who mentions the song "Asmarina"—from which the documentary takes its title—a song by Pippo Maugeri from the 1950s that praises the beauty of a woman from Asmara and an Italian man's love for her. This song reappears later in the documentary, but in its Tigrinyan version, performed by the well-known Eritrean singer Wedi Shaul, who sang it at the Bologna festival in the 1980s. In this version, the words and meaning of the song have been altered: the lyrics have been purged of allusion to the colonial desire of Italian men for the bodies of the Black women of the colonies, and the song is dedicated to the city of Asmara.

Through the voices of the community, the documentary also recounts the recent history of Eritrea, including the dictatorship of Isaias Afewerki, which has erased every pretense of democracy, and the subsequent mass exodus of Eritreans from the country, who must risk their lives first in the desert and then in the Mediterranean to reach Italy. A young man from Eritrea,[112] for example, recounts his own recent voyage and the dangers of the desert[113] and then of the Mediterranean. Thinking back to the crossing he made, this man describes the day he finally landed in Lampedusa as the day he felt the greatest joy of his entire life. However, he then expresses great disappointment because his dream of Italy differed greatly from the reality he encountered, which was strongly characterized by deprivation and marginalization. The documentary also shows the interaction of recent Eritrean immigrants with the established Eritrean community, who have been rooted in the region for decades and who make themselves

---

[112] The names of the interviewees do not appear in the film as superimpositions but only in a list at the end of the film without names being connected to faces. For this reason, I do not specify the name and identity of the person interviewed here and in another instance.

[113] In this regard, see, among others, Leogrande (2015).

available to come to the aid of the newcomers (through practical assistance, but also by providing translation and mediation services).

Asmarina recounts an original part of Italian life, that of the Eritrean community of Milan, one of the oldest communities of immigrants and their descendants existing on Italian soil. One of the central messages of the film, articulated primarily through the voices of the Eritrean Ethiopian community, is that, if it is true that Italy is important for the history of the past and the present of Eritrea, the opposite is also true (a woman interviewed comments, "Probably without us Italy would not be what it is today, and we would not be what we are today."[114]). Through personal archives and narratives, the documentary reconstructs the difficult relationship between Eritrea and Italy at the time of colonialism—which also remains a little-known chapter in the Italian culture at large—but also the settlement of the Eritrean community in Milan starting in the 1970s, its organization, and the valuable contribution that this community has offered and continues to offer to the city and the country. This representation overturns the dominant discourses on immigration, in which immigrants are always considered a problem and never a resource.

The Sri Lankan Italian director Suranga Deshapriya Katugampala abandons the genre of the documentary—which characterizes the early filmic production of second-generation directors—and turns to fiction in *Per un figlio* (*For a Son*) (2016), winner of the Premio Mutti—AMM 2015. This film, as Katugampala points out, is aimed at the Sinhalese, as well as the Italian, community and is the result of a complex interaction between the two. The film portrays a specific aspect of immigration in Italy and the life of second generations: that of Sri Lankan women who came to Italy in the 1990s to work, usually in domestic contexts, and who later brought their children with them and raised them in Italy. *Per un figlio* is set in an unidentified province in Northern Italy, where a Sinhalese woman named Sunita (Kaushalya Fernando) works as a caregiver. Sunita's teenage son (Julian Wijesekara), who now lives in Italy, was raised in Sri Lanka. When the boy begins to show contempt for the life they are leading in the home of the elderly woman (Nella Pozzerle) from whom Sunita is caregiver, she rents an apartment, where she goes (often secretly) several times a day to bring groceries, cook, and, in particular, convey to her son the importance of a home and a family structure. Sunita, however, cannot live in this

---

[114] "Probabilmente senza di noi l'Italia non sarebbe quella che è oggi, e noi non saremmo quello che siamo noi oggi."

apartment because her employment contract requires her to reside full-time in the home of the person she is assisting.

The son has a very hostile relationship with his mother, based particularly on the different expectations the two generations have regarding the country in which they live. While Sunita wants to maintain distance from Italian culture and wants her son to remain attached to the traditions of their country of origin, he wants to be free of the heavy burden of the past and to lead the life his Italian peers lead. Sunita does not want to betray her culture and traditions: she always speaks to her son in Sinhalese (usually, he does not reply, and when he does, he does so in Italian), wants the boy to spend time with his Sinhalese peers, and rejects his Italian friends. In contrast, the boy is embarrassed by his past and by his mother's estrangement from the society and culture in which they live ("Mom, you don't even know how to speak Italian,"[115] he tells her during a fight [Katugampala 2016]). At a certain point in the narrative, he slaps another boy of Sri Lankan origin in the street for no reason other than to prove to his friends his distance from his community of origin and his belonging to Italian society. Sunita's son has internalized the hatred toward migrants he sees every day and has thus developed a desire to wear a metaphorical white mask over his Brown skin, thus enacting a violent suppression of his past.[116]

The film's narrative is sparse: the scenes are drawn from everyday life—shot mainly in the apartment that Sunita shares with her son, in the one she shares with her employer, or in the street—and the dialogue is reduced to a minimum, often diminishing to silence where the mother and son are concerned. The son uses the freedom his mother affords him by force of circumstance not to go to school and instead to loiter with his friends. His feelings toward his mother, and indeed toward the world, reveal a strong ambivalence. On the one hand, the teenage boy constantly shows anger toward his mother; on the other, certain moments reveal that the anger is a stratagem for dissimulating his vulnerability and need for affection. The distance between the two generations is underscored in a scene in which Sunita calls on two men from the Sinhalese community to perform a ritual to ward off demons from her son in their apartment. During the ceremony, the boy is present but detached, playing with his telephone. Even though this rite is adapted to the diasporic context in which it is

---

[115] "Mamma, non sai parlare neanche italiano."
[116] The reference here is to Fanon (1952).

celebrated, the sequence in which it is portrayed still conveys a sense of estrangement, as becomes evident from the remarks of the neighbors, who complain about the noise, and from Sunita's subsequent warnings to the two Sinhalese men to be quiet, to lower the volume.[117] When Sunita forces her son—who was disrespectful of the whole event—to sleep on the landing, her neighbors call the authorities, who arrive to investigate the situation. Their inspection and the anxiety it produces highlight the precariousness of immigrants' lives.

Although the film is articulated through the rigid opposition between first and second generations, there are moments when the characters show that they are not completely locked within their separate worlds. At the end of the ritual, for example, Sunita is given a small candle that she is told must stay lit for three days for the rite to take effect. Having observed her son's disregard for the ceremony, Sunita extinguishes the candle immediately after the two men leave her apartment. Her skepticism seems to suggest her awareness of the fact that such rituals have no value in places so far removed from where they originated and that in the new world it is necessary to develop new strategies. Conversely, at a certain point in the film Sunita's son shows a cautious curiosity about his mother's diasporic version of the world when he goes to a party also attended by members of the Sri Lankan community. When he meets the Sinhalese boy he had previously slapped in the street, his attitude is almost apologetic. Although Sunita's son merely observes as an outsider the people at the gathering, he nevertheless shows a certain curiosity about his culture of origin.

The desire for both physical and metaphorical whitening in a society that, like Italy's, has constructed itself as homogeneously white is the focus of the film *Ambaradan* (2017), directed by Amin Nour and Paolo Negro and winner of the MigrArti 2017 prize. The film developed from an idea by Amin Nour, and some of the events depicted are drawn from his personal life or that of Germano Gentile, who plays the main character, Luca, one of three young neo-Nazis. The film, which has strong Fanonian echoes, investigates the psychological implications and the profound sense of ambivalence that derive from being a Black Italian and from realizing that one's Blackness is perceived in a negative way. Luca, who comes from

---

[117] The ritual is Hindu, even though Sunita appears to be Buddhist. Sri Lanka is home to many religions, and they influence one another. My thanks to Suranga Deshapriya Katugampala for an email conversation we had in November 2017, from which I derived the information in this note and other information included in this text.

an unspecified African country and was adopted by an Italian family, transforms his anger at having always been marginalized and racialized in Italy into hatred for recent immigrants, all of whom he and his neo-Nazi friends would like to send back "home." Scenes of the present are interposed with flashbacks of Luca as a child: his poor performances at school as a consequence of the racism he experienced daily, his assertion of his own Italianness that is constantly denied by the world around him, his desire to hide.

The film's editing emphasizes the ambivalence that Luca experiences on a psychological level, which generates an evident contradictoriness in his behavior. The flashbacks of when, as a little boy, he obsessively washed himself with soap in a vain attempt to whiten himself and thus please a society that convinced him that his Blackness was "wrong" show how the psychological violence he suffered then transforms into the violence he himself perpetrates against immigrants, from whom he feels different because of his Italian citizenship. The external world, however, does not seem to grasp this difference and instead associates his Blackness with that of recent immigrants. During one of the neo-Nazi group's punitive expeditions, an old man intervenes in support of the group of thugs, but it is Luca whom he tells to go back home, not understanding that Luca is one of the thugs and not one of the targeted immigrants. As happened many times throughout his childhood, Luca again finds his Italianness unacknowledged because his Blackness is so visible to Italians of Italian origins that it prevents the processing of any other information.[118] Even one of his neo-Nazi friends reacts in a violent manner when he notices Luca's interest in his sister, showing that the specter of the interracial unions of colonial memory hovering in the film constitutes a further reason for violence. At the end of the film, Luca rebels against two of his supposed friends when they racially abuse a presumably South Asian child on the beach of Ostia. When the child claims to be Italian, the two start yelling, "There are no Italian n*****s,"[119] while they salute with their right arms extended. Luca's identification with the child—who reminds him of his younger self struggling to assert his Italianness—this time prevents him from distancing himself from the targeted subject, who in this case is an Italian with

---

[118] See, in this regard, the epigraph to this chapter, taken from Maria Abbebù Viarengo's "Scirscir N'Demna?".

[119] "Non ci sono negri italiani."

dark skin like him and not an immigrant. This causes him to question his affiliation with neo-Nazi racism.

In addition to the constant references to Frantz Fanon, the film presents other colonial echoes, starting with the title, *Ambaradan*, a term uttered by Luca in a conversation with the child at the end of the film ("it's all an *ambaradan* [mess]"[120] [Nour and Negro 2017]). The everyday use of this term to indicate great confusion—Amba Aradam is the name of a tableland in Ethiopia, where, in February 1936, the Italian army carried out a massacre of Ethiopian soldiers and civilians through the use of mustard gas—shows at a linguistic level the process of revisionism and normalization of colonial violence implemented in widespread Italian culture. The film also contains a subtler allusion to Italian emigration to the United States through a reference to *The Godfather* (1972), the iconic Italian American film by Francis Ford Coppola. A scene of violent devastation—loud and frenzied—is intercut with a scene—silent and still—of Luca's mother in church praying and crying during a mass in memory of her husband and Luca's adoptive father, which her son was expected to attend but did not. A very similar montage in Coppola's film combines a scene—filled with violent, impassioned images—in which Michael Corleone orders the settling of scores before he takes the place of his recently deceased father, Don Vito, at the head of the family with one in which Michael Francis, Connie Corleone's second son to whom Michael has agreed to be godfather, is being baptized—rich in spiritual, solemn atmospheres. Although the context and the type of violence perpetrated differ, this implicit allusion to the film considered the ultimate representation of Italian emigrants in the United States functions as a reference to the migratory continuum that has characterized and still characterizes Italy, connecting the various diasporic movements and creating a temporal continuity between past and present and a spatial continuity between the different Italian diasporas.

The closing song of the film also draws together disparate, contradictory elements, combining the typically Roman popular musical form, the *stornello*, with lyrics by Matteo Persica that speak of the changed social conditions of the capital and the way in which the Roman population has changed ("There was a handsome Negro boy / he was Roman / but inside his heart / there was pain"[121] [Nour and Negro 2017]). This ability

---

[120] "è tutto un ambaradan."

[121] "C'era un negretto bello / era romano / ma dentro ar core suo / c'era 'n dolore."

to blend new themes with traditional forms, including local folklore, shows how these cultural hybridizations are able to give voice to the profound changes that for years have been taking place in Italy and that have radically transformed local as well as national communities and cultures.

Bangla (2019), written and directed by and starring 22-year-old Bangladeshi Roman Phaim Bhuiyan, is the first film by a second-generation director to achieve great popular success while receiving numerous critical awards, including the 2019 Silver Ribbon (Nastro d'argento) award for Best Comedy and the 2020 David di Donatello award for Best New Director. Set in one of the most multiethnic neighborhoods in Rome, Torpignattara, the film has a strong autobiographical vein and tells the story of a young Roman Muslim of Bangladeshi origins, Phaim (played by the director himself), who, from the beginning of the film, describes himself, with a strong Roman accent, as "50% Bangla, 50% Italy, and 100% Torpigna."[122] Phaim lives within a rather traditional family and community. At the center of the film is the theme of "integration" and the often difficult relationship between the first and second generations, but the film's novel element is that, for the first time, these themes are represented through the genre of comedy. Using humor, irony, and self-deprecation, the director examines the conflict between a Roman youth of Bangladeshi origin and his parents and community of origin, while also ridiculing certain aspects of both his community of origin and Italian society. The life of the protagonist, who works as a museum attendant and who, to supplement his income, plays traditional music at Bangladeshi community events with a group of friends, takes shape in this daily divide until the day when Phaim meets Asia at a concert, and they fall in love. This encounter creates existential doubt in Phaim for the first time, as he finds himself on the verge of his first sexual encounter, something completely irreconcilable with the rules of Islam, which instead mandate chastity before marriage. Regarding the role the film has played in contemporary Italian cinema, *Bangla* has been compared to such turning points in British cinema as the film *My Beautiful Laundrette* (Frears 1995) (screenplay by Hanif Kureishi) and the BBC television series *The Buddha of Suburbia* (Michell 1993) (based on Hanif Kureishi's 1990 novel of the same title), which, from the

---

[122] "50% Bangla, 50% Italia e 100% Torpigna." Torpigna is a Roman slang term for the neighborhood of Torpignattara.

mid-1980s onward, have raised the issue of immigration and integration in large urban centers in Europe such as London (Finos 2021).[123]

* * *.

In recent years, second and third generations have also made an appearance in Italian television series. The presence of Tezetà Abraham, an Ethiopian Italian actress born in Djibouti, in the series *È arrivata la felicità* (Happiness Has Arrived) (Milani and Vicario 2015)[124] was hailed by Igiaba Scego as a revolution through which present-day Italy is finally telling "stories of inclusion, of everyday racial mixing, of multicultural society"[125] (2015, para. 9). In this series, Abraham plays Francesca, a young, Black Roman woman who manages a bookstore with her two best friends. Her presence reflects the diversity of the Italian population and represents second generations as an integral part of the country in which they were born and raised and to which they actively contribute. The Italian imaginary, moreover, is enriched by new representations that no longer associate the Blackness of women with conventionally marginal roles, such as housekeeper, caregiver, or prostitute. In another television series, *Tutto può succedere* (Pellegrini and Angelini 2015–18),[126] which aired immediately after *È arrivata la felicità*, Esther Elisha, an Italian actress originally from Benin, plays Feven Neghisi, a musician of Eritrean origin, who in the first season reveals to Carlo Ferraro (Alessandro Tiberi) that their very brief relationship a few years earlier resulted in a son, Robel (Sean Ghedion Nolasco). The appearance of this child, and the marriage

---

[123] The film *Bangla* was recently adapted as a television series of the same title (produced by Fandango and Rai Fiction), for which Bhuiyan collaborated on the screenplay. Two of the eight 30-minute episodes were presented at the Torino Film Festival in November 2021. As of early 2022, the series is available on RaiPlay. In an interview (Finos 2021), Bhuiyan states that the series, which was the originally intended format, delves into themes presented in the film, but also other themes and characters that were not as central in the film.

[124] The series *È arrivata la felicità* aired in prime time on Rai 1, from October 8 to December 17, 2015. The second season of the series aired in 2018 and was less successful than the first. Both seasons are currently available on RaiPlay.

[125] "storie di inclusione, di meticciato quotidiano, di società multiculturale."

[126] The series *Tutto può succedere* was inspired by the American television series *Parenthood*. The first season aired in prime time on Rai 1, from December 27, 2015, to March 13, 2016; the second, also in prime time on Rai 1, from April 20 to June 29, 2017; the third, also in prime time on Rai 1, from June 18, 2018, to August 6, 2018. All three seasons are currently available on RaiPlay.

of Feven and Carlo in the second season, mark the advent of the first generation of both African and Italian descent and the representation of an interracial family. Feven is not confined to her maternal role: she is determined to pursue her career as a violinist and, as a result of her efforts, is offered a position of great professional responsibility and prestige, one even higher than that of her future husband. Like Francesca in *È arrivata la felicità*, Feven also inscribes the presence of Black women's bodies outside the asphyxiating and stereotypical space of care work and sexual work, suggesting that Black women are an integral part of Italian postcolonial society.

The year 2021 marks the release on Netflix of *Zero*, the first series in which the protagonist, Omar/Zero, is a Black Italian youth played by a Black Italian actor (Giuseppe Dave Seke).[127] Omar has Senegalese origins, lives in Milan, is passionate about manga, and works as a delivery rider. Following a strong emotional reaction one day, he discovers that he has the power to become invisible. Omar/Zero is portrayed as a *sui generis* superhero, who uses his superpower to help the young people in the suburb where he lives, the Barrio, combat the process of gentrification gradually forcing the inhabitants of the neighborhood to abandon it because of the continuous increase in rental costs. The series focuses on social issues such as the perception of the so-called second generations in Italy, land use, and housing policies in urban contexts. Even the superpower he is given is imbued with social concerns, in that it raises the issue of the invisibility of Black bodies in predominantly "white" societies as a desire to disappear in order to erase a Blackness perceived as undesirable. The success of the series, apart from the initial launch, fell short of expectations, so much so that the second series was canceled. This can be ascribed to an "overall two-dimensional character construction, filmic writing that leans lazily on the notes of sultry songs, and the unexpected revealing of a mystical, religious subplot that unearths a highly problematic exoticizing repertoire," which complicated and lessened the potential impact of the series on the imaginaries of viewers, of adolescents in particular (De Franceschi 2021, 179).

---

[127] The series is inspired by Antonio Dikele Distefano's novel *Non ho mai avuto la mia età* (I Was Never My Age) (2016).

4.4   Strategies of Invisibility and Aesthetic Practices of Italian Transdiasporic Blackness

Writing about the intersections between Blackness and Italianness from two unique yet overlapping perspectives, Kym Ragusa and Igiaba Scego— the former an African Italian American, the latter Italian of Somali origin—open their respective memoirs *The Skin Between Us* (Ragusa 2006) and *La mia casa è dove sono* (*My Home Is Where I Am*) (Scego 2010), with a series of pointed questions[128]:

> What are you?
> Black and Italian. African American, Italian American, American.
> Other. Biracial, Interracial. Mixed-Blood, Half-Breed, High-Yellow, Redbone, Mulatta. N*****, Dago, Guinea. (Ragusa 2006, 25)

> What am I? Who am I?
> I am Black and Italian.
> But I am also Somalian and Black.
> Then am I African Italian? Italian African? Second generation? Uncertain generation? Meel kale? A nuisance? A Black Saracen? A dirty n*****?[129] (Scego 2010, 31)

The first intersection in which both authors recognize themselves is the one between their Blackness and their Italianness ("Black and Italian," writes Ragusa, and Scego: "I am Black and Italian"[130]), which creates continuity between the (hi)stories of mobility the two authors examine. Both are Black, and their families are part of the Italian diaspora, whether Italy is their families' point of departure or arrival. In Ragusa's case, the intersection of Blackness and Italianness is considered undesirable to both the communities in which she grew up (African American and Italian American in New York City) and to American society at large. This is also true for the Italian society into which Scego was born and raised. Read as a

---

[128] Kym Ragusa and Igiaba Scego met in Rome in August 2009 while Ragusa was in Italy to receive the John Fante Prize, awarded to her for the Italian translation of *The Skin Between Us*, entitled *La pelle che ci separa* (Ragusa 2008a), translated by Clara Antonucci and Caterina Romeo.

[129] "Sono cosa? Sono chi? Sono nera e italiana. Ma sono anche somala e nera. Allora sono afroitaliana? Italoafricana? Seconda generazione? Incerta generazione? Meel kale? Un fastidio? Negra saracena? Sporca negra?"

[130] "Sono nera e italiana."

continuum, the racial history of transdiasporic Italy the two memoirs recount differs notably from the narrative of a presumed hegemonic Italian whiteness. Such a narrative constitutes the principle by which Black Italians who do not conform to the Italian chromatic norm are generally perceived as foreigners and the children of migrants are denied citizenship and kept outside the national body. As Ragusa contends, however, the presumed whiteness of people of Italian origin has historically been challenged in the United States, where the color assigned to Italian Americans (who have been considered almost white but not quite, to borrow Homi Bhabha's phrase) was a symbol of their subalternity and where the intersection of her Italianness and Blackness was rejected by both sides of her family, albeit for different reasons. Ragusa and Scego each denounce the social pressures through which they have been kept at the margins of their communities and societies and show how the hypervisibility of their Blackness—and the sense that no positive trait has ever been associated with it—induced them to adopt complex strategies of invisibility.

Ragusa, who is African American on her mother's side and Italian American on her father's side, writes of the ambivalence she faces in the United States because of her race, both in her two communities of origin and in the broader context of the dominant American culture. In her blood, as the author herself claims, two ethnic groups converged that were never meant to come together, even though they occupied contiguous spaces in New York City, only a few blocks apart from one another (Black and Italian Harlem). At the time of Ragusa's birth, her father had yet to reveal her existence to his family, fearing their rejection. If her father's Italian American family discriminates against her because of her Blackness—which, the author contends, her paternal grandmother manages to forget only by availing herself of "an almost acrobatic capacity" (Ragusa 2006, 223; Romeo 2008)—her mother's African American family, who played a very active social role in Harlem's Black community and were very light-skinned, considers the author's Italian American relations to be "white trash" (Ragusa 2006, 29). Even though the color assigned to Italians in the United States was white by law (see, among others, Guglielmo 2003), their whiteness was not considered equal to Anglo-Saxon whiteness, but rather a whiteness "of a different color" (Jacobson 1998) characterized by a dark complexion (DeSalvo 2003).[131] Such processes of racialization enacted by the mainstream culture on African American and Italian

[131] See note 18 in this chapter.

American communities did not, however, lead to solidarity and collaboration between them. Italian immigrants, considered "white ethnics," chose instead to make a "possessive investment in [their] whiteness" (Lipsitz 2018),[132] which involved distancing themselves from the other migrant communities occupying lower social positions, such as the African American, Hispanic, and Asian communities.

Ragusa explores her own complex sense of not belonging—white among Blacks, Black among whites—which is dependent on the constant conflict between her two communities of origin and on their both being kept at the margins of the dominant culture. For Ragusa, as is evident in the list of adjectives she uses to define herself at the beginning of *The Skin Between Us*, her own difference is not inscribed within a reductive white/Black dichotomy but within an array of identifiers in which color and race constantly intersect with other categories—gender, ethnicity, and social class primarily, but also sexuality, physical beauty, religious affiliation, and level of education. Within such a complex context, telling one's story solely from a racial point of view can lead to dangerous essentializations. Still, race and color are central to the ways her two families and communities perceive her and each other. African American children at school call Ragusa "whitey" and urge her to return to the land of the whites (2006, 156). However, when she plays with Italian American children, she is often called a n*****, as happens in one scene in which another girl from the neighborhood uses that derogatory term to refer to her. Kym's cousin Marie quickly intervenes to reassure their playmate that young Kym is not Black but rather her cousin—indicating the impossibility of her being both—and that she only seems Black because it is dark outside (Ragusa 2006, 179).

If Ragusa's Blackness must be erased in order for her to be able to claim her Italian heritage in the United States, Igiaba Scego shows how Blackness and Italianness are considered mutually exclusive in contemporary Italy. In the earlier short story "Salsicce" (Scego 2005) ("Sausages," 2005b), Scego's female protagonist expresses the disorientation she felt when she observed hordes of people lining up in front of the police station to have their fingerprints taken, which the newly passed Bossi-Fini law had made a mandatory requirement to obtain stay permits. Her physical resemblance

---

[132] For an analysis of the structural advantages that "white" Americans have historically derived from their presumed whiteness, see Lipsitz (2018). For an analysis of the racial status of Italian immigrants in the United States, see Roediger (1991), Orsi (1992), Vecoli (1995), Luconi (2001), Guglielmo and Salerno (2003), Guglielmo (2003), and Caiazza (2018).

to the migrants standing in line makes her wonder whether she should also be lining up, despite her Italian citizenship. In *La mia casa è dove sono,* the doubt runs even deeper, becoming almost Hamletic: the author examines the process by which her own subjectivity as a Black person growing up in Rome has been constructed, showing how her Blackness has always prevented her from acquiring full Italianness. Scego's awareness that her Blackness is at the root of the social rejection she faces begins to take shape at school in her interactions with the other children. The author is constantly othered, marginalized, and compared to Kunta Kinte, the protagonist of the first television series on American slavery broadcast in Italy at the end of the 1970s[133]: "You're like Kunta Kinte, a dirty n*****—we're going to whip you. You were born to be a slave"[134] (Scego 2010, 151–52).[135]

To avoid being insulted ["You don't talk; you make monkey calls. We can't understand anything ... you're weird. You guys are like gorillas"[136] (Scego 2010, 150)], Scego tries to make herself invisible, and since her skin color does not allow her to become lost in the crowd, she chooses the strategy of silence. She utterly rejects the Somali language and only speaks in Italian when absolutely necessary. Trying to attain invisibility through inaudibility is a strategy also used by Rwandese Italian writer and activist Espérance Hakuzwimana Ripanti, who claims, "I have deceived myself ... into thinking that if I didn't make too much noise, I could have been invisible, too"[137] (2019, 10). Both Scego and Ripanti enact a synesthetic process of de-racialization: since their skin color does not allow them to neutralize people's sense of sight, they try to disappear by neutralizing people's sense of hearing through remaining silent. Whether inherited by parents and/or imposed by society, silence leaves indelible scars, as Burkinabe Italian writer Leaticia Ouedraogo points out in her memoir

---

[133] See also note 65 in this chapter. As Scego (2010, 151–52) notes, for Italian children the Kunta Kinte character left none of the deep sense of freedom that enlivened him, but only the fact that he was a slave. This ended up legitimizing the equation Black = slave in children's eyes in Italy.

[134] "Sei come Kunta Kinte, una sporca n****, ti frusteremo. Sei nata per essere schiava."

[135] The same kind of insult is directed at Daniel, the narrator of Jadelin Mabiala Gangbo's novel *Due volte* (Two Times) (2009). He is called "lurido schiavo" (filthy slave) by the other children at the religious institution where he lives with his twin brother, David.

[136] "Voi non parlate, fate i versi delle scimmie. Non si capisce nulla ... siete strani. Siete come i gorilla."

[137] "Mi sono illusa ... che se non avessi fatto troppo rumore avrei potuto essere invisibile anche io."

"Nassan Tenga": "We were emotionally illiterate. Unable to speak about ourselves, not able to verbalize our feelings. Our pain"[138] (2019, 112).

Nigerian Irish author Emma Dabiri (2019, 12–16), following Ayana Byrd and Lori Tharps (2014), contends that the true marker of Blackness is not skin color, but rather hair texture, and that tightly coiled natural hair identifies people as Black (as, for instance, in the case of African albinos) more than dark skin (as is the case for South Asians, who are not considered Black even when they are darker than Africans and African Americans). In Ragusa's prologue to *The Skin Between Us*, the author writes of traveling on a ferry from Calabria to Sicily (her family's regions of origin) and knowing that her olive skin is hardly visible in Southern Italy, where people mostly have a similar skin color. Her tightly coiled hair, however, is tied back to avoid prying eyes, a camouflage tactic deployed by Ragusa since she was a child in order to make herself invisible (Giunta 2003). Ragusa's hair has often constituted a battlefield and has taken on a symbolic meaning precisely because it is the distinctive trait that most reveals her African origins. Yet, as her light-skinned African American maternal grandmother, Miriam, contends, those thick, intricate curls were inherited from her father ("those damned Sicilians with their African blood" [Ragusa 2006, 56]) and are presumably a sign of her Sicilianness rather than of her Africanness. Later, a couple she meets in Palermo complicate Miriam's remark by observing that the author's Sicilianness reconnects her to her Africanness: "Palermo is like your Harlem—we are the Blacks of Italy" (Ragusa 2006, 235).[139] This statement, which highlights the subaltern position of Southern Italians— here of Sicilians specifically—fails to account for the uniquely traumatic heritage of most people of African descent in the United States, a heritage that Ragusa's numerous references to her maternal family's history within the institution of slavery underline. In the same scene with the Palermitan couple—in which an African prostitute appears who has powdered her face white in order "to make herself more beautiful to Sicilian men" (Ragusa 2006, 236)—readers are reminded that Southern Italian and African

---

[138] "Analfabeti emotivi, non sapevamo parlare di noi, non eravamo in grado di verbalizzare i nostri sentimenti. Il nostro dolore."

[139] Expressions such as "Calafrican" ("Calabrese" and "African") to refer to people from Calabria are meant to assimilate Calabria, and by extension Southern Italy, to the subaltern position of the African continent and to attribute to the South an (almost) colonial status vis-à-vis Northern Italy. Such subalternity rests on a number of factors, mainly a presumed racial difference and a lack of "civilization" and culture. Writer and anthropologist Geneviève Makaping (2001), however, who is originally from Cameroon and who lived in Calabria for decades, has remarked that being African and Calabrian in Calabria grants access to very different social positions and levels of privilege. See also note 18 in this chapter.

"Africanness" imply very different processes of racialization and have historically traced very different trajectories.

Even if Ragusa's hair texture were indeed inherited from the Italian American side of her family, as Miriam claims, it is in any case a trait that she shares with the Black community in Harlem. In preparing to comb her hair once a week, her Aunt Gladys would assemble on the table "all the objects of a ritual that has been passed on from black women to black girl children across the generations, across centuries, across the weeping Atlantic" (Ragusa 2006, 57). The "taming" of the hair is considered a transhistorical, transnational ritual that connects the author to the other Black girls in the neighborhood through their common inheritance of abduction, violence, and slavery. This connection to African diasporic women creates a sort of Black Atlantic of aesthetic practices through the rituals of everyday life. Such rituals, shared with those same girls who would otherwise consider her too light-skinned to belong, contribute to structuring Ragusa's process of identity formation, although the effect they produce is only provisional: "My hair would be tamed momentarily just as my identity would be fixed momentarily. In that mirror I would be a six-year-old black girl-child who lived in Harlem. It would be enough, for a time, to hold all the contradictions and questions at bay" (Ragusa 2006, 58).

In a later text, the author reveals that the powerfulness of her hair as a race signifier becomes more evident to her once she grows up. She performs visual experiments by repeatedly going to a photo booth to take pictures of the back of her head and of her hair: "From the time that I wore my hair, as now, in a few lopsided braids, to the time I cut it short and bleached it until it glowed a sickly orange, to the time I shaved it off completely. After that, I recorded the patterns and shadows the stubble made on the back of my head" (Ragusa 2008b, 59–60). Ragusa had been inspired by Lorna Simpson's photographs, in which Black women pose with their backs turned to the camera as if in refusal of the gaze (Ragusa 2008b, 60). To this gaze, which historically has exoticized, objectified, and violated Black women's bodies and beauty, Ragusa offers a sequence of images that shift from a recognizable hair style (lopsided braids), to an unrecognizable one (very short and bleached hair), to an annihilation of her hair (shaved head) reminiscent of the shaving of slaves' heads by the slave traders before they were boarded onto slave ships (Byrd and Tharps 2014, 10).

Wearing untamed hair for Ragusa comes at the end of a long process of self-awareness and self-fashioning. Her natural hair powerfully appears in her memoiristic documentary *fuori/outside* (Ragusa 1997), in which she employs "the narrative techniques of storytelling and the imagery of personal memory" in order to revisit "a past that is broadly historical, yet anchored in the intimate relationships between a granddaughter and her [grandmother]" (Tenzer 2002, 213). The documentary is Ragusa's attempt "to cross the lines of time, memory, and color" (Ragusa 1997, 00:1:05) and is framed as a letter to her paternal grandmother, who had exerted the strongest resistance in accepting her granddaughter as blood of her blood. Ragusa's relationship with her paternal family is one of exclusion; the possibility of inclusion exists, but it would require the denial of part of her heritage and her complicity in the stigmatization of the African American community (concerned about the imminent arrival of new neighbors, for instance, the author's Italian American grandmother, Gilda, had said to her Black granddaughter, "I hope they're white") (Ragusa 2006, 223).

In *fuori/outside*, Ragusa is no longer hiding: she appears with her natural hair loose while conversing with her paternal grandmother, walking around the neighborhood with her and filming both inside and outside her house. The image on the cover of *La pelle che ci separa* (Ragusa 2008a), the Italian translation of *The Skin Between Us*, is a still frame from the documentary: the author's face, partially hidden by the camera, is surrounded by her untamed, tightly coiled hair, left free in affirmation and acceptance of a cultural heritage that has always been divisive to both sides of her family and to society at large (at one point, Ragusa's extradiegetic voice says to her grandmother: "You grew up in a time when Southern Italian immigrants were lynched along with African Americans" [Ragusa 1997, 00:09:39]).

Claiming the right to wear one's hair natural can signal a constructive process of individual and collective identity formation, as well as a quest to articulate an aesthetic that does not mimetically reproduce the canons of whiteness. In her article "Capelli di libertà" (Freedom Hair) (2016), Scego scrutinizes the processes of skin whitening and hair straightening with chemical products as camouflaging techniques and encourages Black Italian women to adhere instead to an aesthetic aimed at rediscovering the uncompromised beauty of their own bodies rather than those proposed by Western and Eurocentric canons. In the article, Scego discusses the Nappytalia website, which was established in 2014 by Ghanaian Italian Evelyne Sarah Afaawua as an extension of the Facebook page Afro-Italian Nappy Girls.[140] On the website, Afro-Italian Nappy Girls is described as "the first Italian community born for girls who have decided to wear their

---

[140] For the origins and development of Nappytalia and Afro-Italian Nappy Girls, see the Nappytalia website and Hawthorne in Frisina and Hawthorne (2015, 2018).

natural Afro-curly hair"[141] (Nappytalia n.d.). This website is specifically intended for African Italian women (and men) "with Afro hair, daughters and sons of mixed couples, a new generation of Italians who do not want to forget their origins, who want to claim their forgotten identities"[142] (Nappytalia n.d.). As Afaawua observes in the short documentary *Nappy Girls* (Coppola 2014), African Italian women like her have internalized Italy's negative perception of their bodies and, as a consequence, have learned to "discipline" their hair (through relaxation or extensions) so as to be able "to pass," at least in part.[143] Their desire to claim their African

---

[141] "la prima community italiana nata per riunire le ragazze che hanno deciso di sfoggiare il loro riccioafro al naturale."

[142] "con i capelli riccioafro, figli di unioni miste, una nuova generazione di italiani che non vogliono dimenticare le proprie origini, rivendicando la propria identità ignorata."

[143] In spite of the documentary's intention to show the existence of African Italian women and valorize Afaawua's process of self-awareness and determination in creating a community of African Italian women, the ways in which the film stereotypically essentializes, sensualizes, and sexualizes Black female bodies appear problematic. To give an example, at the beginning of the narrative, Afaawua introduces herself, discusses her origins, and is shown going about her daily routine. Later, the narrative transitions from her individual story to stories from the community of Black women she has gathered together, who discuss their African Italian identity. For reasons left unexplained, the main narrative is cross-cut with scenes of some of those women dancing sensually in what appears to be a dark, empty disco. Their bodies are intermittently illuminated in different colors for the pleasure of the (presumably white, male) viewer. In the film's narrative, the discussion these women have about their heritage and identity takes place, again for unexplained reasons, in a public restroom—presumably the one in the disco. These details necessarily alter how the viewer perceives these Black women, whose bodies are unwittingly bearing traces of racist and sexist stereotypes, while the intrusion of the camera, and therefore of the white, male director into this highly gendered space, appears as a violation of these women's privacy and intimacy. The bathroom location further suggests that a conversation that should be taking place publicly—as a way to promote positive change—is instead being confined to a private and secluded space. When the narrative transitions from the individual Black subject (Afaawua) to the Black community, one of the women sings to the excitement and enjoyment of the others. In this scene, as well as in the dance scenes, the association of Black women with music and rhythm is enforced and marks their absence from other symbolic and physical spaces. For instance, while Afaawua introduces herself at the beginning of the documentary, the other women do not say their names, nor do they discuss their backgrounds or reveal their origins. This produces the perception that they have no identity or history of their own, that this group is an amorphous body that exists only as part of the community that Afaawua has created, and that their stories are only an extension of hers. Thus, the narrative of the documentary singles out one exceptional individual Black woman and authorizes—at least in part—her upward mobility, while at the same time it represents the larger community of Black women in Italy as mute, inarticulate, rhythmically adept, and sexualized. The colonial imaginary of the Black Venus deployed in the documentary is in stark contrast to the self-representation of Afaawua's website, where African Italian women are portrayed as resourceful, independent, intelligent, and endowed with self-awareness and agency.

heritage emerges from a process of self-awareness, acceptance, and empowerment, and produces aesthetic counter-canons through which these historically racialized bodies demand that their presence in the physical and symbolic space of the nation be legitimized, thus rewriting a very long history of institutionalized oppression.

Examining the blog featured on the Nappytalia site along with the Hijab elegante Facebook page, which was created in 2012 by K.N., a 21-year-old Moroccan Italian, Annalisa Frisina and Camilla Hawthorne (2015, 2018) claim that race is constantly reconstructed through "readings" of hair, body shape, and specific pieces of clothing, and that practices of self-representation such as the way women wear their hair and how they dress (including "the veil") reproduce and consolidate (or, conversely, call into question) the privilege of whiteness and Catholicism in Italy. Disseminating representations of counter-canonical Italianness through the internet has played a crucial role in recreating diasporic connections across Europe (and beyond) and in enacting counter-hegemonic practices (Frisina and Hawthorne 2018, 727). These are acts of daily anti-racism that have the function to counteract "everyday racism" (Essed 1990, 1991). The resignification of daily aesthetic practices "is a process of unlearning and breaking free from internalized regimes of normativity and oppression, which construe afro-textured hair as 'bad,' 'ugly,' and 'inferior' compared to long, straight, Caucasian hair" (Lukate 2019, 123). Such a process contributes to redefining the very concept of the "somatic norm" (Puwar 2004), to establishing which bodies have the right to occupy what spaces in accord with what functions, and to asserting which bodies can be considered to belong to the nation and which bodies should be excluded—if any—or differentially included. Far from being a superficial matter, the creation of new aesthetic canons contributes to constructing new transnational imaginaries and to establishing new practices of inclusion based on the physical characteristics of (re)subjectified bodies.

*   *   *

Reading the reflections of Igiaba Scego (but also of other African Italian writers, intellectuals, activists, and entrepreneurs such as Leaticia Ouedraogo, Espérance Hakuzwimana Ripanti, and Evelyne Sarah Afaawua) in continuity with those of Kym Ragusa emphasizes how these women's Blackness deeply questions and opposes along a transnational and transdiasporic trajectory the construction of the Italian national body as white. The diasporic continuum of which these authors are part shows that the racial history of Italy—as well as Italian national identity and culture at large—has been shaped both inside and outside national borders. These authors' performances of invisibility at earlier stages in their lives constitute their attempt to deflect attention away from physical features, such as skin color and tightly coiled hair, which are markers of racial categories and of a difference from the white norm that has historically been socialized as undesirable. Through counter-hegemonic aesthetic practices that connect African American, African Italian, and other African diasporic women,[144] Scego and Ragusa question and redefine hegemonic national aesthetic canons in ways that do not allow the systematic erasure of Blackness and that instead demand its inclusion in the process of shaping Italian and European identities. This process sets the notion of Italianness apart from an obsolete, racist conception derived from biologism and links it to daily lives, education, cultural practices, and the individual and collective desire to belong and to imagine national and transnational communities as encompassing subjects whose diverging characteristics from the (presumed) national norm radically challenge the very existence of a (presumed) national homogeneity (Lombardi-Diop and Romeo 2012), thus enabling new ways of participation.

4.5   Conclusion

The (mainly) Black postcolonial writers since the beginning of the twenty-first century have redesigned the monochromatic Italian cultural space through their authorial presence and that of their characters, a presence that does not conform to the presumed Italian chromatic norm. If Paul Gilroy claimed that *There Ain't No Black in the Union Jack* (1987), thus metonymically denouncing the invisibility of Black people in the national imaginary, and therefore in the British nation, we could say that these

---

[144] I am not claiming here that African American, African Italian, and other African diasporic women perform the same aesthetic practices, nor am I claiming that hair must necessarily constitute for them a symbol of their "Africanness," or that it constitutes such a symbol for all of them in the same way. I am claiming that counter-aesthetics (here connected to natural hair) has the potential to create powerful counter-narratives, and that this practice has been performed—often in different ways—by African American, African Italian, and other African diasporic women. On the complex ways through which Afro-Europeans construct narratives that are different from both a white European and an African American paradigm, see, among others, Scarabello and de Witte (2019).

writers are creating such symbolic space in the Italian tricolor flag.[145] To this end, it is important not only to condemn overt acts of racism but also to make visible all those subtle mechanisms—predominantly of the colonial type—that daily reinforce the racist structures on which the Italian society is founded.

For over 30 years now, postcolonial writers, intellectuals, and artivists have denounced racism— which is expressed through processes of exoticization, paternalistic attitudes, microscopic and macroscopic discriminatory acts, and systematic marginalization—as a pervasive element in Italian society; they have implicitly or explicitly denounced the symbolic space of history and literature as a white space; they have partly rewritten Italian colonial history, producing what David Theo Goldberg calls a "new racial counter-history" (2006, 356); they have redesigned the Italian social space as plural and diversified, a space in which the combination of "Black" and "Italian" does not constitute an oxymoron; they have mobilized in favor of reforming the citizenship law so that it will become more inclusive of differences; and they have created connections between their own cultural production and other Black diasporic cultures in Europe and around the world, thereby strongly challenging the very notion of national culture. Such contributions over time have opened a breach in the national collective imaginary that makes possible new conceptions of Italianness.

BIBLIOGRAPHY

adnkronos. 2021. Euro 2020, Italia si inginocchia? Azzurri verso il sì. *adnkronos,* June 28. https://www.adnkronos.com/euro-2020-italia-si-inginocchia-azzurri-verso-il-si_7MPQXqJrEJxIrfKHRZByhh?refresh_ce.

Ag, Valentino. 2011. Sono nato qui. Produced by Valentino and Filippo Saccucci. Soundtrack for the documentary *18 Ius soli* directed by Fred K. Kuwornu (Struggle Filmworks). YouTube video. https://www.youtube.com/watch?v=uwCX3K9RUt0&feature=youtu.be.

Ahmed, Sara. 2007. A phenomenology of Whiteness. *Feminist Theory* 8 (2): 149–168.

Ali Farah, Ubax Cristina. 2004. Rapdipunt. In *La letteratura postcoloniale italiana. Dalla letteratura d'immigrazione all'incontro con l'altro*, ed. Tiziana

[145] Gilroy (1987) strongly challenges the presumed whiteness of the population of Great Britain. As previously noted (see note 82 in this chapter), in the "sheep poster," the flag in Switzerland was also metonymically equated with the national territory. See El-Tayeb (2011) and Michel (2015).

Morosetti, 127–130. Vol. 4 of *Quaderni del '900*. Pisa: Istituti Editoriali e Poligrafici Internazionali.

Ali Farah, Ubah Cristina. 2014. *Il comandante del fiume*. Rome: 66thand2nd. Trans. Hope Campbell Gustafson as *The Commander of the River* (Bloomington: Indiana University Press, forthcoming in 2023).

Andrews, Travis M. 2016. 'How Do I Explain This to My Children?': Van Jones Gives Voice to the 'Nightmare' Some Are Feeling. *The Washington Post*, November 9. https://www.washingtonpost.com/news/morning-mix/wp/2016/11/09/how-do-i-explain-this-to-my-children-van-jones-gives-voice-to-the-nightmare-some-are-feeling/.

Angrisano, Nicola, dir. 2010. *Il tempo delle arance*. InsuTV. https://vimeo.com/8812128.

Arquinigo Pardo, Elizabeth. 2018. *Lettera agli italiani come me*. Gallarate: People.

Aru, Silvia, and Valeria Deplano, eds. 2013. *Costruire una nazione. Politiche, discorsi e rappresentazioni che hanno fatto l'Italia*. Verona: ombre corte.

Associazione Il Razzismo è una brutta storia. 2020. L'Italia e i suoi George Floyd. Articoli, June 7. http://www.razzismobruttastoria.net/2020/06/07/litalia-suoi-george-floyd/.

Avati, Pupi, dir. 2015. *Le nozze di Laura*. Italy: Rai Fiction. Relased in English as *Laura's Wedding*.

Balibar, Étienne. 1991. Is There a 'Neo-Racism'? In *Race, Nation, Class: Ambiguous Identities*, ed. Étienne Balibar and Immanuel Wallerstein, 29–40. London: Verso.

———. 2004. *We, the People of Europe? Reflections on Transnational Citizenship*. Princeton: Princeton University Press.

Ben-Ghiat, Ruth, and Stephanie Malia Hom, eds. 2016. *Italian Mobilities*. New York: Routledge.

Bhabha, Homi K. 1994. *The Location of Culture*. London: Routledge.

Bhuiyan, Phaim, dir. 2019. *Bangla*. Italy: Fandango.

Blow, Charles M. 2016. Trump: Making America White Again. *The New York Times*, November 21. https://www.nytimes.com/2016/11/21/opinion/trump-making-america-white-again.html.

Bonavita, Riccardo, Gianluca Gabrielli, and Rossella Ropa, eds. 2005. *L'offesa della razza. Razzismo e antisemitismo dell'Italia razzista*. Bologna: Pàtron.

Bonilla-Silva, Eduardo. 2014. *Racism without Racists: Color-Blind Racism and the Persistence of Racial Inequality in America*. Lanham, MD: Rowman & Littlefield.

Bordin, Elisa, and Stefano Bosco, eds. 2017. *A fior di pelle. Bianchezza, nerezza, visualità*. Verona: ombre corte.

Bouchane, Mohamed. 1990. *Chiamatemi Alì. Un anno a Milano nella vita di un clandestino venuto dal Marocco*. In collaboration with Carla De Girolamo and Daniele Miccione. Milan: Leonardo.

Brunetti, Bruno. 2010. Modernità malata. Note su 'Tempo di uccidere' di Ennio Flaiano. In *Fuori centro. Percorsi postcoloniali nella letteratura italiana*, ed. Roberto Derobertis, 57–71. Rome: Aracne.

Brunetti, Bruno, and Roberto Derobertis, eds. 2014. *Identità, migrazioni e postcolonialismo in Italia. A partire da Edward Said*. Bari: Progedit.

Burgio, Alberto. 1998. *L'invenzione delle razze. Studi su razzismo e revisionismo storico*. Rome: manifestolibri.

———, ed. 1999. *Nel nome della razza. Il razzismo nella storia d'Italia (1870–1945)*. Bologna: il Mulino.

———. 2001. *La guerra delle razze*. Rome: manifestolibri.

Burgio, Alberto, and Luciano Casali, eds. 1996. *Studi sul razzismo italiano*. Bologna: CLUEB.

Byrd, Ayana D., and Lori L. Tharps. 2014. *Hair Story: Untangling the Roots of Black Hair in America*. Rev. ed. New York: St. Martin's Press.

Caiazza, Tommaso. 2018. Are Italians White? The Perspective from the Pacific. *California Italian Studies* 8 (2): 1–15.

Campani, Giovanna. 2008. *Dalle minoranze agli immigrati. La questione del pluralismo culturale e religioso in Italia*. Milan: Unicopli.

Capitani, Flavia, and Emanuele Coen, eds. 2005. *Pecore nere*. Rome-Bari: Laterza.

———, eds. 2008. *Amori bicolori. Racconti*. Rome-Bari: Laterza.

Caponetto, Rosetta Giuliani. 2012. Blaxploitation Italian Style: Exhuming and Consuming the Colonial Black Venus in 1970s Cinema in Italy. In *Postcolonial Italy: Challenging National Homogeneity*, ed. Cristina Lombardi-Diop and Caterina Romeo, 191–203. New York: Palgrave Macmillan.

———. 2013. Zeudi Araya, Ines Pellegrini e il cinema italiano di seduzione coloniale. In *L'Africa in Italia. Per una controstoria postcoloniale del cinema italiano*, ed. Leonardo De Franceschi, 109–123. Rome: Aracne.

———. 2014. 'Blaxploitation' all'italiana. La Venere nera nel cinema italiano degli anni Settanta. In *L'Italia postcoloniale*, ed. Cristina Lombardi-Diop and Caterina Romeo, 178–191. Florence: Le Monnier-Mondadori.

Carpignano, Jonas, dir. 2015. *Mediterranea*. DCM Productions.

Cassata, Francesco. 2008. *"La Difesa della razza." Politica, ideologia e immagine del razzismo fascista*. Turin: Einaudi.

Cazzato, Luigi. 2008. 'Questione meridionale' and Global South: If the Italian South Meets Its Global Brother. *Italian Studies in Southern Africa/Studi d'Italianistica nell'Africa Australe* 21 (1–2): 102–133.

Centro Furio Jesi, ed. 1994. *La menzogna della razza. Documenti e immagini del razzismo e dell'antisemitismo fascista*. Bologna: Grafis.

Choate, Mark I. 2008. *Emigrant Nation: The Making of Italy Abroad*. Cambridge, MA: Harvard University Press.

Chohra, Nassera. 1993. *Volevo diventare bianca*. In collaboration with Alessandra Atti Di Sarro. Rome: Edizioni e/o.

Cittadinanza italiana. 2021. Riforma della cittadinanza italiana, ecco il testo della nuova norma. https://www.cittadinanza.biz/riforma-della-cittadinanza-italiana-ecco-il-testo-della-nuova-norma/.

Clayton, Dewey, and Sean Welch. 2016. Post-racial America and the Presidency of Barack Obama. *Endarch: Journal of Black Political Research* 1 (Fall), article 3: 6–47. https://radar.auctr.edu/islandora/object/endarch%3Afall_2017.003.

Clough Marinaro, Isabella. 2014. 'Sporco zingaro'. I rom e l'integrità del corpo della nazione. In *L'Italia postcoloniale*, ed. Cristina Lombardi-Diop and Caterina Romeo, 91–106. Florence: Le Monnier-Mondadori.

Coppola, Francis Ford, dir. 1972. *The Godfather*. USA: Paramount Pictures.

Coppola, Massimo, dir. 2014. *Nappy Girls*. Corriere della Sera, September 25. https://video.corriere.it/nappy-girls/5291ec12-4416-11e4-bbc2-282fa2f68a02.

Curcio, Anna, and Miguel Mellino, eds. 2012. *La razza al lavoro*. Rome: manifestolibri.

Dabiri, Emma. 2019. *Don't Touch My Hair*. London: Allen Lane.

Dawson, Michael C., and Lawrence D. Bobo. 2009. One Year Later and the Myth of a Post-racial Society. *Du Bois Review: Social Science Research on Race* 6 (2): 247–249.

De Franceschi, Leonardo, ed. 2013. *L'Africa in Italia. Per una controstoria post-coloniale del cinema italiano*. Rome: Aracne.

———. 2018. *La cittadinanza come luogo di lotta. Le seconde generazioni in Italia fra cinema e serialità*. Canterano: Aracne.

———. 2021. Cinema e cittadinanza negata. Oltre il tunnel dell'italianità bianco-normata. In *Politica e antipolitica: cinema, televisione e cultura visuale nell'Italia del nuovo millennio*, ed. Francesca Cantore, Damiano Garofalo, and Christian Uva. Special issue, *Quaderni del CSCI* 17: 173–180.

De Lorenzo, Giuseppe. 2017. Io islamica d'Italia vi dico: lo ius soli è una sciocchezza. *Il Giornale*, August 26. https://www.ilgiornale.it/news/politica/io-islamica-ditalia-vi-dico-ius-soli-sciocchezza-1434052.html.

De Napoli, Olindo. 2009. *La prova della razza. Cultura giuridica e razzismo in Italia negli anni Trenta*. Milan: Mondadori.

Derobertis, Roberto. 2012. Southerners, Migrants, Colonized: A Postcolonial Perspective on Carlo Levi's *Cristo si è fermato a Eboli* and Southern Italy Today. In *Postcolonial Italy: Challenging National Homogeneity*, ed. Cristina Lombardi-Diop and Caterina Romeo, 157–171. New York: Palgrave Macmillan.

DeSalvo, Louise. 2003. Color: White/Complexion: Dark. In *Are Italians White? How Race Is Made in America*, ed. Jennifer Guglielmo and Salvatore Salerno, 17–28. London: Routledge.

Distefano, Antonio Dikele. 2016. *Non ho mai avuto la mia età*. Milan: Mondadori.

Djumpah, Benedicta, host. 2020–. *The Chronicles of a Black Italian Woman* (podcast). First episode aired November 27. https://podcasts.apple.com/it/podcast/the-chronicles-of-a-black-italian-woman/id1542310843.

Dyer, Richard. 1997. *White*. New York: Routledge.

Efionayi, Sabrina, host. 2022. *Storia del mio nome. La storia incredibile e vera di Sabrina Efionayi* (podcast). Released on May 19 (5 episodes). https://chora-media.com/podcast/storia-del-mio-nome/.

Eggers, Maureen Maisha. 2005. Ein Schwarzes Wissensarchiv. In *Mythen, Masken und Subjekte. Kritische Weissseinsforschung in Deutschland*, ed. Maureen Maisha Eggers, Grada Kilomba, Peggy Piesche, and Susan Arndt, 18–21. Münster: Unrast.

Ellison, Ralph. 1952. *Invisible Man*. New York: Random House.

El-Tayeb, Fatima. 2011. *European Others: Queering Ethnicity in Postnational Europe*. Minneapolis: University of Minnesota Press.

Essed, Philomena. 1990. *Everyday Racism: Reports from Women of Two Cultures*. Alameda, CA: Hunter House.

———. 1991. *Understanding Everyday Racism: An Interdisciplinary Theory*. Newbury Park, CA: Sage Publications.

Fabbri, Giulia. 2020. L'afrofuturismo tra Stati Uniti e Italia: dalla memoria storica ai viaggi intergalattici per re-immaginare futuri postumani. *California Italian Studies* 10 (2): 1–16.

———. 2021. *Sguardi (post)coloniali. Razza, genere e politiche della visualità*. Verona: ombre corte.

Fanon, Frantz. 1952. *Peau noire, masques blancs*. Paris: Les Éditions du Seuil. Trans. Richard Philcox as *Black Skin, White Masks* (New York: Grove Press, 1967).

Farnesina and Ministero degli Affari Esteri e della Cooperazione Internazionale. 2021. Cittadinanza. https://www.esteri.it/mae/it/servizi/italiani-all-estero/cittadinanza.html.

Fernando, Natasha, Nadeesha Uyangoda, and Maria Catena Mancuso, hosts. 2021. *Sulla Razza* (podcast). Aired February 12 to July 16. https://www.sullarazza.it/episodi/.

Finos, Arianna. 2021. Al Torino Film Festival la serie 'Bangla,' dal film di Phaim Bhuiyan: 'Risate e conflitti delle seconde generazioni.' *La Repubblica*, November 27. https://www.repubblica.it/spettacoli/cinema/2021/11/27/news/bangla_la_serie-328085026/.

Fiore, Teresa. 2012. The Emigrant Post-'Colonia' in Contemporary Immigrant Italy. In *Postcolonial Italy: Challenging National Homogeneity*, ed. Cristina Lombardi-Diop and Caterina Romeo, 71–82. New York: Palgrave Macmillan.

———. 2014. La post'colonia' degli emigranti nell'Italia dell'immigrazione. In *L'Italia postcoloniale*, ed. Cristina Lombardi-Diop and Caterina Romeo, 61–74. Florence: Le Monnier-Mondadori.

———. 2017. *Pre-Occupied Spaces: Remapping Italy's Transnational Migrations and Colonial Legacies*. New York: Fordham University Press.

Flaiano, Ennio. 1992. *A Time to Kill.* Trans. Stuart Hood. London: Quartet Books. Originally published as *Tempo di uccidere* (Milan: Longanesi, 1947).

———. 2000. *Tempo di uccidere.* Milan: BUR. First published 1947 (Milan: Longanesi). Trans. Stuart Hood as *A Time to Kill* (London: Quartet Books, 1992).

Fondazione Migrantes. 2021. *Rapporto italiani nel mondo 2021.* Todi: Tau.

Fortunato, Mario, and Salah Methnani. 2006. *Immigrato.* Milan: Bompiani. First published 1990 (Rome: Theoria).

Fracassa, Ugo. 2012. *Patria e lettere. Per una critica della letteratura postcoloniale e migrante in Italia.* Rome: Giulio Perrone Editore.

Frankenberg, Ruth. 1993. *White Woman, Race Matters: The Social Construction of Whiteness.* Minneapolis: University of Minnesota Press.

Frears, Stephen, dir. 1995. *My Beautiful Laundrette.* Screenplay by Hanif Kureishi. United Kingdom: Working Title Films.

Frisina, Annalisa, and Camilla Hawthorne. 2015. Sulle pratiche estetiche anti-razziste delle figlie delle migrazioni. In *Il colore della nazione,* ed. Gaia Giuliani, 200–214. Florence: Le Monnier-Mondadori.

———. 2018. Italians with Veils and Afros: Gender, Beauty, and the Everyday Anti-Racism of the Daughters of Immigrants in Italy. *Journal of Ethnic and Migration Studies* 44 (5): 718–735.

Gabaccia, Donna R. 2000. *Italy's Many Diasporas.* Seattle: University of Washington Press.

Gangbo, Jadelin Mabiala. 1999. *Verso la notte bakonga.* Fossa: Portofranco.

———. 2005. Com'è se giù vuol dire ko? In *Italiani per vocazione,* ed. Igiaba Scego, 137–185. Fiesole: Cadmo.

———. 2009. *Due volte.* Rome: Edizioni e/o.

Garane, Garane. 2005. *Il latte è buono.* Isernia: Cosmo Iannone Editore.

Gaye, Cheick Tidiane. 2013. *Prendi quello che vuoi ma lasciami la mia pelle nera.* Milan: Jaka Book.

Ghebreghiorges, Lucia. 2019. Zeta. In *Future. Il domani narrato dalle voci di oggi,* ed. Igiaba Scego, 89–96. Florence: Effequ.

Gilroy, Paul. 1987. *"There Ain't No Black in the Union Jack": The Cultural Politics of Race and Nation.* London: Hutchinson.

———. 1993. *The Black Atlantic. Modernity and Double Consciousness.* Cambridge, MA: Harvard University Press.

Giuliani, Gaia, ed. 2015. *Il colore della nazione.* Florence: Le Monnier-Mondadori.

Giuliani, Gaia, and Cristina Lombardi-Diop. 2013. *Bianco e nero. Storia dell'identità razziale degli italiani.* Florence: Le Monnier-Mondadori.

Giunta, Edvige. 2003. Figuring Race. In *Are Italians White? How Race Is Made in America,* ed. Jennifer Guglielmo and Salvatore Salerno, 224–233. New York: Routledge.

Goldberg, David Theo. 2002. *The Racial State.* Malden: Blackwell.

———. 2006. Racial Europeanization. *Ethnic and Racial Studies* 29 (2): 331–364.

———. 2009. *The Threat of Race: Reflections on Racial Neoliberalism*. Oxford: Wiley-Blackwell.

Golderer, Lalla, and Vito Scifo. 1985. *Stranieri a Milano. Volti di una nuova immigrazione*. Milan: Mazzotta.

Grechi, Giulia, and Viviana Gravano. 2016. *Presente imperfetto. Eredità coloniali e immaginari razziali contemporanei*. Rome: Mimesis.

Griffin, Gabriele, and Rosi Braidotti. 2002. Whiteness and European Situatedness. In *Thinking Differently: A Reader in European Women's Studies*, ed. Gabriele Griffin and Rosi Braidotti, 221–236. London: Zed Books.

Grillo, Ralph D., and Jeff C. Pratt, eds. 2002. *The Politics of Recognizing Difference: Multiculturalism Italian-Style*. Farnham: Ashgate.

Guglielmo, Thomas A. 2003. *White on Arrival: Italians, Race, Color, and Power in Chicago, 1890–1945*. Oxford: Oxford University Press.

Guglielmo, Jennifer, and Salvatore Salerno, eds. 2003. *Are Italians White? How Race Is Made in America*. London: Routledge. Trans. Chiara Midolo as *Gli italiani sono bianchi? Come l'America ha costruito la razza* (Milan: Il Saggiatore, 2006).

Hawthorne, Camilla. 2019. Prefazione. In *Future. Il domani narrato dalle voci di oggi*, ed. Igiaba Scego, 19–32. Florence: Effequ.

Hawthorne, Camilla, and Angelica Pesarini. 2020a. Black Lives Matter anche da noi? Trans. Pina Piccolo. *Jacobin Italia*, September 24. https://jacobinitalia.it/black-lives-matter-anche-da-noi/. Originally published as Making Black Lives Matter in Italy: A Transnational Dialogue. *Public Books*, December 11, 2020. https://www.publicbooks.org/making-black-lives-matter-in-italy-a-transnational-dialogue/.

———. 2020b. Making Black Lives Matter in Italy: A Transnational Dialogue. *Public Books*, December 11. https://www.publicbooks.org/making-black-lives-matter-in-italy-a-transnational-dialogue/.

Herero, Alesa. 2019a. Alesa Herero: 'La bianchezza non si auto-nomina mai, ma definisce ciò che è al di fuori, appropriandosene.' By Giulia Parini Bruno. *Nuove radici*, November 27. https://www.nuoveradici.world/cultura/alesa-herero-bianchezza-auto-nomina-mai-definisce-fuori-appropriandosene/.

———. 2019b. Eppure c'era odore di pioggia. In *Future. Il domani narrato dalle voci di oggi*, ed. Igiaba Scego, 147–167. Florence: Effequ.

Hine, Darlene Clark, Tricia Danielle Keaton, and Stephen Small, eds. 2009. *Black Europe and the African Diaspora*. Urbana: University of Illinois Press.

hooks, bell. 1998. *Elogio del margine. Razza, sesso e mercato culturale*. Trans. Maria Nadotti. Milan: Feltrinelli.

Jacobson, Matthew Frye. 1998. *Whiteness of a Different Color: European Immigrants and the Alchemy of Race*. Cambridge, MA: Harvard University Press.

Kan, Djarah. 2019. Il mio nome. In *Future. Il domani narrato dalle voci di oggi*, ed. Igiaba Scego, 55–65. Florence: Effequ.

———. 2020a. *Ladri di denti*. Gallarate: People.

———. 2020b. Non chiamatemi afroitaliana. *Latte Riot* (blog), September 1. https://latteriot.wordpress.com/2020/09/01/non-chiamatemi-afroitaliana/.

Katugampala, Suranga Deshapriya, dir. 2016. *Per un figlio*. Italy: Gina Films. http://www.perunfiglio.it/. Released in English as *For a Son*.

Khouma, Pap. 1995. Intervista di Graziella Parati a Pap Khouma. In *Margins at the Center: African Italian Voices*, ed. Graziella Parati. Special issue, *Italian Studies in Southern Africa/Studi d'Italianistica nell'Africa Australe* 8 (2): 115–120.

———. 2006. *Io, venditore di elefanti. Una vita per forza tra Dakar, Parigi e Milano*, ed. Oreste Pivetta. Milan: Baldini Castoldi Dalai. First published 1990 (Milan: CDE). Trans. Rebecca Hopkins as *I Was an Elephant Salesman: Adventures between Dakar, Paris, and Milan* (Bloomington: Indiana University Press, 2010).

———. 2009. Io, nero italiano e la mia vita ad ostacoli. *la Repubblica*, December 12. https://www.repubblica.it/cronaca/2009/12/12/news/io_nero_italiano_e_la_mia_vita_ad_ostacoli-1820188/.

———. 2010. *Noi italiani neri. Storie di ordinario razzismo*. Milan: Baldini Castoldi Dalai.

Kilomba, Grada. 2008. *Plantation Memories: Episodes of Everyday Racism*. Münster: Unrast Verlag.

Kureishi, Hanif. 1990. *The Buddha of Suburbia*. London: Faber and Faber.

Kuruvilla, Gabriella. 2005a. India. In *Pecore nere*, ed. Flavia Capitani and Emanuele Coen, 69–82. Rome-Bari: Laterza.

———. 2005b. Ruben. In *Pecore nere*, ed. Flavia Capitani and Emanuele Coen, 83–94. Rome-Bari: Laterza.

———. 2008. *È la vita, dolcezza*. Milan: Baldini Castoldi Dalai.

———. 2018. Ruben. Trans. Victoria Offredi Poletto and Giovanna Bellesia-Contuzzi. *The Massachusetts Review* 59 (3): 438–446.

Kuwornu, Fred Kudjo, dir. 2011. *18 Ius soli*. Struggle Filmworks.

———, dir. 2016a. *Blaxploitalian: 100 Years of Blackness in Italian Cinema*. USA, Italy: Blue Rose Films.

———. 2016b. Blaxploitalian. Intervista con Fred Kuwornu. By Camilla Hawthorne. *Doppiozero*, June 17. https://www.doppiozero.com/materiali/why-africa/blaxploitalian-intervista-con-fred-kuwornu.

Labanca, Nicola. 2002a. Nelle colonie. In *Storia dell'emigrazione italiana. Arrivi*, ed. Piero Bevilacqua, Andreina De Clementi, and Emilio Franzina, 193–204. Rome: Donzelli.

———. 2002b. *Oltremare. Storia dell'espansione coloniale italiana*. Bologna: il Mulino.

Leogrande, Alessandro. 2015. *La frontiera*. Milan: Feltrinelli.

Lipsitz, George. 2018. *The Possessive Investment in Whiteness: How White People Profit from Identity Politics*. 20th anniversary ed. Philadelphia: Temple University Press.

Lombardi-Diop, Cristina. 2012a. Igiene, pulizia, bellezza e razza. La 'bianchezza' nella cultura italiana dal Fascismo al dopoguerra. In *Parlare di razza. La lingua del colore tra Italia e Stati Uniti*, ed. Tatiana Petrovich Njegosh and Anna Scacchi, 78–96. Verona: ombre corte.

———. 2012b. Postracial/Postcolonial Italy. In *Postcolonial Italy: Challenging National Homogeneity*, ed. Cristina Lombardi-Diop and Caterina Romeo, 175–190. New York: Palgrave Macmillan.

———. 2014. Postcoloniale/Postrazziale. Riflessioni sulla bianchezza degli italiani. In *L'Italia postcoloniale*, ed. Cristina Lombardi-Diop and Caterina Romeo, 165–177. Florence: Le Monnier-Mondadori.

———. 2015. Transoceanic Race: A Postcolonial Approach to Italian American Studies. In *Transcending Borders, Bridging Gaps: Italian Americana, Diasporic Studies, and the University Curriculum*, ed. Anthony Julian Tamburri and Fred L. Gardaphé, 84–94. New York: John D. Calandra Italian American Institute.

Lombardi-Diop, Cristina, and Caterina Romeo, eds. 2012. *Postcolonial Italy: Challenging National Homogeneity*. New York: Palgrave Macmillan.

———. 2014. The Italian Postcolonial: A Manifesto. *Italian Studies* 69 (3): 425–433.

———, eds. 2015a. *Postcolonial Europe*. Special issue, *Postcolonial Studies* 18 (4).

———. 2015b. State of the Union: Survival Blankets and Falling Stars. In *Postcolonial Europe*, ed. Cristina Lombardi-Diop and Caterina Romeo. Special issue, *Postcolonial Studies* 18 (4): 337–352.

Lorde, Audre. 1984. The Master's Tools Will Never Dismantle the Master's House. In *Sister Outsider: Essays and Speeches by Audre Lorde*, 110–113. Freedom, CA: The Crossing Press.

Love, Bettina L., and Brandelyn Tosolt. 2010. Reality or Rhetoric? Barack Obama and Post-Racial America. *Race, Gender & Class* 17 (3–4): 19–37.

Luconi, Stefano. 2001. *From Paesani to White Ethnics: The Italian Experience in Philadelphia*. Albany: State University of New York Press.

Lukate, Melissa Johanna. 2019. 'Blackness Disrupts My Germanness.': On Embodiment and Questions of Identity and Belonging Among Women of Color in Germany. In *To Exist is to Resist: Black Feminism in Europe*, ed. Akwugo Emejulu and Francesca Sobande, 116–128. London: Pluto Press.

Maglio, Alan, and Medhin Paolos, dirs. 2015. *Asmarina*. Italy.

Makaping, Geneviève. 2001. *Traiettorie di sguardi. E se gli "altri" foste voi?* Soveria Mannelli: Rubbettino. Republished in 2022 (Soveria Mannelli: Rubbettino). Trans. Giovanna Bellesia-Contuzzi and Victoria Offredi Poletto as *Reversing the Gaze: What If the Other Were You?* (New Brunswick: Rutgers University Press, forthcoming in 2023).

Menniti, Alessandra, and Wanees Mousa, hosts. 2020–2021. *CalabriaMondo* (podcast). Aired November 7, 2020, to April 2, 2021. https://www.spreaker. com/show/calabriamondo.

Michel, Noémi. 2015. Sheepology: The Postcolonial Politics of Raceless Racism in Switzerland. In *Postcolonial Europe*, ed. Cristina Lombardi-Diop and Caterina Romeo. Special issue, *Postcolonial Studies* 18 (4): 410–426.

Michell, Roger, dir. 1993. *The Buddha of Suburbia*. Aired November 3–24, on BBC.

Milani, Riccardo, and Francesco Vicario, dirs. 2015–2018. *È arrivata la felicità*. Season 1 and 2. Italy: Rai Fiction.

Moe, Nelson. 2002. *The View from Vesuvius: Italian Culture and the Southern Question*. Berkeley: University of California Press.

Mohanram, Radhika. 2007. *Imperial White: Race, Diaspora, and the British Empire*. Minneapolis: University of Minnesota Press.

Moïse, Marie. 2019. Abbiamo pianto un fiume di risate. In *Future. Il domani narrato dalle voci di oggi*, ed. Igiaba Scego, 35–53. Florence: Effequ.

Morrison, Toni. 1993. *Playing in the Dark: Whiteness and the Literary Imagination*. New York: Vintage Books.

———. 2016. Making America White Again. In Aftermath: Sixteen Writers on Trump's America. *The New Yorker*, November 21. https://www.newyorker. com/magazine/2016/11/21/making-america-white-again.

Moutamid, Elia, dir. 2022. *Maka*. Written by Simone Brioni. Italy: 5e6 Film.

Mubiayi, Ingy. 2005a. Concorso. In *Pecore nere*, ed. Flavia Capitani and Emanuele Coen, 109–138. Rome-Bari: Laterza.

———. 2005b. Documenti, prego. In *Pecore nere*, ed. Flavia Capitani and Emanuele Coen, 97–107. Rome-Bari: Laterza.

———. 2008. Nascita. In *Amori bicolori*, ed. Flavia Capitani and Emanuele Coen, 67–97. Rome-Bari: Laterza.

Nappytalia. n.d. Chi siamo. http://www.nappytalia.it/afro-italian-nappy-girls/. Accessed 2 May 2021.

New Yorker. 2016. Aftermath: Sixteen Writers on Trump's America. November 21.https://www.newyorker.com/magazine/2016/11/21/aftermath-sixteen-writers-on-trumps-america.

Ngũgĩ wa Thiong'o. 1986. *Decolonising the Mind: The Politics of Language in African Literature*. London: James Currey.

Nidi, Alessandro. 2021. Italia e Austria, perché azzurri non si inginocchiano contro razzismo/ 'Faremo altro.' *il sussidiario.net*, June 26. https://www.ilsussidiario.net/news/italia-austria-azzurri-in-ginocchio-o-non-si-inginocchiano-contro-il-razzismo-perche-significato/2188564/.

Nour, Amin, and Paolo Negro, dirs. 2017. *Ambaradan*. Italy: Rain Dogs Film.

O'Healy, Áine. 2012. Screening Intimacy and Racial Difference in Postcolonial Italy. In *Postcolonial Italy: Challenging National Homogeneity*, ed. Cristina Lombardi-Diop and Caterina Romeo, 205–220. New York: Palgrave Macmillan.

———. 2014. Intimità interrazziali nel cinema postcoloniale italiano. In *L'Italia postcoloniale*, ed. Cristina Lombardi-Diop and Caterina Romeo, 192–206. Florence: Le Monnier-Mondadori.

———. 2015. Imagining Lampedusa. In *Italian Mobilities*, ed. Ruth Ben-Ghiat and Stephanie Malia Hom, 152–174. London: Routledge.

———. 2019. *Migrant Anxieties. Italian Cinema in a Transnational Frame*. Bloomington: Indiana University Press.

Obasuyi, Oiza Queens Day. 2020. *Corpi estranei*. Gallarate: People.

Opitz, May, Katharina Oguntoye, and Dagmar Schultz, eds. 1992. *Showing Our Colors: Afro-German Women Speak Out*. Amherst: The University of Massachusetts Press. Trans. Anne V. Adams, in cooperation with Tina Campt, May Opitz, and Dagmar Schultz. Originally published as *Farbe bekennen: Afro-deutsche Frauen anf den Spuren ihrer Geschichte* (Berlin: Orlanda Frauenverlag, 1986).

Orsi, Robert. 1992. The Religious Boundaries of an Inbetween People: Street Feste and the Problem of the Dark-Skinned Other in Italian Harlem, 1920–1990. *American Quarterly* 44 (3): 313–347.

Ouedraogo, Leaticia. 2019. Nassan Tenga. In *Future. Il domani narrato dalle voci di oggi*, ed. Igiaba Scego, 97–124. Florence: Effequ.

Parati, Graziella. 1997. Looking Through Non-Western Eyes: Immigrant Women's Autobiographical Narratives in Italian. In *Writing New Identities: Gender, Nation, and Immigration in Contemporary Europe*, ed. Gisela Brinker-Gabler and Sidonie Smith, 118–142. Minneapolis: University of Minnesota Press.

———. 2005. *Migration Italy: The Art of Talking Back in a Destination Culture*. Toronto: University of Toronto Press.

Pellegrini, Lucio, and Alessandro Angelini, dirs. 2015–2018 *Tutto può succedere*. Seasons 1, 2 and 3. Italy: Cattleya.

Pesarini, Angelica. 2019. Non s'intravede speranza alcuna. In *Future. Il domani narrato dalle voci di oggi*, ed. Igiaba Scego, 66–77. Florence: Effequ.

———. 2020. Questioni di privilegio: L'Italia e i suoi George Floyd. *Il lavoro culturale*, June 6. http://www.lavoroculturale.org/questioni-di-privilegio/angelica-pesarini/2020/.

Pesole, Elisabetta. 2015. Genere, 'razza' e crisi albanese a Telenorba. In *Il colore della nazione*, ed. Gaia Giuliani, 106–122. Florence: Le Monnier-Mondadori.

Petrovich Njegosh, Tatiana. 2012. Gli italiani sono bianchi? Per una storia culturale della linea del colore in Italia. In *Parlare di razza. La lingua del colore tra Italia e Stati Uniti*, ed. Anna Scacchi, 13–45. Verona: ombre corte.

Pezzarossa, Fulvio. 2014. Gemelli d'Italia. Jadelin Gangbo scrive *Due volte*. In *Identità, migrazioni e postcolonialismo in Italia. A partire da Edward Said*, ed. Bruno Brunetti and Roberto Derobertis, 152–174. Bari: Progedit.

Pivetta, Oreste. 2006. Introduzione. *Io venditore di elefanti. Una vita per forza tra Dakar, Parigi e Milano*. By Pap Khouma, ed. Oreste Pivetta, 7–9. Milan: Baldini Castoldi Dalai.

Poidimani, Nicoletta. 2009. *Difendere la "razza." Identità razziale e politiche sessuali nel progetto imperiale di Mussolini.* Rome: Sensibili alle foglie.

Portelli, Alessandro. 2000. Le origini della letteratura afroitaliana e l'esempio afroamericano. *L'ospite ingrato. Globalizzazione e identità: Annuario del Centro Studi Franco Fortini* 3: 69–86.

———. 2003. The Problem of the Color Blind: Notes on the Discourse on Race in Italy. In *CrossRoutes—The Meanings of "Race" for the 21st Century*, ed. Paola Boi and Sabine Broeck, 29–39. Münster: LIT.

———. 2010. Sulla linea del colore. *Alessandro Portelli* (blog), October 11. http://alessandroportelli.blogspot.com/2010/10/web-dubois-sulla-linea-del-colore.html.

Proglio, Gabriele, Camilla Hawthorne, P. Ida Danewid, Khalil Saucier, Giuseppe Grimaldi, Angelica Pesarini, Timothy Raeymaekers, Giulia Grechi, and Vivian Gerrand, eds. 2021. *The Black Mediterranean: Bodies, Borders and Citizenship.* Cham: Palgrave Macmillan.

Purtschert, Patricia, Barbara Lüthi, and Francesca Falk, eds. 2012. *Postkoloniale Schweiz: Formen und Folgen eines Kolonialismus ohne Kolonien.* Bielefeld: Transcript Verlag.

Purtschert, Patricia, Francesca Falk, and Barbara Lüthi. 2016. Switzerland and 'Colonialism without Colonies': Reflections on the Status of Colonial Outsiders. *Interventions: International Journal of Postcolonial Studies* 18 (2): 286–302.

Puwar, Nirmal. 2004. *Space Invaders: Race, Gender and Bodies out of Place.* Oxford: Berg.

Ragusa, Kym. 1997. *fuori/outside.* Ibla Productions: Video.

———. 2006. *The Skin Between Us: A Memoir of Race, Beauty, and Belonging.* New York: Norton. Trans. Clara Antonucci and Caterina Romeo as *La pelle che ci separa* (Rome: Nutrimenti, 2008).

———. 2008a. *La pelle che ci separa.* Trans. Clara Antonucci and Caterina Romeo. Rome: Nutrimenti. Originally published as *The Skin Between Us: A Memoir of Race, Beauty, and Belonging* (New York: Norton, 2006).

———. 2008b. Three Women, Three Photographs. In *About Face. Women Write of What They See When They Look in the Mirror*, ed. Anne Burt and Christina Baker Kline, 55–61. Berkeley: Seal Press.

Ricatti, Francesco. 2018. *Italians in Australia: History, Memory, Identity.* Cham: Palgrave Macmillan.

Ripanti, Espérance Hakuzwimana. 2019. *E poi basta. Manifesto di una donna nera italiana.* Gallarate: People.

Rivera, Annamaria. 2003. *Estranei e nemici. Discriminazione e violenza razzista in Italia.* Rome: DeriveApprodi.

———. 2009. *Regole e roghi. Metamorfosi del razzismo.* Bari: Dedalo.

Rochat, Giorgio. 1973. *Il colonialismo italiano.* Turin: Loescher.

Roediger, David. 1991. *The Wages of Whiteness: Essays on Race, Politics, and Working Class History*. London: Verso.

Romeo, Caterina. 2006. Il colore bianco. La costruzione della razza in Italia e la sua rappresentazione nella letteratura di scrittrici migranti e postmigranti. In *L'italiano lingua di migrazione. Verso l'affermazione di una cultura transnazionale agli inizi del XXI secolo*, ed. Anna Frabetti and Walter Zidaric, 79–88. Nantes: CRINI, Nantes.

———. 2008. Una capacità quasi acrobatica. Afterword to *La pelle che ci separa*, by Kym Ragusa, 249–270. Rome: Nutrimenti.

———. 2012. Racial Evaporations: Representing Blackness in African Italian Postcolonial Literature. In *Postcolonial Italy: Challenging National Homogeneity*, ed. Cristina Lombardi-Diop and Caterina Romeo, 221–236. New York: Palgrave Macmillan.

Rushdie, Salman. 1980. *Midnight's Children*. New York: Penguin.

Sabelli, Sonia. 2010. Quando la subalterna parla. *Le Traiettorie di sguardi* di Geneviève Makaping. In *Fuori centro. Percorsi postcoloniali nella letteratura italiana*, ed. Roberto Derobertis, 131–148. Rome: Aracne.

Santos, Boaventura de Sousa. 2002. Between Prospero and Caliban: Colonialism, Postcolonialism, and Inter-Identity. *Luzo-Brazilian Review* 39 (2): 9–43.

Scarabello, Serena, and Marleen de Witte. 2019. Afroeuropean Modes of Self-Making: Afro-Dutch and Afro-Italian Projects Compared. *Open Cultural Studies* 3 (1): 317–331.

Scego, Igiaba. 2005. Salsicce. In *Pecore Nere*, ed. Flavia Capitani and Emanuele Coen, 23–36. Rome-Bari: Laterza. Trans. Giovanna Bellesia and Victoria Offredi Poletto as Sausages. *Metamorphoses: The Journal of the Five College Faculty Seminar on Literary Translation* 13 (2, Fall 2005): 214–225.

———. 2008. Identità. In *Amori bicolori. Racconti*, ed. Flavia Capitani and Emanuele Coen, 3–33. Laterza: Rome-Bari.

———. 2009. *Il Terzo Anello—Fantasmi: Black Italians*. Radio broadcast. Rai Radio Tre. https://podcasthall.forumcommunity.net/?t=33286585.

———. 2010. *La mia casa è dove sono*. Milan: Rizzoli.

———. 2015. La rivoluzione degli afroitaliani parte dal piccolo schermo. *Internazionale*, October 31. https://www.internazionale.it/opinione/igiaba-scego/2015/10/31/afroitaliani-seconde-generazioni-tv.

———. 2016. Capelli di libertà. *L'Espresso* 42 (1): 34–36.

———, ed. 2019. *Future. Il domani narrato dalle voci di oggi*. Florence: Effequ.

———. 2020. *La linea del colore*. Milan: Bompiani.

Scego, Igiaba, and Esther Elisha, hosts. 2021. *Tell Me Mama* (podcast). Aired 2021. https://www.storytel.com/it/it/series/63028-Tell-Me-Mama?gclid=CjwKCAiAiKuOBhBQEiwAId_sK0x4IppE8jXRkauM92yD1DB-2_wwY6haM8J87Lk7MKdXR-THu9q0SxoCA-4QAvD_BwE.

Schneider, Jane, ed. 1998. *Italy's "Southern Question": Orientalism in One Country*. Oxford: Berg.

Segre, Andrea, dir. 2010. *Il sangue verde*. Italy: ZaLab-Aeternam Films.

Sibhatu, Ribka. 2004. *Il cittadino che non c'è. L'immigrazione nei media italiani*. Rome: EDUP.

Sòrgoni, Barbara. 1998. *Parole e corpi. Antropologia, discorso giuridico e politiche sessuali interrazziali nella colonia Eritrea (1890–1941)*. Naples: Liguori.

Stefani, Giulietta. 2007. *Colonia per maschi. Italiani in Africa Orientale: una storia di genere*. Verona: ombre corte.

Taguieff, Pierre-André. 1999. *Il razzismo. Pregiudizi, teorie, comportamenti*. Milan: Cortina Editore.

Tekle, Ariam, and Emmanuelle Maréchal, hosts. 2020–2022. *Blackcoffee* (podcast). First episode aired May 7. https://linktr.ee/blackcoffee_pdc; https://linktr.ee/blackcoffee_pdc.

Tenzer, Livia. 2002. Documenting Race and Gender: Kym Ragusa Discusses *Passing* and *Fuori/Outside*. In *Looking Across the Lens: Women's Studies and Film*. Special issue, *Women's Studies Quarterly* 30 (1–2): 213–220.

Teti, Vito. 1993. *La razza maledetta. Origini del pregiudizio antimeridionale*. Rome: manifestolibri.

Tintori, Guido. 2016. Italian Mobilities and the Demos. In *Italian Mobilities*, ed. Ruth Ben-Ghiat and Stephanie Malia Hom, 111–132. New York: Routledge.

Tirabassi, Maddalena, and Alvise Del Pra'. 2014. *La meglio Italia. Le mobilità italiane del XXI secolo*. Turin: Accademia University Press.

Umuhoza, Marilena Delli. 2020. *Negretta. Baci razzisti*. Rome: Red Star Press.

Uyangoda, Nadeesha. 2021. *L'unica persona nera nella stanza*. Rome: 66thand2nd.

Vecoli, Rudolph. 1995. Are Italians Just White Folks? *Italian Americana* 13 (Summer): 149–165.

Verdicchio, Pasquale. 1997. The Preclusion of Postcolonial Discourse in Southern Italy. In *Revisioning Italy: National Identity and Global Culture*, ed. B. Allen and M. Russo, 191–212. Minneapolis: University of Minnesota Press.

Viarengo, Maria Abbebù. 1990. Andiamo a spasso? *Linea d'Ombra* 54: 74–76.

———. 1999. 'Scirscir N'Demna?' (Let's Go for a Stroll). Trans. Anasuya Sanyal. In *Mediterranean Crossroads: Migration Literature in Italy*, ed. Graziella Parati, 69–78. Madison, NJ: Fairleigh Dickinson University Press.

Visconti, Luchino. 1960. *Rocco e i suoi fratelli*. Italy and France: Titanus-Les Films Marceau. Released in English as *Rocco and His Brothers*.

Viscusi, Robert. 2010. The History of Italian American Literary Studies. In *Teaching Italian American Literature, Film, and Popular Culture*, ed. Edvige Giunta and Kathleen Zamboni McCormick, 43–58. New York: MLA.

Wadia, Laila. 2005a. Curry di pollo. In *Pecore nere*, ed. Flavia Capitani and Emanuele Coen, 39–52. Rome-Bari: Laterza. Trans. Monica Hanna as Chicken Curry. In *Other Italies/Italy's Others*, ed. Thalia Pandiri. Special issue, *Metamorphoses: The Journal of the Five College Faculty Seminar on Literary Translation* 14 (1–2, Spring and Fall 2006): 150–57.

————. 2005b. Karnevale. In *Pecore nere*, ed. Flavia Capitani and Emanuele Coen, 53–65. Rome-Bari: Laterza.

Wekker, Gloria. 2016. *White Innocence: Paradoxes of Colonialism and Race.* Durham, NC: Duke University Press.

Wise, Tim. 2010. *Colorblind: The Rise of Post-Racial Politics and the Retreat from Racial Equity.* San Francisco: City Lights Books.

Yimer, Dagmawi, Giulio Cederna, and Fabrizio Barraco, dirs. 2011. *Soltanto il mare.* Rome: Archivio delle Memorie Migranti di Asinitas, Marco Guadagnino, Alessandro Triulzi. Released in English as *Nothing But the Sea.*

CHAPTER 5

Geographies of Diaspora
and New Urban Mappings

We're not British, we're Londoners.
—Stephen Frears (and Hanif Kureishi), *Sammy and Rosie Get Laid*

5.1   INTRODUCTION

In Kym Ragusa's memoir, *The Skin Between Us* (2006), the author, who is African American on her mother's side and Italian American on her father's side, claims that the construction of her own subjectivity began in the places where she was born and grew up, characterized by divisions between her two communities of origin. These fractures, the author claims, have remained imprinted on her body, the mapping of Harlem literally lies under her skin:

I DON'T KNOW where I was conceived, but I was made in Harlem.
    Its topography is mapped on my body: the borderlines between neighborhoods marked by streets that were forbidden to cross, the borderlines enforced by fear and anger, and transgressed by desire. The streets crossing east to west, north to south, like the web of veins beneath my skin. (Ragusa 2006, 26)[1]

[1] Ragusa's memoir has been translated into Italian by Caterina Romeo and Clara Antonucci and published in Italy. See Ragusa (2008).

© The Author(s), under exclusive license to Springer Nature   219
Switzerland AG 2023
C. Romeo, *Interrupted Narratives and Intersectional*
Representations in Italian Postcolonial Literature, Italian and Italian
American Studies,
https://doi.org/10.1007/978-3-031-10043-7_5

On one side is West Harlem, the Black Harlem of her mother's family; on the other East Harlem, the Italian Harlem (now Spanish Harlem) of her father's family; two contiguous yet very distant places, separated by invisible yet impassable lines. Ragusa finds herself in the middle, and the topography of Harlem is mapped onto her body because that body is the result of a crossing of borders that were never meant to be trespassed. When she was still a child, the Italian side of her family had moved to The Bronx and then to New Jersey in an attempt to put some distance between themselves and the new immigrants that were arriving in Harlem and in general in New York City. Their decision to move to The Bronx and then to the suburbs of New Jersey in the 1970s was part of the "white flight" that, starting in the 1950s and 1960s, had led various communities of European origin in the United States to leave the urban areas where they lived—quite diverse from a racial standpoint—to settle in the much more homogeneous city suburbs and exurban areas. For Italian American communities—and for others—this move away from cities stemmed from a desire to consolidate their whiteness. As Robert Anthony Orsi (1992) argues in a study on the racial perception (and self-perception) of Italians in Harlem from the 1920s to the 1990s, in terms of race, Italians from the South (who constituted the majority of migrants to the United States) and their descendants were characterized by a dangerous "inbetweenness" that made their whiteness (sanctioned by law) too labile and their white privilege too weak for them not to fear the proximity of African Americans, Caribbean peoples of African and Hispanic origin, and later Puerto Ricans, Mexicans, and Hispanics.

The flight of Italian Americans to the suburbs therefore represented a two-fold strategy: to eliminate a dangerous proximity to the dark-skinned "other" and to create pathways to greater social mobility free (at least in part) from an uncomfortable racial ambiguity. This process, however, was not without consequences, in that Italian Americans' effort

> to establish the border against the dark-skinned other required an intimate struggle, a contest against the initial uncertainty over which side of the racial dichotomy the swarthy immigrants were on and against the facts of history and geography that inscribed this ambiguity on the urban landscape. (Orsi 1992, 318)

As Ragusa explains, her family's strategy of strengthening their whiteness produces an even deeper sense of ambivalence in her, since it is precisely from bodies like hers that the family wants to distance themselves.[2]

Ragusa eloquently narrated that migrations induce a certain level of preoccupation, as they always alter power relations within and between communities and society at large. Teresa Fiore (2017) has observed that the spaces occupied by migrants are both *pre-occupied* (with a hyphen)—in the sense that they have been previously occupied and are therefore already inhabited when the migrants arrive—and *preoccupied* (without a hyphen)—in that they are imbued with preoccupation caused by the new arrivals in the native inhabitants, who fear that the new cohabitation might generate friction, conflict, and violence. Francesco Ricatti (2018) has also highlighted some characteristics common to the various migrations using homophonic terms, in this case, *intention* (one word) and *in tension* (two words). Analyzing outgoing migrations from Italy to Australia, Ricatti points out that most migrants are motivated by *intention*, a desire, for example, to improve their living conditions, but that their lives are also *in tension*, that is, subject to the tension created by relocating from their country of origin to the country in which they intend to settle. The tension Ricatti identifies as a driving force for migrants is in turn perceived by the population of the country of arrival—and is undoubtedly a tension of a different type, very close to what Fiore calls *preoccupation* (without a hyphen).

This tension/preoccupation increases and becomes structural in society if, at the political and communicative level, the myth of "invasion" is generated. This myth is nurtured in Italy—not least by xenophobic political parties and the media that support them—despite a steady increase in outbound migration, which since 2013 has consistently exceeded 100,000 people per year (Mancino 2018). What should be a cause for concern, then, is not any false narrative about inbound migration but the number

---

[2] For a reflection on the racial connotations of urban spaces in Kym Ragusa's memoir and for a critical analysis of the text, see Romeo (2008).

of Italians leaving the Bel Paese[3] for other places where it is possible to find work or imagine a different life.[4] The fact that the number of Italians residing abroad is slightly higher than the number of foreign residents in Italy—even though debate on the new mobilities is still scarce—clearly shows how Italy implements protectionist and securitarian policies designed to hinder immigration and "integration" of migrants and subsequent generations,[5] while it should on the one hand approve a new law on the attribution of citizenship, and on the other promote social and economic policies that would induce many young Italians to seek a future in their own country.[6] As the data in the notes highlight, incoming and outgoing migrations need to be examined through a continuity perspective that takes into account that the remapping of the spaces of a nation—Italy in this case—is carried out on the basis not only of new presences but also of new absences.

Since the 1980s, when incoming migrations became a consistent phenomenon, migrants, refugees, and asylum seekers (and their descendants) in Italy have remapped physical and symbolic national spaces and rewritten colonial history, starting with the locations they inhabit. Because of the high concentration of migrants in cities, the remapping of urban spaces is frequently represented in postcolonial literature—think of the London of *The Satanic Verses* (1988) by Salman Rushdie, *The Buddha of Suburbia*

---

[3] Almost 197,800 Italian citizens were enrolled in the Registry of Italian Residents Abroad (Anagrafe degli italiani residenti all'estero; AIRE) in 2020, 130,936 of them for expatriation, with an increase of 3.6% as compared with 2019 (Fondazione Migrantes 2020, 4–19). Here and below in this section, I provide the data from 2020, although the 2021 data are available (and I use them in other chapters of the book) because the COVID-19 pandemic has changed the migration trends of Italy and has affected both incoming and outgoing migrations in ways that are too complex to be analyzed here. On the subject, see, among others, Tirabassi and Del Pra' (2020). See also the afterword in Raffini and Giorgi (2020).

[4] The primary destination for Italian migrants in 2019 was the United Kingdom, followed by Germany, France, Brazil, Switzerland, Spain, the United States, Argentina, and Australia (Fondazione Migrantes 2020, 24).

[5] Compare the data of the *Dossier Statistico Immigrazione 2020* with those of the *Rapporto italiani nel mondo 2020*, which show that the number of foreign residents in Italy at the end of 2019 was 5,306,584, or 8.8% of the total population, while the number of Italians who were enrolled in AIRE at the beginning of 2020 was 5,486,081, or 9.1% of the total population (Centro Studi e Ricerche IDOS 2020; Fondazione Migrantes 2020). According to the *Rapporto italiani nel mondo 2020*, there was a 76.6% increase in the number of Italians enrolled in AIRE from 2006 to 2020 (Fondazione Migrantes 2020, 4).

[6] Of those who left Italy in 2019, 40.9% were between the ages of 18 and 34, 23.9% were between the ages of 35 and 49, and 20.3% were minors (Fondazione Migrantes 2020, 19).

(1990) by Hanif Kureishi, and *White Teeth* (2000) by Zadie Smith, to name but a few. In Italy, for instance, the narratives of Amara Lakhous (2006, 2010, 2013, 2014) are focused entirely on the cities where they unfold, first Rome and then Turin. In Lakhous's novels, the heterogeneity that migrants bring to urban spaces comes to corroborate and enrich the already existing heterogeneity of the native population and of the pre-existing urban communities. Dagmawi Yimer's Rome in *Come un uomo sulla terra* (*Like a Man on Earth*) (Segre et al. 2008), however, is the city where newly arrived asylum seekers, migrants, and refugees rebuild their sense of self through the narration of the traumas they experienced during the crossing of the desert, the detention in the camps in Libya, and the crossing of the Mediterranean, while Florence in *Va' pensiero. Storie ambulanti* (*Va' Pensiero—Walking Stories*) (Yimer 2013) is depicted as a place where street vendors become prey to racist criminals.

Added to these narratives, beginning in the 2000s, are those by second-generation authors. These new narratives are no longer marked by a consciousness and sensibility linked to migration; instead, they are grounded in a widespread sense of belonging to the urban spaces in which the authors rewrite alternative geographies, which are both transnational and postnational. Such geographies ideally connect to other urban environments in Europe and around the world in which the children of migrants undergo similar experiences, albeit in places far distant from one another, experiences that are rooted in the diasporic histories of their families of origin, in cultural and religious differences, and in their divergence from the national chromatic norm. Exploring these narratives involves analyzing how the representations of postcolonial cities have changed and how they construct imaginaries that redefine the very notion of belonging to the Italian nation.

5.2   Postcolonial Urban Countermapping

In analyzing the concept of place and the articulation between space and power in colonial contexts, Bill Ashcroft (2001) observes that the colonial "obsession" with maps is an expression of the colonizers' anxiety about controlling the conquered territories. The map, argues Ashcroft, offers visual imagery of the territory, and the common etymology in Greek of the verbs "to see" and "to know" suggests that being able to see means being able to know, and thus to control. For the colonial powers to be able to dominate the space, however, the simple act of looking was not sufficient and needed to be followed by the act of "inscribing," both literally and symbolically. Through maps, not only could colonizers reimagine and remap territories, the written language also allowed them to erase the presence of the colonized in such spaces by replacing the language of the colonized with their own (think, for instance, of the process of renaming colonial cities). In this way, colonial territories were transformed from "inhabited places" (by the native populations) into "empty spaces" (from which the native presence had been erased) and then again into "inhabited places" (this time by the colonizers) (Ashcroft 2001, 132).[7] Through the retextualization and resignification of spaces, colonial powers exercised a discursive control over places (134). In this process, maps are a necessary first step for exercising the power of surveillance over territories that become accessible as texts. Once the territories have been remapped, they must be made physically accessible. Significantly, one of the expressions of colonial anxiety about controlling spaces by the Italian government—as well as others—was the construction of thousands of kilometers of roads in the colonies.

While the need to impose their control and surveillance on colonized countries was a priority of colonial empires, at the time of postcolonial transnational migrations, this need travels along with the migrants to the heart of Fortress Europe. Here, nation states exercise what Henri Lefebvre considers one of the main functions of modern states: "the organization of space, the regularization of its flows, the control of its networks" (1991, 383). This means that modern states that were once colonial empires—and this includes Italy—today exercise their control over the lives of migrants who come from nations that were once colonized and over the spaces to which they have (or do not have) access.[8] As Ashcroft notes, however, "the transformation of imperial conceptions of place, and of imperial technologies of spatial representation, has often been carried out successfully in imaginative acts of resistance through the *creative* representations of place" (2001, 156; italics in the original). The present chapter is devoted to examining such creative representations.

---

[7] Ashcroft defines a "place" as "a process intimately bound up with the culture and the identity of its inhabitants," "a result of habitation, a consequence of the ways in which people inhabit space, particularly that conception of space as universal and uncontestable that is constructed for them by imperial discourse" (2001, 156).

[8] For an analysis of how space and place are racialized in Italy, and of how such racialization affects the lives of migrants, refugees, and African Italians, see Merrill (2018).

Igiaba Scego, Ubax Cristina Ali Farah, Jadelin Mabiala Gangbo, and Gabriella Kuruvilla are the second-generation writers analyzed in this chapter who carry out "the transformation of imperial conceptions of place" (Ashcroft 2001, 156). Through their representations of the social changes taking place in contemporary postcolonial Italy, these authors draw urban countermappings that redefine living conditions in cities. What I intend to examine specifically is the way in which, by populating narratives and urban landscapes with migrant and second-generation characters who do not conform to the everyday representations of undesirability produced by securitarian policies and disseminated by the media, these authors contribute to the creation of new imaginaries linked to cities. Through remapping urban spaces as places of cultural significance and questioning traditional articulations of power in those spaces, second-generation authors also challenge traditional representations of the assumed homogeneity of the Italian population, producing narratives in opposition to those that see migrants as threatening and dangerous subjects, as well as to those that see them as victims deprived of agency. Second generations radically contest the attribution of citizenship according to the principle of *ius sanguinis* (or biological descent) and suggest instead the existence of "new ways of being Italian, whether by virtue of being born in Italy, through everyday experiences and practices, or through participation in the educational system and a dynamic use of the national language" (Lombardi-Diop and Romeo 2012, 9–10). This dynamism is also deeply connected to the way in which urban spaces are occupied and represented and to how these processes contribute to the creation of new Italian national identities.

Igiaba Scego and Ubax Cristina Ali Farah rewrite the conventional representations that consistently relegate migrant women to caregiver or sex worker roles by creating new imaginaries associated with them. In doing so, these authors restore complexity to the migrant experience and to the possible articulations of social relationships in the country of arrival. Even though conventional roles are not entirely absent from Scego's first novel, *Rhoda* (2004), the text also presents a broad representation of different gender roles, diasporic places, and relationships between migrant and native women. In the novel, the Somali Italian protagonist is a woman unable to heal the inner fracture that the diaspora has created: Rhoda becomes a sex worker, contracts AIDS, and dies following an assault (her narrative is presented post-mortem from the grave in Mogadishu). For Aisha, Rhoda's younger sister, the fracture has had less devastating effects, which has allowed her to build a sense of belonging in her city, Rome. The urban spaces of Naples and Rome depicted in the novel are not simply the background against which the story develops, they profoundly influence the processes of subjectivity construction in the characters, who, in turn, shape the spaces "out of the densely woven web of language, memory, and cultural practice" (Ashcroft 2001, 156), thus through the daily practices that come to life in those spaces.

A feeling of belonging to the Italian nation is absent in the novel, replaced by a strong sense of local identity. The novel opens in Rome, where Aisha goes to a hairdresser who is located "in an anonymous street dedicated to an anonymous leader of some surely useless war"[9] (Scego 2004, 7). In the second chapter, Rome is juxtaposed with Naples—"Naples was not breathing that night despite the sea"[10] (12)—and the mention of the Mediterranean Sea immediately brings to mind the thousands of migrants who lose their lives daily trying to reach the southern coasts of Europe, mainly from Africa. The reference to the illegal status of these migrants and the fact that the Mediterranean is a space of connection but also of disconnection between the two continents is made explicit earlier in the narrative:

> The city that night was covered by a thick layer of dust. A yellowish dust that caused allergies, fear, mistrust, anguish, and gossip. The TV said it was desert sand; the TV also said it came from Africa like the illegal immigrants who now landed daily on the Italian coasts. The TV, however, often lied. Or rather, omitted. Maybe that dust was just a symbol of the decay of a nation, or, who knows, even of the entire world. It was the symbol of global incomprehension.[11] (Scego 2004, 15)

While the "degradation" that comes from Africa, symbolized by the yellowish sand of the Sahara, is linked to the presence of migrants, the heat and dust of the city are associated with the hypersexualized image of African sex workers, the only ones who continue to work in such adverse weather conditions. The representation of Naples as a place of

---

[9] "in una via anonima dedicata a un condottiero anonimo di qualche guerra di sicuro inutile." [All translations are the translator's unless noted otherwise].

[10] "Napoli quella sera non respirava nonostante il mare."

[11] "La città quella sera era coperta da uno strato spesso di polvere. Una polverina giallastra che provocava allergie, paura, diffidenza, angoscia e pettegolezzo. La TV diceva che era sabbia del deserto, la TV diceva pure che proveniva dall'Africa come i clandestini che sbarcavano ormai giornalmente sulle coste italiane. La TV però spesso mentiva. O meglio, ometteva."

perdition—for example, Somali immigrants call prostitutes *reer Napoli* (Scego 2004, 102)—is combined with the city's frequent association with a generic elsewhere in the Global South: Naples is called a "brutal forest"[12] (57) and a "Neapolitan jungle"[13] (59). Through images that recall the process of colonial remapping—a process that is articulated through the essentialization of conquered territories' wild nature and the erasure of a previous human presence in those spaces—Scego here reinforces orientalizing ideas about both Africa and Southern Italy.[14]

The representation of Rome in the novel is more complex. When the city is shown through the eyes of Aisha—the most Roman character and the author's alter ego—streets, squares, parks, and public transport routes outline a geography of daily life in which people's existences constantly converge and diverge. Rome acquires a global dimension connected to its being a place of destination for migrants. As Isabella Clough Marinaro and Bjørn Thomassen argue, even though Rome is usually marginalized in the field of global studies focused on economic analysis, it must be considered a global city from different perspectives, because it is "a hub for global diplomacy … immigration, religious pilgrimage, and tourism, and it is one of the world's most known and 'imagined cities,' playing a central role in cinema and popular literature around the globe" (2014, 3). In the novel, Rome is not represented in the traditional way as an international icon of culture, history, and art but rather as a center of global migrations whose geography is constantly remapped by the daily practices of migrant and postcolonial subjects.

Aisha and Rhoda's aunt Barni and her friend Faduma share Rhoda's strong sense of uprootedness, not only because of their distance from their country of origin but also because domestic work confines them to a narrow space of near invisibility. However, their strong connection with the Somali community creates a sense of what I term a "rooted uprooting," which allows them to exercise their agency and thus improve their lives both materially and immaterially. At the end of the novel, Barni and Faduma open an "ethnic" store (Scego 2004, 185), which they call "Rhoda," in the suburban district of Primavalle,

---

[12] "selva brutale."

[13] "giungla napoletana."

[14] For an analysis of Southern Italians constructed as the Other at the intranational level and of orientalizing representations through which the subalternity of the South was consolidated, see, among others, Verdicchio (1997), Schneider (1998), and Brunetti and Derobertis (2009).

where Barni lives with Aisha. By becoming entrepreneurs in their own neighborhood, characterized as it is by the cohabitation of different cultures, the two Somali women create a deeper connection with their adopted city and contribute to redesigning its geography. While marriage to an Italian man—as in the case of Barni's friend Nura Hussein—enables social advancement but no legitimization or empowerment, Barni and Faduma change their social status through a complex process of collaboration and affiliation with other women, both immigrants and natives (the store is owned by Rhoda's friend Sandra, who is Italian of Italian origin). The store's sign, "Rhoda," visually stands out and testifies to the presence of Somali women in the entrepreneurial space of Rome. The shift from the domestic space to the urban space marks an important transition from social invisibility to social visibility and, as a result, establishes the right of migrants and subsequent generations to occupy new spaces, both physically and symbolically.[15]

The process of mapping and remapping the colonial and postcolonial space of the city of Rome is the center around which Igiaba Scego's memoir, *La mia casa è dove sono* (My Home Is Where I Am) (2010), revolves. All the chapters in the book whose titles contain references to city locations ("Teatro Sistina," "Piazza Santa Maria sopra Minerva," "La stele di Axum," "Stazione Termini," "Trastevere," "Stadio Olimpico") are a tribute to the capital and can be read as a reply to the first chapter, "Il disegno ovvero la terra che non c'è" (The Sketch; Or, the Country That Does Not Exist), in which the protagonist and some family members draw a map of Mogadishu to prevent their memories of their city of origin from

---

[15] The transition from social invisibility to social visibility, according to Jacqueline Andall (2002), is an important moment for migrant communities that can, however, encounter hostility and resistance from native communities. This occurred, for example, in Italy at the end of the 1980s, when migration became a visible phenomenon mainly due to two different reasons: (1) the number of migrants had risen sharply; (2) migrants became more visible. In the 1970s and the early 1980s, migrants were mainly women from the Horn of Africa and Asian women (and men) who were employed mostly as domestic servants and lived in the houses where they worked. It was the arrival of migrants predominantly from Morocco and Senegal toward the mid-1980s—who were instead highly visible, as they were Black and worked as street vendors—that provoked the hostility of the native population.

dissolving. To this paper city, which serves as a repository of memories, Scego juxtaposes a tangible city. The author selects places that are crucial to her personal story, as well as to the history of her family, and analyzes the importance of reconnecting the colonial traces scattered throughout the city of Rome with a still often forgotten chapter of Italian history.

As Nicola Labanca argues, "in almost all the cities on the Peninsula, the toponymic memory of the colonial enterprises of unified Italy lives on: a Piazza Adua, a Corso Tripoli, or a Via Mogadishu, or similar, still feature in the Italian street directories"[16] (2002, 7). The fact that these signs are scattered throughout Italian cities, however, does not make them inherently meaningful. As Ruth Ben-Ghiat (2017) argues, the amnesia regarding colonial and Fascist history has caused the connection with the past that these signs/monuments symbolize to be lost, and this has led to a dangerous process of normalization.[17] The American historian urges reflection on the fact that the permanence of symbols of Fascism in Italy, including imposing edifices such as the Palazzo della Civiltà Italiana and stadiums such as the Foro Italico, indeed risks normalizing Fascism and its ideology if not accompanied by an associated critical reflection. At a time when the xenophobic European right grows stronger every day, it is indispensable to reflect on the need to confer new meaning to buildings and symbols from a historical period that has not been sufficiently processed by Italian society and culture—a period that includes the brutality of the Fascist regime, racial laws, and war crimes committed in the colonies (the Palazzo della Civiltà Italiana in Rome is in fact a symbol of the fascist invasion of Ethiopia). As Igiaba Scego argues, "the monuments of Fascism are not neutral relics, as Ruth Ben-Ghiat has pointed out, and it is not right to leave them at the mercy of deviant meanings, as is now the case. From the

---

[16] "In quasi tutte le città della Penisola permane il ricordo toponomastico delle imprese coloniali dell'Italia unita: una piazza Adua, un corso Tripoli o una via Mogadiscio, o simili, fanno ancora mostra di sé negli elenchi stradali italiani."

[17] Ben-Ghiat's (2017) article has given rise to a lively discussion in which prominent figures of Italian culture, such as Roberto Saviano (2017) and Igiaba Scego (2017), have taken part.

Foro Italico to the Fascist Party headquarters, pathways that shine light on the uncomfortable history of those monuments are lacking"[18] (2017).

Constructing such pathways is the objective pursued in *Roma negata* (Rome Denied), a critical essay with text by Igiaba Scego and photographs by Rino Bianchi, which Scego herself defines as "an emotional journey through the city" (Bianchi and Scego 2014, 50).[19] In this text, Scego and Bianchi observe and listen to places in Rome in order to rediscover the traces of a colonial history that has been systematically erased. Rino Bianchi's photographs, from which the narrative unfolds, depict Italians of African origin—many of whom are artists and cultural producers—in places throughout Rome that are connected to the history of Italian colonialism, which in the present are profoundly redefined through the presence of the descendants of those who were once colonial subjects. In the wake of postcolonial studies, Scego argues that contemporary racism cannot be understood without a deep knowledge of the processes of racialization enacted in the colonies, nor can the contemporary imaginary relating to Black women be understood without knowledge of the imaginary of the Black Venus of colonial memory.

Starting with the observation that the monument now standing where the Obelisk of Axum stood from 1937 to 2003 does not commemorate the history of Italian colonialism but rather the victims of September 11,

---

[18] "I monumenti del fascismo non sono tracce neutre come ben ha fatto notare Ruth Ben-Ghiat e non è giusto, come avviene ora, lasciarle alla mercé di significati deviati. Dal Foro italico alle case del fascio mancano percorsi che mettano in luce la storia scomoda di quei monumenti." An interesting, though much discussed, proposal came in 2017 from the city of Bolzano, which launched an art competition for projects that would "depotentiate" ("depotenziare") the frieze on the Palazzo delle Finanze, in Piazza del Tribunale—the former local headquarters of the Fascist Party. It is the largest marble frieze in Europe, commissioned from Hans Piffrader by Benito Mussolini, and it tells the story of the rise of Fascism from the end of the First World War to the March on Rome. The winners of the competition were Arnold Holzknecht and Michele Bernardi. The solution proposed by the two artists to give new meaning to the frieze, which has since been completed, was to place in front of the frieze an illuminated inscription in three languages (Ladin, German, and Italian) with a quote by Hannah Arendt, one of the greatest opponents of Nazi-Fascist totalitarianism: "Nobody has the right to obey" ("Nessuno ha il diritto di obbedire"). This undertaking, which has not failed to arouse debate and criticism, has the indisputable merit of offering a solution that allows preservation of these monuments bearing witness to an important but tragic chapter of Italian history without, however, allowing the monuments—and thus the ideology that they represent—to undergo a process of normalization. On conferring new meaning to the Bolzano frieze, see Marsala (2017).

[19] "un viaggio emozionale attraverso la città."

2001, Scego denounces the fact that the systematic cancellation of the memory of colonialism taking place in Rome and throughout Italy has in fact rendered places such as this mute. Scego and Bianchi oppose this silence through images that depict these places inhabited by descendants of the colonized and through a broad narrative of the historical events connected to them: Piazza di Porta Capena, which until 2003 had been the site of the Obelisk of Axum, taken by Mussolini from Ethiopia as a spoil of war and only returned in 2008; Piazza dei Cinquecento and the Dogali Obelisk, which commemorate the nearly 500 Italian soldiers who fell in Dogali, Eritrea, at the hands of Ras Alula's army; the Cinema Impero in the Roman neighborhood of Torpignattara, which had an identical counterpart in the city of Asmara, where there was a system of apartheid in which the rights and privileges of Italians and natives were rigidly separated; the Ponte Duca d'Aosta, which is a tribute to Amedeo d'Aosta, who succeeded Rodolfo Graziani as viceroy of Ethiopia and was considered "the kind and refined face of Italian Fascism" (Scego 2017, 100)[20]; the mausoleum in Affile (in the Lazio region), erected in 2012 with public funds to commemorate General Rodolfo Graziani, Fascist Party official and war criminal responsible for, among other crimes, the use of gas prohibited by the Geneva Convention on the Ethiopian population. *Roma negata* enables Romans to look at their city with new eyes and to understand that the construction of memory is a process that must necessarily—and deliberately—be undertaken, because only through knowledge of the past can these same atrocities be prohibited from happening in the future.

The legacy of colonial history is also visible in the way in which space is produced in contemporary postcolonial metropolitan contexts. The center/periphery dichotomy is at the core of Ubax Cristina Ali Farah's first novel, *Madre piccola* (2007) (*Little Mother*, 2011), and its representation of the Roman urban space. In a scene in the novel, Barni, one of the Somali Italian protagonists, tries to reach the top of the Capitoline Hill, where the seat of Rome's municipal government is located, to attend the funeral of a group of Somalis drowned in the Mediterranean while attempting to escape the war in their country.[21] The climb up to that place,

---

[20] "il volto gentile e raffinato del fascismo italiano."

[21] Ali Farah here refers to a shipwreck occurred on October 17, 2003, when a boat with Somali refugees on board capsized off the coast of Lampedusa. The 13 bodies that were recovered (although Ali Farah speaks of nine coffins) were taken to Rome for the funerals, which, at the behest of the then mayor of Rome, Walter Veltroni, were held with an official ceremony in Piazza del Campidoglio. See Mattone (2003).

however, turns out to be more difficult than expected, because Barni experiences a sense of malaise and vertigo, and the more she tries to reach the center, the more she is pushed toward the periphery: "It was as if a centrifugal force were pushing me in the opposite direction. I was trying to go toward the center"[22] (Ali Farah 2011, 14). The colonial center/periphery dichotomy is rearticulated here according to an official spatiality of power, which allows the Somalis once subjugated by the Italian colonizers to be at the center of the empire and commemorated by contemporary institutions only once they are dead. While attempting to ascend the Capitoline Hill, Barni feels pushed toward the periphery, where the Somalis, who are being commemorated on this occasion, would also be if they had survived the sea crossing. Had that happened, they would have found themselves in Italy occupying a social space of clandestinity and marginalization. As observed by the narrator[23] in the short film by Ethiopian Italian director Dagmawi Yimer entitled *ASMAT—Nomi per tutte le vittime in mare* (*ASMAT—Names in Memory of All Victims of the Sea*) (2014)—dedicated to the shipwreck of October 3, 2013, off the coast of Lampedusa, in which 368 people (mostly Eritreans) lost their lives and an unknown number (approximately 20) went missing—migrants are "more visible dead than alive."[24] The inadequacy of an institutional place such as the Capitoline Hill for the funeral of the Somali shipwreck victims is also highlighted by Igiaba Scego, who points out in *La mia casa è dove sono* (2010, 94–99) that the appropriate place would have been Termini Station, the only space in the capital where Somalis have been welcomed and feel at home.

The inside/outside dichotomy is further articulated in Ali Farah's novel to remind readers that the concept of margin and center changes over time. One of the officials, while delivering a commemorative speech,

---

[22] "Era come una forza centrifuga che mi spingeva fuori. Io cercavo di procedere verso il centro" (Ali Farah 2007, 15).

[23] The narrator speaks in the Tigrinya language.

[24] Director Dagmawi Yimer's project in the documentary is based on his determination to bring the victims of this tragic shipwreck out of anonymity by remembering their names, which near the end are recited one after the other in the manner of a celebration and a prayer. This long recitation by the narrator produces an effect that contrasts deeply with what David Theo Goldberg terms the "massification" of death (2006, 341). On the ways in which access to grieving signals the social value attributed to those who have lost their lives, see Butler (2009). On the politics of grieving that has taken place in Italy to commemorate the victims of shipwrecks and the postmortem reception of migrants, see Salerno (2015).

reminds Italians of the times when it was they who were forced to flee from desperate situations and to emigrate in search of prosperity:

> I warn you, I have a selective memory. I remember what I want to remember. And what I want to remember is one of their voices urging you Italians not to forget your emigrant past. History repeating the story of poor people spurred on by yearning, such total yearning that it uproots you, it defies sea storms. (Ali Farah 2011, 14)

Clarissa Clò (2012) observes that the connection between immigration in contemporary Italy and the mass emigration that in the century spanning 1870 to 1970 saw approximately 26 million Italians leave their country (see Choate 2008) is present and clear in the analyses of second-generation authors. This connection is crucial for understanding how the intersections between the different diasporas have influenced the process of shaping an Italian national identity. Immediately afterward, Ali Farah adds another important detail to the representation of immigration by providing a list of objects found after the shipwreck:

> You know, dying of dehydration, gasping for air, is no small matter. I imagined those rickety boats, and the list of things they found in the hold. Handbag, notebook, photograph, leather shoe, baby bottle, shirt, backpack, watch, shoelace. Details that tell a story.[25] (2011, 14)

The details provided by the author—the list of everyday objects that belonged to the people who were on the boats that sank in the Mediterranean—produce an effect very similar to the scenes shot at the boat graveyard in Dagmawi Yimer's documentary *Soltanto il mare* (*Nothing But the Sea*) (Yimer et al. 2011). In the film, the camera lingers first on the wreckage of the boats and then on the objects found on those boats—shoes, photographs—without any soundtrack, in an almost religious silence. These images confer physicality to migrations, turn them into personal stories, with human actors, and shape very different narratives from the impersonal and disembodied information contained in the official news reports disseminated by the media about these events.

---

[25] "Sa? Morire disidratati, annaspare, non è cosa da poco. Io immaginavo quelle barche malmesse e l'elenco degli oggetti trovati nella stiva. Borsetta, quaderno, fotografia, scarpa di cuoio, biberon, camicia, zaino, orologio, stringa. Dettagli che scrivono una storia" (Ali Farah 2007, 15).

While the protagonists of the novel *Madre piccola* (2007) (*Little Mother*, 2011) are mostly migrants—even though the end of the novel announces the imminent birth of the succeeding generation—it is the second generations who are remapping the capital's urban spaces in Ali Farah's short story "Rapdipunt" (2004) ("Punt Rap," 2006) and in her second novel, *Il comandante del fiume* (2014) (*The Commander of the River*, 2023). The first-person narrator and main character in the short story is an unnamed female adolescent who joins a gang of youths of African origin, all male, inspired by the Flaminio Maphia.[26] In the story, urban spaces are not just a background to the unfolding narrative. The fact that the events take place in historic sites, such as the Pincio and the Botanical Garden in Trastevere, that the members of the group live in a squat, and that the main male character, Mauro, speaks in Roman dialect shows that the children of immigrants are familiar with the city in which they live and that they are rooted in the social and cultural environment they inhabit. At the same time, the roaming of these youths in transitional, and thus temporary, spaces (Flaminio, Piramide, and Ostia metro stations, and the Roma Termini train station) and the frequent reference to faraway locations that ascend to ideal—almost mythical—places suggest that the restlessness of the group is linked not only to the age of its members but also to their feeling perpetually out of place in an urban—and national—geography that does not welcome them but instead holds them constantly at the margins.

The female narrator embodies the moral authority of the story. Like Mauro, for whom the female protagonist harbors an adolescent passion, she is Italian of Somali origins and is well aware that the boys in the group are watched with distrust in Italian society and are perceived as dangerous because they are different from the assumed national chromatic norm. At

---

[26] Flaminio Maphia was a group of Black youths that was formed at the end of the 1980s near the entrance to the station of the Metro A line in Rome and made its presence felt in the square and the surrounding area in the 1990s. While the element that the boys and girls in the group shared was the color of their skin—most of them were Black—in terms of social class, the group included the children of ambassadors as well as the children of housekeepers and waiters. There were also African Americans and African French transplanted to Rome, children of non-African immigrants and native Italian youths. On the genesis of this group and on the birth of the Roman hip-hop associated with it, see Issaa (2017). On the Flaminio Maphia and the presence of Black youths in Rome, see, among others, Caccia (1997) and Braccini (2000). Flaminio Maphia is also the name of a Roman hip-hop group, formed in 1994 and still active.

the same time, however, unlike the young men in the group who have succumbed to its fascination, the narrator is not seduced by facile glorifications of transnational Blackness. When some young Black men from the United States and Cuba arrive one day among the group and claim that Blacks are respected in their countries, the critical voice of the female protagonist mocks the assumed traditional Africanness of which these boys believe themselves the guardians ("and since he was a Black man, everyone believed that he knew all sorts of traditions and listened to him with attention"[27] [Ali Farah 2006, 278]), understanding that their stories represent for her friends, the Roman boys, a possibility of escape to an elsewhere where their somatic difference would disappear or would no longer constitute a factor of undesirability.

At the conclusion of the story, two events lead the young protagonists to rediscover a sense of belonging by forging a stronger tie with the past and creating a sense of (partial) rootedness in the present: an old man Mauro encounters in Villa Borghese shares a mythologized account of the Somali anticolonial resistance and of their valiant leader Said, whose physical appearance supposedly resembles Mauro's. The old man later takes Mauro to see a little incense plant in the Botanical Garden in Trastevere—a plant that, like Mauro and the narrator, originates in Somalia and was raised in captivity ("cattività"). When Mauro later shares his experience with the narrator, it is evident that the knowledge he has acquired about his own country of origin has made him proud of his family's past and has instilled in him the desire to reclaim his history.

The same centrality of urban spaces in the short story "Rapdipunt" is present in Ali Farah's second novel, *Il comandante del fiume* (2014) (*The Commander of the River* 2023), a Bildungsroman that focuses on the process by which the protagonist, Yabar, constructs his identity in the city of Rome, the novel's second protagonist. The continuity between *Il comandante del fiume* and "Rapdipunt" is evident in the perspective the narrative adopts, which is again entrusted to an Italian adolescent of Somali origins (this time a boy), and also in the presence in both texts of the Piazzale Flaminio community of Black youths. Echoes of the urban atmospheres in "Rapdipunt" also resonate in *Il comandante del fiume*: the river of the title—which is also the river of the Somali legend that acts as a common thread in the novel—becomes the Tiber of contemporary Rome, a pulsing

---

[27] "e siccome era uno nero, tutti si credevano che conosceva chissà quale tradizione e lo ascoltavano con attenzione" (Ali Farah 2004, 128).

vein that provides the lifeblood for daily existence. In the second chapter, the Tiber is undisputedly the main character, depicted as a living being ("I feel the breath of the river around the island."[28] [12]). Here, Yabar observes "the true inhabitants of the river"[29] (22), a community of homeless people, whose alienation Yabar shares—even though his social positioning is quite different—and to which he feels drawn. Rosa and Sissi, who constitute his adoptive family, go running on the banks of the Tiber, and the difference between this space in Rome and the Somalia of their origins narrows when Yabar compares the women to two gazelles running in the savanna: "But this is not the savanna, we're in Rome, this is the Tiber, over there is the Gazometro"[30] (38). The hospital from which Yabar tells the story is located on Tiber Island. The river of the legend and the Tiber River confer unity and meaning to the novel.

As in "Rapdipunt," here the second generations' sense of belonging is much more connected to the local dimension of the city, with its places and its dialect, than to a national one. The distrust regarding a possible transnational global connection with other Black communities in the world, expressed by the narrator of "Rapdipunt," is again articulated here, now by Yabar, who is suspicious of those who call him "brother" ("fratello") just because they have the same skin color. At the same time, the young man is also suspicious of the Somali community he meets in London, where he spends a few days with his mother's family. It is here that Yabar learns his father's story, which his mother had always kept hidden, and finally is able to understand his own. In Rome, his mother had severed all contact with the Somali community, which may be why Yabar is initially fascinated by the Somali community in London. However, his initial interest soon passes as he observes how this community is characterized by hypocrisy, internal fragmentation, self-ghettoization, and ghettoization by the British society on whose margins it lives and moves.

The relationship that the London youths of Somali origin maintain with their country of origin, at first glance closer than his own, soon shows itself to be characterized by great hypocrisy. Yabar develops a deep distrust of the way in which the Somali community in London—which has elected to recreate the same clan division that in Somalia had led to civil war—has built its sense of identity on a connection with the country of origin that

---

[28] "Sento il respiro del fiume intorno all'isola."

[29] "i veri abitanti del fiume."

[30] "Ma questa non è la savana, siamo a Roma, questo è il Tevere, lì c'è il gazometro."

is only superficial and on ghettoization (both self-imposed and imposed by the native population) within the British social context. This produces in him a strengthening of his own sense of belonging to the city of Rome and its urban spaces: "Rome is our city"[31] (204). The author also characterizes the relationship of the exiles—and not just of Somalis—as being complicated by nostalgia: the migrants feel a sense of deprivation that leads to an idealization of the country they have fled, transforming that country into a place of memory that is distant and therefore unreachable both spatially and temporally, a fictitious but reassuring place where everything remains always identical to itself and immutable.

In the novel, a Cape Verdean young man whom Yabar meets in an acting class tells him that his parents had used the savings they had accumulated in Italy to open a restaurant in Cape Verde. But then, every time they returned to their native island, they were left disappointed by the constant changes they perceived in both the landscape and the society.[32] As in the novel *Madre piccola*, immigration to and emigration from Italy in *Il comandante del fiume* are considered part of the same continuum. This point is emphasized in the dialogue Yabar has with Ghiorghis, a young Italian of Ethiopian origin, who shares what he had learned earlier from an Italian American teacher: that he must define himself in relation to the country in which he lives—Italian therefore, not Ethiopian—and claim his own Italianness without waiting for others to grant him the right to do so. The reference to Italian emigration (the Italian American teacher) reminds the inhabitants of the Bel Paese that, long before Italy was a land of immigration, it was a country of mass emigration. Such reference also triggers a new reflection on the way in which migratory movements reposition hegemonic and subaltern relations among social groups.[33]

As already seen in Ali Farah's first novel, the sites mentioned in *Il comandante del fiume* map a "cartography of diaspora,"[34] which includes not only transitional places, such as train stations, but also other locations linked to migrant communities, both in the collective imaginary and in daily life. Examples are agencies for transferring money abroad and call centers. It is precisely in a call center that one of the most intimate and

---

[31] "Roma è la nostra città."

[32] On the gap that exists between real places and the way in which they are imprinted in the memory of exiles, see Rushdie (1991, 9–21).

[33] On the repositioning of hegemonic and subaltern relations in the context of Italian diasporas, see, among others, Capussotti (2007), Viscusi (2010), and Fiore (2012, 2014).

[34] This phrase is taken from the title of Avtar Brah's *Cartographies of Diaspora* (1996).

moving scenes of *Il comandante del fiume* takes place. Yabar accompanies Libaan, a young Italian man of Somali origin whom he has just met, to telephone his mother. Libaan has not seen or heard from her in many years, since at the age of 10 he moved to Italy with his father, who then left him at an institution for minors. When the boy, years later, contacted his mother, the two were not able to communicate because they no longer had a shared language. When Libaan asks Yabar to act as an intermediary on the call with his mother, Yabar is both reluctant and moved by a strong desire to speak his native language, which he has not used in years. The language, which he believes is buried inside him, is in fact only dormant; hearing the Somali flow from his own mouth restores in him a strong connection with his country of origin and a willingness to discover his family's past, about which he knows so little (Ali Farah 2014, 126).

The feeling of belonging to the Italian nation is almost entirely absent in the protagonist (and in those rare instances when it does emerge, it is highly conflicted), replaced instead by a desire to be part of a local dimension on the one hand (that of the present in the city of Rome) and of transhistorical and transnational dimension on the other (that of his family's past in Somalia). Such lack of affiliation with Italy is the result of national policies that regulate the acquisition of citizenship, which work to exclude, or differentially include, second generations from the national body. These legal factors are combined with a total inability on the part of Italian institutions—and often of widespread culture as well—to consider the intersection between Blackness and Italianness as a viable option.

In the scene where Yabar returns to Rome from London, the officials stationed at the airport stop him for a check, thinking that he could be an illegal immigrant. Given his difference from the assumed Italian chromatic norm, they are unable to recognize him as an Italian citizen even when the young man shows them his Italian passport. While in "Rapdipunt" the Blackness of the group is perceived as detrimental and creates tension in an urban space constructed as homogeneously white, this type of tension and rejection in *Il comandante del fiume* rises to institutional levels. The airport episode exposes how Italian identity based on blood relations is strenuously defended by national institutions and how Italy resists inclusion of migrants and second generations in both symbolic and physical terms.

The issue of identity-building is central in the novel and is also firmly linked to history and the past. There are frequent references not only to the civil war in Somalia—the origin of the Somali diaspora and thus of

Yabar's personal life—but also to Italian colonialism, to Fascist racism,[35] and to the period of the Italian Administration of Somalia (Amministrazione Fiduciaria Italiana della Somalia; AFIS): "The history of Somalia is linked so much to Italy's. But nobody seems to know it"[36] (Ali Farah 2014, 99). Such historical references ensure that the individual aspect of the protagonist's search for identity is firmly interwoven with the collective one. Fragmented images recur several times in the novel, and these images often reflect the abjection the displaced characters are made to feel as migrants. The only portrait of his father that Yabar possesses, for instance, is composed of fragments of different photographs that his mother has torn up and that Yabar has put back together; the resulting image, however, is deformed and monstrous. Just before an attempt to have his first sexual encounter, which is a particularly important rite of initiation, Yabar glimpses his fragmented reflection in a mirror. The image that he sees appears to have been assembled from different bodies after a bomb explosion: there are parts of the bodies of his father, of his mother's brother, who had been killed during the civil war, and of a suicide bomber about whom he had read in the newspaper.

Only through the search for his past and an understanding of his own story can the main character achieve physical integrity, a healing of body and spirit that is, in fact, announced in the final chapter. The narrative in *Il comandante del fiume* connects the legend of the commander of the river, the eponymous title of the novel, to Yabar, to the Tiber, and to the city of Rome. In the Somali legend, the commander is elected so that the inhabitants of the region and the crocodiles could live together peacefully, all drinking from the same river. The commander, therefore, is the one who makes the coexistence of good and evil possible. He is the one who heals any fractures in the present by acknowledging and reconciling the wounds and troubles of the past. At the end of the novel, Yabar realizes that the role of the commander of the river does not fall on his father, as he had believed up to that point, but on him. It is he who, in the future, will be invested with this great responsibility. The fact that in these texts the narration is often entrusted to adolescent characters emphasizes the

---

[35] Aunt Rosa's Italian father was a Fascist racist who married an African woman. He later shut her away in an institution because she was suffering from tuberculosis and thus permanently separated her from her daughter. Rosa's unconditional love for everything that was African or that reminded her of Africa sprang from this separation.

[36] "La storia della Somalia è così legata a quella italiana. Ma pare che nessuno lo sappia."

importance of this age of transition—especially for the children of immigrants—during which time their individual subjectivities are constructed through complex negotiations with the culture of their country of origin and the society and culture of the country where they live, as well as with their families of origin and the new social structures established in diasporic contexts (such as Yabar's chosen family).

5.3   "HATE BREEDS HATE": NARRATIVES FROM THE PERIPHERY[37]

The discourse of space is one which we enter as we enter ideology. (Bill Ashcroft, *Postcolonial Transformation*)

"You are murderers! It's easy to gun us down, we have no weapons, we've only got rocks!"[38] (Kassovitz 1995) shouts a man in an archival image, his right arm raised against a line of police officers at a distance. Slowly, on a dark and silent screen, the title of the film appears, followed by the names of the three principal actors. Then, the voice-over states: "This is the story of a man who falls off a 50-floor building. On his way past each floor, the guy keeps saying to reassure himself, 'So far so good ... so far so good ... so far so good.' It's not how you fall that matters. It's how you land!"[39] (Kassovitz 1995). While these words are being spoken, a planet appears on the screen, presumably Earth, with a Molotov cocktail hurtling toward it. Upon impact with the planet, the bomb explodes and the screen ignites. While the opening credits are rolling over images of urban guerrilla fighting between police and protestors, Bob Marley's song "Burnin' and Lootin'" plays. As Marley sings of curfews and prisoners brutalized by the police, the audience sees the crowd on the screen responding by doing just that—burning and looting.

This is the opening of the cult film *La Haine* (*Hate*), directed by Mathieu Kassovitz in 1995 and set in the early 1990s, almost entirely in

---

[37] "La haine attire la haine." This line is spoken by Hubert in the film *La Haine* (Kassovitz 1995).

[38] "Vous êtes que des assassins! Vous tirez, c'est facile hein, nous on a pas d'armes, on a des cailloux."

[39] "C'est l'histoire d'un homme qui tombe d'un immeuble de cinquante étages. Le mec, au fur et à mesure de sa chute, il se répète sans cesse pour se rassurer: 'Jusqu'ici, tout va bien ... jusqu'ici, tout va bien ... jusqu'ici, tout va bien.' Mais l'important c'est pas la chute. C'est l'atterrissage."

one of the Parisian *banlieues*, areas which have historically been the site of high social tension. Here live the film's three protagonists: Vinz (Vincent Cassel), Hubert (Hubert Koundé), and Saïd (Saïd Taghmaoui), respectively of Jewish, African (the country is not specified), and Maghrebi origins. The connection between the initial archival images showing the guerrilla warfare and the fictional images of the film is established through the voice—at first extradiegetic and then diegetic—of the journalist announcing the urban unrest that followed the brutal beating of a male Maghrebi youth by the police at the Muguet district police station in Paris, an incident that sets off the events that unfold in the film.

Kassovitz's film is the subtext of the short story "Com'è se giù vuol dire ko?" (What If Down Means KO?) (2005) by Jadelin Mabiala Gangbo, an Italian writer of Congolese origin who later moved to London. Gangbo's story contains numerous implicit textual references to the film. Both the film and the literary text highlight the "the centrality of space as an idea and of territory as a concrete field of investigation and study"[40] (Ilardi 2007) to analyze not only the contemporary metropolis but also the control exercised over this space to assert political and ideological hegemony in a given social context. Taken together, the transmedia narrative driving the two texts and the transnational context that narrative represents raise important questions about the ways in which the construction of urban spaces in contemporary Europe and access to those spaces (or the lack thereof) reproduce colonial hegemonic dynamics that find new articulations in the securitarian policies implemented throughout contemporary Europe. If, as Bill Ashcroft (2001, 129) argues, maps in the colonial era (and at other times) represent not only space but also the *power to create* a universalized space, such power is opposed by practices that include forms of urban countermapping like those presented in Kassovitz's film and Gangbo's short story. These two texts interrogate the means of access and question the permanence in urban spaces for bodies perceived as distant from the somatic and chromatic norm of the individual European states and of the continent as a whole,[41] bodies that, for many reasons, are a constant source of preoccupation.

---

[40] "centralità dello spazio come idea e del territorio come campo concreto di indagine e di studio."

[41] For a definition of Puwar's "somatic norm" (2004) and my "chromatic norm" (Romeo 2012), see note 6 in Chap. 1.

The film and the short story both place at the center of their narratives presences that in many respects have been at the margins of the metropolitan scenarios of many European cities for decades. The new mappings these texts propose favor local and global dimensions, while at the same time they create a certain distancing from the national dimension. The local contexts in which the two stories unfold are the Parisian *banlieue* on the one hand and the city of Bologna on the other, while the global dimension is highlighted by the similar experiences of second (and subsequent) generations around the world—even though these groups live in places far apart from one another—experiences that are rooted in the diasporic stories of their families of origin, cultural and religious differences, and divergence from the national chromatic norm. Inscribed in this context is the transmedia and transnational narrative woven by Kassovitz's film and Gangbo's short story.[42]

"Com'è se giù vuol dire ko?" is set in Bologna, where the urban mappings and the contexts of marginalization are profoundly different from those of Paris, and where the colonial dichotomy between the center and the periphery, in which mostly immigrants reside, is not reproduced as rigidly. Gangbo's short story emphasizes the existence of the social issue linked to the "integration" of second generations, even in the absence of an urban spatial dichotomy. The protagonists are two 19-year-olds, Antonio, who is Bolognese of Italian origin, and Aziz, who is Bolognese of Maghrebi origin. The narrative unfolds as the two young men stroll through the center of the city one Sunday afternoon. Like the characters in Kassovitz's film, Antonio and Aziz are angry, filled with hatred toward anyone who conforms to a desire for "normality" but also toward anyone who implements discriminatory practices against them: "We feel hatred, B. Admit it. You fear people. You're scared. Why? This is the first issue to resolve. The question we owe an answer to is 'Why do we hate them so much?'"[43] (Gangbo 2005, 146). Aziz is frequently racialized as a Maghrebi, but in Northern Italy, in Bologna, his difference is often assimilated to that of Southern Italians: "Twelve years ago [Aziz] asked his father why

---

[42] Kassovitz's film has also been inspiring for the writer and artist Gabriella Kuruvilla, born in Milan to an Italian mother and Indian father. Her novel *Milano, fin qui tutto bene* (Milan, So Far So Good) (2012) already makes explicit reference to the film in the title, which quotes the line spoken by Hubert at the beginning and the end of the film ("So far so good").

[43] "Noi proviamo odio, B. Ammettilo. Temi la gente. Hai paura. Perché? È questa la prima questione da risolvere. La domanda a cui dobbiamo una risposta è: 'Perché li odiamo così tanto?'"

his schoolmates said that he and another Sicilian boy were shitty Moroccans."[44] (149).

The social tension represented by Gangbo is certainly on a smaller, more localized scale than that in Kassovitz's film, and the conclusion of the short story is not as tragic. However, such social tension is rendered palpable in the text through a crescendo of narrative tension that culminates in a scene in which Antonio and Aziz are stopped by two policemen for a document check and find themselves compelled to confront the arrogance and racism directed at them by the two men. Aziz's sneer, which deeply irritates the policeman who wants to exercise his authority over the boys and to control the space they occupy, stems from his sense of outrage against Italian institutions, which keep him, a second-generation Maghrebi Italian adolescent, at the margins of society, and do not allow him—or only allow him with great difficulty—to become an Italian citizen. Therefore, whenever Aziz is asked to show his residence permit, he does so with defiance: "Every time Aziz has been forced to pull out his residence permit, he has always pulled it out with insolence"[45] (173).

The editing in this high-tension scene is almost cinematic: the reader's attention is first drawn to the gun that one of the officers has unholstered for no apparent reason and is then quickly redirected to the hysterical reaction that the sight of the weapon triggers in Aziz. The gun in Gangbo's short story is a reference to Kassovitz's film: in the film, it is Vinz's discovery of the gun lost by a policeman during the unrest caused by the protestors that sparks the narrative. The entire film revolves around the possession of that weapon and its possible use, which in the end determine the conclusion of events. There is also a reference to a real-life incident that inspired *La Haine*: on April 6, 1993, an inspector of the Parisian police, Pascal Compain, brought an 18-year-old boy of Zairean origin, Makomé M'Bowolé, into the station for questioning about an illegal cigarette trade and ended up killing him with what was presumed to be an accidental gunshot (just like the shot from the gun of the policeman at the end of Kassovitz's film is accidental). From the reaction of the community to yet another episode of police violence against immigrants and their children, the director took the idea of representing the social unrest of the *banlieues*

---

[44] "Dodici anni fa [Aziz] aveva chiesto a suo padre perché i suoi compagni di scuola dicessero che lui e un altro bimbo siciliano fossero due marocchini di merda."

[45] "Ogni volta che è stato costretto a estrarlo, Aziz il permesso di soggiorno l'ha sempre estratto con insolenza."

and what for him had long been a phenomenon requiring immediate attention and reflection (Coccia 2015).

In Gangbo's story, it is Aziz's nervous laugh at the sight of the gun that sets off a chain reaction. While his body, unlike the "conventional" (2005, 175) ones of the policemen, is different from the national somatic and chromatic norm, the language that Aziz speaks and raps identifies him as Bolognese. And, indeed, it seems that it is precisely his perfect Bolognese accent—his linguistic mimicry (Bhabha 1994)[46]—that causes the policeman to feel threatened. In order to reestablish Aziz's estrangement from the nation, the policeman suddenly starts creating stereotypical associations: "What are you? ... Moroccan Italian? Check out the Bolognese accent this guy has. Come on, empty your pockets on to the hood, Ali Baba"[47] (176). At the peak of tension, Gangbo inserts an oblique reference to Kassovitz's film, when, suddenly, something breaks and Antonio reacts to the arrogant and discriminatory attitude of the policemen toward Aziz: "By now Antonio has gathered the momentum to plummet headlong from the top of a skyscraper. It is physically impossible to avoid the collapse"[48] (176). The reference to the skyscraper here evokes the fall of the man from the fiftieth floor in Hubert's words at the beginning of *La Haine*. In Gangbo's story, it is not, as in the film's opening sequence, the Molotov cocktail that explodes but Aziz, who reacts not only to the discriminatory language the policeman uses in this moment but also to the many prior episodes of marginalization and racialization he has suffered. The memory of when "that ice cream parlor on Via Zamboni hadn't sold him an ice cream"[49] (173)—since the owners believed that Aziz, as a Maghrebi, might be a drug dealer—recurs several times in the short story to emphasize how it is small daily gestures of this type that fuel the tension that ends up resulting in violence. Aziz's violence, though, is verbal, not physical. Spurred on by Antonio, who speaks to the importance of second generations to the country's future ("You are fundamental for the evolution of this country"[50] [177]), Aziz responds to the xenophobic attitude of the policemen by improvising a rap. By using hip-hop—a language of

[46] For the use of mimicry in Italian postcolonial literature, see Romeo (2018).

[47] "Che sei, un marocchino italiano? ... Senti un po' che accento bolognese ha, questo. Forza, svuota le tasche sul cofano Alì Babà."

[48] "Ormai Antonio ha preso lo slancio per precipitare a capofitto dalla cima di un grattacielo. È fisicamente impossibile evitare il collasso."

[49] "la gelateria in via Zamboni non gli aveva venduto il gelato."

[50] "Tu sei fondamentale per l'evoluzione di questo paese."

protest that spread over time from the New York City of the 1970s to the suburbs of the United States and from there to the suburbs of other metropolises around the world, including the French ones in Kassovitz's film—Aziz creates a connection between his own individual rage and that of Black youths in the United States, youths of the Black diaspora throughout the world, and those in the Parisian *banlieues*.[51]

Following Aziz's response in freestyle, the two 19-year-olds are forced into the car by the two police officers, who intend to take them to the outskirts of the city, far from prying eyes, to teach them a serious lesson. Unlike Kassovitz's film, however, here the police violence is halted by an unforeseen event—Antonio defecating on himself—that causes the policemen to unload the two boys from the car as quickly as possible. This event produces both comic and bitter relief in the readers, as the defecation is caused not only by fear but also by yet another act of discrimination the boys have suffered: not long before their encounter with the police, they had been refused the use of a public restroom. This episode at the end of Gangbo's story recalls a rather enigmatic scene in Kassovitz's film in which Vinz, Saïd, and Hubert meet an elderly man while in a club's restroom. The stranger, who comes out of a stall doing up his pants to the sound of a flushing toilet, starts off with the line "Nothing like a good shit"[52] (Kassovitz 1995). Then, for no apparent reason, he begins to tell them a story about a friend of his, a certain Grunvalski, who years earlier had frozen to death because he had not been able to jump back on the train that was deporting them both to Siberia and from which he had jumped down to attend to his physical needs. Whereas in the film this bodily need leads to death, in the grotesque and comic narrative reversal of Gangbo's story it leads to salvation for the two boys.

In the end, Antonio and Aziz are let go unharmed, but the final sentences in the story—"Hatred rises. I understand the reasons why. Anyway, there's time for many things"[53] (Gangbo 2005, 186)—emphasize that hatred is far from dormant and that, as Hubert states, "Hate breeds hate"[54] (Kassovitz 1995).

---

[51] For an analysis of Aziz's rap as an expression of the transnational cultural production of second generations, see Clò (2012).

[52] "Ça fait vraiment du bien de chier un coup!"

[53] "Sale l'odio. Ne capisco le ragioni. Tuttavia c'è tempo per molte cose."

[54] "La haine attire la haine."

In the film, two elements underline the circular nature of the narrative: at the beginning, right before the events involving the three young men begin, Saïd's face with his eyes closed is framed in the foreground and then, suddenly, he opens them. At the end, the camera brings Saïd's face back into the foreground as he watches the concluding events, his eyes wide open with terror, and then, just before the screen goes dark and the shot that ends the film is heard, he closes them. Furthermore, Hubert's words from the opening about the story of the falling man are repeated almost identically in the closing, again on a dark and silent screen, but with a significant difference: "This is the story of *a society* that is falling, and as it falls, it keeps saying to reassure itself, 'So far so good … so far so good … so far so good.' It's not how you fall that matters. It's how you land"[55] (Kassovitz 1995; emphasis is mine). The passage from a *man* to a *society* that is falling underlines that the events in the film do not concern only Vinz, Saïd, and Hubert, just as the events in the short story do not concern only Antonio and Aziz. Kassovitz's film and Gangbo's story contain much broader references to the social condition of second generations and invoke the need on the part of the French and Italian governments to implement inclusive policies that take into account the profound changes generated by contemporary transnational migrations and that lead to a differential inclusion of non-normative bodies in contemporary Europe's postcolonial societies.

As Guido Caldiron argues, the frequent unrest in the *banlieues* cannot be treated like a public order issue, but rather as the outcome of the growing tension that results from systematic marginalization (2005, 13). What occurs in these peripheral spaces, including the violence, must be integrated within a broader social analysis. Maurizio Ambrosini, also in reference to the riots in the French suburbs, has stressed the danger of keeping second generations at the margins of the Italian nation:

The second generations problem is growing in importance in our country. There are at least three reasons for this. The first is demographic: the number and age of adolescents from immigrant families is rapidly rising, due to the combined effect of family reunifications and the natural evolution of the foreign population in Italy. The second refers to the echoes of the revolts in the French *banlieues* and the pressing matter of the possibility that similar events could also occur in Italy. The third, more internal to the political debate, is the initiation of a revision of our citizenship law supporting a

---

[55] "C'est l'histoire d'une société qui tombe et qui au fur et à mesure de sa chute se répète sans cesse pour se rassurer: 'Jusqu'ici, tout va bien … jusqu'ici, tout va bien … jusqu'ici, tout va bien.' L'important c'est pas la chute. C'est l'atterrissage."

more rapid inclusion in the national community of young people of immigrant origins.[56] (2007, 87)

The interaction with the surrounding space, the ability to freely move within it, and the feeling of belonging to certain places—in other words, the local dimension—are very important for the processes of individual and collective identity-building in second generations, as highlighted in both the texts under discussion here, which represent the conflict and ambivalence around which these subjectivities shape themselves. At the same time, however, the transmedia narrative that the film and the short story construct underlines the relevance of the strongly transnational nature of the social marginalization of migrants and subsequent generations. Jadelin Mabiala Gangbo's short story interrupts established traditional narratives and creates new ones based on temporal and spatial connections between the various incoming and outgoing migrations that have affected Italy—reminding Italians of how such migrations have historically placed them in positions of both hegemony and subalternity. At the same time, the transmedia narrative that the story constructs with the film establishes connections between different post-diasporic subjectivities around the world and underscores the need for a dialogue among second generations in Italy and in other European countries (and beyond) that seriously questions the very concept of national homogeneity through the development of transnational aesthetics.

Gabriella Kuruvilla's novel *Milano, fin qui tutto bene* (Milan, So Far So Good) (2012) is also inspired by Mathieu Kassovitz's *La Haine*. The explicit reference to the famous line spoken by Hubert at the beginning and end of the film—"So far so good"—suggests in the novel's title the idea that, as in the film, the assertion that everything is going well can perhaps be legitimate only if the full context is not considered, if space—and time—are subdivided into small segments that do not give back a full

---

[56] "La questione delle seconde generazioni sta crescendo d'importanza nel nostro paese. Le ragioni sono almeno tre. La prima è demografica: stanno aumentando rapidamente il numero e l'età degli adolescenti provenienti da famiglie immigrate, per l'effetto combinato dei ricongiungimenti familiari e della naturale evoluzione della popolazione straniera in Italia. La seconda rimanda agli echi delle rivolte delle *banlieues* francesi e al pressante interrogativo sulla possibilità che eventi simili abbiano a prodursi anche in Italia. La terza, più interna al dibattito politico, è l'avvio di una revisione del nostro codice della cittadinanza in senso favorevole a una più rapida inclusione nella comunità nazionale dei giovani di origine immigrata."

image and that, for a moment, allow for the inevitability of the conclusion of events to be disregarded. The novel is divided into four sections—"Via Padova," "Via Monza," "Sarpi," and "Corvetto"—each of which centers around one of the protagonists (Anita, Samir, Stefania, and Tony), whose lives are inseparable from their positioning in the urban geography of Milan. Each of the four protagonists tells a story, at first glance unrelated to the others; gradually, as the narrative proceeds, however, it becomes clear that the different narratives intersect, even if only tangentially. Collectively, the four stories offer not only a representation of present-day Milan but also of its historical stratifications: on several occasions, readers are shown the social changes that have occurred over time in the city's spaces.

Uniting the stories of the four principal characters are migrations that, in different ways, have affected and continue to affect Milan: Anita Patel (like Kuruvilla herself) is the daughter of a Milanese woman and an Indian man; Samir is an Egyptian immigrant who landed in Lampedusa and then settled in Milan; Stefania is Milanese but lives in Chinatown, where Italians constitute a minority; Tony comes from a Neapolitan family and is part of the intranational diaspora that brought many Southern Italians to the industrialized North after the Second World War. The city and its neighborhoods carry the signs of these migrations. As Anita argues, at the beginning of the twentieth century, Milan was the destination of intraregional migrations from Bergamo, Mantua, and Brianza; after the war, as a consequence of the economic boom that followed, intranational migrants from Southern Italy arrived in Milan; finally, in the 1980s, it was the turn of transnational migrants from various countries, "Filipinos, Chinese, Egyptians, Peruvians, Senegalese, Romanians, Moroccans, and Indians, mostly"[57] (Kuruvilla 2012, 7). It is as if the internal migrations were "the grand rehearsal for later dramatic changes in place" (Parati 2017, 190).[58]

The continuity between intranational migrations from Southern to Northern Italy and international migrations is also highlighted in the last section, where Corvetto is presented as a neighborhood that has witnessed a high rate of social deterioration, whose geography, as Tony states, "doesn't depend on topographical rules but on the rules of drug dealing"[59]

---

[57] "filippini, cinesi, egiziani, peruviani, senegalesi, romeni, marocchini e indiani, soprattutto."

[58] See Parati (2017) for an analysis of Kuruvilla's novel.

[59] "non dipende dalle regole topografiche ma da quelle dello spaccio."

(Kuruvilla 2012, 141–42). While Corvetto was once characterized by the migrations of Sicilians—and by the investments of Cosa Nostra in the narcotics market centered in the area—in contemporary times the neighborhood has been "invaded by Africans"[60] (142). Tony has a deeply racist attitude toward African migrants, as, in his mind, the fact that both his family and the Africans are part of a migrant continuum is the main reason that he and his family are relegated to a subaltern position. However, through what Kym Ragusa calls "an almost acrobatic capacity" (2006, 223), Tony's racism toward Africans coexists with his presumed affiliation with Rastafarianism—complete with dreadlocks and hip-hop music—whose features of Black culture go utterly unrecognized. To distance himself from the social subalternity of his family and the neighborhood where he grew up, Tony is about to move to another area of the city, thus facilitating the social mobility he craves, while at the same time creating the possibility of a break with the narratives of migration and poverty that have defined his identity to this point.

The motorcycle ride he takes in the neighborhood before leaving is a mapping of memory, in which each place is linked to episodes from his childhood and his past. In the first section of the novel, Via Padova is associated with marginal, dangerous, violent places, but also with European capitals such as Paris and London: "For some people it's the ghetto, the casbah, the Far West, or the most devastated Italian banlieue. For others, however, it represents Milan's East End: a model of possible coexistence."[61] (Kuruvilla 2012, 47). In the last section, Corvetto becomes Detroit's Eight Mile Road, which, as Tony explains quoting Eminem in the film *8 Mile*, is "the notorious road in Detroit that divides the white neighborhood from the Black neighborhood"[62] (168). Tony, however, is not only aware of the differences that exist between Milan and Detroit in terms of the population's racial composition; he also understands that such composition in his city has undergone profound changes over time: "It was there that I realized that I was living in Milan's 8 Mile: only at the time it seemed all white and it wasn't half Black yet"[63] (168).

---

[60] "invaso dagli africani."

[61] "Per alcuni è il ghetto, la casbah, il Far West o la banlieue italiana più disastrata. Per altri, invece, rappresenta l'East End milanese: un modello di convivenza possibile."

[62] "la strada malfamata di Detroit che divide il quartiere bianco dal quartiere nero."

[63] "È stato lì che ho capito che io stavo vivendo nella 8 Mile di Milano: solo che all'epoca sembrava tutta bianca e nunn'era ancora mezza nera." Here and elsewhere, Tony speaks a mix of standard Italian and Neapolitan dialect.

The social tension and the parallel with the Parisian *banlieue* in Kassovitz's *La Haine* provide background to the entire novel through continuous references to the decline that characterizes some of the neighborhoods in question and to the news reports about them that emphasize such decline. In the first and third sections, for instance, reference is made to two cases of urban guerrilla fighting that erupted in high-tension areas in Milan: the uprising by the Chinese community that occurred on Via Paolo Sarpi on April 12, 2007, and the consequent reaction of the police; and the uprising that occurred in Via Padova on February 13, 2010—compared to those in the Parisian *banlieues*—when a group of Maghrebis overturned and set fire to cars after a Dominican man killed a young Egyptian following a trivial dispute.[64]

Corresponding to the change in the city's geography is a repositioning of its inhabitants and a deconstruction of the native/immigrant dichotomy. Stefania, a Milanese who lives on Via Paolo Sarpi and photographs the Chinese community, feels like a foreigner in Milan's Chinatown, where the official language is some kind of "Chinese dialect" (Kuruvilla 2012, 98) and the vast majority of the businesses are owned by Chinese entrepreneurs. Stefania is treated like a foreigner by a restaurant owner, who tells her that the dishes she ordered are among those served to tourists. The native/immigrant dichotomy here has been replaced by the native/tourist dichotomy: "I was going to tell her that in reality we, here in Milan, are natives, not tourists, even in Paolo Sarpi"[65] (107). The counter-mapping in this area of the city has produced a repositioning of its inhabitants: the position of native is now occupied by the Chinese, while the Milanese have become guests in their own city.

5.4   Conclusion

Toward the end of the second millennium, Edward Soja wrote that "the landscape has a textuality that we are just beginning to understand, for we have only recently been able to see it whole and to 'read' it with respect to its broader movements and inscribed events and meanings" (1989, 157).

---

[64] See the coverage from the two most important Italian newspapers: "Milano, rivolta a Chinatown. Scontri, feriti e auto distrutte" (*La Repubblica* 2007) and "Milano, ucciso 19enne egiziano. Dopo la rissa è rivolta nelle strade" (*Corriere della Sera* 2010).

[65] "Stavo per dirle che in realtà noi, qui a Milano, anche in Paolo Sarpi, siamo nativi, non turisti."

To read the textuality of the urban landscapes that shape the narratives examined here, it is necessary to analyze the way in which these landscapes profoundly influence the processes of identity formation in the different subjects that occupy that space—especially when those subjectivities are linked to diasporic movements—as well as the interactions between such processes. The authors examined in this chapter are themselves part of the so-called second generations: they come from families and cultures linked to an elsewhere; at the same time, they structure their process of identity formation in Italy. The possibility of developing a feeling of belonging to the nation openly contrasts with the protectionist policies of Italy; here the difficult route of reform of the laws surrounding the attribution of citizenship shows the unease with which the Italian collective imaginary is able and willing to share the "privilege" of Italianness with subjects who present a different phenotypic aspect but who also share the national language, educational path, daily practices, and widespread culture. The narratives under discussion in this chapter speak of this exclusion, just as they do of the conflict and ambivalence around which these subjectivities take shape. At the same time, however, the authors promote and develop transnational aesthetics that are deeply rooted in the urban contexts in which they develop. Their narrative structures are based on representations of present-day Italian urban landscapes characterized by conflict but also by great diversity and versatility, discovery and re-evaluation of peripheral and interstitial spaces, and possible interactions with profoundly different subjectivities. These texts therefore interrupt established narratives and generate new ones based on temporal and spatial connections that link the different incoming and outgoing diasporic movements in Italian history. These new narratives—literary and cinematic—remind Italians how positions of hegemony and subalternity have alternated over time. They also generate points of contact between different post-diasporic subjectivities and between the living conditions of second generations in Italy and those in other countries. These narratives take shape, as do the subjectivities that produce them, from the remapping of Italian postcolonial cities and develop in parallel with the ways in which the second generations are redrawing new urban topographies in the rest of Europe (and around the world). By undertaking such a significant project, second-generation authors strongly question the very concept of "national literature" and give shape to a postnational literature and aesthetics that promote a vision that is as much political, social, and spatial as it is cultural, a vision capable of confronting the challenges of the present, as well as those of the future.

BIBLIOGRAPHY

Ali Farah, Ubax Cristina. 2004. Rapdipunt. In *La letteratura postcoloniale italiana. Dalla letteratura d'immigrazione all'incontro con l'altro*, ed. Tiziana Morosetti, 127–130. Vol. 4 of *Quaderni del '900*. Pisa: Istituti Editoriali e Poligrafici Internazionali.

———. 2006. Punt Rap. Trans. Giovanna Bellesia-Contuzzi and Victoria Offredi Poletto. In *Other Italies/Italy's Others*, ed. Thalia Pandiri. Special double issue, *Metamorphoses: The Journal of the Five College Faculty Seminar on Literary Translation* 14 (1–2, Spring–Fall): 276–280. Originally published as "Rapdipunt" in *La letteratura postcoloniale italiana. Dalla letteratura d'immigrazione all'incontro con l'altro* (Pisa: Istituti Editoriali e Poligrafici Internazionali, 2004).

———. 2007. *Madre piccola*. Rome: Frassinelli. Republished in 2022 (Rome: 66thand2nd).

———. 2011. *Little Mother*. Trans. Giovanna Bellesia-Contuzzi and Victoria Offredi Poletto. Bloomington: Indiana University Press. Originally published as *Madre piccola* (Rome: Frassinelli, 2007).

———. 2014. *Il comandante del fiume*. Rome: 66thand2nd. Trans. Hope Campbell Gustafson as *The Commander of the River* (Bloomington: Indiana University Press, forthcoming in 2023).

Ambrosini, Maurizio. 2007. Oltre l'integrazione subalterna: la sfida delle seconde generazioni. In *Le banlieues. Immigrazione e conflitti urbani in Europa*, ed. Umberto Melotti, 87–108. Rome: Meltemi.

Andall, Jacqueline. 2002. Second-Generation Attitude? African-Italians in Milan. *Journal of Ethnic and Migration Studies* 28: 389–407. https://doi.org/10.1080/13691830220146518.

Ashcroft, Bill. 2001. *Post-colonial Transformation*. London: Routledge.

Ben-Ghiat, Ruth. 2017. Why Are So Many Fascist Monuments Still Standing in Italy? *The New Yorker*, October 5. https://www.newyorker.com/culture/culture-desk/why-are-so-many-fascist-monuments-still-standing-in-italy.

Bhabha, Homi K. 1994. *The Location of Culture*. London: Routledge.

Bianchi, Rino, and Igiaba Scego. 2014. *Roma negata. Percorsi postcoloniali nella città*. Rome: Ediesse.

Braccini, Barbara. 2000. *I giovani di origine africana. Integrazione socio-culturale delle seconde generazioni in Italia*. Turin: L'Harmattan.

Brah, Avtar. 1996. *Cartographies of Diaspora: Contesting Identities*. London: Routledge.

Brunetti, Bruno, and Roberto Derobertis. 2009. *L'invenzione del Sud. Migrazioni, condizioni postcoloniali, linguaggi letterari*. Bari: Edizioni B.A. Graphis.

Butler, Judith. 2009. *Frames of War: When Is Life Grievable?* London: Verso.

Caccia, Fabrizio. 1997. Noi, i cattivi ragazzi del Flaminio Maphia. *La Repubblica*, December 3. http://ricerca.repubblica.it/repubblica/archivio/repubblica/1997/12/03/noi-cattivi-ragazzi-del-flaminio-maphia.html.

Caldiron, Guido. 2005. *Banlieue. Vita e rivolte nelle periferie della metropoli.* Rome: manifestolibri.

Capussotti, Enrica. 2007. Sognando *Lamerica*. Memorie dell'emigrazione italiana e processi identitari in un'epoca di migrazioni globali. *Contemporanea* 10 (4): 633–646. https://www.jstor.org/stable/24653298.

Centro Studi e Ricerche IDOS. 2020. *Dossier statistico immigrazione 2020*. Rome: Edizioni IDOS.

Choate, Mark I. 2008. *Emigrant Nation: The Making of Italy Abroad*. Cambridge: Harvard University Press.

Clò, Carissa. 2012. Hip Pop Italian Style: The Postcolonial Imagination of Second-Generation Authors in Italy. In *Postcolonial Italy: Challenging National Homogeneity*, ed. Cristina Lombardi-Diop and Caterina Romeo, 275–291. New York: Palgrave Macmillan.

Clough Marinaro, Isabella, and Bjørn Thomassen. 2014. *Global Rome: Changing Faces of the Eternal City*. Bloomington: Indiana University Press.

Coccia, Andrea. 2015. *L'Odio*, 20 anni dopo non siamo ancora atterrati. *Linkiesta*, May 6. https://www.linkiesta.it/2015/05/lodio-20-anni-dopo-non-siamo-ancora-atterrati/.

Corriere della Sera. 2010. Milano, ucciso 19enne egiziano. Dopo la rissa è rivolta nelle strade. February 13. https://milano.corriere.it/milano/notizie/cronaca/10_febbraio_13/milano-nordafricano-ucciso-coltellate-1602458972870.shtml.

Fiore, Teresa. 2012. The Emigrant Post-'Colonia' in Contemporary Immigrant Italy. In *Postcolonial Italy: Challenging National Homogeneity*, ed. Cristina Lombardi-Diop and Caterina Romeo, 71–82. New York: Palgrave Macmillan.

———. 2014. La post'colonia' degli emigranti nell'Italia dell'immigrazione. In *L'Italia postcoloniale*, ed. Cristina Lombardi-Diop and Caterina Romeo, 61–74. Florence: Le Monnier-Mondadori.

———. 2017. *Pre-occupied Spaces: Remapping Italy's Transnational Migrations and Colonial Legacies*. New York: Fordham University Press.

Fondazione Migrantes. 2020. *Rapporto italiani nel mondo 2020*. Todi: Tau.

Frears, Stephen, dir. 1987. *Sammy and Rosie Get Laid*, written by Hanif Kureishi. London: Cinecom Pictures.

Gangbo, Jadelin Mabiala. 2005. Com'è se giù vuol dire ko? In *Italiani per vocazione*, ed. Igiaba Scego, 137–185. Fiesole: Cadmo.

Goldberg, David Theo. 2006. Racial Europeanization. *Ethnic and Racial Studies* 29 (2): 331–364.

Ilardi, Massimo. 2007. *Il tramonto dei non luoghi. Fronti e frontiere dello spazio metropolitano*. Rome: Meltemi.

Issaa, Amir. 2017. *Vivo per questo*. Milan: chiarelettere.

Kassovitz, Mathieu, dir. 1995. *La Haine*. Paris: Les Productions Lazennec. Released in English as *Hate*.

Kureishi, Hanif. 1990. *The Buddha of Suburbia*. London: Faber and Faber.

Kuruvilla, Gabriella. 2012. *Milano, fin qui tutto bene*. Rome-Bari: Laterza.

La Repubblica. 2007. Milano, rivolta a Chinatown. Scontri, feriti e auto distrutte. April 12. https://www.repubblica.it/2007/04/sezioni/cronaca/milano-rivolta-cinesi/milano-rivolta-cinesi/milano-rivolta-cinesi.html.

Labanca, Nicola. 2002. *Oltremare. Storia dell'espansione coloniale italiana*. Bologna: il Mulino.

Lakhous, Amara. 2006. *Scontro di civiltà per un ascensore a Piazza Vittorio*. Rome: Edizioni e/o. Trans. Ann Goldstein as *Clash of Civilizations Over an Elevator in Piazza Vittorio* (New York: Europa Editions, 2008).

———. 2010. *Divorzio all'islamica a viale Marconi*. Rome: Edizioni e/o, Roma. Trans. Ann Goldstein as *Divorce Islamic Style* (New York: Europa Editions, 2012).

———. 2013. *Contesa per un maialino italianissimo a San Salvario*. Rome: Edizioni e/o. Trans. Ann Goldstein as *Dispute Over a Very Italian Piglet* (New York: Europa Editions, 2014).

———. 2014. *La zingarata della verginella di via Ormea*. Rome: Edizioni e/o. Trans. Antony Shugaar as *The Prank of the Good Little Virgin of Via Ormea* (New York: Europa Editions, 2016).

Lefebvre, Henri. 1991. *The Production of Space*. London: Blackwell.

Lombardi-Diop, Cristina, and Caterina Romeo. 2012. Introduction: Paradigms of Postcoloniality in Contemporary Italy. In *Postcolonial Italy: Challenging National Homogeneity*, ed. Cristina Lombardi-Diop and Caterina Romeo, 1–29. New York: Palgrave Macmillan.

Mancino, Davide. 2018. Chi arriva e chi parte: i flussi migratori spiegati bene. *Il Sole 24 Ore*, July 5. https://www.infodata.ilsole24ore.com/2018/07/05/arriva-parte-flussi-migratori-spiegati-bene/.

Marsala, Helga. 2017. Abbattere no, coprire sì. L'arte contemporanea depotenzia il bassorilievo del Duce a Bolzano. *Artribune*, November 10. https://www.artribune.com/progettazione/architettura/2017/11/fascismo-monumenti-abbattere-no-coprire-si-arte-contemporanea-depotenzia-il-bassorilievo-del-duce-a-bolzano/.

Mattone, Alberto. 2003. Roma piange gli immigrati morti. Oggi funerali in Campidoglio. *La Repubblica*, October 24. https://ricerca.repubblica.it/repubblica/archivio/repubblica/2003/10/24/roma-piange-gli-immigrati-morti-oggi-funerali.html.

Merrill, Heather. 2018. *Black Spaces: African Diaspora in Italy*. London and New York: Routledge.

Orsi, Robert Anthony. 1992. The Religious Boundaries of an Inbetween People: Street 'Feste' and the Problem of the Dark-Skinned Other in Italian Harlem 1920–1990. *American Quarterly* 44 (3): 313–347.

Parati, Graziella. 2017. *Migrant Writers and Urban Space in Italy: Proximities and Affect in Literature and Film*. New York: Palgrave Macmillan.

Puwar, Nirmal. 2004. *Space Invaders: Race, Gender and Bodies out of Place*. Oxford: Berg.

Raffini, Luca, and Alberta Giorgi. 2020. *Mobilità e migrazioni*. Milan: Mondadori Education.

Ragusa, Kym. 2006. *The Skin Between Us: A Memoir of Race, Beauty, and Belonging*. New York: Norton.

———. 2008. *La pelle che ci separa*. Trans. Clara Antonucci and Caterina Romeo. Rome: Nutrimenti.

Ricatti, Francesco. 2018. *Italians in Australia: History, Memory, Identity*. New York: Palgrave Macmillan.

Romeo, Caterina. 2008. Una capacità quasi acrobatica. Afteword to *La pelle che ci separa*, by Kym Ragusa, 249–270. Rome: Nutrimenti.

———. 2012. Racial Evaporations: Representing Blackness in African Italian Postcolonial Literature. In *Postcolonial Italy: Challenging National Homogeneity*, ed. Cristina Lombardi-Diop and Caterina Romeo, 221–236. New York: Palgrave Macmillan.

———. 2018. *Riscrivere la nazione. La letteratura italiana postcoloniale*. Florence: Le Monnier-Mondadori.

Rushdie, Salman. 1988. *The Satanic Verses*. New York: Picador.

———. 1991. *Imaginary Homelands: Essays and Criticism 1981–1991*. London: Granta Books.

Salerno, Daniele. 2015. Stragi del mare e politica del lutto sul confine mediterraneo. In *Il colore della nazione*, ed. Gaia Giuliani, 123–139. Florence: Le Monnier-Mondadori.

Saviano, Roberto. 2017. Quella paura dei simboli fascisti. *L'Espresso*, October 23. https://espresso.repubblica.it/opinioni/l-antitaliano/2017/10/18/news/quella-paura-dei-simboli-fascisti-1.312385.

Scego, Igiaba. 2004. *Rhoda*. Rome: Sinnos.

———. 2010. *La mia casa è dove sono*. Milan: Rizzoli.

———. 2017. La nostra solitudine davanti ai simboli del fascismo. *eastwest.eu*, November 4. https://eastwest.eu/it/monumenti-fascismo-italia-significato/.

Schneider, Jane, ed. 1998. *Italy's "Southern Question": Orientalism in One Country*. Oxford: Berg.

Segre, Andrea, Dagmawi Yimer, and Riccardo Biadene, dirs. 2008. *Come un uomo sulla terra*. Rome: Archivio delle Memorie Migranti e Asinitas-ZaLab. Released in English as *Like a Man on Earth*.

Smith, Zadie. 2000. *White Teeth*. London: Vintage.

Soja, Edward W. 1989. *Postmodern Geographies: The Reassertion of Space in Critical Social Theory*. London: Verso.

Tirabassi, Maddalena, and Alvise Del Pra'. 2020. *Il mondo si allontana? Il COVID-19 e le nuove migrazioni italiane*. Turin: Centro Altreitalie.

Verdicchio, Pasquale. 1997. The Preclusion of Postcolonial Discourse in Southern Italy. In *Revisioning Italy: National Identity and Global Culture*, ed. Beverly Allen and Mary Russo, 191–212. Minneapolis: University of Minnesota Press.

Viscusi, Robert. 2010. The History of Italian American Literary Studies. In *Teaching Italian American Literature, Film, and Popular Culture*, ed. Edvige Giunta and Kathleen Zamboni McCormick, 43–58. New York: MLA.

Yimer, Dagmawi, dir. 2013. *Va' pensiero. Storie ambulanti*. Rome: Archivio delle Memorie Migranti. Released in English as *Va' Pensiero—Walking Stories*.

———, dir. 2014. *ASMAT—Nomi per tutte le vittime in mare*. Rome: Archivio delle Memorie Migranti. https://vimeo.com/114849871. Released in English as *ASMAT—Names in memory of all victims of the sea*. https://vimeo.com/114343040.

Yimer, Dagmawi, Giulio Cederna, and Fabrizio Barraco, dirs. 2011. *Soltanto il mare*. Rome: Archivio delle Memorie Migranti di Asinitas, Marco Guadagnino, Alessandro Triulzi. Released in English as *Nothing But the Sea*.

INDEX[1]

[1] Note: Page numbers followed by 'n' refer to notes.

Printed in the USA
CPSIA information can be obtained
at www.ICGtesting.com
LVHW011639161123
764105LV00006B/338